GROW ASPEN

Adventures of the Unsupervised

WRITTEN BY:

ANDY COLLEN | CHRIS POMEROY
DEAN JACKSON | LO SEMPLE

TWIST AND TURN PRESS

GROWING UP ASPEN:
ADVENTURES OF THE UNSUPERVISED

Keep in touch!

We invite you to subscribe to our mailing list at TwistAndTurnPress.com to get news and blog post updates from the authors every now and then.

INTRODUCTION

This collection of stories as told by four friends whose lives and experiences overlapped during Aspen's last-stand in the 70s–80s. Our stories come from the real heartbeat of what it was like growing up in Aspen. Funny how such a remote place could shape the lives of kids growing up in a world-class resort. Our parents gave us an amazing childhood, but they had no clue about what we witnessed or took part in—we were junior league spies under the influence of Aspen. This is a fresh, honest look at what went on "backstage" and how it shaped our young lives.

TABLE OF CONTENTS

Contributor: Dean Jackson

Contributor: Lo Semple

FOREWARD:
GREG POSCHMAN

IT'S A REUNION OF SORTS ... FOR ALL.

Growing Up Aspen brings together 4 men who share fond memories of their childhoods in the place we love.

It is what happens when old pals get back together. The stories begin to flow ... the tales of misspent youth ... the unique taste of freedom experienced in the small mountain town—the compilation of memories is the next best thing to being here in the late 70s or mid 80s...

Try to imagine skitching on snow-covered streets, ascending the fire escapes to the rooftops, sitting at the feet of Nick and Maggie Dewolf, Patti and George Stranahan, Dr. Whit and Polly Whitcomb, Herbie and Marcie Balderson, or Sandy and Mary Lynn Munro, to name just a few. Roaming the old mine tunnels around Aspen, and hawking Bill Dunaway's Aspen Times... These stories will take you there and make you feel a part of something magical. This book and these writers give us confirmation that Aspen is indeed heaven.

When I was a kid I heard old-timers talking about how they had the best of it ... the best snow, the best town, the best life, living free in our small town. My dad and his buddies claimed they'd had the best of it in the 1950s until it "went to hell" in the late 1960s. Or maybe later if they were a bit more open-minded.

The first I heard this sort of banter, it was related to me secondhand. I was told that in the quiet years of the 1920s and early 1930s, Mr. Tidwell owned the general store at the top of the mesa on Main and 4th streets in Aspen. He grubstaked the miners through the hard times and when they went bust, died, or gave up, he ended up with their claims. In the mid-1930s the first skiers began to arrive. When Tidwell saw them he told his family "that's it. This place has gone to hell—we are *out* of here!" And they decamped to the tiny ghost town of Crystal, Colorado. Apparently, his collection of acquired claims made up most of what was left of the town.

In due course, the first generation of powder skiers were upset when snow grooming equipment was introduced. And those same post-war locals from the 1950s were incensed when the Hippies upset their dreams of utopia by arriving in the late 1960s.

And it goes on and on ... I can't help but think my AHS Class of 1977 had it best ... but then along comes this group of 4 miscreants from its Class of 1985-86 who make a similar, audacious claim.

The common sentiment seems to be that Aspen is going to hell, but I think every generation agrees that the rest of the world is going to hell faster. Our love for the Aspen we knew, grows stronger with each telling.

I still argue that we are "special" here in Aspen and the Roaring Fork Valley. This unique place has attracted eccentrics, including outcasts from Eastern society, the uncomfortably wealthy, the ski bums, the intellectuals, and artists, and to some extent it still does. Our remoteness, or what is left of it in this age of accessibility, is considered to be an advantage. Those who make the herculean effort and expense of moving here, have something special going— they don't settle for less, they avoid mediocrity, and in the best circumstances, they become passionately committed to our town. I think they may also be truly hypoxic ... we live at 8,000' and the lack of oxygen in our air tends to make one a bit high, or at least a bit irrational, which can explain our love of beauty and the passion we exhibit for political intrigue and interminable arguments. Of course, extended periods of hypoxia do permanent damage to the brain ... and it's perhaps no coincidence that the longer one lives here, the more special one feels. This could explain our unusual sense of pride, entitlement, and ownership.

The stories in Growing Up Aspen will take you back to a time and place that no longer exists. Arguably the best of times and I can't disagree. In indulging in the book, I find myself back in our old Aspen on silly, foolhardy, daring adventures that would make any young Aspenite proud ... and make the more mature survivors weep with joyful sadness.

Some of these kids went to the Aspen Community School where they were taught to think independently, to create, and to become remarkable adults. They had the tutelage of some of Aspen's great characters—eccentrics and geniuses who became their mentors and North Stars.

I am grateful for the work that Andy, Chris, Dean, and Lo have done in these pages to preserve their memories of growing up in our town. Other generations have done it, and more will do it ... each claiming that they had the best times in Aspen... And they'll be right.

Buy the book, and share the memories of Growing Up Aspen.

ABOUT GREG POSCHMAN
Colorado's Pitkin County Commissioner of District 3

Greg was born and raised in Aspen. He graduated from Aspen High School and earned his Civil Engineering degree from the University of Colorado, minoring in business and filmmaking. Greg is a familiar face around the town of Aspen and knows the community well, having made many biographies and documentaries about local individuals and non-profits, including The Aspen Institute, Music Festival, Challenge Aspen, and the Aspen Hall of Fame.

For his directing and camerawork, Greg won three National Emmy Awards for Camera/Cinematography and Best Direction, as well as a Gold Apple Award, two Cindy awards, ACE nomination, 1998 Fellow. Colorado Council on the Arts.

Greg's father, Harry Poschman, helped construct the first chairlift in 1946 and was in the 10th Mountain Division. He taught skiing to the troops at Camp Hale, Colorado, then fought in the major battles in the Italian Alps. Greg's mother, Jony, still lives in the valley and was an avid skier, journalist, and artist. Greg's parents started a ski lodge and his father was the sole operator of the Aspen Chamber of Commerce in the early 1950s, tasked with promoting our then-unknown ski resort.

Greg lives with his wife Maureen and twin daughters, who attend Aspen High School. He hopes his children and their friends will grow up having the incredible healthy environment and opportunities his childhood in Aspen offered.

CONTRIBUTOR:
ANDY COLLEN

ANDY CUT HIS ENTREPRENEURIAL teeth at the age of 16 by becoming Burton Snowboard's first Aspen distributor. After his college years, he discovered a culture of independent animators in Portland, Oregon, and moved there, working at Teknifilm, the local 35mm film processing lab while connecting with the local artists and studios. He freelanced for Will Vinton Studios (Claymation, *California Raisins, The PJs*), Blashfield Studio (Photo cut-out, MTV music videos), and mentored with Tom Arndt of Merlin's Hammer.

Andy met Amy Blumenstein while producing *It's About Peace*, a collaborative short film that Amy and many other local artists contributed animated scenes to. Andy and Amy soon married (at the Portland Zoo) and started their boutique studio, Happy Trails Animation. Ever the innovator, after several "nose to the grindstone" years of producing and directing commercial animation for ad agencies, Andy developed a distinct, low-cost, high-production value approach to generating Motion Comics and Motion Posters. This creative venture resulted in a stretch of work for Disney (*Tron, The Muppets*), Starz Entertainment (*Spartacus, The Crazies*), and BBC Worldwide (*Doctor Who, Torchwood*).

Andy continues to explore and innovate through digital storytelling. He finds writing truthful tales about his childhood, perspective, and work to be a total blast.

DEDICATION

This book is dedicated to my mom, dad, and bro.

And for my nieces, nephews, and cousins!

*I would also like to acknowledge my brother-in-law
Bruce Blumenstein (Big Brother) who on many hikes
in the Oregon Cascades enjoyed sharing stories
of our childhood adventures. I learned that
sharing stories can bring us all together.*

*And this book is a big thanks to the town
that shaped who I am.*

AUTHOR'S INTRODUCTION

Whenever I'm asked, "Hey Andy, what was it like growing up in Aspen?" it's like being handed a whole roll of quarters—it's always fun to share my collection of "Aspen's Greatest Hits" with folks. Aspen in the 70s was truly outstanding. It's easy to recount all the good times, but, as with most things, there's a flip side. It's hard to have experienced such an integral place as a kid and see it change so dramatically.

Nick DeWolf's digital/organic fountain
©Melanie Malone Love

WHEN IT COMES TO THE TOPIC of Aspen, we locals usually talk about new Aspen and old, comparing which one's better. Well, since I'm always interested in digital organic experiences, I wanted to create one for *Growing Up Aspen* and play with presenting a past and future experience. Like a portal, this creative merging of ideas with technology was first presented to me by Aspen's dancing fountain—a cutting-edge, experiential water feature downtown, designed by Nick DeWolf who showed me the magic of connecting art and technology.

In *Growing Up Aspen*, I reflect on the Aspen childhood that made me who I am today. My words on paper are the organic method of storytelling. The QR codes that follow are links to digital images and movie clips which, when scanned by your smartphone's camera and digital devices, turn them into a time-traveling tardis for captured emotions and moments of a time gone by. The QR Codes become Easter eggs for an *experiential* style of storytelling.

MY MOM'S BOOK, "Storm of the i: An Artobiography" was my inspiration for producing *Growing Up Aspen*. Here's a QR link to her book if you'd like to check it out; you know what they say about the "apple and the tree."

*Storm of the i:
An Artobiography
by Tina Collen
(website).*

SO LONG BEACH BOYS, HELLO JOHN DENVER
AND THE NITTY GRITTY DIRT BAND

Moving from the surf-side streets of California to the Rockies of Colorado as a boy immersed me in events and adventures I could never have imagined. And I soon found out that Aspen was in the midst of change. Aspen back then had a great, supportive, supply and service dynamic with its tourist industry. The locals cherished their off-season like most sports fans relish the Super Bowl. Half the town would close down except for those places frequented by the local community.

Even though Aspen was the playground for the rich and famous, it was the mountains and the Norman Rockwell pool-hopping locals that gave Aspen its true color and unique spirit.

Aspen had its famous tourists, but it also had some local stars like Jack Nicholson, John Denver, George Hamilton, Jimmy Buffet, and later on, Kurt Russell and Goldie Hawn. Heck, Aspen was even home to Dionne Warwick for two years, back in the day.

In the 70s, true locals managed to hold the line between play and fun with respect for the valley and the land itself. The first Chart House, with its famous bottomless salads and locally sourced culinary creations started in Aspen before branching out as a chain. Locals created environmental centers like Windstar and equitable non-profits like the Aspen Institute. While it is now a private think tank for international groups, institutes like these used to go out of their way to include locals and were designed to unite local and international mindsets. Now Aspen attracts the 1%.

I've collected a group of stories from three friends I grew up with, the idea being to share how our stories played out, what it was like to be a local kid back in the day, and how the local-tourist relationships worked. We grew up during a time when an Aspen grocery clerk might've been your neighbor. Now there's no chance a clerk could afford a house anywhere in Aspen. Times are always changing, but I'd like folks to know what made Aspen so special to us.

BEFORE ASPEN

It was the summer of 1976 in Southern California—Los Angeles, to be exact. I was eleven, my brother Mark was nine, and my mom was designing and manufacturing fashion jewelry in a small office on Hollywood Blvd. The Century City law firm my dad worked for just settled a big case, which meant we had an opportunity to change our lives. My parents sat us down and talked about all our options, with "Option A" being Aspen so we could leave the big city and do the rest of our growing up in the great outdoors. Not saying we hadn't had a few outdoor adventures in California, but Aspen, Colorado, was, at that time a much smaller, more grounded community.

My last summer camp experience in the Malibu Hills of California was unforgettable. Cottontail Ranch was a rustic place away from everything, just like the kids' camp in the movie *Meatballs* with all kinds of crafts, mini-bikes, horses, and a great big catfish pond for fishing. As is typical of California summer camps, there were plenty of teenage counselors. I have a crystal clear memory of riding in a VW van with them, cruising down the Pacific Coast Hwy. No seats in the back—just shag carpet on the van's floor with camp kids piled in and the sun dropping down with a nice orange glow. The windows were wide open and the salty sea air blew over me as I munched my quintessential PBnJ— you know—where the jelly and peanut butter has fused with the bread molecules from sitting in its brown paper bag for the better part of a day in a hot van, while we tried our hand at surfing and swallowing sand.

The Beach Boys "Surfer Girl" played on the radio, followed by Seals & Crofts "Summer Breeze." I had no idea what our new life in Aspen would be like, but my 11-year-old brain believed it'd be like *The Wilderness Family* movie I'd seen last Christmas—a great adventure.

The Wilderness Family movie trailer (1 min). ©Lionsgate Entertainment Company

A scene with Venice High School in Grease (1 min). ©Paramount Pictures

Every time I see the movie *Grease* I get a flashback of learning to ride my Schwinn Scrambler around Venice High where that movie was filmed.

I was one of those kids attending the very first west coast Montessori School in Santa Monica (now it's the Sony building). Some of my fellow students were children of famous people, like Jennifer who had Cary Grant for a dad and Matthew who was the son of Robert Altman.

So much of our life back then was about getting out to the beach— it was hard to imagine what it would be like being landlocked. My old neighborhood would later become part of a crazy skateboard culture called Dogtown while my brother Mark and I kicked our heels in the high altitude of one of the best ski towns in America.

EARLY DAYS OF ASPEN

MY POPS HAD LINED THINGS UP so Mark and I would arrive in Aspen just ahead of the tryouts for Little League, believing baseball would be the best way for us to get connected with the local kids. Trick was, we'd need to be able to play right away if we were going to make it on the team. Us "city boys" were about to get acclimated to the mountain way.

While our parents drove a moving truck full of all our belongings to Colorado, my brother and I stayed with our grandparents to finish out our last days of school.

Grandma Sonny was a stout, no-nonsense Jewish woman whose love was so intense, I swear my ribs are still recovering from her hugs. Grandpa Saul had a soft spot for us as well, of course, but Grandma's love was formidable. She never hesitated to take care of us. She took us and our two cousins to Disneyland twice a year without fail. We were a carload of noisy, wound-up Grandkids but she *still* got us on the rides we wanted and stuffed us with ice cream.

Grandma could not have been happy about our moving away but when the time came, she did usher Mark and I across the tarmac to the boarding stairs of the plane. It was early June of 1977 when we waved goodbye, buckled up, and flew off to our new life in Aspen, Colorado. No turning back.

My parents met us at the Grand Junction Airport and together we made the last leg of our journey seated four across in the big moving truck. Warm mesa fruit valleys changed to rugged red hills as we went up through Glenwood Canyon through dramatic surroundings, unlike anything Los Angeles had to offer. Our ears popped as we climbed in elevation. It was like heading into the alpine heights of Heidi country.

In Glenwood Springs, Colorado, we stopped at a car dealership. While our parents picked out our new family car, Mark and I got a crash course about Glenwood's history from the rack of travel brochures. Before the miners came, the valley belonged to the Ute Indians and Aspen was originally called Ute City. Glenwood is famous for its hot springs. Doc Holiday is buried in Glenwood— he was battling tuberculosis and the hot springs were thought to be medicinal. Later I went to so many birthday parties there, Glenwood Hot Springs was like a steamy second home to me.

After an hour or so we were back on the road. Our new family vehicle was nothing like the L.A. lawyer's car my pop usually drove. Our new car was a big Chevy Blazer, a mountain vehicle with beefy tires and loads of wheel well clearance which was typical of Aspen at that time.

Before putting down "roots" we'd had a choice between Sonny & Cher's old house, or Peter Brinkman's duplex which was off Cemetery Lane by the Aspen golf course, right on the 5th tee.

The Brinkman duplex by the golf course (image).

To integrate ourselves into our new town, we went for the local footprint. Peter had built the duplex. He was a local contractor during the summer and a ski instructor in the winter. His wife, Dede, was an advertising producer and actually produced a few TV commercials in Aspen with local casting. (I graduated with their daughter, Missy, who now owns Publik Coffee in Salt Lake City, Utah.)

What's Missy up to now? (website)

At this point, Aspen's golf course was only 9 holes. The Brinkman duplex had a magnificent view of Pyramid Peak, picture framed by the slopes of Buttermilk and Highlands. This house turned out to be the right move.

In L.A. we'd lived up Laurel Canyon in the Hollywood Hills where we watched a murky layer of pollution rise and fall each day. In Aspen, we were 8000' above sea level in the expansive Rocky Mountains with a bright blue sky and fresh mountain air. Several times double rainbows stretched across the sky, from the Brinkman house to the mountains. During the day we watched bright white thunderheads roll in and around Highlands Mountain, Pyramid Peak, and Buttermilk Mountain. At night, the sky was absolutely pitch black and filled to the brim with a crystal-clear Milky Way so dense it looked like a cloud made up of a billion stars.

"Rocky Mountain High" by John Denver (4-1/2 minute audio)
©RCA Records

In another month, just after we arrived, the sweet smell of cottonwood permeated the valley floor. All that cottonwood fluff would fill the air and pile up in drifts like snow. We called it our second snow season. A daily rain spell came and went like clockwork around three in the afternoon. Clouds would accumulate, lighten their load, and move on.

Our first induction as Aspenites happened on the second night. It was after midnight. Pop, my brother, and I were sleeping while my mom, a night owl, went on a tear to unpack so we could stop living out of boxes as soon as possible. As the story goes, she was organizing the pantry when she heard rustling sounds coming from the garage. She figured it was deer or raccoons roaming around—no big deal.

About 20 minutes later my mom was startled by a deliberate RAP-RAP-RAP! of knuckles hitting our front door followed by a woman's commanding voice. "It's the Aspen Police!" My mom opened the front door and was immediately greeted by two of Aspen's Finest and their vehicle's flashing lights.

A female officer spoke straight to the business at hand. "Ma'am, a serial killer, Ted Bundy, escaped the county courthouse. We believe he went through your garage—we *know* he stole your neighbor's car."

My mom was stunned.

"Good thing you locked your car," said the officer, lowering her flashlight. "And it's a good thing Ted was in a hurry, you're just his type. Long, dark hair that's parted in the middle."

For two whole weeks, our community traveled around in packs while Ted was on the loose. We thought we'd left that kind of Charles Manson craziness in Los Angeles. (In years to come I'd find Aspen had its own level of crazy. And us kids? We'd see it all—backstage style.)

Ted was a sadistic psychopath—a cold-hearted killer accused of many murders in Washington, Idaho, and Oregon, but it was physical evidence from the murder he'd committed in Snowmass/Aspen that brought him down. Colorado was the first to have a solid case against him. This trial was supposed to get him locked up so they could bring the other cases out of the cold.

"Ted Bundy tales come out of the woodwork" ©The Aspen Times

The Aspen Courthouse (courthouse history website)

"Bundy's escape forever a part of Garfield County history" news article. ©The Aspen Times

The craziest part about the Ted Bundy experience was that half the town said they thought he was a clean-cut preppie dude. Many were duped until he escaped by jumping out of the second-story courthouse library window, injuring his ankle. Word was, he limped up Aspen Mountain and hid on Shadow Mountain until dark, then ran across the golf course, rifled through our garage, and took off in our neighbor's classic Cadillac. Eventually, his ankle injury hindered his driving and the police stopped him, thinking they had a drunk driver on their hands.

Ted could charm almost anyone including reporters, law officers, flight attendants, and people at the courthouse. There are stories about him referring to his leap from the courthouse as "The Great Escape," later telling a reporter he enjoyed reading an account of it (*The Aspen Times*, March 27, 2019).

During the thick of all this activity, my pops had us breaking in our new baseball mitts. It was time to start training—no time to waste worrying about Ted Bundy.

Since there was a little baseball field and basketball court for the neighborhood right next to our house, Mark, my pops, and I would put in a few hours of practice each day and spend the rest of the time unpacking and settling in.

While building our bunk beds my mom found that we needed more bolts. She gave us a sample of what to get at the hardware store and said we could ride our bikes into town. It was our first adventure out on our own. We found Main Street and stopped to ask one of the bench warmers by the Jerome Hotel where the center of town was. "You're in it," he said.

The old guy gave us directions to the hardware store. It turned out to be something right out of *Little House on the Prairie*—it still had horse-hitching posts out front. In fact, I think the Miller beer ad (see QR code) may have been produced by my friend Missy's mom, Dede. Little did we know that we were living in a historic town destined to begin its transformation into a glitzy new future. At this time there were still old buildings standing that had warbled window glass and that had been constructed with square nails. They looked better than any set at Universal Studios.

Miller beer commercial with Aspen's old hardware store in a scene (:30 secs). ©Miller Brewing Company

During this time Ted Bundy was believed to be hiding up in a cabin near the town of Independence, so us kids, especially the girls, would travel in groups. This situation only lasted two weeks but it was the craziest thing, knowing there was some insane dude hiding up in the hills. We could not let Bundy ruin our routines but we were on high alert. One time, when my brother and I were walking on the mall we saw a disheveled dude on one of the benches. He was sitting quietly, eating a brown bag lunch from Tom's Market. As we passed by we got a better look and realized he looked a lot like a disheveled version of Bundy. We circled back to make sure, but he was gone. Was it paranoia, or was it Bundy?

When the authorities caught Bundy he was half-starved from living on next to nothing. They did not lock him up in Aspen's jail again. They moved him to Glenwood Springs where he escaped again. While in Glenwood's jail, he refused to eat. The guards had no idea he was making his next plan for escape. This time Bundy would be so skinny that after he unscrewed the light fixture in the ceiling he fit through the hole. He busted his way through some drywall to a closet in a hallway and quietly snuck out. From there he caught a flight from Grand Junction and took his freak show to Florida to terrorize and murder more people.

After a time, we were settled in enough for our parents to do their own adventuring around the Rockies while Mark and I played ball and stayed at the house. We often cooked our own dinners. Mark was nine and I was eleven ... had the show *MasterChef Junior* existed back then, we'd have been big fans. My bro and I held our own cooking challenges once in a while, like the time we did our own guacamole taste-off for Mom and Dad, or when Clark's Market finally got a lobster tank and we prepared Mom a Mother's Day lobster dinner.

Mark and I rarely fought. In fact, we stood up for each other during baseball and many other situations. We liked making stir-fry with all sorts of fresh and fancy ingredients. One night we were teamed up in the kitchen; me hacking up chicken, Mark on veggie detail. The kitchen was a small area with a framed refrigerator that blocked the view of the front door.

Suddenly I heard a man's voice call out, "Hello?" from the living room. His voice was soft and matter-of-fact, but coming from *inside* our home. This was the second time since moving to Aspen that I began to feel that things could go wrong. The unexpected guest triggered my "stranger danger" training, but I thought, hey, this is Aspen, no need to come at it like Snake Plissken in *Escape from L.A.* ... And yet, some strange man *was* in our house. Mark and I looked at each other. I grabbed the knife I'd been using to cut the chicken and tucked it behind my back. Mark's eyes went wide as I edged around the counter to get a look at who'd come into our house. No knock at all—just waltzed in. I glanced back and saw Mark grab the bottle of soy sauce and raise it like he was ready to play whack-a-mole.

The man was looking for our neighbor Sandra, who happened to be Steve Martin's private secretary in Aspen, at the time. Our units faced each other and looked alike—the man had gone into the wrong one (that little unit lists for about $2 million now). As I directed the man to the right duplex, I saw Mark move from panic to silent spasms of laughter. When the man was out of earshot we laughed. "I grab a knife, and you go for the soy sauce," I said, poking fun, "what was your plan—salt him to death?"

Mark and I did most things as a team but we also had our different school friends. He and a few of his friends took to stashing bags of candy up on the rooftops of businesses downtown. Almost every building had a fire escape, access ladder, or stairwell that made it easy to climb up. Whenever Mark and his friends wanted a snack, they could go up and raid a stash. They had candy hidden on the rooftops of Aspen Square Hotel, Little Nell's, and The Continental, on a roof across from the Playhouse Theater where my mom's first studio was, and a few other places around town.

There came a time when Mark was restocking his rooftop supplies and the police nabbed him. We learned later that a call had come into the station—someone with a gun had tried to hijack a car. The cops were scouring the area, looking for a young man in his thirties with dark hair. Now, my brother was only ten at the time, but when the Aspen Police spotted Mark skulking around on the roof, they were sure they had their man. He was unarmed, of course, so they threatened to charge him with being a public nuisance.

My pops got the call—they had my brother in custody. Good thing my dad had been a lawyer in Century City—they'd no idea who they were dealing with. It didn't take long to get Mark out It was more ridiculous than anything and has become a family joke. In *Mayberry* talk, the Aspen Police pulled a "Barney."

Ever since Hunter S. Thompson brought his "Freak Power" to challenge the old conservative Aspen Sheriff mindset, we kids began to see the force as more of a Barney Fife type. But unlike Barney, some of these guys were capable of busting tourists for having drugs and keeping some for themselves.

My brother and I were actually pretty respectful kids so dealing with the police was kind of an oddity, but we did have our few run-ins. To us they seemed more like concierges of the streets with nothing better to do than challenge us.

We could tell how well our economy was doing by where each season's tourists came from. Each year might be different, but the results were the same—an onslaught of consumers who generally didn't seem to appreciate what the little town of Aspen had to offer as culture. It seems they have now become the locals.

This was the kind of social society lessons we Aspen kids learned from observation on the open street mall, not school. When the stock market was doing well, we got folks from New York, and when oil was doing well we would hear a lot of "Yeehaws" so we knew Texas was doing well. Each year would be a different crowd; the only things consistent were the locals, the locals who owned and ran most of the stores and services Aspen (now out of "syndication," like *Fawlty Towers*). Once the Mountain Chalet sold in 2021 the writing was on the wall.

Since Aspen was a small, quiet town, most people knew each other, and parents were comfortable leaving kids on their own. At this time Aspen was the proverbial village that helped raise us kids. Now that village is owned by corporations, not by individuals.

It was hard to watch companies like Benetton begin to edge out time-honored "Norman Rockwells" like Tom's Market during the early 80s, but it did. Don't get me wrong, Benetton was cool. I did like the international branding they did at the time, and many of my friends had summer jobs there, but the change was a big culture shock.

Whenever my parents went adventuring we'd have the run of the house and cash so we could go out to eat somewhere if we wanted to. Usually, they'd be away for a day or so. To us, it was no big deal. In L.A., Mark and I used to stay with friends. A little extra liberty in Aspen seemed to fit fine with the start of our self-management.

Aspen had many locally run restaurants back then. Our favorite place to eat at was Toro's Mexican Restaurant because we'd still have money left over for Pinball Palace which had it all—video games, pinball, and foosball. Pinball Palace was the creation of George Perry and our friend Ian's mom, Terry Murray, who owned the Whale of a Wash laundromat. They wanted to give us kids in town something to do that did not include mischief and drugs. Well, we still got into some mischief, even with Pinball Palace.

The amazing thing about George Perry and Terry Murray was that they gave us kids a full-on lesson about how to make an Aspen city BMX track. We were told, if we really wanted a BMX track, to draft up some plans and show up at City Hall. George told us there was already land for just such a thing behind the baseball park. The land had been donated by the Moore family (their son Travis was in my high school graduating class). BMX had just become a big craze.

Our bike gang showed up at City Hall and did our pitch with our drawings of how the track would work. We talked about how this sport is taking off and Aspen would be on the map with its own BMX track. We also talked about how there were already amenities at Iselin Park that could handle this new traffic.

"Giving Moore to Aspen," article. ©The Aspen Times

We were all around nine to thirteen years old. It worked! We got some space—the city would bring back loaders and build out what we wanted for the terrain of bumps and jumps. We had one day with the loaders to create Aspen's original BMX track. Ian's brother Chris welded a real pull cable starting gate for us. The Armstrong family ran the Little League baseball program and gave us an extra hose to hook up so we could wet the track as needed.

Well, now that track is part of the AstroTurf field ... evolution I guess. For us, this was the time that Spielberg captured in *E.T.* or *Goonies* and we were those kids on BMX bikes. I think the saddest part was that no other young kids took on the effort to keep the track alive, kind of like the old rope swing up near the Devil's Punch Bowl. Just another reminder of how quickly things slip away.

A year or so later we had another rooftop run-in—this time with water balloons, not candy. The consensus between our friends and us was that we were being overrun with "turkeys" (our nickname for tourists).

One time as we went for dinner at Toros we noticed there was a set of fire escape stairs that went up and over to the top of the Aspen Drug building. We climbed up and found a cool spot for viewing the mall down below. There was this short wall built on the edge of the roof that connected the two buildings and was only waist high.

Part of that wall was worn away. It was old, like most of the buildings downtown at this time. In fact, the Jerome Hotel was so run down that it had its own breed of feral cats living in the hallways before the major remodel. What we noticed here was a hole in the plasterboard, which we agreed would be a great hiding place for some water balloons.

That night the gears continued to click. We hatched a plan, and the day came when we executed that plan. We loaded up a bunch of balloons, stuffed them in our snapped-up coats, and took the local free city bus all the way from Cemetery Lane to downtown. We marched over to Toros, climbed up to our new rooftop hideaway, and set up our arsenal.

We started lobbing water balloons at those turkeys as fast as we could—then ducked down, hiding behind the wall facade to snicker and giggle. The balloons made satisfying splat, splat—splats! We'd wait a few minutes, sneak a peek and lob more balloons. Two or three rounds later, I was busy laughing at our handiwork when someone tapped me on the shoulder.

I cringed. Turned around. Again, two of Aspen's Finest stood glaring down at us. Black boots, blue jeans, button-up rugby shirts, badges. Sunglasses. The taller cop barked, "What are you kids doing?"

We stammered, "It's—it's sss-ummer—we were just having some fun—yeah, uh huh, only a few water balloons," to which he replied, "You do *know* we can take you guys into the station." The other cop grabbed one of our water balloons. "These are weapons," he said, then threw it down hard by his feet as if putting an exclamation point on his lesson. But it didn't break ... it bounced.

Well, as you may know, those little water balloons can be rather sturdy—they'll bounce if they're not filled up all the way. We'd been in a rush, so ours were all sorts of sizes. The cop frowned and stepped on it—but it still didn't break. It blooped out from under his boot, stretched so tight it looked like an angry pus bubble ready to pop.

So, there we were, stunned and staring when he barked, "You DO KNOW this could be considered a missile or a projectile weapon," and stomped that balloon zit with his other boot—and then it sure did pop! The water shot right up his pants and crotch. All I could think was—*if you laugh it's going to be worse*. So, there I sat, holding it in, expecting to be read our rights.

The cop looked down at his wet pants. "Okay boys, get out of here. I do not want to see you here again or I will arrest you. Consider this a warning!"

We all darted out of there, just glad to be off the hook. It was a huge adrenalin rush, but I knew that was our last turkey toss. We'd need to find another way to get that thrill.

These first years were very interesting as we began to acclimate to the local lifestyle. One of the big events that we loved was the World Cup every year. The World Cup came to Aspen in 1950 and was invented by Bob Beattie and Serge Lang in 1966. Some of my school friends' parents were racers during their time. Every class had kids trying and wanting to be that next Olympian. Monique Pelletier was just a class below mine and was in two Olympics, and before her, it was Beth Madsen.

I saw my first FIS Alpine World Cup in Aspen in 1977 along with all the hoopla it caused— Franz Klammer was in town that year. Everyone was there, the Mahre brothers, Ingemar Stenmark, and even the young Leonard Stock. All the locals would gear up with all their warm waterproof gear and huff it up the mountain. They made every effort at real, physical audience participation. They lined the course and watched the racers speed by. There were spectators hanging in trees. They hauled lounge chairs up along the sides of the course.

Aspen World Cup AI art image by Joshua McMahon.

Aspen skilebrity (yes, it's a real word), Andy Mill, was our town's US ski team competitor that year. Some years later, Andy Mill would be our high school class of 1985 graduation speaker and his graduation speech would be a full circle moment—one of the most directly connected messages from one generation to another. He talked about the sports industry; the struggles and pitfalls but told us about the strength of perseverance and grit. It was very special.

It was also amazing to hang with him during my senior year graduation party. Now I realize his own graduation experience must've been closer to what was shown in that seventies movie, *Dazed And Confused*—whereas my own was more like *Fast Times At Ridgemont High*. Andy Mill did have that good hair thing going, though.

Our post-graduation bonfire celebration was at the Gloor's, the glow of the fire dancing off the back side of Aspen Mountain. John Gloor was in our class and he was that survivalist, inventor dude. You know, the guy that shows up in school with a throwing star he made out of a table saw blade. They lived up Ashcroft Valley so we knew there would be no one to bother us that night.

Big bada-boom! Andy Mill showed up with his wife, Chris Evert Lloyd! I'd seen her at the Pro Celeb tournament a few

©Ski Racing (Tom Kelly) – Andy Mill (website)

years earlier at The Aspen Club and she knew some of us kids at this graduation from that event. It felt a little like living backstage. These events were what shaped our town and us kids. Andy behaved as if he was right at home, probably remembering his own Aspen High graduation from not that long ago. Sometimes I wonder, had our parents any idea of what we'd experience when we all left our crazy big-city lives?

Andy Mill must've been in his 30s when he came to speak to us. Now I'm in my 50s thinking about what I, myself, would have said at a high school graduation, given what I've learned. I think I'd talk about how so many of the locals actually helped prepare me for life's battles. For me, Nick DeWolf (Aspen's great brain and early technology wizard) introducing me and my friends to technology so early on was a big one. The first time I grasped a real understanding as to what he'd been talking about was while working on my Amiga computer in the 90s. I was playing with some time-lapse photography captured on ¾ inch tape. At the time, my Amiga 3000 was the only consumer computer capable of pulling in high rez, which was 720 x 480 television pixels. I realized then how a neighborhood parent like Nick DeWolf had made such a difference.

Aspen's parents ran the local stores, sold the property, had construction companies, and ran accommodations for the tourists, much like the Melvilles with their Mountain Chalet. Earlier in Aspen building code history, the Chalet's roof was the building code limit. Folks in the community did not want the view from town to be blocked by buildings. I think that changed somewhere in the 90s when the Melvilles had to replace their roof. The truth was us kids had full access to everything. The things we *saw!* The Mountain Chalet was a true family operation. Every Melville kid, adopted or not, worked at the family hotel and learned the value of truly hard work.

When The World Cup came to town my friends and I felt tied to our international roots. The world was coming to Aspen, and we had some locals representing the US. There were high school nights when we would pool hop and meet up with all these ski racers. Pool hopping was what most of us kids did since we were a 100% tourist town with a ready selection of hotels, motels, and condos with pools. We'd suit up and drive from pool to pool, hot tubs, and all. Let's just say, the high school parties were pretty crazy that time of year. The Continental Hotel back then was like Grand Central Station. CBS would set up in the lobby ... the place was packed. Bob Beattie could be seen walking the hallways elbow to elbow with the skiers as they would get ready for the races during the mornings' and afternoons' prep for the next day's event.

In 1956, Beattie was named acting coach of the Middlebury College school's ski team after coach Bobo Sheehan left to coach the alpine skiers on the 1956 U.S. Olympic Team. In 1957, Beattie became the head skiing coach for the University of Colorado in Boulder, and during his tenure, the team won the NCAA national titles in 1959 and 1960. In 1961, the U.S. Ski Association named Beattie the U.S. Ski Team's head alpine coach.

During his coaching years, Beattie was known as a demanding coach, driving his athletes hard. At the 1964 Winter Olympics in Austria, the Beattie-coached U.S. team won two medals, both in the men's slalom: a silver earned by Billy Kidd and a bronze by Jimmie Heuga. They were the country's first-ever Olympic medals in men's skiing. (Bob Beattie (skiing). (2023, March 26). In Wikipedia. https://en.wikipedia.org/wiki/Bob_Beattie_(skiing))

As middle school kids, we'd run around trading ski lapel pins, swapping Aspen's pins for their international ones. The older pins were worth more, plus they were just plain cool. Lots of us would save batches each year to start circulating in the following years. We were the source for cool pins—since stores at that time mostly sold the current year. I think this was another *Our Gang* moment—Aspen style.

Oh! And the Continental Inn had this sit-down, two-seater, Mrs. Pac-Man tabletop game. We found out that if we struck the coin box we could get a free credit. It had to be tapped in just the right place. We kept a round rock for just this purpose hidden in the lobby, or we would use our ski boots in the winter. While waiting for the bus in town we could literally rap up a few credits and play until our bus was at the main stop next to Wagner Park (yep, consider this a confession).

If it was snowy, at night we had our own serious adrenaline rush style of transportation, practically a rite of passage for growing up in Aspen—mastering the art of "skitching." It was a little like water skiing, but we'd be hanging onto car bumpers in Sorel boots sliding over snow. A snow mode of transportation. Older gens refer to it as "hickey bobbing." This maneuver didn't use a rope.

Of course, skitching starts with the first really big snow. Once the streets are packed and the news report is for snow all night long, this usually means we could start taking night rides in and around town, courtesy of any passing car out braving the conditions.

To skitch, you get all your outdoor gear on, including your best and toughest pair of ski gloves—oh! and goggles, too. As a car drifts by, the skitcher runs, grabs the back bumper, and plants their feet against the snow. The typical position is crouched in a tuck, one hand under the bumper and the other on the outside or trunk so you can stop and start as the car does. Ideally, the driver remains clueless.

True experts would ride on the end or side of the bumper so they could see what was coming and going. It's done as one single motion of running, squatting, and getting your feet to slide on the snow-packed road.

As a kid with no driver's license, this was the first mode of transportation and as a rider, you are trying to predict what the driver would do. You must be ready for every turn or stop. But because you'd be hanging on to the back of the car you could see the brake lights or turn signals so you had some idea of when to let go or move on to another car.

Some got really creative with their dismounts. One time the road was especially slick with a thick layer of ice under the snow and one of my friends let go as the car was making a big turn. He was crouched down on the bumper and did a double 360º spin, stood up, and walked right onto the mall right near Cross Road Drugs (now it's a Ralph Lauren). Skitching was like our underground style of figure skating but with a bit of *Fight Club* grit.

Skitching was fun, but every once in a while my brother and our clan of friends would create new snow devices, contraptions, and sports. The one that most comes to mind was our great idea of "Hefty'ing."

We rode the chairlift up with trash bags stashed in our pockets, all dressed in our ski gear and typical Sorels. We told the lift operators that we were going up to get the ski stuff that we left at the Merry-Go-Round restaurant. The lifts close at around 3:45 p.m. which is when they clear the trails of day skiers, checking all routes, and making sure everyone is off the mountain.

When it got close to that time, we walked out and down one of the trails. As the patrol started their first round of clearing, we jumped and hid in a batch of thick trees—there was no way they'd see us. After the second round of patrollers yelled, "Clear!" we crept out of the woods. When we reached the top of a run we put our feet and legs all the way into the bags and pulled them up to our chests. We had no idea how this would work out. I began to have flashes of some dude going over Niagara Falls in a barrel as I skootched myself toward the slope.

Here's the thing ... with skis you have edges. Even with a toboggan you can lean and have some sort of control over your turns. What we found was, as soon as you started to move in a Hefty bag, it was as if you'd hit warp speed—first thing, you're shooting downhill like a *BULLET*.

The problem starts when in the first 100 feet you are aware of how long ski runs can be—some might be a mile long. Then you fly over one mogul, bounce, land, and clear two more and each time you touch down becomes one brief opportunity to try and dig your fingers into the snow to try and stop or slow or gain any semblance of control.

We finally reached the top of Thunderbowl on Highlands ski area, the run above our house, which meant we were at least getting closer to safety. This adventure was in the spring so the sun would be out till about 6:00 p.m. and the mountain would close at 4:00 p.m. which gave us plenty of daylight to get down the mountain. But this also meant the temperature had dropped and the runs were crusty and icy in spots. We just called it "crispy." Thunderbowl was a part of the mountain that most folks didn't really ski. At that time, it was usually chop that would eventually get shaped into soft, long moguls. It was chop because a few of us locals like to leave some cool tracks in the fresh powder (POW). You could look up and see your line. As times would warm and cool in the spring the snow became soupy cement.

It hadn't occurred to us that *stopping* would be our biggest issue. With almost no way to dig our fingers into the packed snow, our gloves became useless, slippery brake pads. Thunder Bowl was so steep, once our plastic bags hit maximum velocity, our eyes were so teary, not even goggles could handle it. Everything became a giant blur. The trick to this run was that it was both pack and chop.

Each skittering glance off the packed slope left us a bit winded. The packed snow meant pure speed, whereas chop bounced us uncontrollably, rattling our jaws and blasting our asses like flash grenades. We shot through powder that flew up everywhere, and for seconds at a time we'd be left with zero visibility, then bust out of the clouds only to feel gravity pulling us faster and faster.

After the first 50 feet I realized trying to stop was a waste of effort and that my new goal should be staying upright and not facing the wrong way. Eventually, we stopped just before the bottom of our road, right off the slope. Panting and laughing, Mark and I walked the rest of the way down on wobbly legs to our home.

I think this was the first time where I really felt what "out of control" really meant. I feared for my life with every bounce, but what I walked away with was that I could dance on the edge and be balanced. I heard that strength comes from conquering your fears. I also thought about Tom Crum (senior) and his Aikido (more about that later).

Hefty'ing reminded me of the scene in *Christmas Vacation* where Clark greased the metal circle sled. At some point, I knew I could steer toward the water tower at the bottom of the slope. I remembered how sailboats tack and I thought that I had to try and slide across and down the slope at the same time. There is a moment where being out of control becomes slow motion and I saw every second one slice at a time. It kind of took some of my childhood Malibu body surfing skills to the slope. Maybe this is the time I should have seen that I had a mind for animation. This is the first time I began to physically understand the art of mogul skiing and timing.

I remember that by my senior year, I had taken all the credits I needed to graduate to fulfill the minimum requirement which meant I only had algebra with Susan Sanchez, and a few art classes with Barbara Smith. During my last semester, on Mondays, Wednesdays, and Fridays I was out of class by 9:30 a.m.

I would hike up the road to my house through a field. That field now has a chairlift up to Highland Bowl for high schoolers.

We used to just make that hike to Highlands as a warm-up. I would grab my pack, skis, boots, and poles and by 10:30 a.m I could be up at Merry-Go-Round restaurant, home to Gretl's famous apple strudel (her old place on Aspen Mountain became

Bonnie's). When Gretl moved her strudel to Highlands, that marked the time that Highlands officially became the local's mountain.

L to R, Anna Gauba, Andy Collen, ©Melanie Malone Love

Doing my homework by the warmth of the Merry-Go-Round restaurant's stone fireplace on Highlands gave me an idea of the kind of work environment I wanted to create. My studio has an efficient wood stove and I work by a toasty fire every winter. I stacked wood in Aspen and stack it now in Portland. Home is where you make it. It's *how* you make it that's important.

This image from my mom's book, Storm of the i: An Artobiography, shows a sample of our Goonie Skis. ©Tina Collen

Another sport we invented was what we called Goonie Skis. I think I was thirteen, so this would be around 1979. We dug through our mountain collection of beat-up old skis and found two black pairs of my dad's old Head skis. To make a pair of Goonie Skis, what you do is, pull off the bindings and reset them so that the skis are only long enough to secure the bindings and just your boots. These skis are basically just a bit longer than the bottom of your ski boots. Goonies are like a cross between speed skating and skiing.

The best thing about the old Head skis was that they had a solid metal plate that ran all the way down the ski. Hacksawing these took some serious elbow grease. The metal meant we needn't worry about hitting rocks or any other debris. We could confidently rip through anything with those little puppies.

These smaller Goonie skis would let you practice all sorts of aerial tricks without worrying about clearing the rest of your skis. Back in the day, skis used to be at least as tall as your arm's length could reach.

We could now literally ski down some of Aspen's steepest runs. We were even able to do some crazy out-of-bounds exploration. We built a ragtag team of us kids. In art class, I made some silkscreen T-shirts for all of us, and we became Team Goonie.

ASPEN LITTLE LEAGUE

THE ARMSTRONG FAMILY ran Little League and were longtime Aspen residents. Otis Armstrong was probably in his thirties and his little, eventually taller, younger brother Andy was about four years older than me, meaning when I finally hit high school as a freshman he was a senior. The other little league coaches were the Marolt boys—Roger, Steve, and Mike. In movie terms, this would be *Dazed and Confused* and I was the young punk Little Leaguer kid. For me I was coming out of the 70s and heading into high school during the 80s. My class of friends was beginning to see the change in Aspen as we hit high school. For instance, there were stories about Prince Bandar's house having a tile floor that lowered you into the pool rather than having steps. Yep, that kind of change was around in the 80s, however, it really did not take effect till the mid-90s.

The baseball field was pointed right at the backside of Buttermilk ski mountain, facing the side known as Tiehack, on Maroon Creek Road near the James E. Moore pool. Both the park and the pool were made into the Aspen Recreation Center. The cool part was I could see where the ski runs were cut. Lots of wildflowers and other grasses grew on the runs which were lined by tall Aspen groves. The mountain in summer looked like a drunken buzz cut with all sorts of trails winding through the clusters of Aspen trees. The green Aspen leaves would quake, as the wind made its way down the Maroon Creek Valley.

The city stored extra telephone poles at the end of the baseball field. When one of us would hit a home run, this yellow-bellied marmot would pop up, stand on top of those poles, and yell at us like a grumpy old man. This was hilarious when we had teams travel in from out of town. Grouchy Bob would show up and yell at us kids.

So, my pop was right—baseball turned out to be a great way to meet the community and figure out where I stood in the social setting. I had a great arm and could throw far with some accuracy which meant I was mostly in the outfield catching pop-fly balls. I was good but by no means the best player. However, I was able to pull some magic out of the bottle like stealing a few bases and I managed to make the traveling team.

Little League was the first time I began to see how the other communities around Colorado received the Aspen kids. We were considered to be spoiled, rich kids. Which ... some were ... and some were not. Before Aspen became Aspen it had two countercultures ... farmers, and hippies and the Hippie School (aka the Community School) and the Intellectual (Country Day), two small private schools for kids that were not ready for the full-on socialism of public school. Remember, my brother and I came from the very first west coast Montessori School. Full-on public school would be a bit much, but baseball involved the whole community and that made it much easier to blend in.

There was one place our Little League team would travel to for away games: the small, rundown town of Grand Valley. It was a long bus ride just to play one game. This was the first time where the older kids showed some of us younger kids about chewing tobacco. Didn't seem appealing.

At least five of the guys on the opposing team were sporting beards. I mean like, ZZ Top chin huggers. I figured they must've been short players and had to pick up a few extras, but this was crazy. My thirteen-year-old kid brain wondered if the beards were just how those low-altitude kids turned out.

Baseball was a great way to be introduced to our new town. It helped that both my brother and I had something that stood out skillwise. Mark was able to pitch and hit the corners, and since I was able to throw to home from left, center, and right, I was moved around accordingly and could steal a base or two. (These were the same kids I would go to high school and college with. The only thing I like about Facebook is being able to keep in touch with all these folks, and from time to time cross-chat. It's not the same but at least we are still in touch.)

What I got out of baseball was a sense that this little boy could compete with kids much bigger than himself. Always being the smallest kid in my grade was something that became normal, but catching a pop fly has nothing to do with size. It was at this moment that I knew I had to make my own path, if I didn't then these kids would try to do it for me. Some tried but I earned the respect of most of them from the field and later on as I began to lift weights.

In fact, I wonder if my record is still up on the AHS wall I weighed 145 lbs and with Erik Klanderud, the big kid in baseball, and my freshman year bodyguard spotting me, I benched 315 lbs—only once, but man did that change my perspective. Erik called me Mighty Mouse from that point on, and coming from him, the nickname was an honor.

THE NEW NEIGHBORHOOD IN ASPEN

AS KIDS WE HAD IT GOOD. I remember my parents saying while we were still unpacking to go out and play with some of the neighborhood kids. Because of baseball we developed our Little League neighborhood group.

Mike Tache's family was interesting since his dad was on the Canadian ski team. After papa Tache was asked to come run the ski instruction on Buttermilk, he did, in exchange for being the town's Golf Pro when they finally built the golf course. This was the family that started the tradition of offering local kids free ski lessons on weekends. Back then it was called Aspenauts—not sure what it's called now. Mike's older brothers were crazy good skiers like their dad, only with the U.S. ski team (currently the entire Tache family is involved with high-level ski training throughout Aspen, Vail, and Telluride).

One of my first real, powerful moments of acceptance by the special folks that made up Aspen was a situation with our neighbor, John Keleher, the older brother of our buddies, Chris and Brian.

As the new kids on the block, my brother and I walked over to ask the Keleher kids if they'd like to go skateboarding with us on the basketball court alongside our house. Chris and Brian's older brother John was about my age. He'd been diagnosed with Muscular Dystrophy (MD) very early in life and went everywhere in an electric wheelchair. Earlier in Santa Monica, California, my brother, good friend Erik Luvstad and I had literally worn our feet out during the Montessori School's March of Dimes fundraiser. John was the first friend I'd made who had MD. I found out later that he was the reason the town of Aspen had an elevator installed in the middle school.

While we were skateboarding, John came rolling up and said, "Let's play Crack the Whip." We were all like—*YEAH!!*

So, there we were, the whole Cemetery Lane clan on boards, with John pulling all of us around the courts—his kid brothers, Chris and Brian, Mike Tache, Erik and Tina Tevetia, Ian Murray, Mark and I—one slight turn of John's chair would "send" us all. It was us trying to stay on our boards while John tried to take us all down with his version of Crack the Whip.

I remember these first Aspen kid incidents well, and the sad part; John would eventually pass by the time I hit seventh grade. One thing I learned from good ol' Johnny Boy was to make the best of what you've got. It's up to you to have a good time, and we sure did. So many matter-of-fact situations in normal Aspen kid life shaped us. Aspen was real people trying to have a normal life in an amazing outdoor setting.

Neighborhood kids. Photograph by ©David Brownell

Every view in Aspen is postcard-worthy, but it can get tough to see five feet in front of you once the snow comes. I experienced my first major blizzard late one night. From our window, I saw a flurry of snow passing through the street light creating a cone of glowing light ... the area beyond became a dark purple. I put on my headphones, slapped a Pete Seeger cassette tape into my Walkman, and went for a walk. Visibility was ten feet, at most.

Here's a clip about my neighbors, big John Keleher and Little John (15 mins). ©Aspen Hall of Fame

As I marched around the little park alongside our house I noticed how the light affected the snow. I could see waves forming, much like a surfer looking for that perfect wave before paddling out.

As I basked in the cone of snow and light, Pete Seeger's "Snow Snow" song came on. The opening lines are: *"Snow, snow, falling down. Covering up my dirty old town ..."* I think I was about thirteen at the time. I stood there, all bundled up, looking at the street light and snowflakes as they came down. I sensed this part of my life was going to be amazing. It was a major storm and Pete's song seemed to be talking about the storm of changes in my life.

I was first introduced to the folk music of Pete Seeger through

"Snow, Snow," by Pete Seeger (3 mins) ©Columbia Records

Sandy Munro, one of the many talented parents linked to the Community School. Sandy brought his banjo on the school's Yampa River float trip and sang a bunch of folk tunes. Sandy was the owner of the local music store, The Great Divide, and soon became Aspen's music historian. All musicians at one time or another would need to pick up supplies at the music store, which was run by Sandy and his family.

Pete Seeger letter to Happy Trails Animation

Below is a QR link to *Aspen Unstrung*, Sandy's second memoir which dips into the town's history and times surrounding musicians who "gained their stripes" playing in our little valley. *Aspen Unstrung* is a look back in time that's well worth every page.

Sandy Munro's encore memoir, Aspen Unstrung (website) ©Sandy Munro

I got to know the Munro family even better after we had a field trip to the almost-finished new home of Sandy and Mary Lynn Munro. We had read *Little House On The Prairie* in Rhett Harper's class and she wanted to impact us kids beyond the pages. She orchestrated a way for us to see how they would bake bread with fire in those old days. For me, this was another magical moment.

During the late 70s, there was a trend of blending old and new ways including building homes with an intent to conserve and preserve. The Munros were unique. They installed an old 40s Aspen School District gas flame cook stove in their new home. It had a *Little House On The Prairie*-style kitchen.

I think baking bread at the Munros as a class field trip is what Bill Gates would eventually call CORE education. The idea was, with physical experiences, and stories from books, deeper lessons could find fertile ground. The more we read or imagine some individual's journey, the more events along the way spark interest, and interest becomes the fuel for knowledge.

So, while we were reading about baking bread for a dinner or some old-west celebration, our class got to watch Mary Munro go through her Martha Stewart imitation with a Mountain Mom's flair.

THE ASPEN COMMUNITY SCHOOL

IT WAS A TRUE COMMUNITY that raised the Aspen Community School. Eren Gibson's dad (David F. Gibson), an environmental engineer, designed this 70s version of a raw-cut log cabin-like school. The land in Woody Creek was donated by the family of Champion Auto Parts, a continual supporter of the Community School. George Stranahan even gave the town's most notorious journalist and author, Hunter S. Thompson a good deal on purchasing Owl Farm, a patch of land that was just a few 100 feet from our math class. The school sat on a hill looking upvalley towards Aspen. Woody Creek was the last plateau in the Aspen valley created by the melting glaciers. The view from the school was plateau grasslands that ran right into the big, steep cliffs of the Rocky Mountains and aspen tree groves galore.

The new, remodeled Community School (website).

©Eren with her dad, David F. Gibson who designed the old Community School building (image).

Everything about the Community school was out of the box and done differently, including how it was built—raw, square sawed logs woven together much like a log cabin. The best part was, they built a very cool little crow's nest post so we kids could climb up and look out over the mountains. It was so much fun to climb up there as fall changed to winter and feel the frozen crystals needling your face as the snow blew through the crow's nest.

The community school was like a *Little House On The Prairie* school in many ways, but what struck me most was how fifth to eighth graders were all in the same classroom, just with different assignments for their grades. While figuring out who and what I was going to be, The Community School's unique approach became a crucial influence on how I approached the world around me.

I mean, what grade school performs *One Flew Over the Cuckoo's Nest* as their grade school play? The Community School and Paul Rubin, that's who!

One spring day, we had the first shot of warmth in months. The fresh mountain breeze smelled like new wildflowers. At 8000' above sea level, it takes a while for temperatures to rise in the valley, and that goes for the famous swimming holes we used to haunt too. On this day, the front door of the school, big as an airplane door, was braced wide open. On any given day, if we left the math room door open, a huge draft would blast through whenever the school's front door opened and cause a wind tornado. There were times when the tunnel of wind pushed me right out the front door!

With the doors open, we could also hear almost everything that went on outside. One day we were working on some major algebra equation when all of a sudden we heard the RAT-A-TAT-TAT of gunfire. I jumped in my seat. In fact, we all did. Then there was the sound of a gun firing and the pow-pow-pow of a smaller gun, and so on. Turned out, this was to become a common occurrence—Hunter S. Thompson out on one of his shooting benders. In the 90s, when I learned about school shootings in Chicago I realized I'd already experienced the scary element of gunshots, only for me it was Gonzo style. Hunter was a crazy cat, but he sure knew his way around guns.

One thing that made an impression on me was Juan Thompson's dog Lazlo, a Doberman Pinscher and the first dog that I honestly connected with. Those of you familiar with Hunter will recognize Lazlo as the name of Hunter's lawyer friend in *Fear and Loathing*. Here's the thing, Lazlo was the nicest dog, but if you said "Nixon" Lazlo would go into attack mode. Lazlo had been trained to bite the hell out of a stuffed dummy that had a rubber Nixon head.

Hunter Thompson shooting guns with Conan O'Brien just like Hunter did during our classes (7 mins). ©Late Night with Conan O'Brien

Nick DeWolf (website), ©Aspen Hall of Fame

Nick DeWolf's original company (website), ©Teradyne

John Katzenberger & Nick DeWolf building computers with us kids (image). ©Nick DeWolf Images on Flickr

I liked that Lazlo had short fur, short enough to feel the muscles in some places. I remember Lazlo used to like sitting in our math class in the sun. Hunter's son Juan was one of my first good friends in town along with Brad Laboe. I remember working on some art project outside when Lazlo came up to the school and decided to sit right next to me.

I can't really remember what Brad and Juan were talking about. I just remember sitting there with Lazlo and feeling these little round nodules under the skin.

I asked Juan what they were and he told me, "Hunter thinks there are coyotes in the bushes and really it's Lazlo chasing them away. Lazlo gets caught in the crossfire. Those are shotgun pellets."

Brad, Juan, and I were drawn to computers early on. We were inspired by our math teacher, John Katzenberger, co-founder of the Aspen Global Change Institute, and Nick DeWolf who helped create Aspen's dancing fountain. Nick was the tech guy who built our school's first computer. I think Nick's playing with technology and his fountain's organic motion of water is where my love of combining digital and organic animation first began.

Brad, Juan, and I played John Katzenberger's harvesting game—you had to predict and plant crops to try to save your community. The game was way ahead of its time. Since I was introduced to the computer so early, it was an easy step for me to jump on the tech wagon with the Amiga computer years later when I landed in Portland.

All of the schools had Outdoor Education trips of some sort; another ritual for Aspen students implemented to help kids learn to work together and to get to know each other better.

The most memorable Outdoor Ed event for me at the Community School happened to also be my first real backcountry trip, guided by Rhett Harper and John Katzenberger. They took 12 of us kids out for a weeklong hike over from Maroon Bells to Conundrum Hot Springs. We had to have tent partners and Dean Jackson was mine. He was an interesting character, a skinny, observant kid with an amazing talent for memorizing song lyrics and making me laugh with funny quotes. He'd had cleft lip surgery and came across as quiet and meek in crowds, but when pushed he could stand on his own two feet.

Even at the age of 12, I could see how Dean was able to take on every challenge and persevere. I realized then that the answer to getting what you want is persistence. And that takes patience. Oh boy, at that age, where to find patience? It just so happened, although I didn't know it yet, that the Community School was about to teach me much more than schoolwork.

We set up camp and got a campfire going. Thanks to Rhett Harper, she took a pie pan, put it on a fresh bed of coals, and poured in some brownie mix. Then she placed another pan upside down on it and added some coals over the top and bottom of that pan. How many coals would determine how fast the brownies would cook, so that meant slowly adding smaller coals on top as they burned out. If I remember right, it only took like 20 minutes on the campfire. The brownies were amazing, caramelized in just the right way.

We camped outside, looking up at the night clouds which were actually the Milky Way while John Katzenberger read excerpts from Edward Abby's *Desert Solitaire* to us. No kidding—this was a unique school experience, sitting around a fire above timberline, listening to one of America's best novelists, learning how to be good stewards of nature while watching meteor showers.

While John was reading I was also looking up at those stars, and thinking about my new home and how big our world is. I was reminded of a clay animated film I'd seen in seventh grade at The Aspen Film Festival called *The Little Prince*. That quintessential night by the campfire let me imagine myself as the Little Prince and

The Little Prince film (28 mins), ©Will Vinton

Melting Polar Ice Caps, a clip from Wildfire ©HappyTrailsAnimation

Windstar and John Denver's legacy (website), ©Aspen Journalism

Here's a "Wild Ride!" ... Stein Erickson (Crazy Aspen Characters) Chevrolet Commercial – Corvair in Aspen 1960 (2 mins) ©Chevrolet

John Katzenberger as the Barnstormer. Funny how even then I was pulled by the magic of imagination and animation. After high school I would go on to work as an independent contractor at Will Vinton Studios where *The Little Prince* was made. (I learned so much about the industry by watching how Will maneuvered his business. Truth is, there's no substitute for good old-fashioned creativity. Thanks, "Uncle" Will for creating such a magical place to learn about animation.) Later on, in the mid-90s, John Katzenberger would world premiere my film *Wildfire* at both John Denver's Windstar and The Aspen Institute.

During this same Community School camping trip one of my friends, Andy Marlow, and I went to wash out our pots and pans after breakfast. He was about four years older than me, the kind of kid everyone liked. Funny, fun-loving. If something were wrong he would stand up for just about anyone. So, Dean Jackson had the cleft lip, Andy, the glass eye, and I was super short.

Both of Andy Marlow's eyes looked pretty normal, just that one was slightly off. In a way, he was, at that time, kind of like an older brother since I never had one. So, there he and I were, at the creek's edge washing dishes. I was scrubbing and slinging the soapy water away from the creek into the trees when Andy leans over, shows me his tin cup, and says, "Does my cup look clean?"

I peered right into his cup and his glass eyeball was staring back out at me, bobbing and bouncing around in the cup's watery oatmeal remnants. I couldn't help but burst out laughing. I think from that day on I made it on his list of being cool. It was so unexpected and a true introduction to the characters that Aspen had to offer at the time. Boy, was I in for a wild ride.

Later, Dean, Andy, and I were in the school play, *One Flew Over the Cuckoo's Nest*. All told, grades five through eight were 12 kids at most, so everybody got a part in the play. Andy Marlow got McMurphy (Jack Nicholson). I'd never been in a play before but tried out for Danny DeVito's character, Martini. I got the part and was psyched to have such a small, but fun part.

Josh Rubin's father, Paul Rubin, was a theater teacher and a general contractor. The word was out that he always wanted to produce a real Broadway play. Instead, he had us—Aspen's own *Bad News Bears*. The amazing thing was, he pushed and pulled us creatively, and yes, he was tough, but truth be told, the theater began to teach me where my strengths and boundaries were. As I got more comfortable on stage, getting into character with my friends, it became clear to me that there was more to a play than memorizing lines.

A scene from One Flew Over the Cuckoo's Nest (after the party) (3-1/2 mins) ©United Artists

Opening night was at the Paepcke Auditorium. During the opening, one of the props broke. Andy Marlow as McMurphy was doing the infamous late-night party scene with all of us "looney bins." McMurphy, having discovered that the Chief character wasn't comatose, just quiet, was trying for the first time to wake him. One of us loonies was passing around the IV bag and we were drinking from it (it was filled with apple juice). Right on cue, another character walked on stage but as he did so, he accidentally bumped the IV stand, disconnecting the tube and it started spraying juice around on stage.

"Martini" waiting for the bus with Ian (image), ©Ian Murray

Scott Reynolds, playing the silent Chief, completely *froze*—so did Andy (McMurphy) who was supposed to deliver the next line. I saw the prop fail, the juice spewing, and jumped right into improv as Martini, making up some lines of nonsense—then worked my character's outburst back over to Andy and he quickly picked the scene back up. These two guys were in some strange way channeling their own real-life characters on stage.

Andy Marlow was, no joke, just like the McMurphy character ... out for a good time. Scott Reynolds was tall, quiet, and distant just like the chief. I think this is the point where I began to see how some actors channel that character they connect with and run wild. I could also see now how Paul Rubin was much more than just a construction guy wanting to produce a play. He found parts for each one of us and we began to learn more about ourselves in that one play. It was very interesting being a kid in Aspen acting in a play with all the locals catching the show—Jack Nicholson himself could be out there. See, we never knew who would show up and when, but BAM! It worked! We'd no idea a New York play director was in the audience and had seen the two of us improvise our way out of a problem—he asked us to work on his play during the summer.

I was happy with my stage success but wanted to be able to play baseball that summer so I politely declined his offer. However, Rhett's sister worked at the local Grassroots Community Television network and had an idea for producing a PBS special where a hearing kid stays at a deaf camp. The Deaf Camp annual picnic is a big, local shindig fundraiser. Her project would only be a two-week production time and I thought, hmmm, I can do that! Eventually, the time came.

The issue was that I had no idea that deaf folks make lots of noises like yelling and grunting while they sleep. We were all sleeping in a barracks-like situation so there was no way for me to get away from all the noises. Night after night the deaf kids would be loud and unconscious while I got no rest at all. After a few days, I snapped (remember, I was 12 at the time).

One day the deaf camp took a trip to the Porsche show on the Snowmass Golf Club Course. This car show was famous in local lore because inevitably some rich dude driving to the convention would go up the back side of Hwy 82 towards Independence, a very long, narrow, and winding road. It was their chance to pretend they were in one of those fancy car commercials. Seemed like every other year someone would launch their Porsche off that final hairpin turn at the top of Independence Pass.

The deaf camp driver parked the bus right next to the barn of the old Anderson Ranch which happened to be where my mom was taking a macramé class. I spotted our Blazer in the parking lot. I felt like I had to make a break for it and escape the madness. I needed some sleep. I felt desperate like Steve McQueen and Dustin Hoffman in the movie *Papillon* as I rolled under our Blazer and waited till all the kids and counselors passed by then went over to my mom. I told her my problem and she said, "Okay, we can go home but we'll need to call both the camp and Rhett's sister and tell them what's going on."

It was like early reality television. I think my struggles as a hearing kid were a good thing, in the end. I did the show, they edited it, and it went to several PBS markets through Denver Broadcast. Being involved with the deaf camp was an amazing lesson, an experience I'm glad I was part of and I am glad it drew attention to the needs of the Aspen Deaf Camp. It was cool.

Deaf Camp PBS Special (11 mins) ©GrassRoots Community Network

Another great experience for me was staying with the Baldersons, it was the closest I ever got to living like *The Wilderness Family.* Herbie and Marcy Balderson were both involved in developing the Chart House Restaurant which became a huge success and an international chain. Their kids, Dylan, and Erica went to the Community School with me. Our parents knew each other from being on the PTA board, which during the 70s was not like that of Santa Monica Montessori School. We had Hunter S. Thompson to contend with, not Cary Grant.

My parents invested their savings in condos with the hope we could slowly sell them off and make that income last a few years. Well, it did! We lived in Aspen for about fourteen years. Each year in the fall my parents drove to Denver to deal with furnishing their condos and that's when my brother and I would stay behind at friends' houses. I generally spent four days out of the year over at Dylan and Erica Balderson's house, and my brother Mark got to stay with the Crum family. The Baldersons lived just below the Smuggler Mine (it made history in 1894 because it's where the largest silver nugget ever mined in the U.S. was found.)

The amazing living room of the Balderson house (image).

Herbie Balderson and his magic bowls (images) ©Balderson Family.

Lou Wille's "bumper art" ©Library of Congress

Lou Wille's famous "Chrome on the Range" buffalo sculpture (image).

The Balderson's place was like a Hobbit house from the 70s with a spiral staircase and handcrafted wood beams that gave the place a log cabin frontier movie set feel. In the center of the room was a big fireplace. Herbie was one of the local artists. Herbie's wooden carved bowls were amazing. He was well respected amongst the community like Tom Benton (Hunter Thompson posters), Richard Carter (involved in creating the Aspen Art Museum), and Lou Wille (the amazing car bumper artist), truly part of Aspen's crazy art scene.

Lou Wille built and decorated the Tyrolean Lodge with his sculptures. Now the lodge is run by his youngest son Pierre and his wife Beth Wille. (I went to school with both and graduated with Pierre.)

The Baldersons lived just past the lower mine dumps on Smuggler Mountain where my brother Mark and I would later ride our motorcycles. They had a circular house with windows all the way around, from which you could see mountain views through the young aspen groves next to the top part of Hunter Creek. It was generally the beginning of hunting season when I stayed with them. I would have to wait at the house with Marcy till Herbie, Dylan, and Erica would come home with a deer. They would show up late afternoon on Saturday. There was never really a long wait and I'd get to hang out with Thea Whitcomb, while Dylan and Erica were out ... Thea, Dylan's older cousin (4 years older than me), lived just down the street in a cool old Victorian house. She also went to the Community School. At this time, she was like an older sister to me.

The thing I remember most about staying with the Baldersons was whenever I would ask, "What's for dinner?" Marcy would generally answer deer, elk, or pork ... this time she said, "Deer liver and onions ... would that be okay?"

I had grown up eating chopped liver at Grandma's, so, whether Marcy was joking or not, I could handle it. I felt like, when in Rome, so I told her, sure! She wasn't joking—dinner turned out to be exactly what she'd said. Usually, dinner also included some veggies from the garden since this was at the end of summer and we were eating the last fresh veggies of the season. Actually, it was not *that* bad—I liked it. Although breakfast was better—it was sausage from last year's pig.

The Baldersons were unique, they tried to live off the land and seemed like they were a blend of Indian spirits with just enough Aspen crazy. I learned a lot from staying with them. In fact, I really liked this particular time of year because of those four fall days, and still do today. When at the Baldersons it was about raiding Herbie's jam-packed shack of hoarder odds and ends and trying to create things, or making spears so we could try to catch trout in the pools nearby. I got to feel like a savage in the woods. I caught a nice-sized trout that Marcy pan-fried for dinner one night. It was great!

One of the best adventures with the Baldersons was inner tubing down the mining culvert that ran from the lower Smuggler Mine which was literally in their backyard and ran all the way along the back of Red Mountain. In the summer that water would get warm. The bottom of the culvert was soft, silty sand. Erica, Dylan, and I would each grab a tube and Marcy would plan to pick us up several miles down the aqueduct.

This little trip reminded me of what Magic Mountain tried to create with their log flume ride, Log Jammer. Only these mountains were real and this flume had long ago been a real, working aqueduct. The best part was, while I would sit in the tube with all my extremities hanging in the water, I could rest my head back and get my hair wet. My view was of a wide, deep blue sky with a few cumulonimbus clouds floating above. The sides of the flume were overgrown with plants and as I drifted downstream, big cottonwood branches reached over the water as we would drift in and out of their shade, reminiscent of what Mark Twain wrote about with *Huckleberry Finn*.

Many years later, these fall days with the Baldersons would give way to spending long weekends up at my wife Amy's brother

Bruce's place on the Santiam River. Life went from Dylan and Erica hunting deer to where I am now—out there *with* the deer, hunting the Pacific Northwest's elusive chanterelle mushrooms. Walking up Hunter Creek in aspen groves with its cool fall scent in the air went from to rummaging through tracks of fir and alder on forest lands just below the Detroit reservoir in the Oregon Cascades. I think as we grow and change through life there are parts that we must try to figure out how to hang on to. It's fun to see where our passions start and how we incorporate them into our adult life.

AI re-envisioning of the old "Gentleman of Aspen" poster.

Pic from ©Erica Balderson of Herbie's fire spirit. The Baldersons were pure physical and artistic adventurers.

When Dylan Balderson was 11 years old or so, he badly wanted to ride a bronco. His dad cabled a bronco barrel between three aspen trees by their house; a training barrel that we all got to play with. These Balderson cats marched to a different tune, and boy was I so glad to have had a chance to drop in. I think Dylan was one of the youngest bronco riders at the Snowmass Rodeo at the time.

When I moved to the public school, Carl Uyehara's family became another sanctuary of sorts. Carl's dad was a Vietnam vet who was injured while trying to escape from his fighter plane as it started to go down. As he ejected from the cockpit both legs got cut off so Carl's dad was in a wheelchair. These two very different families both taught me a few things. I was so impressed with Carl's older brother Corey; he was one of the youngest Gentlemen in Aspen's famous rugby team. From the Uyeharas I learned how to clown around and spar with wisecracks. I learned not to sweat the small things and to try to enjoy life ... let's just say, they are a very punny family.

During my very first winter in the Community School, I had a seizure. Just so happened, Dean Jackson was right near me and saw me fall. I found out later that he went and got help.

This kind of thing could be very traumatic for a young kid, but because it happened in the Community School environment I felt like they all helped me. I realized that family helps folks get through things.

Late one spring, right before school let out, the Community School did a rafting trip down the Yampa River. There was a suspension bridge we had to go over that was a thousand feet up, hanging in the air by support cables. We went across with the bus all loaded with gear, two rafts, a kayak, and us. The bridge was a metal-graded bridge so as you walked across you could see thousands of feet down to the bottom of the gorge. We had to walk to the other side with all the gear to lessen the weight. We watched with our parents as John Katzenberger slowly and carefully maneuvered that bus across the bridge. Even with the weight off we were maxing the limit with the bus and some gear. With John driving the bus it was nothing but fun and adventure at the Community School.

The thing I remember most about this trip was hanging out with Dr. Harold Whitcomb, Thea's stepfather, who we called Whit. Every once in a while I was the odd one out on this trip. Whit told me he'd packed a fishing pole and that, if I wished, I could use it as long as the other kids weren't around.

One day I pulled an 18" catfish from a pool just up from the rafts. It was big enough to put up a fight. When I cleaned the fish, I could tell that he had eaten some of Marcy Balderson's egg rolls from upriver the night before. This is when I learned about how everything flows downstream. Whit's wife Polly was the sister of Marcy Balderson, so there was a big Balderson/Whitcomb presence at the Community School. This whole school sort of made students feel more like we were all family members.

That day I connected with Whit, and later he would become my doctor. Two years after my seizure I developed a reaction to the meds I was given. One day my stomach began to hurt so bad that my mom drove me to the new hospital just off Castle Creek, right next to where all the hang gliders used to land. The doctors did all kinds of tests and could not find why I was in such excruciating pain.

While I was on the gurney in the emergency room I heard a ruckus, and the medical staff swept my curtains around to block our view. I could hear the transporters hurrying to throw some guy on the bed nearby. The guy was breathing hard; all my mom and I could hear was him saying, "Come on doc—just sew it back on so I can get back in the game!!" I knew right then that he was one of Aspen's Gentlemen Rugby Club players (that beat the New Zealand team and put Aspen in the record books).

I ended up stuck in that hospital for two weeks. They had to pump my stomach until the pain went away. One day, Dr. Whit came waltzing in. He was a Doc ahead of his time in our valley. People used to call him Dr. Vitamin C because he believed in preventative measures with vitamins. He was the first doctor who taught me about nutrition. Whit always liked a good project and if it was medical, he was especially in for the ride.

Whit was not even my doctor at the time, but he showed up at my hospital bed every day, once in the morning and again at night to check on me. There I was, in a bed, not knowing what was

©Aspen Hall of Fame - Dr. Barry Mink (website)

wrong—the only way to get some sleep was with a shot of Demerol. I gotta say, when Dr, Whit looked me in the eyes and said, "I am going to figure out what's causing this," he became my doctor right there and then, and for many years to come. Just knowing he was out there trying to figure out what was going on made me feel so much better.

The answer did eventually come, not from Dr. Whit but from Dr. Ann Mass after I mentioned that the meds for my seizures seemed to be giving me acid reflux.

©Aspen Hall of Fame - Dr. Harold Whitcomb (website)

I told Dr. Mass, "These meds are the problem." I'd had two seizures as a kid. Turns out, Dr. Ann Mass's RN had just read in the *New England Journal of Medicine* that another kid in New Jersey had had the same reaction. They switched my meds, and the mystery was solved at last. I've never had pancreatitis again, thank goodness.

THE MOTORCYCLES

MY GATEWAY INTO SMALL ENGINE adventures actually started with a go-cart given to me by Uncle Mike when he saw how much rough range there was between our home and the golf course. There were lengthy patches of rough where all the groundhogs were. They'd stand up right in front of their hole and make their chirp sounds, darting all over, way faster than either Ian Murray's go-cart or mine could go.

Aspen summers are cool, and the sunsets can be rich with reds and oranges. This was the year Mt. Saint Helens in Washington State blew and we had magical sunsets as the sun bounced off the reflective ash. The night skies were all the colors of the rainbow, and from light to dark. It was amazing zooming around on the go-cart watching the sky turn vibrant shades of colors with heat lighting illuminating the distant horizon. Once the golf course was closed for the day, and just before the sprinklers came on, we'd have our chance to be at "home on the range" for an hour.

A few neighbors yelled whenever my friends or I rode in the rough with our go-carts. Both Ian Murray and I shared our carts with all the other kids. This time I decided to go out on my own to whip it up and do a few laps. One day I was out zooming around, and the neighbors called the Aspen Police on me.

By the third lap, I'd made it just past the neighbors' and was blasting through an onslaught of tall grass, debris, and thousands of grasshoppers. I could see the flash of blue and red "jellybeans" between the houses as the police car drove through the neighborhood streets looking for me.

I'd just seen *Smokey and the Bandit* at the Playhouse Theater and, well, maybe I overdid it. I thought if I went way off towards the golf course's shooting range I could draw the police over through the neighborhoods and have a short-cut home since they were forced to use the streets. I thought if I got home fast enough I could stash the go-cart in the garage and run into my house from around back.

This was a great idea, in theory, but when you're on the fly, things happen. I ended up slamming the cart into a railroad tie as I raced to reach the sanctuary of the garage. Hitting the tie threw me over the steering wheel. I landed face-down in the gravel driveway. As I tried to get up I could see a pair of shiny black boots right in front of me. Busted!

It was the same policeman who had busted me before with the water balloons a year or two earlier. He told me about the neighbor's complaint and gave me a warning. "Drive more carefully … and you might want to stay away from the railroad ties."

At 14 I quickly moved on to the 2 wheel pleasure. My death machine was the Yamaha YZ80. The motorcycle group I hung out with were not the real gear heads, but more like the next step up from BMX. This group included Marc Whitley, Ian Murray, Erik Teveta, Brad Barnes, Michael Dayton, my brother, and a few

Andy Collen in his Yamaha jersey (image) ©Tina Collen

others like Bill Sullivan, Jon Fox, Rob Feeley, and, Ted and Stony Davis. It's funny to think back on how we would sneak our bikes through town, walking them behind the elementary school down by Clark's Market to load up on snacks before and after our rides. Whenever a group of us would go into the grocery store wearing heavy-duty cycle boots and coats, they must've known what we'd been up to. But, since this was a small town we were able to get to where we could ride both the lower and upper dumps on Smuggler Mountain Road. We could run into the local grocery store with all our gear on and riding our bikes through town was technically illegal which is why so many of us got good at riding side saddle, and not get busted for riding our bikes. It seemed that the police decided to pick their battles, and we got lucky with this one.

There were so many times when we'd be riding around out on the lower dumps when out of nowhere Curt Caparella, an older kid, would come flying in from what seemed like the clouds and land on the track right in front of us. To us, Curt was the stoner, bike racer, and ninja master who would fishtail in and utter... Fuuuuuuuuck! Curt used the word "Fuck" like Matthew McConaughey uses "Alright, alright, alright!"—a casual greeting that could mean several things, coming from Curt. Whenever Curt heard us out there, he would make one of his masterful appearances. In a crazy way, Curt was our image of a total full-on Moto Cross,

Smuggler Mine Dumps – Steadman Tribute (image) ©Happy Trails Animation

capable of jumping his bike more than fifteen feet up in the air with no problems landing. In fact, he was the first kid with a water-cooled motocross bike in town.

Years later, while attending Colorado University at Boulder I came home to kick around Aspen with my friend David Burson. That weekend we were walking around the brick-stone outdoor mall. There were three trashy fraternity boys causing a ruckus, making disturbing comments to locals, and laughing hysterically, having a great time at everyone else's expense. Dave and I just kept walking past, trying not to make eye contact with them.

Several laps later we were nearing the hardware store when we heard the same laughter mixed with shouts—a fight was going on between the Isis Theater and the old fire station. The same three tourists were hassling Curt who was kicking and swinging, going into ninja master mode, which was only riling the strangers up, making them more dangerous. Dave and I ran and got some cops who broke it up.

Later Dave and I had to ID the guys. They were from Grand Junction and had come to Aspen for nothing but trouble. This was the first time I'd seen a change in culture. It was alarming and I was glad we were able to help Curt. No telling what could have happened. They were not fighting fair—they'd had two, foot-long

pipes in their hands. To me the only difference between then and now is, then it was stupid fraternity guys, and now it's corporate CEOs and ex-Russian oligarchs—what's the real difference? When those corporate CEOs treat Aspen like George Stranahan of Champion Auto Parts, Aspen might have a chance. The path to our future might start by honoring the past in order to create a better new future.

Now that I think of it, we didn't refer to where we lived as "our" house. We called it by the name of the family that actually built it. We were so proud to have an original from a local. So, our first home was the Brinkman house and the second was the Kashinski house. We never referred to either one as the Collen house ... hmmm! We never wanted to tear anything down or build a monstrosity to be used for a corporate think tank or tax write-off. We just wanted to be part of the community, plus, I went to school with all the kids whose parents built the homes we lived in.

Pics of the Kashinski house from my mom's book, Storm of the i: An Artobiography ©Tina Collen

For me, the most memorable moment with the motorcycles was the trip Ian and his older brother Chris planned for us. It was just Chris, Ian, Mark, and I. Chris was several years older than us (the Greg Brady to our Bobby) but he was a true motor-head. He offered to carry gas for an overnight camp-and-ride trip from Ashcroft, up and over Taylor Pass to Little Annie's, and back down Aspen Mountain. This proved to be the most amazing and taxing trip. I didn't grow up with anyone to introduce me to the world of mechanics and motorcycles, and Ian's big brother Chris filled that role.

During the ride, we literally encountered boulders the size of VW Bugs and had to get our little bikes over and around probably a 200 to 300-foot stretch. We were in an X-Games challenge before the X-Games were even invented. It was during this trip that I learned about the difference between all our bikes. Ian had the Honda CR which was all power, a four-stroke that could make it up anything. My brother's bike was a more practical Kawasaki KX, pretty much the all-around best bike. Mine, however, was a Yamaha YZ, a racing bike that needed to be ridden very fast or else it would bog down. This bike taught me how to take things fast which leads me to my next story.

When we moved to Highlands Mountain, there was a horse trail just below the water tower to the left of the Thunderbowl ski run. The T-Lazy-7 horse ranch would use this trail to take folks on rides over to the Ashcroft Valley. I used that trail to practice riding my bike fast.

The trouble with horse trails is that the hooves wear deep U-shaped trenches that taper in at the tops of the trench. When you're riding a kid's 80cc bike, the foot pegs usually glide too low, in this case, under the worn-away trench. The issue is, the curves of the soil would sometimes catch the foot pegs, cram your foot against the pegs, and occasionally, throw you off the trail.

One time I was really cranking through this trail when I popped out and lost control. I shot off the trail, managed to wedge my bike right between two small Aspen trees, and got launched like a slingshot. I landed eight feet away, staring back at my bike raging full throttle, handlebars pinned by the two trees. My bike looked angry, screaming and fishtailing—spraying debris 10 feet up behind. I came to my senses, ran over, and cut the power switch. I felt like a bull rider tossed by a bike that saw nothing but red. How lucky I was for wearing those boots, a heavy leather coat, and a nice Bell Moto-3 helmet. Chris always taught us about safety first.

I think this is where I learned about the trials of producing. At Happy Trails Animation we have always had an overqualified group of "ranch hands." However, when you're in the middle of a project and changes are being made on the fly, sometimes you need to clear your mind and hit the kill switch, and right the wrong. I think it's funny how dealing under pressure is different then and now, but very applicable. Back then it was my bike and now it might be someone like Disney, and to both, I have to say, what a ride!

ASPEN
TENNIS TEAM

ONE OF THE THINGS I like to ask folks who work for me is, "What kind of sports do you like"? If they say they don't play anything I begin to wonder about their ability to be a team player. There are so many things we learn out on the court, and not just from basketball. I was schooled on the Iselin tennis courts just down the street from the Kashinski house. In tennis, it was about who had the best forehand, backhand, or serve and which players you were against. Of course, a good serve never hurts. But knowing the strengths and weaknesses of each team player and learning how, together, they could help each other to become better was a great lesson.

One summer, worn out on baseball, my brother and I dug around in the garage and found some old tennis rackets—one Doris Hart, the other Jack Kramer.

Playing tennis with my dad really got my brother and me to quickly understand the dynamics of the full court. See, my father wore trifocals and has always been fiercely competitive in a fun way.

Seems like the very next weekend my dad had us sent off for a boys' tennis lesson adventure in Jackson Hole, Wyoming. That's where my bro and I figured out that with a little back and forward spin, we could take advantage of Pop's trifocal situation. These games were even better because my pops would come at us with all he had. It was a great feeling to be as young as we were yet able to slay Pop on the court, sometimes. I soon understood there was a strategy to tennis which is why, as soon as you play, you watch.

My brother and I watched the French Open match with Yannick Noah and Wimbledon with Björn Borg against John McEnroe and a match with Ivan Lendl. This was when women's tennis really took off with Billy Jean, Chris Evert Lloyd, and Martina Navratilova. I was this little Jewish boy who wanted to play like Björn Borg and have the composure and heart of Arthur Ashe.

Greatest tie-break in Wimbledon history (22 mins).

We were signed up for the Aspen tennis team during the next three summers. The Moore family donated Fred Iselin Park which included the public tennis courts. Like the Queen of England, Dee Dee McCabe was the ruler of the courts and dubbed them "The Slums of Aspen." The best part was they were literally right down the street from the Kashinski house. The tennis courts became our life for a few summers. I was either at the courts, working at the burger stand, or being a Gant Man (think Matt Dillon in *The Flamingo Kid*, only Aspen style. (More on this as "Odd Jobs in Aspen.")

Arthur Ashe & Björn Borg courtesy of ©Nick DeWolf Flickr images.

So, the tennis team is when I got to re-meet up with both Brian and Chris Keleher. We were connected in an old next-door neighbor kind of way. It was fun since they were very competitive. We had a few great doubles matches—the Collen boys against the Kelehers. Brian had a limp, one which I hadn't noticed before, but like his brother John, he was persistent.

Impromptu "Slums of Aspen" image, Dee Dee style ©Dee Dee McCabe

Here is a poem I wrote in high school using Brian as my subject during my junior year. This was a Bob Simons writing assignment so, of course, I probably got a C grade. Mr. Simons made his mind up when I was in eighth grade that I was a "C" student ... oh well, small town.

BRIAN

Loud, in his quiet way,
The childlike youth greets the day
Cheerfully, with a smile as bright as a puppy's eye.

Standing proudly, yet shakily, atop the wall,
He admits to no weakness.
Allowing his limp to see no witness

To the frailty within which he is bound.
Caring not his imperfection, as his scar,
He lets no sorrow entrap him.

No grudges are held for that frail limb
With which he is so cursed, for he knows no barriers;
For to him life, is life ...

During this time I began to understand that we were living in magic times and that we sometimes got a shot into each other's lives. Living in Aspen was like living backstage and watching the development of both The Nitty Gritty Dirt Band and The Eagles (Lore has it that Maroon Lake, which is just up from the tennis courts, is where Stevie Nicks found the inspiration for "Landslide").

Tennis lessons were so that we could all get ready for the big tournament in Grand Junction. Our ringer was Erin Hood. We had a few kids that would show up every summer and Erin was one. Like the caddies in *Caddy Shack*, we were the students who would help Dee Dee, running after balls and taking care of the courts, working out of one of those pop-up outdoor sheds. This was when those oversized Prince rackets became popular. All the Secrists were decked out with them. Our old rackets quickly became memorabilia like the old skis on the walls of some local restaurants. Eventually, we donated our Doris Hart and Jack Kramer rackets to the bucket of spares. I gave up mine for Martina Navratilova's racket—a new Yonex.

The 1983 Pro Celeb tournament came to The Aspen Club and the tennis team kids were the court managers, ball boys, or girls. It was awesome—we got free, brand-new Reebok tennis shoes that we could only wear for ball boys and ball girls, but that we got to keep afterward. The whole team worked together as a way for us to earn our behind-stage experience.

During the Pro Celeb tournament, the tennis team ran the courts and CBS was there with Howard Cosell. All the great players were there—Vitas Gerulaitis, Pancho Gonzales, John McEnroe, and Björn Borg—generations of greatness. There was a buzz of anticipation because, depending on the draw, the games could dwindle down to be the first rematch of Björn and John. It was mid-July, there was a warm summer breeze, the sweet scent of cottonwood in the air, and aspen trees lined the path up to The Aspen Club's front entrance.

Aspen Tennis Team 1981 (image)

Björn Borg and John McEnroe – Steadman Tribute (image) ©Happy Trails Animation

There was a parking lot just off Hwy 82 for the club. From there a paved road led to a bridge that went over the Roaring Fork River and continued up a slight hill to the front entrance of the club. Amazing to look over the bridge and see trout swimming amidst the rocks below while just a few steps away there was a complex of outdoor tennis courts.

It was the first day of setting up for the matches that would be happening during the following two days. I was walking back to the club after filling up the water coolers on the upper courts. Tennis players and stars like Kenny Rogers were warming up.

As I left the upper courts I walked past an old man wearing a nice suit and tie near the front entrance. He was tan and looked alert—glancing around like he had places to be.

I stopped when I heard him say, "Hey kid—can you tell me where I can get a ceee-garrr?"

I blinked, translating the word "ceee-gar" in my head. As soon as I'd heard his voice I'd recognized who he was. I turned around and said, "A cigar? In town ... this is ... we're at the *athletic club* ...

they don't have cigars here." Hoping to help him out I said, "Mr. Cosell, I can go into town and get you one ..."

He just shook his head woefully and said, "Oh my god, *THIS* is a puhh-lace to *die!*"

———

On the first day of the tournament, the moment I walked up to the front courts, the first person to grab my attention was Dudley Moore. He looked like he'd just walked off the set of 10, decked out in summer slacks, smiling. I'd always been the smallest or shortest in my grade and there I was, a high schooler meeting Dudley who was shorter than me. He was a perfectly proportioned small person. He asked me to show him to the club director. I connected them and at that point, I realized personality and poise made all the difference, not height or size.

Halfway through the last day of the tournament, I was told I might have to take over for a ball boy at the net. Something had come up and they needed someone right away. How lucky was I? Dee Dee, my team coach said, "*COLLEN, YOU'RE UP!*" and shoved two terrycloth towels in my hand. "These are for your knees at the net—put one on either side of the court."

I was ball boying the title rematch of the century in my hometown of Aspen center court, watching the game from the net. The atmosphere was charged. I was having flashbacks of all those amazing games my brother and I had watched on television, games where a point might take 6 minutes. Well, this was definitely another one of those games. Only this time, John McEnroe did all the running and Björn Borg appeared to be coasting—having fun with the audience and doing all sorts of trick shots while John was playing ANGRY of course.

Working the net meant lots of running back and forth, getting balls after they hit the net, but it was the best seat in the house. Eventually, the battle was over, and it was time to clean up the courts. Folks were in the stands and the players went to their benches and were waiting for everyone to clear out. I thought of something I could do for my brother. It was so fun watching these guys go at it from the net. Björn Borg was on fire and just having so much fun, of course, he won.

Mark was on the tennis team but missed the tournament because he was on a three-week bike trip in France. My brother was a big fan of Björn, so I had a game ball I had been getting other players to sign with a Sharpie, like Vitas Gerulaitis and Pancho Gonzales. I figured this was my chance. I approached Björn first. He was quiet, smiled, and signed the ball. I then walked over to John McEnroe who was pissed off and initially told me to F**k Off!! but then signed it. I felt *honored* to have had the wrath of John directed at me. Later that day I heard John on the club phone with Tatum O'Neal having one of their typical spats. I wondered, maybe I'd just found out why he'd been so angry in the first place.

I learned a few things from working at this tournament. The first was from Björn Borg. Even in big events you need to be more like an Aikido master and have fun with the way things are going, and not get tangled up by what's being thrown at you. I learned that there are two ways to win. One is to stress out about needing to win so you are forcing yourself to play hard. Whereas the other way you are there for a fun game and are just going to react to whatever is thrown at you, to effectively bob and weave set after set. Björn was there for pure fun and won with guile and grace. While John probably made more money from the event and told me to F-OFF, from that day on I was going to take Björn's lessons and apply them to my everyday life. I think I was sixteen.

A week later, I went to the club to work out and have a steam. Local folks who pitched in got memberships before the club was even built.

I was heading for the weight room and could hear weights clanking and the groans of a weight lifter barreling down the hall. I'd been working out almost every day for a couple of years and weighed 140 pounds. I was benching over twice my weight. Eventually, I would max 300+ pounds. As I approached the weight room I could see that it was Steve Grabow making all the noise, him and Rich Perez of RP's pizza joint.

On the way into the gym, there was a glass room for spin and yoga classes. Jane Fonda was working out in the yoga area which explained why Steve and Rich were acting like a couple of idiots, grunting and letting the weights clank, trying to impress her like the kids on *Jersey Shore* (I could see they were only benching 185 lbs). When they abandoned the bench I asked my brother to spot me as I swapped their discs off for 45s. My brother raised his eyebrows and said he wasn't sure he could spot me with that much weight (225 lbs)—I told him not to worry.

I jumped on the bench and pulled off a quick set of 10, no grunts, just for show. As I popped up to stretch my arms, Steve Grabow came over and asked if I'd like to work out with him and Rich someday. I said, "Well I've got school and all … not sure when I could."

I sat back down and proceeded to do two more sets, with no grunts or heavy clanking. As I left, Jane looked over at me with a smile. Not sure if she was aware, but it felt like I'd just helped her out with the *Jersey Shores*' goon squad. Years later I'd come to be good friends with her daughter Vanessa through our mutual friend Buzz, one of her old high school buddies.

While we were leaving the gym, my brother asked if we could go shoot some hoops, so we went on down to the courts. We opened the door and there was Bruce Johnson, Jason Perrin, and Jason's dad playing some two-on-one at the far side of the court. Mark and I started passing the ball around and shooting on the opposite side. They asked if we'd like to play a game. As we were getting ready, Martina Navratilova came running in and asked, "Hey—if I get some club guys, would you guys want to play some full court with us?"

We all looked at one another like we'd been asked if we knew our own names, then said, "Sure!" in unison. She ran off and came back in five.

There we were, us kids and a dad against Martina and the club guys. I'd watched a lot of Martina's tough matches with Billy Jean and Chris Evert Lloyd. She was a monster on that court, so I knew we were in for something. Turns out she wanted to cover my brother, so he really had to deal with her.

Truth is, both Bruce and Jason were key players on the high school basketball team and my bro was kind of a ringer as well. It was so awesome to be over-underestimated because we were kids. I was buff, short, and fast so I mostly would drive folks around and dish to either Perrin or Bruce or my bro and set some picks. We kept the game moving and actually won! The funny thing was, Martina was such a fouler, my bro was like, "Wow—she sure pushes the lines!" I laughed.

———

Later in my life, I would spend a summer with my best friend David Burson in Los Angeles where we played a pickup game on the famous Venice Beach courts. Those dudes were always screaming about fouls here and there. The entire game was spent arguing about fouls. This was Crips and Bloods' land, so we were on our best behavior. We had tried calling fouls with Martina and she would just say, "No, I did not." No matter—we still won.

This is when I learned that playing in the streets is a bit different than 8000' above sea level. Later in my life, it would be ad agencies, then big studios. No matter where you are there is always a game being played. When you know the game you can bend the rules. Competitive folks look for those opportunities that can change the game. Be the one to control the change.

I think this really showed up later in my life when I got a crazy call from this guy named Jeff Krelitz who wanted to take our studio in a new direction, that of Motion Comics. So, for about eight years we got to tag team with some pretty big studio's marketing departments. We were working side by side with their marketing teams on some cool campaigns, projects like Tron, Torchwood, Doctor Who, and Spartacus.

Tron Motion Comic trailer (1 min) ©Disney Digital

It was events like the Pro Celeb tournament or pickup game with Martina that made me see, no matter who is standing in front of you, you need to be able to play the game and win. I had so much fun with studios like Warner Bros., Disney, Starz Entertainment, BBC Worldwide, and even Universal Studios. These events helped shape how I began to approach things. Whether it was Martina, or Disney, I was ready.

AI art re-imagining of Jeff Krelitz (image). ©Jeff Krelitz

ODD JOBS IN ASPEN

WORK EXPERIENCE AS A TEENAGER in Aspen gave me some of my most valuable life lessons. Like in the movie *Breaking Away*, back then, what separated the "soches" from "cutters" was having a summer job. Lots of us worked from the earliest stage allowed— I never could understand the whole, "oh, let them be kids" mentality.

I had a motorcycle and needed to buy equipment from time to time. My mom and dad would match funds for us for things like that. It felt great to have that summer job bagging groceries at Clark's Market so I could fix my bike up. During days off we'd go riding around, occasionally stopping at Clark's for chips and Pillsbury cookie dough ... hmmm ... since we worked there, that must be why no one made a big fuss about us swinging through with our gear on, having fun.

Hands down, the one lesson I learned, again and again, was that folks who *made* their money respected what you did for them. Those who'd inherited their wealth wouldn't respect anything you ever did, and I knew this readily by the age of twelve.

The first job I had was as an usher at the Playhouse Theater. We only had two screens in town at the time, the Isis and the Playhouse. Well, okay, the Wheeler Opera House also showed movies but not mainstream blockbusters like the Isis and Playhouse. Each theater got dibs on certain distribution studios. After growing up in L.A. with all the premieres, I now had to wait weeks or even months for one of the latest movies to roll into town. It took ages before we finally got to see *Star Wars*. When I lived in L.A. I got to see the premiere of Lo Semple's dad's film *King Kong* at the Pacific Palisades Theater.

Don Swales, owner of the Playhouse Theater, gave me my first real job. His son, Kevin, went to the Community School. I think Don Swales might've seen me in the Deaf Camp PBS or the Community School play performance and figured I could think on my feet. He offered me an usher job on weekends for winter and all summer.

One of the perks of this job was, when Warren Miller stepped up production on his private 16mm ski movies that he screened at The Slope (a local nightclub lounge), to full-on 35mm feature films that became an industry, they showed at Don's Playhouse Theater to packed crowds. The Playhouse had the biggest screen and a deal with the Ski Corp and Aspen Ski Team and held fundraisers with each premiere of Warren Miller's ski films. As an usher, I got a free ticket to each show and enjoyed a few talks with Warren.

The other fundraiser The Playhouse Theater hosted was John Denver's foray into feature films with the movie, *Oh, God!* John showed up for some fun Q&A at the end of the movie. George Burns played his counterpart of God, but unfortunately, Aspen's altitude made it tough for God, who was in his eighties, to attend. Although I can't recall for certain, the fundraiser was probably an Earth Day celebration through John Denver's Windstar Foundation. John was really a local guy, I mean, he hung out and fished with us all. Around the campfire, he was the kind of guy who'd just play music with whoever was around.

One summer day, Don Swales told me some Edwards Theater corporate dudes were in town all the way from Minnesota to buy his Playhouse Theater. Don was able to get a good deal and he put in a good word for me and my bro so we could both have summer jobs. The new owners split Don's old-fashioned single-screen into four and changed the name to Stage 3. This is when the Isis Theater became the only big screen in town. Eventually, they cut their big screen into four small screens as well.

Both my brother and I worked for that new chain, essentially running it for a season or two. Edwards Theater sent a typical new guy "Jeff" to implement their system and run the theater. He reminded me of David Cassidy with a *Joe Dirt* mullet. He liked how my brother and I were really a team and how well we worked with our friends behind the shows. I started this job at the age of twelve—unheard of now.

My brother was head cashier and worked some concessions. I worked concessions and was the projectionist, although Mark was also trained and helped when we had film jams. Everyone on duty was an usher as well. When it was hopping, the theater usually had a staff of five to run the place.

One night when projecting *Brother From Another Planet* something happened. The film was running fine but there came an issue between the long rollers where the film needed to be able to feed through, heading for the camera. Somehow the 35mm film had snapped or had not been spliced together. There was plenty of slack and the rollers were holding. In a split second, I grabbed the film splicer and tape. I set the two ends on the ground, did a quick splice of the halves, and slapped tape over the break before the camera caught up to the broken section. A rush of glee shot through me. I felt like one of those guys in a rodeo who tackles the cow, ties three of its legs, and throws up his hands. Fixing the film seemed like I was doing the splice in slo-mo, but it had really taken seconds … no curtain drop … no auditorium lights … the audience went uninterrupted while I was silently "yippee-yee hawing" up in the projection booth.

During sophomore year I worked at the burger shack by the baseball park just down the street from my house. I'd open the stand at around nine in the morning, work the grill, then cut out for the tennis team at one in the afternoon. Now I was the kid on the other side of the counter. I'd been one of those Little Leaguers buying sodas and fries. We always said, "twice the price with no ice."

The manager, Kim Doyle Wille, was nice. The phrase "you can do it!" could've been coined for the entire Wille family. Pretty sure they were all long-distance runners and cross-country racers; all podium-worthy.

Kim did a lot of catering so the fridge was full of food that we sliced, chopped, sorted, and stacked in containers. The burger stand had been built with cinder blocks over a concrete slab, like a bunker or one of those Venice Beach public bathrooms. It was painted light gray. Maybe cinder block was all they had at the time.

Bagdad Cafe
movie trailer
(2 mins)
©Island Pictures

The shack catered to the James E. Moore Swimming Pool, the Fred Iselin Baseball Field, and "The Slums of Aspen" tennis courts. It was the only burger stand up on Maroon Creek Road, and I was in charge. Maybe this is why later on I liked the movie *Bagdad Café*—when the burger shack was hopping it was slammed, and when it was slow it was super slow.

Fred Iselin and
Disney film,
Fantasy on
Skis (50 mins)
©Walt Disney

Like Jack Nicklaus designed so many of America's golf courses, Fred Iselin for which the field is named, designed most of Aspen's early slopes. He directed a film in Aspen for Walt Disney's *Wonderful World of Color* in 1963 called, *Fantasy on Skis*. Like in the movie I had a classmate who lived at the top of Aspen Mountain who had to ski all the way down to get to school every morning, much like the little girl in Fred's movie. Only Bridget Birrfelder was skiing down the hill in the 70s and 80s, and she is still skiing there to this day.

Fred Iselin
(website), ©Aspen
Hall of Fame

I had another summer job doing room service at the Sardy House, which used to be a mortuary. One of the rooms used to be the actual embalming room. Then the place was turned into a hip, new, fancy-pants bed and breakfast. This was a cool place with lots of history. It was built in the 1800s during the mining days and was one of the first homes in the country to be outfitted with electricity, central heating, and indoor plumbing. I worked there during its first year of being a top-notch bed and breakfast—and got some of my best tips ever. It was not uncommon to come home with like $300 in tips.

Shelly Mars got me that job. This was the summer my mom and her partner Terry Rose designed the materials for the Coors Bike Classic. I had to work the day of the race, so I missed most of it. That was the year the town closed Main Street and allowed the course to wind through the town and surrounding neighborhoods. Aspen sits at about 8000' so the racers are already high up in the altitude. Shelly and I took a break and got to watch from the deck above the Sardy's front entrance. As luck would have it, this turned out to be one of the best viewing spots in town. Greg Lemond had just won the Tour de France and we got to watch all those racers compete. This was the year The Coors Bike Classic replaced Celestial Seasonings aptly named Red Zinger Race when they had to drop out. The Red Zinger is the race that Kevin Costner's film *American Flyer* is based on, which stars my friend Ian Murray's wife, Alexandra Paul. Kevin Costner has since become an Aspen local and Shelly Mars is now his groundskeeper.

"Coors Bike Classic" poster, designed by T. Collen and T. Rose ©Coors Brewing Company

Although I didn't get to walk the course, I had one of the best seats in town on that upper deck of the Sardy House. Olympic speed skater Eric Heiden showed up as the anchor on the 7-Eleven bike team. His thighs were like tree trunks. All the girls at school said they wanted to check him out. This was the year that we got to see Aspen local, Alexi Grewal, racing for the 7-Eleven team.

This is around the time that I began to notice that the kinds of guests we were getting in town were changing; they wanted surroundings that were even more chic. Our little town was beginning to sink into fashionista hell. The old-style layers of Aspen's history and quirky ways were quickly getting stuccoed over. When I first arrived, there was a small group of buildings called the A-Frames. I remember the day they tore those down. I knew the past would soon get covered in GLAM.

Another cool job my brother and I both had was doing maintenance and driving guests to and from Aspen's airport as Gant Men at Aspen's 80s condo complex for tourists. This was exactly like Matt Dylan in *The Flamingo Kid*, Aspen-style. I was familiar with the layout of the place which was situated off to the left of Aspen Mountain.

Each unit had two or three bedrooms, a small kitchenette, and a living room area. Before the summer season started it was our job to make sure each unit had an appropriate stack of wood. They also had us do all sorts of odd jobs, which brings me to one of my Gant experiences.

Summer Gant workers were recognized in our uniform of green Izods with khaki shorts. One day I was picking up sandwiches at the Butcher Block for all the management staff. On my way out, the owner of a new bike store stopped me to say that he'd give me 20% off any bike in his store if I directed guests his way. I said, "Thanks—I'll tell 'em to check out your shop."

I had other lunches to pick up over at the brand-new McDonald's by Wagner Park. The city had stiff rules for businesses and discouraged franchises but allowed McDonald's as long as its golden arches were diminutive. This was back when the town still cared about its image; Aspen then was a village, not a corporation.

A lot of my school friends worked at McDonald's, and it had just opened so it was a bit crowded. In fact, my friend Chris Pomeroy worked there as one of the first trainees. I was nearing the counter when I heard the Gant management calling me over my walkie-talkie, "Mr. Collen to brain surgery ... Mr. Collen to brain surgery." Of course, everyone in the place looked at me and cracked up.

I grabbed the walkie-talkie. "Getting your lunch—coming back STAT!" Yes, the Gant was a fun group of folks—like family.

Mostly our job was driving folks around in a long van that sat high with a row of windows on both sides like an extra-long bus. Guests needed shuttling to the music tent and wherever else they wanted to be dropped off or picked up in town. (One year my own grandmother came to visit, and she got to see Itzhak Perlman and Pinchas Zukerman with the young protégé of Yo-Yo Ma who was, I think, nine or ten?)

One of my more memorable excursions was for a group of three retired couples who wanted a ride to the music tent where they could enjoy some amazing classical music.

For fun, I decided to make their trip more interesting.

At the west end of town en route to their destination was a stretch of Victorian homes. I began to make things up. I waved a hand and announced, "Over there is Robert Redford's house."

One of my passengers asked, "Doesn't he live in Utah?"

I said, "Yes, but where do you think he got the idea for Sundance? Aspen! He has a house here as well," of course making it up.

We were nearing my friend Will Bennis's old house above Hallam Lake and knew they'd be excited by who Will's neighbor was. "On your right, in that little green Victorian house, is Jack Nicholson."

The group immediately hissed, "Stop! Stop!" So I hit the brakes and all six pressed their faces against the windows—staring wide-eyed at Jack who had just happened to come out of his house in his typical Jack attire—shorts, a Hawaiian shirt, and sunglasses. He sauntered to the edge of his porch and did a stretch as they gawked. He spotted their faces, turned around, and went back inside. I felt like the driver of a Lion Country Safari tour, only Jack was the lion.

At the drop-off point, they all thanked me for the tour and each couple tipped me $50! With this money, I was able to buy a new mountain bike at the store where that guy had promised me a sweet deal. While I felt bad and never did anything like that again, I gotta say—"Thanks, Jack!" I still have the bike in my garage today. It was my first mountain bike and was the first bike made by a BMX frame maker, HARO.

———

Out of curiosity, I put this story into one of those AI art-creating sites and the AI spit this out:

Image inspired by Nick DeWolf and a new AI tool system (Night Cafe).

MY LEMONADE STAND

MY BEST FRIEND DAVE BURSON always had a few jobs. I remember asking him one day about why he had so many. He told me it gave him something to do, and how with cash he could do or get whatever he wanted, permission or not. At this time we all loved to drive to Denver for concerts. Red Rocks was our mecca. Dave liked quality clothes early on and so he'd buy a few nice things, like at the Pitkin County Dry Goods that were made well but cost quite a bit. He had good taste and liked to, once in a while, not be the typical bedhead in a flannel or Izod shirt, like me (in fact, to this day I still have a nice pair of pants from Dave's collection that I wear to special events. He gave them to me when we were roommates at Williams Village at CU Boulder). It was Dave who taught me the value of hard work. I remember him talking to me about working at Sushi Masa. He explained work as if it were done with a Buddhist meditation: making the rice, cleaning the pans, sweeping the floor. It felt like he was using Mr. Miyagi's *The Karate Kid* approach at work.

Because Aspen's community either owned, worked at or catered to tourists, doors opened for us kids to gain experience and learn about entrepreneurship early on. For instance, Anthony Burns had an enterprise gig he developed. He'd put on goggles and dive for golf balls in the ponds on Aspen's golf course. He even invented a ball cleaner that fit in his dishwasher. He'd set up just inside the rough by the fairway with a "3 BALLS FOR $1" sign. He averaged $5K per summer.

I also had an entrepreneurial mindset. My first gig as an artist was when I was around twelve. One day I boarded the Cemetery

Lane city bus into town with a card table and a backpack full of Sculpy Clay and some of my sculptures. I figured, if Pierre Pelletier could find fame slinging lemonade, I could sculpt my clay creatures downtown and maybe sell a few.

Well, I did sell a lot of clay sculptures that day, so after that, I brought ten or so different animal sculptures with me each time. I glued them onto smooth, river-rounded redwood pieces that we picked up during our drive to visit my dad's side of the family in California.

When I was on the outside mall, a bunch of jugglers and performers as well as practicing music students performed downtown for spare change from tourists. Even the Flying Karamazov Brothers, popular in the Pacific Northwest but otherwise unknown, did street performances to branch out and bring folks into their traveling show. (My mom got us tickets to their performance at the Wheeler Opera house one winter. I sat right next to Barbra Walters and her husband.)

With the downtown mall area being so busy it was a great place to try and sell my assortment of Sculpy animals. A large group of folks gathered around to watch me sculpt my miniature clay animals. I even took suggestions from time to time. Turns out, there was a guy watching me sell sculptures who was planning to open a pop-art gallery between the Rocky Mountain Chocolate Factory and Pinocchio's (before they both moved).

A sample of my clay sculptures from my mom's award-winning artobiography ©Tina Collen

One day, two cops came over to my table. One was Dick Kienast. I went to school with his kids, so I recognized him. They told me, "You are going to need to break this down," to which the entire crowd started to boo and jeer that they should leave me alone. It was the craziest feeling to have folks I didn't know defending my honor toward the Aspen Police.

Finally, the police opted to let me stay but told me not to make selling my sculptures a habit unless I got myself a permit. This is when the art gallery guy handed me his card. "I would like to teach you about the gallery world and sell your art for you ... would you be interested?" I told him I'd need to talk with my parents but still said, "Yes, I *would!*"

The next week I went to Davian's Gallery with a considerably bigger selection of sculptures. And he, like my mom, picked his favorites and together we loaded a shelf up with them. My cross-eyed puffins, flamingos, howling coyote, fish-eating pelican, a tongue-tied frog with a fly on the end, and numerous other silly characters sat on their pieces of wood in the gallery, right next to local artist Geoffrey Rose of "Frozen Moments."

My first personal experiences with art were through a few unusual circumstances. Had that crowd not hung around to attract the police, would my clay creations have been on the gallery shelf? I don't know. What I *do* know is that the Aspen that helped lift me into my journey as an artist is long gone.

Later on, when I was in high school and working that job at The Gant, I had to wash my hands in one of the condo bathrooms after stacking wood. While drying my hands I looked over and saw two of my puffin sculptures sitting right there by the mirror! Later I discovered that a few more Gant unit owners were supporters. I suspected my quirky blend of commercial and fine art could connect with people.

Eventually, those sculptures led me to Portland, Oregon, where I would freelance for several animation studios, meet my wife, and build our own studio, Happy Trails Animation. My first hiring was with Oscar winner Bob Gardner and it was to sculpt some old fifties-style cars for a short he was working on for Elvis's Graceland museum.

I've been back to that complex where Davian's Gallery was, and although there was still a gallery nearby, it was full of work by famous outside artists including a huge self-portrait by Chuck Close. Don't get me wrong, Chuck is way cool with me. I've seen his paintings in New York when hanging with family. When I first saw Chuck's fingerprint painting I was amazed at how all those smudges could be blended enough to look like a photograph if you stood far enough away. I was floored by how realistic he could get his portraits to be with just an ink pad and his thumb.

Another foray into early entrepreneurship started with a holiday gift from my parents at sixteen. The year was 1982 and we got brand new Burton Snowboards, and it just so happened my friend Tai Vare got a Simms board. These were the first snowboards to hit the slopes of Aspen, and for some time, the ski industry was baffled. They had no idea how to insure something that was neither sled nor ski. Highlands Mountain allowed us up but only after getting around their safety stipulation for having straps on the boards. The first time we went up we were completely hooked.

Aspen Highlands (22 mins) ©Mac Smith movie.

After that, we knew we needed to get our friends into the action. Our mom let us use her wholesale license, helped us get set up, and voilà! The Snowboard Brothers of Aspen were in business. Our garage literally sat smack at the end of Thunderbowl's slope by the water tower road so that's where we sold boards. Our first two customers were Klaus Obermeyer Jr. and Pierre Pelletier.

Aspen local hero Klaus Obermeyer - true inspiration (3 mins). ©Explore Colorado

There were a few folks from the Alps living in Aspen. Klaus's father Klaus was from the old country ... European Alps. Klaus's father was the supreme local yodeler and creator of Sports Obermeyer. He single-handedly changed ski fashion forever. His son helped us put the word out about our business at our high school. Those first purchases set us up for a bunch of others to follow.

1984 Snowboard Brothers of Aspen (image) including our business card, ©The Aspen Times

With our Snowboard Brothers of Aspen enterprise officially underway, Mom, who studied art at Pratt Institute, stepped in with, "If you guys are going to do this, you need to start right," and designed real business cards and letterhead for us. So, with cards in hand, we hit the slopes to face our new market. We made Xerox flyers. I even designed our own silk-screened T-shirts in Barb Smith's art class.

Earlier, during my freshman year in art class, none other than senior Francoise Pelletier, the big brother of my buddy Pierre, took me under his wing. Francoise and his gang of cohorts had their own enterprise while still in high school. They designed, screen printed, and sold their custom T-shirts at the tourist stores in Aspen. Pierre's

family ran the coolest ski lodge. All the others on these mountains were owned or run by The Ski Corp. The Pelletier's little ski lodge was the only one that was family-owned. In fact, their ski lodge even made it into *National Geographic*—they used a picture of Pierre at his lemonade stand in the article.

Pierre Pelletier at his lemonade stand (image), ©National Geographic

The whole family lived in and ran the lodge on Tiehack/Buttermilk, right at the base of Racers Edge. Even little Nicole, probably eight years old at the time, made change for customers at the till when she wasn't out on the slopes dealing with Zero G's ... she was the *BLUE BLUR*! Mama Pelletier had been the youngest Mouseketeer on television during the Annette Funicello years.

Bonnie Bell ©David Brownell – Little Nicole (image)

We had a lesson in bookkeeping from my parent's accountant. Sorry Mr. Conarroe (Aspen High School accounting teacher), I never took your accounting classes in high school ... oops! Sure would've helped. We passed out snowboard flyers around town and took out a few ads in the local *Aspen Times*. For us, this was more about the process of getting up on that mountain and boarding ... sales were the perks.

In fact, later one summer I went to visit my old friend Erik Luvstad from Santa Monica Montessori School. His family had left L.A. for Phoenix, Arizona. It just so happened that Warren Miller was screening one of his movies there. Erik thought I'd be interested in checking it out, plus, inside the theater, it was nice and cool. We went and at that event, I was able to hand Warren an actual business card. I'd met him at my job with the Playhouse Theater but now I had a product.

He glanced at my nicely designed Snowboard Brothers of Aspen card and immediately got serious. "Can we come and do a piece on you?"

I told him, "Well, actually I live on Highlands Mountain. All you'd need to do is bring some cameras—I can tell my snowboarder friends. We could shoot on Steeple Chase—it would be awesome."

He said "Okay, kiddo! I got your card, let's talk!"

It was my first real promotional meeting ... Warren Miller. Can you believe it?

Warren Miller did call and set up a time to shoot, but when the time came, our gig got preempted by some unusual swells in Hawaii (Warren shot both ski and surf films). The sad part is, one year later I would see the first movie introduction of a snowboard in the new Bond film, *A View To A Kill*. "Missed it by *that much*"!

We had a deal with our friends who all went to school together. Since everybody knew everybody in Aspen, we'd cut them in on a $10 commission per actual locked sale. Our customers would tell us who recommended them. Our little league connections became customers, and our close friends became our sales team. Another *Our Gang* moment.

Our neighbor Scott Voorhies became one of our first salesmen. This was the year we'd had okay snow, but it'd been a while since a real dump had happened. The snow had been rather crusty. That night we got two feet of fresh Colorado POWDER. Full-season passes back then were $120 and had to be bought by Thanksgiving weekend. Scott and I agreed this would be the best day for a little "show and tell" on the slopes.

We hiked up our road just below the water tower on Thunderbowl in our Sorel boots with our Burton Boards, and huffed it all the way over to the Lower Stein Lift. From the lift we could see that the snowfall was beyond Warren Miller—the stuff we were about to experience was going to be historic.

The run below us sparkled in the morning sun. It was *cold*. This was the early 80s and Gore-Tex had really just come on the market which kept us dry during our full day of fresh powder. We decided Lower Stein Run would be our secret target even though it was roped off as OUT OF BOUNDS which meant we'd be blurring the line between right and wrong. Was it wrong to risk our passes for this magical powder day? How could we resist? We were damned if we did and damned if we didn't, a prevailing lesson every Aspen kid grew up with.

Lower Stein is very steep and has this weird corkscrew shape. The left has serious snow drifts with lots of small cornices from where roads cut awkwardly across the run. We had our new Performer Elites and were excited. Toward the top of the first lift, we agreed on where to repack our boots just above that magical fall line. The snowboard bindings of today did not really start showing up until the late 80s and 90s. At least ours were nylon with clips, not leather straps like the *real* old ski days.

Scott and I dropped over the edge, swished a few turns, and floated towards the cluster of Aspen trees we'd spotted from the lift. The snow was so dry and crystallized, it only took a few seconds to get there. It was like surfing on clouds. When we reached the spot, both of us were out of breath. I stopped just below the lip of one of those cat roads, figuring I could pull myself up onto the road as a jumping-off point if I had to. Scott stopped just below me. The next trick would be maintaining a massive amount of speed to make it across the long straightaway at the bottom and cover the distance to the chair lift. Below us was an untracked fall line and scattered trees. I planned to go down the side to miss the Aspen grove.

We were sideways to the slope, pounding our Sorel boots when I noticed that the little "Charlie Brown" tree by Scott was wiggling with each blow. Then I saw a crack in the snow moving up from Scott towards me.

I yelled, "Are you ready?—cuz this bowl is going to go!"

I pulled myself up onto the road above me just as the snow beneath my feet gave way. A cloud of white swept up and Scott disappeared into a blur of snow and Aspen trees. The entire run was zero visibility. The air was suddenly filled with a vast, dazzling display of glittering white speckles. Really quite amazing, but I was freaked out for Scott. I yelled and yelled.

Finally, from waaaay down at the bottom came Scott's faint, "I'm okay ... come on down ... it's *AWESOME!*"

This one run was the closest to surfing with the mountain gods one could ever hope to get. Mother Nature bequeathed us with the most amazing run, and we appreciated it, to which I now say "thanks." That run was so steep the only thing we could do was to float from side to side between a few Aspen trees, kicking up a nice trail of sparkly snow dust all the way down to the bottom.

As a foolish kid moving on to other life events like senior year, The Snowboard Brothers enterprise slowly drifted off as the rest of the world woke up to the amazing new sport. I learned a lot from this experience but the number one rule I learned about business is, it's best to be a fan first.

I may have brought snowboarding to those hills and now one of Burton's early champion boarders, Chris Klug, holds my local footprint. He is my Burton Brother from another mother. As I see snapshots of him skiing and snowboarding with his kids on Facebook I now can see my life being recreated through another family. Actually, it makes me smile to think some other kid will get to experience some of what I did. I hear folks talk about who stayed and who left, but the truth is, those mountains crafted our hearts; it's in us no matter where we go.

"Snowboard Brothers of Aspen" (2 mins), ©Channel 4 News Colorado

Highland – Ralph Steadman Gonzo Art Tribute ©Happy Trails Animation

Snowboard Brothers of Aspen – Steadman style, image, ©Happy Trails Animation

Collen family New Year's card (image). ©Tina Collen

OTHER LIFE
SHAPING EVENTS

EVERYONE HAS A FISH STORY, but mine is a fish *confession*. I was 12 and it was the late 70s. The Mace family, owners of Toklat's Restaurant and Art Gallery, lived way up in one of the old mining areas. They were old Aspen folks, true pioneers. Stuart Mace was known as Aspen's "Mr. Iditarod." He had several teams of dogs and maintained an award-winning dog sled run between Aspen Mountain and Highlands Mountain up Ashcroft.

The Mace family was well known for their wildlife conservation and for living within nature. Their restaurant served fresh, wild dishes that were amazing. Stuart Mace entertained, telling stories about his dogs, and talking about living within nature. He was Aspen's own version of Edward Abbey but with the courage of the 10th Mountain Division.

Meet Stuart Mace
(28 mins), ©Bill
Moyers journal

When we were kids and folks visited from out of town, my parents would take them up to Toklat. The restaurant is up a long and winding road past some huge stands of Aspen groves. As you get closer to the restaurant you can see that the river winds around and flows through several beaver dams—the whole valley funnels through a

Toklat article.
©The Aspen Times

network of dams. Each dam created pools of crystal clear water where you could see the trout hovering over the glacial gravel at the bottom. The water was so clear you could see the reflections of the mountains and sky as though you were looking into an alternate universe.

One summer night during dinner I asked my parents if they could drop me off so I could fish from some of those beaver ponds. The next day my mom drove me all the way up the canyon so I could do some fishing. As we drove up the valley highway my mind began to wonder about the cowboys, Native Americans, and frontier men who'd really lived in this valley back in the day.

Glancing over at my mom who wore dark braids, and aware of the Aspen trees blurring by, for just a moment I could imagine her as Native American. In fact, my mom's great-grandfather was Russian; her great-grandmother was probably Mongolian. These Mongolian-Russian roots gave my mom's Mom a unique look and she ended up being a model for my grandfather's raincoat company in New York. By the time genetics reached my mom, it gave her a slight look of Native American or Eskimo.

Then my mind cut back to the hang gliders. Folks would hang glide off Little Annie's and fly over the town and land near the hospital at the mouth of Ashcroft Canyon. The best part was, if you looked up at the hang gliders while driving up the canyon, you could see the sun behind the hang gliders making them seem like flying stained glass shapes in the sky.

While the L.A. kids were skateboarding city sidewalks and empty concrete swimming pools, us Aspen kids had the road up Ashcroft. In my class, the skater dudes were Blake Gilner, his older brother Garth, Adam Ziets, Lo Semple, Zach and Josh Stevens, Ed Dent, Curtis Kelinia, and a few others. We started this thing called Luge'ing which was performed basically with a really long homemade skateboard, long enough for the rider to lie down on. I was only crazy enough to do this Ashcroft luge maneuver once. Now Longboards are really hot. I know Curtis Kelinna is still cutting it up out there ... somewhere.

The road up Ashcroft starts above Timberline and shoots down to 8000 feet. Let's just say you get to moving feet first so fast you need ski goggles just to see. Like mogul skiing, the further you go, the more speed you pick up. You must try and turn ahead of the actual turn, much like bobsledding.

The most amazing thing to me was when you let go and folded your hands behind your head and just looked straight up, you were sandwiched between two huge mountains, and behind them was a big blue sky with a few white puffy clouds. You could see the trees blow by and as the speed increased you began to notice how quickly the turns came upon you. This was an amazing area to skateboard, go fishing, or cross country skiing.

My mom dropped me off near the end of the road, at what looked like a string of ponds connected by beaver dams. In the middle of the biggest pool was a round beaver lodge. My mom said, "I'll pick you up right here in three hours."

I picked a few pools to fish. I had a cooler with drinks and food and ice for the fish I might catch. I left the cooler in the brush near the edge of the road and went on to the ponds with my fly rod. Each dam had trout you could see. The rocky glacial waters made them so easy to spot.

A few pools had way more fish than others. By the time I was finished fishing, I'd caught 20 or more fish and my cooler was filled to the brim with fresh trout. When my mom finally arrived she asked, "So how'd you do?" In lieu of words I opened the cooler, and her eyes went wide. "Holy *COW*!"

Unbeknownst to us, one of those ponds with the best fish was *stocked* as a supply source for the restaurant. I didn't figure that out until I was already at home cleaning the fish. So, to the Mace family, I would like to say, I am sorry, but thank you so much for shaping who I am and how I feel about the environment and our planet today. I would say the closest person like Stuart Mace of Aspen now is someone I grew up with, Peter McBride. Keep the flames burning, PM.

GEORGIA

One of the things that made a great impression on me was my first real encounter with Georgia Leighton. I was training for my bike tour in France one summer. The trip went from Normandy on through the Loire Valley. My parents bought me an awesome Bianchi bike from Sabatini Sports and decked it out with panniers—the total tourist kit. I geared my bike up with the packs but with nothing inside of them. I think I was 15 at the time. I decided to try and get above timberline, as far up Independence Pass as possible.

©David Burson, Robert Burson, Andy Collen up at Independence Pass (image).

It was the very beginning of summer and I needed to get into shape so I could handle biking fifty miles a day during the trip. On my first day of training, I set out on my new bike going past Mountain Park and The Aspen Club, then off I went, zig-zagging up past the old rope swing towards the pass. In my Walkman was Queen's "Under Pressure," and I was feeling like I could take on the world!

Independence Pass courtesy of ©Nick DeWolf Flickr images.

I noticed someone on my tail, an older lady everybody called Georgia. Since I lived on Highlands Mountain I mostly skied or snowboarded on Highlands and Georgia was a permanent fixture on the slope. She was in her sixties, one of our elder villagers who knew stories from the old country. I think she was from the Alps of Austria or Germany. During midwinter snowstorms Georgia would be skiing in shorts, hence her nickname Leather Legs. Georgia was "old country" strong.

By this point I was exhausted and pretty high up on Hwy 82 when all of a sudden Georgia passes me—not just passes but speeds up! I figured I'd keep my pace and catch her up toward the top. With every traverse, I could see Georgia drifting further and further away. She was about to summit Independence Pass while I was about to hit that last big turn and make that steep grind up past timberline to the top. That day I learned age has little to do with determination. I muttered to myself if Georgia can do it … so can I.

Finally, just as the sun was setting, I summited. There was a warm orange glow in the sky and a cool breeze blowing from the other side of the mountain. I stood atop that last traverse, drank the last of what was in my water bottle, and watched Georgia making her way down, rounding out of view as she passed the old town of Independence. Night clouds were rolling in over the mountain ridges as I shoved off to bike down.

The lesson I peddled away with? Persistence pays off. Setting goals of conquering one turn at a time gets you across the finish line. Georgia helped me realize that persistence is more like fuel; it doesn't matter how new or old the bike is. I also learned that what really pulled me up that hill was the fact that every turn had amazing views from evergreens to Aspens, on past timberline. I also realized, riding in that high-altitude, water can make a huge difference. This ride was my Rocky Balboa moment. I even did a dance with my arms in the air as the sun was going down. Standing at the top looking down towards the old ghost town of Independence is probably one of my most amazing memories.

I never really knew Georgia but always remembered this incident and feel thankful she became part of my journey. Coming down was worth the work of going up.

Events like that made a big impact as to how I approach my world these days. So many of the locals moved away because they couldn't afford to live in Aspen which influenced the change of clientele. Many did not like how the change affected the town and dealt with it by moving elsewhere for a new adventure. For me, I moved to Portland, Oregon in the Pacific Northwest although it too had a fun art culture, like hanging out with those wacky folks at Will Vinton Studios during the California Raisins heyday. The indie vibe of Portlanders eventually changed as well.

The first CA Raisins commercial (:30 secs) ©California Raisins

JOHN DENVER STORIES

I was 12 when I attended my first local summer event, and that was the Deaf Camp Picnic. It was a local fundraiser that would kick off with a grab bag of "whoever was in town" performers like Jimmy Buffet, The Nitty Gritty Dirt Band, Stephen Stills, Graham Nash, and many others. John Denver was the ringleader. The Deaf Camp Picnic was my first introduction to the "real" John Denver, beyond the record album fan version my brain had created. It was John, live on stage.

It was one of those first real warm days with a few clouds building up mid-way through the concert. While John was singing some of his songs, the clouds began to turn gray and a few rolls of thunder came out to play. John finished singing, "Follow Me," looked up at the changeable clouds, leaned towards the mic, and said, "How about we do something about the clouds?" He then sang "Sunshine On My Shoulders" and those clouds parted and disappeared—and in the distance, a rainbow began to appear over the mountains. This was early on in my Aspen experiences—a sign that this country boy, John Denver, was very different. This town of Aspen was magical—like Alice in *Wonderland*, we were living in our dreams.

————

Here's the "John Denver" I grew up with (9 mins). ©PBS Documentary

My next John Denver experience didn't include John, physically. This was much later, in high school. The gondola had just been put in and this was the first summer it was running. Some friends had a family wedding at the Sundeck Lodge at the top of the mountain. I knew the family but was not really dressed for the occasion.

I wanted to see if there were any hang gliders going off Little Annie's and it was an opportunity for a free ride so I jumped into the gondola. As I rode up I had my Walkman and was listening to John Denver's *Greatest Hits* album. His words matched the views, capturing a time in Aspen like no other.

I reached the top and everyone was on the deck overlooking the Ashcroft Valley, an amazing view from Aspen Mountain to the back side of Highlands. I walked to the left and up the trails towards Little Annie's, the area designated for snowcat skiing, not quite helicopter skiing.

There was a view between clumps of trees and branches where I could see across to Steeple Chase, which is now Highlands Bowl. Warm air was drifting up to meet the cool breeze coming down from the clouds. They met precisely where I stood. From that height, I could see alllll the way down to the valley floor. I pushed my headphones off my ears so I could hear the wind and my music at the same time.

Through the evergreens, I could see a bright yellow hang glider suspended on the air currents. It was weird, he was several miles up from the valley floor but hovering at the level where I was standing. I heard the wind whistling. John was singing Eagle and the Hawk into the second verse as the hang glider drifted past. Behind him was a huge golden eagle riding the draft. That sight is still the most amazing thing I've ever seen.

Class of '85 Reunion T-shirt featuring Ralph Jackson. ©Happy Trails Animation

Astounding. I felt like I was standing on the set of a John Denver television special and the director had said, "Cue the epic moment!" I think I understand the magic behind John's passion for nature, and how he found inspiration. The gift was Aspen itself and we need only let it bring out the best in every one of us.

Remembering John Denver (1943–1997) (48 mins) ©Colorado Public Radio

Catching sight of that hang glider with the eagle was a lesson to pay attention. Ideas come from everywhere. I began to feel the power behind what John wanted to do with Windstar. John's best muse may very well have been his many chairlift rides in Aspen. Those mountains certainly became the muse for many of us.

———

My favorite John Denver story is about what he did at the memorial for the town's most radical ski bum, Ralph Jackson (1901–1981) who was famous for ski ballet. Remember Suzy "ChapStick" Chaffee in those Ski Ballet commercials back in the

©ChapStick lip balm commercial from the 70s featuring Suzy Chaffee (:30 sec).

late 70s? Ralph was the guy who *pioneered* that sport—ski dancing down the slopes while dressed like a cross between Red Skelton and Hugh Hefner—with a touch of Phyllis Diller tossed in.

Anyone who spent time on the slopes caught sight of Ralph—you couldn't miss him. Affectionately dubbed the "Clown Prince of Aspen" by fans, he ski-danced his way down the mountain in a top hat and long coat, smoking from one of those long opera cigarette holders.

If he wasn't showing off on the slopes, he was carousing at the bar at Buttermilk's base lodge. He was also a real character as a neighbor; always had a few junker cars in his yard.

My brother and I were relatively new to skiing—we'd been but not very often and never in so much powder. Luckily Aspen had the Aspenauts who gave free lessons to local kids on the weekends.

At our first lesson, we were put into groups. I was in Toad's, which meant we were mostly on Tiehack rather than the basic Buttermilk. I was stuck with the crazy kids like Chris Goss, Rob Feeley, Byron Hawkins, and Lo Semple, who would take jumps and fly way up in the air (they'd eventually be part of my high school graduating class). It was during these days on Tiehack that I first got introduced to the Pelletier clan.

While cruising around with the Aspenauts I'd see Ralph Jackson doing ski ballet in his latest goofball get-up. (Later on, for one of my Class of '85 reunions I produced an illustration of Ralph that the Pelletiers, now in Hood River, Oregon, screen-printed featuring Ralph's toothy grin, his infamous opera-length cigarette holder, top hat, long fur coat, and coat pins galore.) If ever there'd been an Aspen-style cast of *Mayberry* characters, Ralph Jackson would've been one.

After Ralph passed away there was a big hubbub about how to manage spreading Ralph's ashes over Aspen Mountain. It had to do with getting a plane and dealing with the technical issues and permits. If memory serves me right, John Denver jumped in on the conversation and said, "I've got a plane! Just tell me where and when."

So, there we were at the bottom of Lift One with almost the entire town looking down towards Wagner Park when swooping out of the sky ... John Denver in his sparkling blue bi-plane flew by, and behind him, Ralph Jackson floating out across the mountains.

INTRODUCTION TO THE WORLD OF ANIMATION

This next event would eventually lead me on my journey into what I do today as a producer/director at my studio, Happy Trails Animation. My interest in animation started during that time of year when all the theaters get booked up for The Aspen Film Festival, including the Playhouse Theater (later Stage 3).

Dinosaur, a Claymation film by Will Vinton Studios of Portland, Oregon. (13 mins) ©Will Vinton

My mom saw that the Isis Theater was having a private screening of the animation collection and took me to see the films. Several had been made at a Portland studio I'd later walk the halls at, freelancing on projects as an independent artist. Those films were *Dinosaur* by Will Vinton Studios and *The Creation*, a claypainted film by their featured artist Joan Gratz. Another was *The Street*, a superb paint-on-glass film by Caroline Leaf who taught at Harvard and earned grants from the Canadian Film Board. With *The Street*, I began to see how animation as an art form could tackle some pretty tough messages. This was one of the strongest mediums of all, blending reality with imaginary adventures.

The Creation, the amazing claypainted short film, production designer and animator Joan Gratz of Portland, OR. Narrated by James Earl Jones (7.5 mins) ©Will Vinton Studios

The characters in *Dinosaur* were made of clay, like the animals I was selling at Davian's Gallery— all I could think about was how my clay animals could do more than just sit on a shelf ... they could be brought to life as clay animation!

The Street short film (10 mins) ©Caroline Leaf

Starland's "Afternoon Delight" music video (3 mins) (RainShadow Studios) ©RCA

Food Chain (1 min), filmed at RainShadow Studios. ©Happy Trails Animation

My parents said I should make a film and got me some time at a local sound studio that had some video editing equipment. That studio was RainShadow, and I was told it was where the hit pop song, "Afternoon Delight" was produced. In the video (via the QR code below) you can see the stage where we set up my clay characters.

RainShadow also worked for John Denver and many other local artists. At that time I had no idea who RainShadow was—I was more concerned with my high school friends than with what was going on around me.

So, there I was with my clay animals, moving them across the screen, capturing a clip of a few seconds to a minute of video at a time. I would move and tape, move, and tape, for two days straight, then spend two more days trying to splice as few frames together as possible, four to five frames per pose. When the editor and I played the edited frames back it moved clunky, a little like *Gumby and Pokey*, but it was alive, and it worked. Later in Portland, Oregon, I would acquire some old editing 16mm equipment from Art Clokey of *Gumby and Pokey* fame.

We needed to produce the soundtrack. So my brother and I got to sit in the sound booth and make all the animal sounds. This would be my first Folly sound EFX experience. After that, we added back the soundtrack from the quarter mag tracks because RainShadow was a real sound studio. The whole film was shot and edited on three-quarter tape. Ahhhh, 80s technology. I called my film *Food Chain* since it started with a clay fly eaten by my clay frog character, then a fish, and so on.

————

Earlier in my career, I created several short films. *Hero Sandwich* was a sand animation of two stories my parents told me one day when I was testing out a new digital recorder. Their stories were funny, but happened to be about encounters they'd had with disabled parking. While working on the film I remembered those times with John Keleher.

Hero Sandwich was the first-ever colored sand animation film. We wanted the sand to be full color and bright. We finally found an ink that would adhere to the silica of beach sand. The issue we needed to solve was that the size of the sand crystals mattered because, when blown up from 35 mm on a 20 foot screen, one grain might look like a boulder, others like powdery sand. We found the right beach with just the right size range of powder and particles. Technically this film is both historic and illegal since it's not

Hero Sandwich,
sand animation
(3 mins) ©Happy
Trails Animation

okay to remove beach sand, but this was in the 90s and, as I'd once said in Aspen, we were damned if we did and damned if we didn't.

We drew frames, glued sand down, and shot the paper cells on 35mm film using an old Oxberry stand. For the opening title sequence, I sculpted words out of clay and coated them with sand. *Hero Sandwich* premiered at the Denver Int'l Film Festival, and both Amy and I were seated right next to the creator of *Bugs Bunny* ... the master of animated disaster, Chuck Jones. What an amazing experience.

THE DEVIL'S PUNCH BOWL

For us kids, there was summer fun to be had at the Grottos and Rope Swing, but nothing was more life-altering than jumping into the Devil's Punch Bowl. It's at the bottom of a ledge in the Roaring Fork River off Hwy 82, just a couple of turns past the last of the homes beyond The Aspen Club. This part of Independence Pass has amazing views looking down towards the river to a vast expanse of Aspen trees quaking in the wind.

The Devil's Punch Bowl is like a big, washed-out stone bowl with scoured rock sides. As soon as the Roaring Fork's water level was low enough, folks would jump off from many spots to drop

The awe-inspiring Devil's Punch Bowl ©Uncover Colorado (website)

25' into the bowl's ice-cold snowmelt runoff. Gearing up for that jump was intense. Let's just say, I started to think about it in, say, eighth grade. It took me till my junior year to actually jump. But I did it quite a few times.

The hardest part was stepping off that ledge. Also, I must admit, I do have a bit of a fear of heights, but that was not going to stop me. Up top were slabs of stone for some of the best sunbathing spots which was usually where a few of us local kids hung around. Just like the Native Americans have rites of passage to adulthood, so did Aspen and that was The Devil's Punch Bowl.

The Devil's Punch Bowl is a rather large hole worn out of two rocks that jut out and has been cut by millions of years of run-off water and glacial melting. Aspen has several glacier shelves. I remember when Mike Flynn, our meteorology teacher would take us outside and point out the actual plateaus created by the melting of the glaciers. Today my old motorcycle buddy Marc Whitley is in Mike Flynn's footsteps.

In fact, there are places where you can see big scratches in the rock caused by smaller rocks drug across the face as the glaciers melted. The highway leading up to the bowl is lined with aspen and fir trees. The water is crystal clear, and you can see all the different colors of rocks at the bottom of the bowl.

I figured the best time to jump would be when the temperature was in the 90s. It would help make the cold plunge more tempting. The issue was that final jump off the ledge. As a kid, you would stand right at the edge, look down, and think ... *Okay! Here I go... Okay ...* fifteen okay's later and you'd still be up there. *Okay, here I go!*

The first experience for me was interesting. It was one of those hot days and some clouds were coming in. I was a junior in high school and had never "dipped in." This time I figured out how far out I'd need to jump to miss some rocks below (something like 10 feet). As I ran off the ledge of the rocks I noticed clouds starting to come in as I heaved myself over.

So, there I was, out about 10 feet. I spun around in a 360º turn. As soon as I'd heaved myself out over the edge I looked down and it was like I was spinning in slow motion. Some of my senses shut down. I could see all my friends laughing and pointing. Everything went silent as gravity began to grab my feet and pull me down. I could see the rock walls rush by as I finally splashed into the crystal clear snow melt.

If ever there was a part of Aspen that felt a bit Norman Rockwell it was The Devil's Punch Bowl. As a kid what I got out of the Punch Bowl was some fun times with friends but what I really learned from the Bowl itself was about conquering my fears. Safety comes from mastering your fears. This was one of those things that took some time to overcome. But when you finally jumped in it seemed a lot easier the next few times. In the future, this event would help me figure out how to push myself out there and be okay with the splash.

There were a few times when Dave Burson and I would come home to visit from college. We'd take the shortcut from Copper Mountain to Buena Vista and up to Independence, the back way to Aspen. We would pull over on the highway and take a dip in the pool. Usually meant Dave and I cooling off and then heading on into town. It was a cleansing of the soul.

NANCY SPANIER & PAUL OERTEL

As with most kids, my parents did things we had to go along with, some became pretty cool influences. There was a week when our house was 'grand central' for a dance troupe that was run by a friend of my mom's. Nancy Spanier would bring her 12 or more dancers from Boulder to Aspen and present their current show for a few nights at the Wheeler Opera House.

Nancy Spanier and Paul Oertel (website).

They filled our house with chatter and dance moves—it was like living with the circus. They were also really nice to us, and each dancer inspired us with stories about their lives and experiences as performers.

This was my first real "behind-the-stage" experience. Breakfast was a busy blend of cooking, eating, and talking as they joked around and visited with us. After eating, we'd all walk up our road to hike up Maroon Bells, Ashcroft, or Hunter Creek. When we came back they'd all have showers before the show.

I didn't get to watch them practice for the shows but I did catch a few of the performances. Their style was a blend of ballet and modern interpretative dance with a dash of Cirque Du Soleil. The troupe was one of the first to do things like lie on top of each other in the shape of an animal ... then pull apart, becoming different parts of the animal. Most of their performances had themes much like Cirque Du Soleil. Before them, there was a German group called Mummenschanz and Nancy was who brought them to my attention.

Her troupe came to visit two to three years in a row. It was very interesting living in a camping situation in your own house. But for that week our house was alive. It was awesome to hang with them late at night after each performance, as they would go through and critique areas to improve. I think this is where I learned how to take criticism. Both Paul and Nancy would have things to say but everyone there was like a team.

Together they were one mass, and to see how enthusiastically they were to improve was a lesson to me—we are always learning. Why limit yourself to last year's knowledge when it's so much more fun to gather more and more experiences? That is what Nancy and Paul were to me.

Early on with these troupe visits, Nancy's manager, Becci Starr would come and visit us as well. Becci and my mom became friends. Soon Becci and her husband Scott moved to Aspen for a while and lived just up the road from us. This was the road we used to walk up to ski every day, so we would pass their house a lot and every once in a while their place would be a resting stop at the end of some incredible skiing. Scott was an amazing chef ... even his grilled cheese sandwiches were amazing, so needless to say we got close. So many Bronco games, Scott-style. Oh, so good. Let's just say that Scott would beat Bobby Flay, hands down.

At one of these Bronco games, Scott asked Mark and me if we'd be willing to sacrifice our New Year's celebration for $200.

He wanted to throw a bash at the Rock's house which was next door to us just off Maroon Creek Road. We were like, "Sure what do you need us to do?"

He took a deep breath and said, "Well, there's a catch ... you'd be babysitting six or more kids at a nice condo we rented, so all you'd have to do is watch the kids till their parents are done partying. They'll probably start picking them up after the ball drops, and when the gig is over you can stay at the condo if you like."

Mark and I really did this as a favor to Scott. Scott did not have a son and once I was able to ski moguls Scott and I would have some real fun on Highlands. So we said we would do it "no matter what" as a favor. Turns out that a wife of a friend of Scott's managed condos, which Scott rented and paid for. Back in the day, most were owned by individuals who would rent them out during the bulk of the season except for the two weeks when those owners would return for a visit.

Mark and I got to the unit before the kids were dropped off. Scott and Becci's daughter Morgan was one of the kids so mostly it was a pretty easy gig, and Morgan even helped us. So there we were—eight kids not including Morgan, Mark, and myself.

There was this one kid who would not stop taking a knife to the condo owner's locked closet door. It was common practice that the owners would store their things where no one else had access. Time after time my brother, Morgan, and I had to take the knife out of the kid's hand, trying to get him to understand that the locked closet was not for investigating.

Needless to say, between Mark, Morgan, and I we managed pretty well. Most of the kids just wanted to play so we tag-teamed. The next morning all the parents started picking up their kids. Mark and I went home after that. Scott came over and paid us $200. We were in high school, so this was a great one-night haul for us.

The next weekend I'd been watching *M.A.S.H* with my family, a nightly tradition, and this call came in. One of the kids' parents wanted to talk with me. My mom handed me the phone and this guy went off—he was swearing at me! What I could get out of all that swearing was that his kid broke the lock of that condo owner's closet, and because I'd been the sitter, this kid's parents wanted *me* to pay to fix it. I said, "I'm sorry, but we told your son numerous times not to touch that private door and we definitely told him *not* to play with knives."

"I don't care," he said, "you were paid and were responsible for taking care of the kids."

The guy had no ground to stand on. I replied, "We did this as a favor and were paid by Scott. He was very happy with our efforts." The guy got so mad he hung up on me.

My mom looked over and asked, "Who was that?"

"Oh, one of the parents," I said, "I guess it was the dad of that kid who was trying to break into the owner's closet. He broke the lock so now the dad wants *us* to pay."

My mom suggested, "Why don't you call Scott and see what's up," which was good advice. I gave him a call.

"You did what I asked and I paid for everything," said Scott. "If this guy is not willing to cover $50 to fix that damn door that his kid broke, then forget him. He didn't even offer to chip in. Just forget him."

Right after I got off the line with Scott, the guy called back. Again, my mom handed me the phone. Thanks, Mom!

Now this guy was *really* pissed. "Your dad was a lawyer in L.A." he huffed, "he should know about this."

I told the guy, "I talked with Scott and he paid me for my services and was quite happy. I'm sorry your son would not listen to both my brother and me—so many times we told him not to mess with the lock. So, this is your son's problem, and you need to deal with *him*." This speech made the guy blow up even more, to which I then said, "Look, you want to bring this to court? I want Judge Wapner." I hung up, never to hear from him again.

Scott and my parents said they were proud I'd stood on my own two feet. I was, like, 16 at the time. It takes a village; thanks for so many great lessons, Becci and Scott ... and to Mom and Dad for showing me I could fight my own battles.

———

My parents had connections in town, but never to the level of becoming Elks Club members (but I did get a chance to see the inside of the the place when they let our AHS class of '85 hold its 30th reunion there). I think they wanted to stay out of local politics but they'd help out when they could. When my mom, for instance, volunteered at the Aspen Writers Conference, we'd also host writers who would stay with us. We met some amazing folks that way.

Our first guest author was Ted Conover—an interesting journalist who would immerse himself in a place and then write about it. First, he rode the rails with the last remaining old-timer hoboes and wrote, *Rolling Nowhere: Riding the Rails with America's Hoboes*. Then, he crossed the Mexican border with actual "Coyotes" (slang for people smugglers) and revealed the experience, bullets, and all in his book, *Coyotes: A Journey Across Borders with America's Mexican Migrants*.

Where Hunter S. Thompson went full-on Gonzo with his journalistic experiences and bridged the gap between reality and imagination, Ted's approach was to present his experience of places he visited and write the real people of that place—build an experience.

We had no idea at this time that Ted was going to write a book about Aspen, but by the end of his visit he'd crafted an idea, and it became, *Whiteout: Lost in Aspen*.

Whiteout: Lost in Aspen by Ted Conover (website)

Ted's first gig while staying with us was to drive a cab for the local cab company, Mellow Yellow. I remember, after his first night on the job, I'd come back from hanging with some friends and was in the kitchen grabbing snacks when Ted comes walking in.

"Guess what? You wouldn't believe the night I've just had," says Ted. "I got this call to pick up a group at Poppies ..." (Poppies was a fusion restaurant in an old, converted Victorian house. It was known for having very good food but was pretty expensive so we ate there only a few times. This was around 1982).

Poppies (article), ©The Aspen Times

Ted said when he got to Poppies, the owner came out and said the people he was picking up weren't quite ready to leave and was there any chance he could come in and wait. Ted was like, "Sure ... okay" and went inside the bar. The owner asked Ted what he wanted to drink while he waited. Ted said he was on duty and asked for water He said he could barely see the folks at the other end of the bar, but that there was a tall, skinny hippie dude adjusting the water levels in several wine bottles. Then the dude picked up a spoon and fork and proceeded to hit them and play out a Fleetwood Mac tune. Ted then realized the hippie dude was none other than Mick Fleetwood. Turns out, his very first cab fare was Fleetwood Mac, Stevie Nicks, and all the rest of the gang. Ted was floored! (Stevie Nicks actually sang at the AHS graduation for the class of '71 or '73 ... let's just say they were another regular band in town).

Ted did not stay with us long. Once he got into the local culture he really jumped into his research about Aspen. What I learned from Ted was how experiences create the best stories; made me think about that old saying, "truth is stranger than fiction."

Ted surfed through Aspen with the innocent eyes of an outsider and saw the soul of the town selling itself to Hollywood. He wrote about corporate greed taking over the community and about how old Victorians which had once been revered as historic homes and restored, became tear-downs that got turned into 12-bedroom McMansions.

Ted's book was the first time my 16-year-old self looked at my own town through someone else's eyes. I know that so many locals finally felt the stench of change and did not want to admit it, but I think Ted chronicled the exact time at which Aspen started to change. The wonderful, personal community of Aspen literally developed into one big grab bag of corporate sponsorship. Thanks, Ted for the fun times and the clear vision. Telling the truth just a few years before it all came to be.

In the summer of 1985, right after high school graduation, I had one of my very first lessons in producing a stage play. I think this was during the time my friend Gideon Murray's Dad, Bob, ran the Wheeler Opera House and we had an unusual guest become a true local for just that summer. I was working as a Gant man and Lily Tomlin was in town to brainstorm her next Broadway show, *Search for signs of intelligent life in the Universe.*

She opened up our cozy little town to her process. My family loves Lily Tomlin and I was especially interested in her creative approach. That summer we watched her show several times just to see what she was up to. The first stage of her process was to work off creative notes from her yellow legal pad or ring binder. There she was, under basic stage lights reading some of her delivery jokes or acting as characters. Whenever she was unsure of her delivery she would interact with the audience and ask questions about how we felt about the lines.

A few weeks later my family and I caught another run-through, only this time she read from a full script, doing the accents and acting her characters, again asking if it was working for us. We were all sitting there with our mouths open waiting for the next character change.

Lily Tomlin and Jane Wagner's "Search for Signs of Intelligent Life in the Universe." (website)

A few weeks later she would be physically acting out the characters as well as honing in on their personalities. When she felt the need, Lily would break out of character and again ask for audience input. I was sitting there thinking, wow, she really wants to create something that touches her audience. This was the first time I learned how being professional is less about ego and more about capturing the character and audience at the same time.

By the end of the summer, Lily was rehearsing her full Broadway performance with lights, costumes, sets, and amazing lighting. While growing up in Aspen we had backstage passes to so many life-altering experiences. I have to thank "professor" Lily for sharing this generous experience with local kids like me.

———

Later on in my career an industry friend by the name of David Daniels invented a mindbending stop motion animation technique called Strata-cut where colored clay is layered horizontally.

©David Daniels
– Amazing Strata-
cut-animation
(4-1/2 mins).

The result would be a length of clay that he'd then slice and film, frame by frame. There's no way to test the animation. Once the clay gets sliced, that's the end of it! Strata-cut involves so much math it makes my head spin just thinking about it. David was playing with the idea of a clay animated show for Lily Tomlin based around her Edith Ann character.

I don't have samples of that project but here's what David's crazy style looks like (see QR code). You may recognize some of the clips from Pee-wee's Playhouse, Michael Jackson, or Peter Gabriel's music videos from about this time (1985).

―――――

From the Krabloonik dog sledding team to the T-Lazy-7 Ranch and Snowmobiles, there was always fun to be had in that valley. I remember my first time snowmobiling was when our New York cousins from my mom's side of the family were visiting. I was probably thirteen. We all doubled up. My mom and pops, my aunt and uncle, my cousins Rob and Laurie, and Mark and me doubled up on snowmobiles. None of us had ever ridden one before.

I think Zach Stevens' older sister Kelsey was running the winter shift that year at the T-Lazy-7. She gave us a quick operational walkthrough. Mark and I were nodding our heads. Now, this was around the time we'd just gotten motorcycles so we felt like we could handle anything. Snowmobiles would be a lot like motorcycles, I mean, how hard could it be?

We started off with Mark driving. I was on back, one arm around his waist and the other holding onto the bar behind me so I could sort of feel where I needed to shift my weight. We did well until we ventured out into one of the big open fields near Maroon Lake. Mark was really pushing the speed and I could barely see from all the bouncing. Suddenly we hit a small log—or who knows what—all I knew was that I was holding onto Mark's waist as he flew up in the air. I thought, *"Thank God I still have a hold of the back bar.*

The next thing I knew my grip slipped from Mark and I'm hanging off the back with both hands holding onto the bar. Mark is belly down on the seat still holding on by the throttle which means we're going even faster and I'm getting dragged across this bumpy field, fluffy snow flying into every crevice of my clothing. The spinning treads were throwing so much snow in my face I felt like a human snow cone!

Finally, my brain came to its frozen senses and said, "Let go!" Mark got back on the seat and let go of the throttle. Boy was that a real plow in the face. I learned that day that sometimes it's better to just let go. Your instinct is to hold on, and you need to reconnect the neurons that force you to let go.

———

Another natural event was my first experience of an electrical storm at 8000 feet. Mark, our neighbor Erik Tevita, and I had rigged old tent poles and rain ponchos to create our own mini hang glider. We were able to feel just a little lift as we'd leap off an aluminum ladder. A storm had started to blow in, but we were having so much fun we really had no idea, not until it was right on top of us.

At some point we stopped and caught a whiff— there was a dry, dusty metallic smell in the air. I looked over at Erik; his blonde, long hair was standing straight up—he looked like the Statue of Liberty. We all three looked at each other and started to laugh. Suddenly we could feel this little magnetic energy in our muscles. They were twitching ever so slightly. We could actually *feel* the electricity.

Right as my mom yelled for us to come inside there was this extremely loud roll of thunder that ended in an even bigger CRACK—*BOOM*! We looked over at my mom and saw a huge bolt of lightning strike the mountainside behind her, across from the Cemetery Lane Bridge.

We ran inside the house and heard two more loud BOOMS as we dried off. The energy from the frequency of the boom would almost push you over. It was amazing to be at that high of altitude and to be that close to a lightning strike.

When the thunder stopped we went back out. Over at the spot where the first bolt hit we could see some smoldering. We all got on our BMX bikes and rode down Cemetery Lane to where it was. Ian Murray grabbed a shovel and met us at the bridge. When we got there someone was stomping the fire out so we helped a bit, then hopped on our bikes and went home.

———

What I learned from this storm was how, in life, things blow by and you need to be ready for the strike. Now I know why they told us to get out of the James E. Moore pool when the clouds would show up. That day I definitely learned to respect the power of electricity. I also felt honored to have been part of the stomp out. I also realized that culture and people might change in that valley but it's Mother Nature who's *really* in charge.

CHARACTERS OF INFLUENCE

WHEN I THINK BACK ON FOLKS who made a big influence on my early years, I would have to say that Tom Crum (senior), father of little Tommy, was significant. Tom was an Aikido master and John Denver's friend, spiritual influencer, "brother," and bodyguard.

Meet Tom Crum, best-selling author of the Magic of Conflict and Three Deep Breaths.

Tom incorporated Aikido into everyday life. He has always been about centering energies. I also think he was a big influence at Windstar. Windstar was developed to speak about the green future and quickly became a passion project for both Tom and John. It was their way to share with the world how they think things should be. I got to attend a few events at Windstar and it was magic.

We used to go home for lunch with little Tommy and the gang after Little League. Before lunch, Tom would wrestle with us kids, maybe eight of us against him. I just remember running at him and then suddenly finding myself rolling over one of the other kids. Tom quickly had us all piled up. It was amazing—he would just stand there, and one by one, with a simple shift here and there, we were gone.

I think this is when I began to realize that we have a choice to move in different directions. Tom was showing us how to roll and protect ourselves. Truth is, he did it so simply that I began to anticipate the motions automatically and it was a blast. He made us aware of flow and energy which really helped me later in many other sports, especially snowboarding.

I find that even today when I go looking for wild mushrooms here in the Pacific Northwest, I am always dealing with balance. Be they rotted logs underfoot, ankle-grabbing vine maple, or steep brushy inclines, we are always bushwhacking through life.

I also credit Tom's influence as to why, at a young age, I really connected with *The Little Prince* by Antoine de Saint-Exupéry, *Zen and The Art of Motorcycle Maintenance* by Robert Pirsig, and *Illusions* by Richard Bach.

Tom always seemed like he was cool—nothing could bother him. I learned that Aikido is more than physical. It is also mental. It's an approach in life and there are many parts to practicing it. The trick is to live your life with balance and if flying down the mountain wrapped in a thick plastic bag, you can put some of those lessons to the test.

One of my greatest influencers was my high school art teacher, Barb Smith. She is an artist, but I think her best work shows in how much she inspired her students. We all call her "Smithy." I spent more time in her art class during my freshman and sophomore years. Smithy gave me a place to hide and explore at the same time. I was the smallest kid in my high school, that is until I grew taller than David Hauer, and not by much.

Thanks to Smithy I got to do a lot of silk screening. Including a certain type of screening with glue and a grease pencil called the Tusche and Glue Method. You draw with a grease pencil and then put this clear glue all over the silk screen. Afterward you would use a solvent to remove only the grease pencil and it would leave your screen open to ink. You would get a replica of your grease pencil art resulting in a style very much like pointillism.

I really enjoyed how simple this technique was. It reminded me of the artwork on the menus at the Red Onion which looked very much like pointillism. I created an onion and cleaned up the outside edges with tape on the screen and made a prototype on some material. I showed it to the manager of the Red Onion and asked if he would like to do some shirts.

The manager liked my spunk and ordered a whole box of T-shirts. That was the first time my mom's wholesale license came in handy (the second was the Snowboard Brothers of Aspen) and I bought a bunch of Fruit of the Loom shirts for the gig. It was my first time creating merchandise. Not sure if Red Onion sold them? Maybe they became shirts for the softball team.

The best part about Smithy's methods was that she would set some challenging criteria for her art assignments. I was always pushing those parameters and would get that "sparkle" that teachers always eye students with when they take on too much.

Barb Smith, Art Teacher ©Aspen High School

Another one of Smithy's assignments was to, "Use plaster of Paris to make a sculpture that's very much *about* something ... GO!"

What I decided to make went way outside of the box, as always. My mom had shown me sculptures by Duane Hansen, the artist who made realistic people and posed them in real-life situations. That got me thinking.

Who is Duane Hanson? (website)

"I want to do my full-on torso ..." I said, "and have myself climbing out of a trash can."

Smithy gave me "that look" but replied, "Okay, but I'm going to have to run the show on this one."

We chose a time. I put a long john shirt on and a shower cap. I think Smithy had Rene Pelletier and Kim Quirk assist. It took an hour just to get me covered with plaster properly. Then I had to hold my "climbing out of an imaginary trash can" pose

©SFMOMA - Duane Hanson audio clip (2 mins).

for something like 30 minutes while the plaster set up. It took another half-hour to cut the cast in half and get me out. My long john shirt was toast.

Even though they'd greased me up like a pig at Wink Jaffee's rodeo it was still tricky to get the plaster cast off. I felt like that kid in *A Christmas Story* trying to run with all that clothing on. Only my arms weren't sticking straight out—they were stuck in this weird, contorted pose. I needed to make it look like I was pushing myself as if I was climbing up out of the trash. Well, it all worked out just as planned.

Both halves of my body cast came off perfectly and I just stitched up the sides with more plaster gauze straps and left it white. I used up most of Smithy's plaster but it came out great better than I would've expected. Nowhere near as amazing as Duane Hanson's work, of course, but it was a fun project. My trash can sculpture lived in the art room for quite a while. It was one of the most creative but also *eerie* sculptures I've ever made ... almost felt like it was moving.

Smithy taught us how to think about what we were making and fueled our grandest ideas. From Smithy, I learned that you get to decide how big your fish bowl is. Some dreams need collaboration. This is when I learned that my favorite place is in pushing the edge and working with a team. Later in life it would mean jumping from traditional hand-painted animation cels to the tap and fill of the Amiga computer. These lessons would come in very handy when my wife Amy and I built our studio.

Video of Juan Thompson talking about his book (25 mins).

Juan Thompson's book: Stories I Tell Myself: Growing Up with Hunter S. Thompson (website)

Many noteworthy characters came and went from Aspen in those days. Hollywood locals ranged from old-time locals Goldie Hawn and Kurt Russell to the new styles of Don Johnson and Melanie Griffith. But the most indelible Aspen character I ever encountered was Hunter S. Thompson. His son Juan was my first friend in Aspen. Juan recently wrote an autobiography called, *Stories I Tell Myself: Growing Up with Hunter S. Thompson.* His perspective and observations captured a time in Aspen so well.

Hunter marched to his own tune but seemed ahead of his time. I liked his Gonzo approach to journalism or whatever you call it.

The best story I have about Hunter comes from an old family friend, deputy Bill McCrocklin.

Now, our friend Bill stood over six foot six and had a handlebar mustache. The Sam Elliot of the Aspen Police force. The story starts with what would usually be a typical call from one of Hunter's neighbors. There were so many—mostly noise complaints or calls about him shooting his guns.

On this day an emergency call came into the station about smoke pouring out of Hunter's house. When life was smooth Hunter was cool, but when things got aggro so did Hunter. He apparently had a spat with Sandy, his then-wife, and had gone full on "Hunter" and a neighbor had called the police.

Bill said, "Okay guys—pick a straw and let's see who gets to go deal with Hunter."

Well, big, tall Bill drew the short straw and had to drive off to Hunter's place out in Woody Creek. On his way, the staff was alerting him over the radio. This was during the time when SAAB sponsored the police fleet. When Bill got there he saw the front door was open and smoke was billowing out through it and all the windows. The smoke was a chemically purple color.

Bill walked in and asked, "Hunter what are you doing?"

Hunter responded, "I am roasting some hot dogs. Want one?" Hunter was burning a huge pile of Sandy's garments in the living room. He'd poured some gas on the clothes, lit them on fire, and was sitting in one of those typical outdoor aluminum lounge chairs holding a long stick with a hot dog on it. He looked over at Bill and smiled.

Bill persuaded Hunter to put out the fire and clean up the mess. This was just another one of the many Hunter visits by the Aspen Police. It seemed that the community gave Hunter his space and that allowed him to do his thing. We never knew why he did what he did.

Later on in life Bill and Judi McCrocklin ended up with an Aspen-style place just outside of Boulder up in the Sugarloaf area. So when Dave Burson and I went to C.U. Boulder, any time we felt like looking up at the stars and sitting in a hot tub, we'd head on up to Bill and Judi's. It was from one of these hot tub sessions that I heard this Hunter tale. Bill not only was a police deputy in Aspen but was a volunteer at the Sugarloaf Fire Department. In grade school I hung out with their daughter Leah McCrocklin, in fact, our families shared blankets at the Deaf Camp Picnic.

———

Another character of Aspen was its biggest cocaine dealer, Steve Grabow. Everyone in town knew what line of business he was in. He was careful. Lore had it that he would land his little plane up on an old mining road on Aspen Mountain and unload it during the summer, backpacking it down one kilo at a time. He was a huge mover.

Drug Busts, Past and present (Steve Grabow), ©The Aspen Times

One time, my friend and I were at The Aspen Club snack bar watching one of our schoolmates, Nikos Hecht, play indoor tennis on a court below us. Steve Grabow was nearby at the snack bar.

I was a sophomore. In Aspen we had two guys competing for the best tan in town and that was Steve Grabow and local award winner George Hamilton.

My friend was one of those kids who would push the limits of a conversation. It was funny to see him at work. I wasn't really surprised when he busted right out and asked Steve Grabow, "When will you retire?"

"What?" asked Steve.

"Well you know ... when do you think you will stop doing what you do and *retire*?"

"Well maybe when I have enough money?" quipped Steve.

My friend dove for more. "How much money do you have now??"

Mr. Playboy Grabow considered, then said, "Oh about ... $50 million."

Incredulous, my friend pressed on. "How much do you *need*?"

Steve rattled off, "Oh ... $70 million."

My friend and I went wide-eyed, looking at each other like, "$50 million scot free and he's not willing to quit?! WOW!" At this point I was thinking, sometimes folks get caught up in things they can't get out of, like in *The Godfather*.

The crazy part is, two years later in the summer of '85, Grabow got set up in a sting by the DEA, and by that winter he was dead—

blown up in The Aspen Club parking lot. One of my other school friends witnessed the hideous sight of Grabow pulling himself towards the outside parking lot pay phone which was near the bridge and bike trail. What a crazy place for kids. Again, I wonder if our parents really had a clue what kinds of things we saw.

Not long ago, Chris Pomeroy told me about a show on TV called *Cocaine Cowboys*. Chris recognized Griselda Blanco with one of her bodyguards in an episode. I finally got to watch it and Chris was right. I remember seeing them in the back of Cooper Street Pier at the bar, which was next to the Donkey Kong video game during my senior year. I was at Cooper Street to play a few games of pool with friends but decided to play some video games first.

I remember the picture of Speed Boat Betty along the sidewall. I was standing at the end of the shuffleboard next to the pay phone. I could see Griselda talking on the phone. This was right before Steve was about to get blown up. Funny coincidence that right after we see this crazy lady from Miami with her bodyguard, Grabow gets whacked. Aspen's Finest to this day never made the connection. Again—Keystone Cops or did we see things they did not?

Watching how crazy Steve Grabow's life was … who to trust, who to buy off? We were the eyes and ears. I could see how the drug culture was really a dead-end road. I always think about how Steve Grabow seemed to move the goalposts, till it was too late.

TIMES HAVE CHANGED

I think what I have as a takeaway from those early Aspen years to now, is that times are always changing and that's just the way it is. We are all part of some fantastical web of experiences. We are no longer looking at who we are, but what we are about. Life is the path, but you get to choose where to turn. Some of us plowed into issues and some got to learn from others.

As kids, Chris Pomeroy and I hung out from time to time on the outdoor mall and between classes, but our circle of friends had been slightly different. I reconnected with Chris after his brother Jimmy came up to me at our tenth high school reunion and said,

"You should give my brother a call—he's really into animation." I'm glad I took his advice. Chris came for a visit and ended up being one of our Photoshop grunts for the week at my studio. Turns out, being sleep deprived while working under a pressure-keg deadline is a really great way to reconnect.

So, there we were, getting reacquainted while battling who could color and crank out the most Photoshop frames in four days' time for an animated commercial we had to finish for "1-800-CALL-DOC." There's something about being in a team and working on a project that creates a natural family—we had the same task at hand, which was to create some cool shit.

The "1-800-CALL-DOC" ad by Happy Trails Animation ©1-800-CALL-DOC

That visit was a working vacation for Chris ... oh! Except for the one movie we decided to see. Our supposed break was seeing *Battlefield Earth*, which was an epic fail. I mean, we did get distracted, because we were so unimpressed with everything about the movie. I would find out later from meeting Claude Sandoz of Bridge Publications about how that movie went down. He told me that the script got bastardized and that he learned about licensing rights and Hollywood game-playing very quickly. They say everything "shows up" in the film—guess that's true.

When we'd finished coloring "1-800-CALL-DOC," I composited the scenes and rendered them in After Effects, and Chris headed home to Fort Collins.

Once the animation was cut I dumped it out on VHS for Greg Ives, our go-to soundtrack guy, and sent it off to the client with a few Oregon voice talent samples. The client picked Lester B. Hanson for the voice of the commercial, and right there in Greg's studio, I soon found out that Lester and I had lived in Aspen at the same time. Turns out, he'd been one of the local voices of Aspen's KSNO radio. "I got to be the voice for the Ski Splash for a few years," he said.

I remember my very first Ski Splash. Once again, I think I was like, twelve. It was part of the annual Wintersköl celebrations and was held at Snowmass Mountain over by a condo complex near the small outdoor mall that had a rather nice, steaming, warm pool. We'd all crowd around its perimeter to watch as hyped-up Ski Splash contestants launched themselves off a huge jump. They'd fly way out over the pool, hang in the air, do their tricks, and plunge into the water. It was crazy! Women did the challenge in bikinis and would often end up leaving half their suits in the pool—that would get the best audience applause. And no matter what, over the loudspeaker, Lester B. Hansen was there as the event announcer to make us all laugh.

As soon as Lester finished voicing the "1-800-CALL-DOC" soundtrack, I took the final edit to Portland Post and overnighted the beta to be broadcasted "live" in San Diego. The client was thrilled. Two weeks later I checked back to see how things were going with their ad buy, but was told they'd had to pull the ad off the air! I was rather worried until the guys in the background began to laugh. "We got too many calls! It got such a great response, the phones jammed. We have to hire more staff and get more phone lines before we can run it again."

Ultimately, the success of that project was due to a blast from the past with Chris, an old fellow mall rat. I couldn't have made that deadline without him and we've been great friends ever since.

In revisiting our past, we begin to see how our lives unfolded in the first place. It's true, what Joni Mitchell said: "You don't know what you've got till it's gone." But it's also true we're in charge, regardless of whether or not we can tolerate change. We go on, interpreting decisions we've made in the past as part of our guiding force for the future. Oddly, seeing that we all do "life on the fly" reminds me of that time I decided to learn how to ski moguls.

The thing about mogul skiing is, you're really learning to see and think fast, looking three moves ahead like a radical game of chess while attempting to aim your feet and skis between the bumps. There's this natural thing that happens when you get on a ski run like Floradora, you've no choice but to let go and accept that you'll be sliding from side to side between the bumps all the way down. You have no control of speed, only the motion which is your knees firing up and down—they call it "sewing machine legs." You quit resisting and just let gravity pull you down the slope.

Trying to slow down or stop is how I'd run into problems in the first place; too much front-on jarring impact on bump after bump. Moguls are a chance to practice Tom Crum's Aikido ways of making the force work for you, not against you.

Highlands Mountain had local competitions almost every week. Back then, the pro tour would show up and the moguls would quadruple in size. So, I decided I would go for it and learn from real mogul pros. The next day I peed some blood, so I went to see my doctor. This time I saw Dr. Ann Mass, known around town for being a good doctor and a mogul skiing champ.

Watch mogul skiing, the way it should be done (2 mins).

Dr. Mass asked, "What happened?!" I explained about the moguls. The funniest thing (and this is so Aspen), was that my medical advice that day from Dr. Mass was a prescription for how to 'mind the kidneys' while mogul skiing. Dr. Barry Mink had shown me the importance of exercise, Dr Whit was all about nutrition, and Dr. Ann Mass? A great sports doc. From that point on I was able to ski moguls.

Johnny Moseley on mogul skiing (article), ©SkiMagazine

How I approached the slope ran parallel with how I needed to approach life. It's quite a challenge, to learn how to let go while taking charge. I'll bet everyone has these sorts of great stories in the chapters of their lives.

I'm in a few Aspen groups on Facebook and it's quite funny to hear the slightly different variations of life there. I would say, rather than think about the specific year, think about a time ... a time where old-country mixed with new Aspen business when the folks that lived there also owned and ran the restaurants and hotels that were not connected to big conglomerate chains. We all sat at the joiners table at the Wienerstübe.

It's so interesting because, as I look back on my Aspen experience I've got to say, I've sure had a crazy ride of it here in the Pacific NW as well. It seems my tattered tales of Aspen followed me to Portland.

The idea for this book really started while exchanging stories via Zoom and phone calls with Chris and Dean about the good old days. I was having chemo, and everyone was hunkered down, beginning to deal with Covid. One thing I realized while dealing with cancer, like so many before me, was that the things that keep you going, you know, what gets you out of bed in the morning, that's what's important.

To my way of thinking, Hunter S. Thompson had been fighting cancer for quite some time. I can clearly say that his heart for staying in the fight was gone the minute he opened his eyes to the change in clientele at his local haunts; the J Bar and Woody Creek Tavern.

Hunteresque – Mad World, Gary Jules (3 mins) ©Sanctuary Records

My first experience with the reality of cancer was as a kid when Herbie Balderson dealt with pancreatic cancer. Where our medical system is now with treating cancer is a world apart from what it was then. Now, in my adulthood, I know I was lucky—mine was more manageable (stage three colon cancer). Many thanks to Herbie for showing me how to power through with a strong spirit. Even though Herbie lost his battle, I have to say, "Thanks" for showing me how to be tough and stay in the fight as best as you can.

Teachers are often the first to help us start blazing a trail in life, but few so much as my history teacher, George Burson. He worked with thousands of kids and is a comrade of politics— always ready for a great discussion. Everyone who had George as their teacher learned how to think and voice an opinion. And he was sure to do the same. His son David and I became close friends early on and had the most amazing discussions and excursions as kids. We also had our share of *Animal House*-like experiences in college together. There was a great stint there in Greeley, and then Boulder where we had the opportunity to bring friends back with us to Aspen now and then.

There will always be a difference between being young and old. We grow and learn to change perspective as we see what works and what doesn't. There are still folks living in that valley who carry the culture I've spelled out in these pages. For instance, the last time I spoke with Tom Crum (senior) he still had a strong hope for the community.

Frank Beer, eighth-grade science teacher (image)
©Aspen MS

I've lived in Portland, Oregon since the 90s but I still cross paths with Aspen in the weirdest ways. Two of my wife's great-nieces, Alissa and Andrea, graduated from McNary High School in south Salem, which turns out to be where my eighth-grade science teacher (Frank Beer), started his teaching career. I count myself lucky to have gone on outdoor ED trips with Mr. B, looking up at the stars scattered in the pitch-dark desert sky with him showing me all the constellations. Also, my nephew-in-law, Jeff, grew up in Colorado. He's huge into rock climbing and biking. Every so often I see him in an old Coors Classic T-shirt my mom's company designed. What are the odds? Jeff has also been hauling around a hardbound copy of *The Aspen Book*, which has the timeless photo of Stacy Thorp, Ian Murray, and I from up on Red Butte just off Cemetery Lane. Amy's niece brought Jeff to the very first screening of our short film *Winter/ En Hiver* at McMenamins Mission Theater in Portland. Jeff recognized me from that old photo when we were introduced. (The photo in *The Aspen Book* was taken by local Aspen photographer, David Brownell, to whom I also want to thank for letting us share his work in this book.)

Everyone's always talking about old and new Aspen, and what's better. Well, to me it was always about community. We all lived there year-round, everyone's parents owned and ran it all. I suspect the hope for Aspen now will be when the folks of today reach out to those of the past. Funny, this is exactly what happens at most hackathons. Coders of all ages converge, working together to solve a real problem. There's no allowance for attitudes, who's too old or too young, they simply get to work, pushing each other toward the solution. Learning strengths as part of a team with a common goal.

Bear in mind, I'm a student of Nick DeWolf and we had technology and computers in Aspen in the late 70s and early 80s. Being mindful of the past does not mean being clueless about the future, it only means you're not doomed to repeat the same mistakes of the past in the new environments of the future.

There was a time when Aspen was like John Cleese's *Fawlty Towers*. This series always made me think of the Mountain Chalet and the Melville family. The lesson I've learned is that it's not about the past but the journey. This is different for everyone; it just so happens I got lucky and mine started in Aspen.

A scene from *Fawlty Towers* that reminds me of the Mountain Chalet

As I left Aspen for Portland, I had no idea my reflection of Aspen in the 70s and 80s was going to be such an influence, that those years would mirror my social and learning experiences with independent animation studios through the 90s.

There are so many songs that would be great to sum up how I feel about Aspen's influences on who I am, but I think I am going to leave you with this gem from John Lennon. I think this song best describes my view of where I stood with both my family in Aspen and in Portland. In Aspen, my art influences were Lou Wille, Tom Benton, and Judy Hill and in Portland, they were Tom Arndt, Jim Blashfield, and Joanna Priestley. I have learned to be thankful for my time slot in Aspen's history. I feel lucky with both lives. The one from Aspen buried deep inside my heart, or the new one in Portland with its indie animation movement. I think I will share that chapter next with another collaboration with a group of cool guys. No matter where you are, everything is always changing. I think the question is, how much change, how fast, and whether it will change the culture.

As I see what Aspen meant to me and what I got out of it. I sure hope other folks got the same. I know my classmates did.

Watching the Wheels Go Round and Round by John Lennon (3 min).

CONTRIBUTOR:
CHRIS POMEROY

CHRIS WAS BORN IN THE MOUNTAINS and raised from infancy in Aspen, Colorado. He left the valley in the 1990s to pursue a career in Newspaper management. He worked at three newspapers over the span of a decade, *The Aspen Times*, the *Fort Collins Coloradoan*, and the *Athens Banner-Herald*. He shifted away from the industry in the early 2000s with a short stint in agency work, and then to his current job of 15+ years, consulting in Internet Banking for Digital Insight, Intuit, and now NCR.

He has won many awards for campaigns, layout, and illustration throughout the years, and has done illustrations for national companies, newspapers, and magazines for a myriad of uses.

When not "slaving for the man" he has worked in the art of animation, one of his true passions, for the better part of 30 years. As any animator can tell you, animation is a love of the art and the art of sacrifice. Caffeine and bad music are a staple for projects with near-impossible deadlines and endless pressure to not only meet the challenge but to walk away proud of the effort and the finished project. In the end, the work is fun. But it is work. Lots of it.

He currently resides in Athens, Georgia with his wife, two sons, a dog, cats, and a bunch of fish. He is proud to boast that he can still pull off the coveted "bedhead" style of the late 70s, and often does.

DEDICATION

*I dedicate this portion of our book to my parents,
Joan Bigelow Pomeroy, and James Pomeroy,
the drafters of the dream.*

And to my brother and sister, the keepers of the flame.

**With a special shout-out to Cameron Burns,
and the many times he's mentioned me in his books.*

HOW MANY
"OLD ASPENITES"

Q: How many 'old Aspenites' does it take
to screw in a lightbulb?

A: 12,000. One to replace the bulb and 11,999 to
reminisce about how great the old one was.

So goes the joke ...

Reflecting on the years I lived in Aspen, it's now apparent to me that I have lived elsewhere for more years than I did in that town. Granted, I did come back to live in Carbondale and Basalt in the mid-nineties, but I've now lived in Athens, Georgia for longer than I did in my hometown, where I grew up. Weighing my experiences, however, it almost seems like I lived two or more lifetimes in the valley, when I compare it to my adult life, which consists mostly of work, and raising my own children.

As most upbringings go, on many levels it was standard—teenagers hanging out in front of the McDonald's, playing at the park, swimming lessons, little league, and when I was older, keg parties, and cruising around in cars. But in other ways, we had a unique upbringing built on experiences and events both magical and horrifying, when compared to the standards of helicopter parenting and suburban ideals of today.

Take for example the recollection my mom shared with me that when she brought me home as a baby, she gently placed me in her lap in a wicker laundry basket, wrapped in a blanket. And that's how it was for the whole ride home.

By today's standards and laws, you *can't* do that. When my children were born, there were strict laws surrounding the type of baby seat you could buy, and whether it had "expired" due to age. We had a class we needed to attend, websites, pamphlets, rules, regulations, and laws. In fact, we had to pass an inspection before we could take our child home from the hospital—which is within five miles of where I live.

What I failed to mention, is that I was adopted. When my parents brought me home, it was from DENVER. They drove us home over high mountain passes, with wild animals capable of jumping out into traffic, and in those days, some two-lane winding roads, for a 200-mile trip that likely lasted four or more hours—in a wicker basket.

But that was the beauty of it, too. There was a certain amount of freedom our parents enjoyed that we may never know. Living in Aspen was both idyllic, and fraught with potential scenarios you would think were fiction had you read about them in a book.

We were latch-key kids in a town with no locked doors. Some were children of the elite, while others were like free-range carny kids in the Disneyland of the rich and famous. Others still, most of us in fact, fit somewhere in between. But Aspen of the 70s and 80s was a melting pot for all of us. While school could be very cliquish, rarely was there a time when we weren't all in it together, as a community.

Nevertheless, when people find out I grew up in Aspen, there is often the misjudgment that we were all fabulously wealthy. This simply wasn't the case. Aspen of those days was a tight-knit community, and people were there for each other. Call it small-town sensibility. Or maybe call it an actual community. Perhaps it came about with the influx of hippies. Whatever it was, people pulled together, in good times and bad, to somehow make it work.

I'm often reminded of the notion my mom would share, that during those years when there really was an off-season, the same $100 bill would pass through the hands of just about everyone in town. Someone would use it to pay their rent. Someone else deposited it in the bank, where someone else withdrew it shortly thereafter to pay to fix their Jeep. The mechanic would stock up on groceries. The grocer would use the $100 for payroll for an employee. The employee would spend it on new gear at the ski swap, and the lucky person who made that much from their gently used skis might have used it to pay his three-month tab at Tom's Market for groceries needed during the previous "off-season."

In those days "off-season" meant no tourists, no snow and for many people, no income. For anyone who relied on ski season to stay afloat, it could be a long few months. Families would have to budget with 3–4 months out of the year generating no money coming in. Many held multiple jobs. As I recall, even a few of our teachers would work construction when school was out, living the ideal that "the best three things about being a teacher are June, July, and August."

Off-season in Aspen could be a struggle. But it was quiet. It was serene. And for a small amount of time, by God, it was ours.

Though Aspen's first boom was borne of a silver rush, its next iteration was a quiet time that lasted around fifty years. Before the glitz, glam and drugs of the 70s and 80s, Aspen was essentially a town of old-timers and ski bums. Stories of ranchers running cattle up the dirt road named Main Street abound in the lore of the era's inhabitants and their children.

Then came the hippies, the wealthy elite, the royalty of Hollywood as well as those of the music industry. Granted, the arts culture, and skiing attracted tourists of old. And the town had its start with the help of folks like the Paepckes, it was reborn as a center of philosophical thought, outdoor paradise, ecological sensibility, and the arts.

As early as the late 1940s, the town was born anew with the advent of the Aspen Skiing Company, who in league with the 10th Mountain Division, opened the ski mountain in 1946 (skifederation.org). Soon followed by The Music Association and the Aspen Institute (aspeninstitute.org) (1949), and Aspen Center for Physics (aspenphys.org) (1961), and Hallam Lake Conservancy (aspennature.org) (1968 donated by Elizabeth Paepcke).

Eventually, however, the dreams of an earlier generation gave way to larger crowds with new ideas. The 1980s presented new opportunities for land speculation and many of the old buildings such as the Hotel Jerome and the Wheeler Opera House, were again revamped to appeal to larger, more affluent crowds.

Eventually, however, the dreams of these earlier generations gave way to larger crowds with new ideas. The 1980s presented new opportunities for land speculation and many of the old buildings such as the Hotel Jerome and the Wheeler Opera House were again revamped to appeal to larger, more affluent crowds.

It was a magical time and place when you look back. Where else could the "average Joe" bump elbows with heads of state, world-famous musicians, A-list celebrities and renowned scientists, professors, politicians, and sports legends from around the globe?

We all had our share of experiences and run ins with someone famous. But it was an unwritten rule to treat them as though they lived there. A paparazzi could have made millions from the sightings, yet it was a free-range vacation spot where they knew they'd be left alone—for the most part, anyway.

As it turned out, many celebrities had made Aspen their home and contributed to the community. Goldie and Kurt raised kids, Glen Frey had his dude ranch, Hedy Lamarr had her villas (Hedy's Beddies), and of course you had Hunter. S. Thompson.

But it was a greater chance still that you could see Jimmy Buffett playing in the local softball leagues, your casual conversation with Jack Nicholson or Arnold Schwarzenegger, and most notable of all, John Denver, who was influential and committed to our beloved community. Whether he was playing guitar for us kids while we sawed our graham crackers at the local school, reintroducing wolverines to the ecosystem, or his works at Windstar Foundation, he was a constant presence and a hero to most.

As seasons change, so do the people. Seemingly suddenly, things started to look different. What was once a thriving small community, was slowly transforming into a vacation spot for a more transient population. And overnight, the divide between the haves and the have-nots began to widen.

Now workers shifted to more affordable accommodations in the bedroom communities downvalley or piled up and slept in shifts in the hostel-like employee shanties that were once someone's income property but that hadn't quite commanded a large enough price to sell as a tear-down.

For every small-town local business that didn't survive that year's off-season, another tourist-based business popped up in its place. Instead, items that were useful to guests and locals alike began to be replaced with T-shirts and "luxury" items. Eventually, there were only a few places where someone could buy things like scissors, socks, and jeans. Places like Bill Bullocks went away, and more and more trinkets with the Maroon Bells printed on them, took over shelf space that once served our guests and our community. Even the grocery stores replaced mundane wares and staples with selections of high-end maple syrup or charcuterie from foreign nations.

As the changes morphed our small town into a "mini-city" you could sense subtle differences. But like a frog in a pot of boiling water, it happened over a long enough time that it wasn't immediately obvious to most. The middle-class families that were the lifeblood of the tourist industry, slowly became priced out of their beloved vacation spots, and the old hotels and condos with that comfortable Scandinavian flair, were razed to the ground and replaced with more modern, albeit soulless buildings in their stead. The days of partnerships and co-pollination between local businesses, the Ski Co, and community services began to dry up. And new faces each year represented a wealthier and more entitled lot in life. As prices rose, so did expectations.

Neighborhoods that once hosted friendly camaraderie, became quieter, and the homes of the hangers-on became surrounded by empty "McMansions." These large and mostly vacant vacation homes replaced more humble abodes of everyday families who sold and moved downvalley—or out of the area altogether. In short, "the billionaires ran the millionaires out of town."

The town had slowly become a place where the locals would be treated like the hired hands. It became a double-edged sword. We had unlimited access to nature and beauty, but had to struggle to make ends meet, and to afford to live in a place where only the increasingly wealthy could live. We needed the tourists for the steady influx of cash that kept the local economy going, yet after the 1980s, it was many of those same tourists that made it no longer enjoyable to be there.

There were those that tended to make us feel unwelcome in our own town. Like when the Aspen Club made it abundantly clear that the locals were no longer needed, and summarily priced them out once the club had a solid footing financially. Or that local kids were not allowed in the clubhouse at the golf course. Or in stores without the accompaniment of their parents. Or at the fine restaurants, unless you were hidden away in the kitchen or the back alley with the dumpsters.

Recently I've read there is now limited access to the parks—unless you play polo.

Monstrous homes of the ultra-rich began popping up, to honor and congratulate themselves for being born lucky. The new monoliths, occupied for only part of the year, loomed over the adjoining, now meager properties, jutting out with ostentatious appeal, to the other would-be billionaires in a gesture not unlike the painted roof of the barn in Woody Creek, flying the middle finger to all who could see it. One could be reminded of the behavior of the kid in Middle school who always took two chocolate milks, and laughed maniacally while telling the others, "Look what I got! You can't have one!"

Perhaps it's a slightly smaller model of the shift in our capitalist culture. Maybe it's just shit luck. But the shift in demographics in Aspen, as well as most of the other covetable locales in our country, points to a shrinking middle class. The trend continues until the final rung in the middle of the ladder is now much lower on the steps. The widening gap between the haves and the have-nots becomes more apparent the older I get. I chose to move on, but many friends and family remain—soon to be priced out of the bedroom communities downvalley.

Now I'm told and read in the papers, that Aspen has transformed into something different still—what some would describe as a soulless town of entitlement and greed. Sure, the mountains and beauty of the area still thrive, but the community, in many respects, has lost its way. The dream of the Paepckes gave way to the dreams of our parents, and now has given way to something wholly different.

Being immersed for the formative years in a culture of so-called exceptionalism, has taken its toll on many of us. Living at 8,000 feet, I tended not to notice the uniqueness and true beauty of the area, until I left and lived in the flatlands for several years. The opulence, sophistication, and mirage of greatness that Aspen represented in those years, has left many of us with a lifelong quandary: the belief that all of us were somehow "special," and that with hard work we could accomplish the same level of success that was evident all around us. This was our "normal."

However, in contrast to the ordinary lives we lead now, we will never be able to produce the level of wealth and opportunity afforded to those who visited, and later transformed our town into a soulless shell of empty mansions and struggling locals. In place of an excited enthusiasm to go out and achieve, those of us who left had a rude awakening into the world of the "ordinary."

Many of us fell into a phase of self-medication through alcoholism, substance abuse or alternate methods of self-destruction. Others moved far away to escape the pain, while still others, in fact too many, lost the battle to suicide. Hopefully by now, we've found healthy ways to work through the damage. Personally, through a combination of those methods, I have finally come to terms with the tremendous fortunes we had and use that experience to balance the negative treatments endured while working for the world's elite; those who knew just how easy it was to put us in our place and remind us that we are not "exceptional" like them.

Somehow the myth of the American dream on steroids was imbued into us kids during our formative years. Yet many of us were not fortunate enough to truly understand the irony in the cliches, "it takes money to make money," and with a little luck you could be in "the right place at the right time." The latter is clearly not a recipe for success by its own merit. We were led to believe that with enough effort and hard work, we could accomplish anything we dreamed of being. Just like all the rich, beautiful celebrities that frequented our town.

Instead, we were both fortunate and cursed to live in a place and time that was a melting pot of intellectual thought and an artistic paradise. We had access to some of the world's most innovative and influential minds of that century. And yet, they were just people around our town; people who hung around with our parents and frequented our favorite places. The most unfortunate truth has become, that many from that time have passed on, and were gradually replaced by people who were merely there to "see and be seen." Those who own homes only to honor themselves and to have bragging rights to the great successes they were fortunate enough to be blessed with; fortunes almost no one else could gain on their own.

To put the current level of wealth and the disparity in perspective, consider the following:

An average career lasts 55+/- years. The curve of income trends up, but let's take an average of $70,784 per year:

55 x $70,784 = $3,893,120 over the lifetime of the earner.

$3,893,120 would be the amount saved if said worker never spent any of the money he/she earned.

$3,893,120 may still seem like a lot until you remember that $1 billion dollars is **1000** million dollars. The "average Joe" wouldn't earn that much in 250 lifetimes. Not accounting for interest-bearing accounts and strict saving rituals, or a head start in the form of generational wealth, most will never be wealthy.

As of writing this, the median home price in Aspen was $14,550,000[1]. For an 80% loan, a mortgage would be approximately $77,500 per month (7% 30 yr fixed x $11,640,000). That is more than the median income in the United States for a year ($70,784)[2].

[1] src: https://issuu.com/slifer.smith.frampton/docs/rfv_monthly_stats_february_2022)
[2] (src: US Census Bureau, 2021)

My stories of growing up in Aspen may seem to have occurred in slow motion, and many are of adventures in solitude. There is some truth to that notion, particularly in the off-season. With our parents working double time to make ends meet, and partying as hard in their off time, we largely had to find ways to occupy ourselves. For me, a lot of that time was spent exploring every square inch of that town and its surroundings with friends and siblings. When I wasn't working to be able to afford the things the other kids had, I was doing what most kids did. Just hanging out.

Our upbringing was not unique in that most of our stories are relatable for many people. However it was unique in that **all** of these things happened in a small, quiet mountain town with a population of 2000 or so full-time residents—seemingly all at once.

Sadly, our Aspen is gone, as is the Aspen from the quiet times, and the original silver boom. Now our town lives on in the memories of the families and people who made it great. And regrettably, we are forever priced out of a lifestyle we can never again regain.

Some might say we squandered our future by leaving, while still others might state we didn't know what we had when we had it. But in truth, as the town changed and the new 'locals' offered huge amounts of money for the land, and made Aspen less enticing to be in, the more tempting it became for the holdouts to leave.

We all tend to think "our Aspen was the best." Unfortunately for us, the new Aspen is 'cool' to the new folks. It seems to work for them. What they don't seem to understand, is that everything that made Aspen cool and appealing in the first place, has been strip-mined and sold off to the highest bidder. In short, our town's people sold out, and took off, and with them, the soul of the place is now, for the most part, gone. And who can blame us? We saw the limitations of the future, the writing on the wall. And when the price was right, many of us suddenly had a chance to get out from under the costs of the days of old. A chance to move on, with a new ideal, and clear of old debts.

When we say "the old Aspen," which Aspen is it exactly we are nostalgic about? Was it the "old" Aspen the Utes knew? The "old" Aspen of the miners in the 1880s? Or could it have been the "old" Aspen of the ranchers? The Paepkes' vision? The ski bums? Or maybe the hippies? Or the millionaires? And now the billionaires?

When my wife and I first moved to the South, it became immediately apparent that there were certain, unspoken animosities toward outsiders, that only the locals could explain. Aside from the more obvious resentments which bizarrely remain from the Civil War, what it comes down to is the fact that when people from the North arrive, more often than not, a certain transition happens. The tendency for "Northerners" to fall in love with the place morphs quickly into a new desire to change it. Like, "this place is great! I can't believe how far my money goes here. The only thing that would make it better, is if I make it a little bit more like where I came from." And no sooner than the ink dries on the sale of a new property, the new occupant begins mulching trees and painting the place in colors that go against the norms and look of the neighborhood, the culture, and the town.

When one looks back and revels in their own idealism, we tend to forget that each iteration is the perception of that time's reality. Each is unique, and some may or may not actually have been better or worse.

Unfortunately for us, the Aspen our parents built was not good enough for the new occupants. Nor was the Aspen of the next short era. Or the next. Fads and times change. One adapts, resists, or moves on.

It's as though they heard about an awesome party. They showed up, turned on the lights, changed the music, invited all their friends, and switched the beer out for fine wine. Essentially, it became their party.

Just like our families changed the community from what it was in "the quiet years," the millionaires changed if from our dream, and later still the billionaires changed it from theirs.

One thing is certain, the Aspen we all knew in our own vision is now gone. And any Aspen experience is now completely out of reach for all but the wealthiest, or the diehards. And if we perpetuate as a society the wholesale worship of wealth, celebrity, youth and exceptionalism, places like Aspen will remain as such. Out of touch and out of reach for almost everyone.

And as an "old Aspenite" I am unabashed when I say that I choose to reminisce about the old lightbulb. At least the one I remember. Those family members and friends who remain, carry the burden of maintaining the last embers of a light that once shone so brightly. And what a glorious light it was.

Growing up in Aspen was unique. Mother Nature was our backdrop. As I raise my own children in suburbia, that fact becomes more apparent with each year they grow. Our playgrounds were the peaks of the Rocky Mountains. School trips consisted of camping, cross country skiing, downhill skiing, hiking, mountaineering, long-distance bike riding, rafting, and rock climbing to name a few. Utah and New Mexico were also destinations for weeklong trips to Canyonlands, Arches, Mesa Verde and more. Our education included and sometimes revolved around nature and the outdoors.

Our extracurricular lessons consisted of winter survival tactics, nature conservancy, biological diversity, hikes, and history in the form of nearby ghost towns, and exploring the mining ruins of the area's past. The great outdoors was not something we learned about in books, instead we lived it in real-time.

A certainty that I am aware of from experience in nature: there are places you can find that are so remote, so free of human contact, that they will take your breath away. No photo I have ever seen comes close to the experience I've felt looking over a cliff that drops hundreds of feet to a babbling brook. Sounds, smells, even tastes propel the vision into a realm of the impossible that not even the world's greatest technology can capture. I only wish my children could experience a small slice of the joys I've found in my youth alone in the wilderness.

When I look back at the Aspen I remember, I think of miles of Aspen groves, hills that turn into mountains, and mountains that turn into craggy peaks, the landscape changing colors with every season. Winter resembled a grey, white, and black sleeping army of aspen trees, a landscape pocked with the blue-grey footprints of birds, fox, deer, elk, snowshoe hare and the very rare bobcat, moose or even one of John Denver's wolverines. Summer brings greens from every myth, toadstools, hummingbirds, and wildflowers litter the dew-fresh meadows. Spring starts with melting ice and the buds of tiny leaves, a rebirth of nature, life blossoms with fecundity. Autumn explodes with color and paints the landscape with the hues of Mother Nature's dreams. Wherever there are no aspens, the terrain spreads out with large cottonwoods, scrub oak and pine trees that drop needles to bake in the fall heat. The smell of sap and pine bring fresh senses and memories that never fade.

My one ask of the new owners of our wonderful town, is that they not squander that which we will never have unlimited access to again. Resist the urge to see and be seen. Instead experience Mother Nature in her finest form. Learn from your surroundings and please respect the land. Your homes may be beautiful in your eyes, and in the ledgers of your accountants, but nothing compares to what our planet makes available to you every day.

"Only when the last tree has been cut down, the last fish been caught, and the last stream poisoned, will we realize we cannot eat money."
– Alanis Obomsawin

"BORN TO SKI"

MY PARENTS WERE SKI BUMS.

If there was an adequate definition for Ski Bum in the late 1950s it might be close to this:

Ski Bum:

Syllabification: ski-bum

Pronunciation: skee/bum

Definition: Someone who abandons "normal" life ambitions to pursue living in a winter destination; one that revolves around the sport of skiing— willing to work for a small pittance in exchange for the opportunity to spend time on the ski slopes instead of pursuance of a more lucrative career and lifestyle that their parents had hoped for them.

Mom and Dad both arrived in Aspen in the late 1950s along with a generation of crazies from around the same time as the beatniks. They arrived well before the hippies. There was no Jazz or artistic movement that drove the ski bums. There was just a roving desire to experience life in the mountains, and to go really, really fast down the fresh, untouched powder unique to this part of the country.

Dad grew up in Los Angeles but discovered the beauty of the Rockies while in a year of college at CU Boulder. He is an avid sportsman and considers himself a cowboy born in a city. He feels out of place where he can't be around horses, a good fishing stream or a place where he can take the dog for a 6-mile walk.

Mom came from St. Paul, Minnesota, after a year in nursing school and a stint at Ma Bell. She was born into a once wealthy family, who were friends, and neighbors to railroad titan, James J. Hill. Several of the homes on the famous Summit Avenue in Saint Paul were once owned by her relatives. However, after losing almost everything in Italy in WWII, the family landed squarely in the middle class. She came to Aspen with little more than a dream, and an enthusiasm for the area and its people.

GiroInfoto Magazine (Italy) Issue 66, April 2021, La Casalta – page 108, (article in Italian)

My parents were two sides of the same coin. Similar in most respects, but they could never see eye to eye.

Like a badge of honor, I wear the notion that I was raised by two people who wanted so much to have children and share their love and experience. In a town where many kids were treated like commodities, and others were raised by nannies, I am blessed to have been raised by my parents.

My brother and I arrived in the late 1960s. My sister was born three years later in 1971. Summers were short. Three months at best, the remaining months of the year involved lots of snow, lots of clothing and before the height of the 1980s, lots of skiing before the tourists arrived in droves. My siblings and I were brought up on skis. From as early as we could walk, my parents held us between their legs, strapped to boards and taught us to ski. Before I can remember, my motor skills intended for walking, running, and occasionally skipping were fine-tuned to the art of carving, cutting, turning, and slowing down in attempts at total control on the slopes. You could say we were born to ski.

Well, my brother and sister were anyway.

There is an allure to the pure driven and freshly fallen snow which can only be understood by someone who has experienced it in its raw fashion in nature. Only in areas where the snowfall is measured in feet and yards can it be understood what "snow" really is. Our counterparts in the states closest to the equator can only imagine what a "snow day" is or what it means to drive on ice. That, or they pay dearly for the opportunity to spend a week or two with their families or friends to get but a glimpse of the lifestyle they once saw on TV. A lifestyle many of us took for granted when it was at our fingertips.

True, spiritual beauty can be experienced while floating in a snow drift and watching the sun glint off the glitter-like particles of snow too light for gravity's hold. The air stings your nose as you try to smell the wind and breathe in tiny ice crystals. By moving, you not only disturb the silence, but allow the cold to permeate your shallow shell of clothing. The snow drifts into the empty crevasses of your clothes, like water in a frozen landscape. As you grasp to climb out of the pitted banks after a wipeout, and regain your balance, there is a certain serenity to the task of finding your soul at the same time you search for your lost poles, skis, hat, and goggles.

A wipeout in the snow can be humbling, and an experience of great joy and solace. Often the only source of stress is to find your skis, hat, poles, and sunglasses before the other members of your entourage arrive to ensure your safety. Or it is the pressure of reassembling so as not to be the last one in the group—and catching up.

Skiing may be a way of life. But reality dictates, "it costs money to live."

During the early years, Dad began working in the local ski stores in the winter, tuning skis and assisting customers with the best fit for their rental equipment and the most modern styles of the day. At some point, he made the decision to stop "working for the man" and open his own shop at the base of Aspen Mountain, just across the street from the ski lifts. It was about the most convenient place for a ski store, aside from being on the mountain itself. The store had Dad's name, but the venture was a partnership with Mom, both in sacrifice and "sweat equity." Pomeroy Sports was a mainstay for quite a few years.

Dad's raison d'étre was, "You'll never get rich working for someone else." He employed that philosophy throughout the extent of his career.

As we got old enough, my brother, sister and I would help in the shop. It was not so much for reasons of economics, really, but more a way for my dad to instill a work ethic into each of us. And for something to do to keep us out of trouble. I can still remember the chores as though they were yesterday. Many of his lessons remain with me to this day. I don't remember if we were compensated in any way financially. There may or may not have been an allowance at the end of the day, but that really wasn't the point. What I do remember is the work itself and the lessons I learned from my dad about life, effort, and people.

A typical summer break day for me at the store, although minimal in actual physical effort, seemed like a mountain of work for an 8-year-old. The jobs my dad gave me were minor, and often not necessary. Nonetheless, I took them most seriously. I knew I "had" to do them if I was to be able to impress my father. His modus operandi was that work was life, life was short, and work was waiting. And I aspired to be like him.

At first, the store was just a ski shop–that is to say, Dad had a small area where he and a couple of guys waxed and repaired skis. They would help fit customers into the skis and bindings, and he had a small inventory of ski boots, poles, gloves, jackets, and hats. Soon the volume outgrew the space.

To my memory, the store next-door was some sort of Spanish themed store. In short, they sold leather pants, jackets, boots, and those fringe outfits that pervaded the 1970s like a bad habit. I will always remember the giant oak/cedar door that separated the two stores. My dad would open the top half of the door by sliding a huge iron bolt and the petite, Hispanic man from the adjoining leather clothing store would flamboyantly show up and say, "Hellooooooo!!!"

Eventually, my dad bought out that space and expanded to sell more clothing and seasonal sporting equipment relevant to the times. The "shop" side remained, for the most part, the same as always, only now there was more room for rental skis and machinery. In its heyday, Pomeroy Sports served throngs of families with their ski apparel needs, from the locals all the way up to the world's elite, including the Kennedys.

During winter, our activities outside of school were skiing, sledding, building snow forts and mostly playing in the snow. Sunday mornings were devoted to church at St Mary's. This was a huge part of our upbringing.

In the summer, and after school later on when I was older, work was the main focus. I got my start at Pomeroy Sports. The shop was quiet, and relatively clean. An average day would begin at about 7 a.m., before the store was open, with mowing the lawn out front of the store. The plot of grass was small by modern standards, really no bigger than a postage stamp, but to an eight-year-old kid, it was formidable. I'd start out by going through the back, out by the trash to grab the mower. After unlocking the gate, I would drag the heavy tool across the sidewalks to the front.

There were no pull chords, there were no spark plugs and there was no need for gas. This was an "old-school" mower, made of two rings of blades. When pushed, its blades would scrape against each other and cut the grass, much like if you had a giant pair of scissors. In short you would push, and you would turn. There was no "quick" way to mow the lawn. For a little kid, it was actual work. I would mow back and forth, up, and down until my sneakers were green with fresh clippings.

I knew I was done when my shoelaces were soaked and the tiny mushrooms that grew closest to the curb were adequately mulched.

Then came watering the sidewalks. Dad knew that cleanliness translated to sales. If the sidewalk outside showed signs of the drunken debauchery of tourist revelry from the night before, his products behind the window showed less promise to the family-oriented trade of the daytime hours. Dust, grass clippings, cigarette butts and broken glass alike needed to be dealt with.

Among many things, inadvertently or otherwise, my dad taught me the ways that water could be tamed and manipulated. The power of water grows with its flow and its volume. We had a small cone-shaped nozzle that intensified the water pressure from the hose. While the mathematics and physics of the action may have eluded my dad, or possibly he did not care, what he showed me was a lesson in the way the world works. Even if it was on a small scale in a seemingly silly action.

As we turned the pressure of the hose up, the spigot made the water exit the hose at an even higher velocity, even though the amount of liquid leaving the hose remained the same. As such we were able to make a stream on the ground. To wash every inch of the sidewalk with the spigot pointing in a line or a grid would take days to accomplish and untold hundreds, if not thousands of gallons of water. Instead, Dad taught me that by moving the stream back and forth and allowing the water to collect, I could push the water over itself and in effect create a mini tsunami. The miniature waves would swell and grow with each movement and in the end the sidewalk was clean within minutes. The waves did the work for us. The filth of the night before rolled down the gutter and into the storm drain. Each day was a new day.

I would then pocket the spigot and roll the hose into a tidy pile out of the sight of potential customers. Then I would roll the mower back around to the trash area and stow it, walk into the shop, place the spigot on the nail where it belonged and then proceed to the back of the store where the boxes had been collected from the day before.

My next chore was to crush the boxes down and dispose of them in the trash area in a neatly stacked pile. Shoe boxes were the best. They had sturdy corners that collapsed easily under my wide tennis shoe. I would step on each corner until the box was flat and stack them in a pile of similar boxes. Then, when finished, I'd take the stacks back and out of the store across the courtyard to the dumpster. The more boxes there were, the happier Dad was, and the more fun it was to break them down. Empty boxes meant lots of sales.

Next, I would use the shop vac to clean the shirt needles from the floors under the racks and shelves. There were hundreds of them. When someone opens a new shirt, after the plastic is taken off, the needles need to be removed too. For some reason, customers and employees alike dropped the needles on the short-knit, orange and black carpet, instead of throwing them in the trash. My job was to get them all out of the carpet, so no one got stuck in the toe while trying on shirts or shoes. After that was done, I'd vacuum the whole floor. I hated that vacuum. Aside from the nasty gunk caked on the sides from the ski wax and petox from the shop, it smelled of chewed gum, wet cigarettes, and dirt sludge—peppermint nightmares.

The vacuum had to be emptied, along with all the trash cans throughout the store. The trek to the dumpster was well traversed, this time with trash bags and that stinky vacuum I would drag by its hose on shaky wheels to the dumpster. More than once I ended up dumping the vacuum canister of dust, needles, cigarettes, and chewed gum all over myself since I was too short to reach the top of the dumpster. The plastic handles on the trash bags allowed me to hurl them over the top of the dumpster. Occasionally a bag would split and dump half-empty coffee cups filled with cigarette butts and stale liquid down on me.

As the sleepy-eyed and often hung-over employees of the store would slowly show up, Dad would have me take their coffee orders. There was also a coffee pot in the breakroom, but it was an afterthought. The crew preferred fresh brew and I was the best way to get it.

I'd take the list to the Weinerstube, (a Nordic-themed breakfast restaurant that held great appeal for decades) and wait patiently for the waitress to fill the orders. My eyes barely reached the top of the bar where they poured coffee, wearing their Oktoberfest dresses, their pens stuck behind their ear, and their hair in a bun.

The staff was happier when the coffee returned hot. On the days the orders were small I would ride my bike. On days everyone showed up on time, I walked the few blocks, laden with as many cups I could balance. Upon my return I felt like I was the most popular kid there ever was. It's possible not even one of those employees would remember me now. Such as it is with coffee; people forget the pusher. They only remember the drug.

As we got ready to open the shop, my last chores were to clean the bathroom, and organize the break room. Other random chores included dusting the tops of the racks, shelves and displays, pulling weeds from the flower bed out front, washing the windows (inside and out), cleaning the mirrors, and sweeping the sidewalks as needed.

When I was older, I used to inventory rental skis, boots, and poles. All of which required engraving numbers for reasons of theft. I enjoyed setting the type stencils for the serial numbers and engraving each ski/boot/pole, and so on. While usually done only once a year it was one of my favorite chores. Waxing and repairing skis became responsibilities, as did occasionally fitting customers for skis, boots, or bindings.

Often Dad would have me walk with him to run an errand. I could never keep up with my dad. His pace was faster than my gait could contend with. I often found myself literally running behind him on the way to the bank or the doughnut shop. Dad's pace was twice what I could cover, no matter how long my inseam ended up. Many other people, older and taller than myself have told me the same. Dad's pace left many of us in the dust. The only thing that ever slowed him down was a quick conversation with someone in town. And Dad knew everyone.

Before I was old enough to get a "real" job, but just after I spent years of my early life helping my dad at Pomeroy Sports, my mom offered to help me earn extra money for the things I wanted. The things I needed were taken care of, thanks to Mom and Dad.

Bear in mind, in Aspen in the late 1970s and early 1980s, it was easy to get a job in the kitchens by the early teens or so. My first "real" job was washing dishes at a place called Joe's Diner at the ripe old age of 11 or 12. Before that, I had an allowance, supplied by my mom, of $5 per month. But, by God I had to work for it.

In the winter, my chores were simple. Keep your room clean, take out the trash cans once per week, and keep the driveway and the decks clear of snow. By now I should explain. No child should be paid to clean their room. That part was more of a ransom issue. As in, if you don't clean your room, you don't get jack squat.

A standard job for me was taking the trash cans located next to the decks to the end of the driveway. Trivial as that may seem, for a small kid it was not easy. We lived in a remote neighborhood on the west side of town–more toward the untamed mountains leading to Independence Pass and the Continental Divide. On the other side of our house, was the view of the valley that opened up and poured out downvalley and eventually to the flatlands before Utah. Our neighborhood was sparse and our views of the mountains and of the valley were enviable. As such, our driveway was about 50 yards to the street and was almost two-lanes wide. We could park cars two-by-two, eight deep if we wanted to. During our high school years, my brother and sister and I put that to the test by entertaining our friends. For a good laugh about why that driveway was so big, read Jack Brendlinger's book, *Don't Get Mad, Get Even*.

Of the many pranks my parents' friends were involved with, the Duck Boat (jon boat) Incident is hilarious in hindsight, but it was odd to be on the other side as children.

Don't Get Mad... Get Even: Stories of the Aspen Practical Joke Years by Jack Brendlinger.

Before I was old enough to know better, I would often 'sell' things to the neighbors to make small change. I would load up my Western Flyer wagon with old toys, rocks or any such thing and go door to door hawking my wares. Our neighbors were very kind, patient, and generous. They would often oblige and give me a quarter for an old matchbox car or some other treasure.

As I was too young to understand or appreciate the nuance of basic ethics in business, it was not beyond me to pluck "fresh cut flowers" from the neighbors' gardens, and then sell them back to the very neighbors who took the pain to grow them in the first place.

This was often followed up with a call to my parents from a concerned neighbor.

I would also often "help" Gene and Rita Clausen in their woodworking and pottery studios. And of course, there were countless days when I would "help" Richard Powell with his painting projects, and gladly accept cookies as payment from

Angelina, his wife, who lived a few doors down from us. They lived in a home owned by Tom Anderson. *(Angelina has remained a close friend for the entirety of my life. She officiated our wedding in 2002)*

Soon after, my parents convinced me of better ways to make money. Activities like shoveling snow from decks, driveways, and an occasional roof from which I may or may not have fallen off of, were better suited for a happier neighborhood.

For years, I would clear the deck with a plastic, wide faced shovel and an "ice chipper." The shovel was great when the snow was dry. However, when the snow was wet, it got heavy and often unruly. The ice chipper, which was basically a hoe straightened out, became the tool of the trade when the Ice hardened, and the shovel couldn't push it off the deck. The deck was a moody beast. On good days it took 5 minutes. On bad days it took hours.

Then came the driveway. Two lanes of snow packed sludge, eight cars deep. ...

One year my mom bought an electric snow blower. Most patrons opted for the gas-powered version but for some reason, she insisted on the electric model. (She also once bought an electric chainsaw). A snow blower is essentially a winter version of a real lawn mower (not the kid-powered version of my youth). The main difference is, in a healthy snow year, I got to "mow the lawn" every day. In heavy snows, the height of the snow would reach in the measure of feet rather than inches. It was common to have to clear 2 to 3 feet high, 40 yards long by 12 feet wide. It took most of the day. And that was with the snow blower. I did this for years. While occasionally my brother helped, the duty was largely mine. I enjoyed it.

Mom didn't have much money coming in. We didn't have a lot of extras for a lot of years. I was happy to get my monthly allowance. $5 didn't go far, but it meant a hell of a lot to me. Occasionally I would shovel the back deck too. It was less trafficked in the winter, so I only did it when it was necessary to keep it from caving in from the weight of the massive snow pile. The third deck, on the third floor, remained packed with snow until spring. I think Mom was afraid I would fall off, so she let it slide each year.

Later, as I was anxious to earn more money and get a "raise" in my allowance, I started helping my mom with her own bookkeeping business. Mom had a modest, but regular influx of clientele that not only kept her busy but kept us in shoes and clothes when there was little money to do so. The lean years were tough. While we always had a roof over our heads, hand-me-down clothes and sports equipment were appreciated and welcomed, and duct tape made for great shoe repairs. My brother and I also had the opportunity to work in the middle school cafeteria, washing trays and helping with whatever cooks Angie Caparella or Mary Clapper needed. This ensured we had a meal ticket and could eat lunch at school on most days.

It was obvious that she could not afford it, yet Mom gave me a "raise" in my allowance and began teaching me her trade. While I can't recall for sure, I think she raised my $5 per month to $7. But once again, the experience was greater than the immediate reward. My first responsibility was to go through the note cards in the plastic holders and alphabetize the client's receipts and match them with the folders in the file cabinet. Mom recorded each ledger on grid paper. Each ledger matched with each receipt. If there was a discrepancy, Mom would set it aside and have me track it down.

"Aspen Welding Works is off by $2.47 for the fiscal year." My job was to root through both the plastic case and the filing cabinet to find the receipt.

About once per year, my sister and I would assist Mom in balancing the ledgers for each and every client she had. While the two of us swelled with pride in the service we provided for our mom, I'm certain she went back and double checked our work. Nonetheless she paid us our allowance, whether or not she could afford to do so.

One year Mom was able to give me "paying" work at her full-time job. While it did not include actual bookkeeping tasks, it was related to taxes and was therefore "important." Ok, so it wasn't anything earth shattering. It was Inventory. My Job was to count each item in all the drawers the welders used for their job. After hours of counting, sorting, and identifying anomalies, I had gone through every nut, bolt, and rusty welding rod the company had. Each item was accounted for and listed on my Big Chief notepad; mom tallied the items and balanced the books. I walked away with $20 for the day's work, paid in full by an 'actual' business owner. I was a "professional."

It was about this time I realized I could make real money and spend my earnings on the things Mom and Dad could neither afford, nor had any interest in buying for me. I was hooked. It was not too much longer before I had my first "job" at age 11 or 12.

Aspen in the late '70s and early '80s could be a double-edged sword. While on one hand the town was now a destination resort for the rich and famous in the tourist season, it was also a seasonal struggle for those who chose to make it a year-round home. One by-product of this phenomenon was the lack of year-round funds for the local poor and middle-class families. The other by-product was a glut of menial labor jobs that had no viable applicants. Toward the mid-eighties, undocumented immigrants from Mexico and South America discovered the ski towns of the mid-continent and filled the need. But until that time, my friends and I had our pick of jobs during the high seasons of the summers and Ski Season, and this work provided my siblings and I with the opportunities to earn our own money to buy the things that we couldn't otherwise afford. We bought everything from Jeans to T-shirts to comics, skateboards to records to books to candy and video games; I finally had money to buy the things the other kids all seemed to have. Anything I wanted that my parents couldn't afford was pretty much up to me ... and I was lucky to be so privileged.

The lessons one can learn from hard work are unlimited. And the people I met, some of whom are life-long friends, broadened my perspective. Of the jobs I did, many concurrently, here are a few that come to mind: babysitter, newspaper hawker, pamphlet hawker, seafood case cleaner, manual laborer, dishwasher, prep cook, pizza cook, line cook, sous chef, McEmployee, ski restaurant worker, sandwich maker, sandwich delivery boy, grocery bagger, retail sales, sign painter/pothole filler/ecologist, pop art sculpture maker, t-shirt maker, newspaper designer, graphic designer, and later, liquor store retail sales ... And of course, shoveling lots and lots of snow.

A few places I worked at through the years: Retail at Pomeroy Sports, *The Aspen Times*, cleaning at Amelia's Hair Salon, handing out rack cards for multiple companies, dishwasher at The Diner, Joe's Diner, Schlomo's, construction hand for multiple jobs, demolition/construction at the Aspen Club, McDonald's, together with classmates Mark and Pedro, dishwasher and Pizza cook at Pinocchio's, prep/line cook at The Paragon, prep cook/sous at The Hotel Jerome, cook at Merry-Go-Round Restaurant (three days), bagger/stocker City Market, sign lackey at the City of Aspen, Liquor pusher at Mr C's in Carbondale, Pop Art Sculpture maker for Frozen Moments, T-shirt printer for The Shirt Stop, and later on, Designer at *The Aspen Times*.

Through all the different jobs I worked, I met people from all corners of the world. Among my coworkers were many Europeans, hailing from France, Italy, Germany and a ton of Swedes. I worked with people from South America to Canada, Spain to South Africa. There were people from Vietnam, India, Australia, New Zealand, and Austria among other places. Many were drawn to Aspen for the mystique the town held at the time, while still others were drawn to the area for "the best skiing aside from the Alps," as more than one told me. Some of my favorite coworkers from those times included Swedish Fred the Jazz Dance enthusiast, Olsa (also from Sweden), Hathanh, Philip and Marie from France, Pedro from El Salvador, and of course, Johan 'the cheesehead,' also from Sweden. The good old-fashioned 'yanks' provided a lot of color and humor to otherwise thankless jobs in the back of the kitchen. Tom, Bernie, Mark, Mitch, Warren and many others provided me with an early education in off-color jokes, while the Swedes taught me how to swear in their native tongue. I have remained in contact with some of my European friends to this day, more than 30 years later.

Some might say that at the cost of my childhood, I traded my early years for minimum wage. But my odd jobs kept me busy in those years. They also kept me humble and made it possible to buy records, skateboards, lunches and other luxuries that enriched my childhood. By the age of 16, I had already worked at more places than many adults do in the span of a career. Ironically, while the town was fertile with jobs that kept us busy for the formative years, there were few that one could make into a well-paying career. For that, I needed to leave the valley.

When we weren't working, or in school, we were undoubtedly either playing in the snow or skiing.

Even the school had worked out a deal with SkiCo to ensure the kids had access to the slopes. Each year, we'd line up to get our photo for our $5 ski pass. It allowed us to ski for $5 each time. School didn't end in the classroom. While they were not affiliated with the education system, our instructors on the slopes through "Aspenauts" could claim no less credit for our upbringing. On weekends we learned to ski. Skiing was a part of life. It's what we did.

THE HOUSE
IN EASTWOOD

IN THE EARLY 1970s my parents bought a house that was a step up from our meager abode on 4th street in the West End of Aspen. Our new house was a fresh, modern design of the times at the foot of the mountains about a mile from downtown. But as is true for most things designed in the 1970s, the judgment of time proved harsh. By today's standards, the house might be considered unattractive by some. As was true of many 1970's styles, the house was as unique as it was bizarre, but still it had its merits.

Built three stories up from the dugout basement, the square roofed house towered above an Aspen grove native to the neighborhood. It had two full walls of eight-foot windows, stacked three-high, a wall of glass with stunning views of the mountains and pine forests across Hwy 82. Its magnificent views of the valley also meant for astronomical heating bills in the winter. The roof stood 28 feet high from the floor in the living room.

When we moved in, the builders were still putting the roof on the home. This did not stop my parents from lugging all our belongings and their three small children into our new future. Prior to that, the home had been featured in a magazine highlighting the modern design and the trendy locale.

My brother and I shared the room on the southwest corner on the first floor. My sister had the room across the hall facing north. Directly above her room was the master bath. The master bedroom had a loft-style end wall overlooking the living room.

By far, the most dominating feature of the home was its three-story rock fireplace that started in the basement and rose up through the living room which meant it was three stories tall. So from the living room we had a two-story rock wall which we were not allowed to climb on, but frequently did anyway. Dad had a phrase, "they'll only fall once." I find myself using that very phrase these days, while observing my own kids.

To the left of us lived the Blauls, and on the right were the Scheers. To the top of the hill lived the Clausens, Bil Dunaway and Bobby Mason. On the other side, Richard and Angie Powell (later Tom Anderson), and the Desorceys (later Bill McEuen). Across the street live the Colonys. And in a large house that had many different owners throughout the years, they used bedsheets for curtains and hushed whispers told tales of prurience and misdeeds. One owner truly stands out as she was from the South and loudly yelled every morning for her dog, "Miss Muffin! Oh Miss Muffin! Come on home...." Her yelling proved to be hilarious to our mom due to the accent. Mom was a solid Midwesterner from St Paul, Minnesota. We kids hesitated to tell her, but her dialect from that part of the country often came out in the euphemisms she would utter.

Ours was a quiet street. One where we could sled in the winter, ride bikes in the summer and rarely see anyone drive through, except neighbors. I remember fondly chopping logs for firewood with the Scheers. We would use the raw, large logs to build forts in the middle of the road. It's a wonder they didn't collapse on us kids, peering out of our full-scale Lincoln Log windows, while we watched our dads chainsaw them into smaller cuts, and then split them into wood ready for our fireplaces.

After my parents split up, my dad moved just down the road to live with Suzanne Mathias, whom he later remarried. They remained married for 25+ years until Suzanne passed in 2003. While she could seem strict, and at times a seemingly intolerant stepmother, in truth she was a very generous and kind person who had endured a lot in life. On some weekends I opted not to ski with my dad, brother and sister and instead spent time with Suzanne. I enjoyed her company. I credit Suzanne with rounding out my upbringing. She was a classy lady, and generous to the core. For someone who didn't *have* to be there for us, she put forth a lot of effort, and truly cared about my siblings and myself. I'd like to think that some of the better aspects of my personality are a byproduct of her influence.

Our stepsisters Libette and Linda were mostly a mystery to us when we were younger. They were older than us and had their own lives. However, as adults, we became closer and spent quality time with both when Dad and Suzanne moved to Arizona. They are both fantastic people and we remain in touch.

There were decks on three sides of our house: one in front, one outside of the third-floor loft, and one huge back deck that provided a startling view of the valley. The best part, in my opinion, was Crystal Lake across Hwy 82—not more than 500 yards from our back door. While my mom referred to the lake as nothing more than a mosquito hatchery, the lake was one of my favorite places in my own little world. All four seasons offered new experiences at the pond. Winter iced it over for a great, yet scary ice playground we really weren't allowed to be on, while summer offered an inviting world for exploration into microscopic species and amphibian friends. We spent countless hours trying to catch frogs, salamanders, crayfish, minnows, garter snakes, water skippers, various aquatic bugs, and well, anything we could snare with a net.

Although it was a small lake, there were areas that were "off limits" mom and dad forbade us to go to. Mostly across the way and toward the road on the other side, this was the "forbidden zone" well into our early teens. It turns out that that part of the pond was on private land which had been purchased by investors who would later turn it into a god-awful development that backed up to a health club.

On our end of the pond was a beaver dam. This provided us with endless curiosity and a healthy dose of fear. We would quietly walk across the stick and earthen structure and jump back with a start every time we heard rumblings from below as the beavers would dart out from under the structure and swim for dear life.

My fascination didn't stop when seeing recently cut off Aspen saplings that had been cultivated for the miniature fortress. We used to grab the ones on the ground and pretend they were spears. I often tried to imagine the life the little beavers lived beneath the dirt and water but could never really picture it without the help of the illustrated visuals we saw in our textbooks at school.

At some point, someone had disassembled the bike path fence, and fashioned large wooden rafts from the wood. We spent many hours on the lake just floating. I never could understand why the city didn't crack down on us for those large rafts.

One year it all changed at the lake. My brother and I took a familiar walk down to the beaver dam to see if we could spot them and noticed something new. An alien sign, hard nailed into a large Aspen tree. The words shocked us. "Posted: No trespassing. Violators will be shot." With casual shrugs and a careless nonchalance, we trudged on and walked down the slight incline to the beaver dam and tossed small stones into the water.

This would be the first time someone ever shot at me deliberately. The Doppler Effect created a delay, and we heard the pellets landing all around us before we heard the report. Someone was shooting a shotgun in the air in our general direction. Pre-teens that we were, we snapped to, looked at each other in terror and ran faster than any Olympic runner ever could. We high tailed it across the highway and back to the safety of our house. We freaked out for hours. Only in my adult life did I realize that it had to have been salt, not birdshot that scattered around us. The new owners of the adjacent land had decided that the lake views were not enough. They wanted the lake too.

As it turned out, access to the pond was owned by the county for all with the exception of the land around the inlet of the waterway. Anyone could look at the lake, photograph the lake, and even fish or swim, but they could only do so from the access that was still considered public. Eventually the signs came down and we were never threatened again as long as we didn't jump in the lake from the south side–by the multi-million-dollar condos. Nonetheless it scared the living crap out of us for a good long time.

Shortly thereafter, we went to the pond only to find that 99% of all life in the water was floating belly up and smelling rank. The "owners" had sprayed the water surface with pesticides to kill the thriving mosquito population and inadvertently killed everything—everything but the mosquitoes.

It was the first time the reality of an ecological catastrophe hit home for me. My heart broke for all the creatures I had previously tried to catch and domesticate for most of my youth. In fact, I had never seen or imagined many of the species, now floating, had lived in the lake. Large fish and minute creatures alike hung lifeless, suspended and rotting. It smelled terrible in the aftermath of the failed culling and attempts to make the tennis club look more appealing to potential real estate prospects.

———

As was always the case at 8000+ feet in elevation, summer only lasted a few short months. Soon thereafter, winter reared its ugly head and swept away the toxins with weighted snow. The pond iced over and forced all remaining living things into hibernation. The next spring, I couldn't wait to see if the pond again flowered with life. As the ice inched its way back and chilly water began to flow again, new signs of life slowly began to stir. Small puddles gave way to mudskippers and other insects mostly in the larval stage. Low and behold, I was sure I spotted a tiny minnow or two skittering its way around the current of the melting snow.

I broke away large chunks of ice and tried to hurry Mother Nature along. After a while my brother sauntered up the path, climbed down the bank and started breaking the ice with me. We knew we had only a few minutes more before dinner would be ready. With the no trespassing signs now gone, we knew it would be a great year. We returned to the house we called home.

In short, our house was our castle. My siblings and I spent the better part of our youth there. In 2021, the home was sold as a $2+ million-dollar teardown and is no longer standing.

A few houses down from our home on Eastwood Drive was a grandiose home built for the Desorcys. It stood at the top of the great hill where in the summer we neighborhood kids would routinely speed down on our bikes, and in the winter, risk our lives on our Western Flyer sleds.

When it was first built, the Desorcys imported hundreds of giant boulders from the surroundings of Independence Pass, to create an expansive boulder field, or "rock garden", that covered the hill and stretched below the home to connect with Hwy 82. The rocks were all rounded and massive. Between 3' and 5' wide, they were likely filched from the debris fields of glacial moraines. The features of the beautiful interior could only be bested by the astounding views from the glassed rear of the home, which overlooked not only the boulders, but the aspen groves that lined the Roaring Fork River.

We spent quite a lot of time in the beautiful home as kids. My parents were close friends with the Desorcys. "Uncle David" as we kids knew him, had made it his life goal to become a millionaire by the age of 30 and had accomplished the feat. As such, it was always an adventure visiting our neighbors, and taking in the sights that they had adorning their home. Mr. Desorcy was an avid Hunter (or collector, I never really knew which) and decorated the living area with taxidermy of his conquests. His then wife had a particular affinity for art and artifacts from the native cultures from the regions of the North Pole. They always had a warm fire in the rock fireplace. We kids spent a lot of our time playing pool on the huge billiards table, while our parents chit-chatted for what would seem like hours. Later, they added the first tabletop video game of the era, and a huge pile of quarters on the glass top for us to play Pong until it was time to go. When things got boring for us kids, my sister and I would entertain ourselves by playing with their one-eyed dog named Monlicker.

The adjoining lot to the right of the home was undeveloped at the time and host to a large Aspen grove meadow that sloped down to the highway. It proved to be a magical place for me as a child. I spent a lot of time in the summers running through the knee-high grass and soaking my tennis shoes in the morning dew. As a kid, I had a fascination with "creepy crawlers" and found that meadow to be a fruitful hunting-ground in which to catch garter snakes, the harmless reptilian denizens of the high Rocky Mountains.

From time to time, I would wander over into the base of the boulder field and spot one or two sunning on the rocks. Much to my now adult horror, I would often find nooks and crannies in which to hide under the boulders themselves and make a "cave" or hideout where for hours, I would listen to the rocks shift and settle as the late spring snows would melt. It's a wonder the rocks never crushed me and rendered me never to be seen or heard from again.

As it turned out, the decade proved to be torturous to both families. Aspen's trials and struggles of long winters and slow off seasons gnawed their way through matrimonial bonds and eventually, both unions ended in divorce. And thus perpetuated the division of assets and the sale of the beautiful home on the top of the hill to another owner. It's possible that the new owners never saw me playing in their rock field, but I doubt it. The 70s and 80s were a special time in Aspen, and it was rare that someone would bark at a kid to vacate their land. Folks were either oblivious, or cool with it. I still spent a lot of time in that meadow, and in those boulders, despite the presence of new owners.

One day, when I was quietly trying to catch a garter snake, I realized I wasn't alone. I turned around to notice a shy kid standing there, not 15 feet away, watching me intently.

"Whatcha doin'?" The kid asked quietly.

"Shhhh. Catchin' snakes. C'mere. I'll show ya."

Within seconds we were both crouching. I caught a small one and handed it to him. He promptly dropped it, and I picked it up again and gave it to him. His eyebrows were high with excitement and instinctual fear, but he was grateful. I quickly caught another one.

"Whoa! We gotta show my dad!!!" he said, hightailing it up the grassy hill to the driveway where some men were unloading guitar cases and equipment from a van.

"Dad! My friend and I caught snakes!!!!"

To which the man calmly examined the scene and asked, "Aaron, what's your friend's name?"

We quickly became buddies. The only thing was, Aaron was seldom there, and when he was, it was only for short periods of time—a day or two—sometimes only a few hours. So, when he did come to town, we made the most of it.

One day, when I saw that Aaron was there, I rushed up the hill to see what he was up to. Aaron quickly announced, "My dad said we could watch them work this time if you want, but we have to be reeeeeeally quiet." My curiosity was piqued. I had no idea what he was referring to. After the Desorcys moved, there was a period of time when the new owner had a lot of construction work done to the lower floor of the house which was an area largely unfamiliar to me, other than that it used to be David's workshop.

Aaron quietly opened the giant wooden door, and we descended the stairs to just barely peek our heads around into the room. Large panes of glass served as walls, and we could hear Aaron's dad sitting by himself in a room on a stool playing a mandolin. The owner of the house occupied another room and was focused on some type of electronic machinery.

There was loud music, to which the man would occasionally look up. The music would stop, and all would be silent. Then he would play a few notes. And sometimes re-play them.

I would wonder why I couldn't see the other musicians and looked around for the woman behind the vocals singing "Make A Little Magic."

Magic indeed. The basement of the house had been converted into a recording studio.

There were only a few times when I could watch, but it was always exciting. Until it wasn't. For the musicians, this was work. It often times took a lot of takes to get it right. Which to a couple of kids, was sorta boring after a while. So, Aaron and I would go back out to play in the road, or ride bikes or try to catch snakes.

In between albums, it became rarer when Aaron would come with his dad, and eventually not at all. His dad was always nice and would say "hi from Aaron!"

I never really thought much about it, except that eventually my buddy didn't come back. By this time, we were both beginning jr. high school and our paths had taken different routes.

Many years later, at the Mountain Fair in Carbondale, I ran into Aaron's younger brother after he played a set on the main stage and was able to reconnect with his dad. Aaron now owns his own animation company and enjoys success and family life in another state.

Many of the band's songs from that era, along with the comedy albums of a friend of Aaron's dad, were recorded in that studio.

But I'll always remember that on Halloween each year, instead of candy, the McEuens would give out 45 RPM vinyl recordings of the Nitty Gritty Dirt Band, and we could not be more thrilled. Also recorded in that studio, I still laugh every time I hear Steve Martin singing "King Tut."

———

Note: An unwritten rule in Aspen was always to treat celebrities and their families as you would anyone else. This was a main draw to the town for them at the time. I chose not to write about the many occasions of crossed paths with heads of state, A-list celebrities, and members of the wealthiest families in the world. Many of these kids went to school with us or joined us in our off-time activities. This story has personal significance for me, in that Aaron was and likely still is one of the nicest people I've had the pleasure to meet. I chose to include it to honor an old friend.

THE ORIGINAL GANG, PRANKS AND TOMFOOLERY

FOR EVERY PRANK OR JOKE, there's inspiration from a generation that did it first. And they in turn learned from their predecessors before them.

Aspen of the 60s and 70s was a place where pranksters thrived, and the antics that wreaked havoc on the unsuspecting victims were legendary. Far more creative, far more shocking than a white elephant gift at Christmas (although those certainly made the rounds), the pranks dreamed up by our parents can best be described in Jack Brendlinger's book, *Don't Get Mad, Get Even*. The Brendlingers owned the Applejack.

The camaraderie among my dad's group of friends was heavily nuanced in ornery humor—"Throwing barbs" if you will. While they all took part, Ken Sterling, who owned and operated the Heatherbed Lodge with his wife Martie, was the ringleader and king of jabs. In place of a simple hello, there was usually an off-the-cuff comment about one's appearance or some other ribbing that, if taken out of context, might otherwise ruin a friendship. Good-natured chidings took the place of normal and polite congenialities.

If Sterling was the king of insults, Jack Brendlinger had to have been the king of pranks. Which left Dave Hoff as the king of crazy antics and reckless stunts. Dave owned and operated Aspen Rent-All. Much of this has been written about in Brendlinger's book (Seriously. Read it.), but the mark they left on us kids was indelible. There were examples like the duck boat Incident at our house, the casual and good-natured insults we grew accustomed to, and the stunts like Jeep jumping the fountain on the mall or driving a pal's Willys up the spine of Red Butte and ditching it there. We were first-hand witnesses to head-scratching events and shameless tomfoolery.

And of course, there were the "gifts" that made the rounds in Aspen during the previous generation. Aside from the "Golden Boy" mentioned below or gifting a tired old horse to your friend's kids (who didn't already have horses), another treasure that left an impression, was the statue of Hercules wrestling Diomedes, which we were not supposed to see as kids (I'm not sure what dad it was eventually re-gifted to, but a similar gag gift is now circulating through the ranks of my closest friends).

If one were to show up at a Pomeroy party in the mid-seventies, you might expect to see a cast of characters like the Sterlings, the Brendlingers, the Hoffs, the Whitcombs, the Odens, the Decorcy's, the Clausens, the Henrys, the Mencimers, Bev Mars, Peter and Barbara Guy among countless others.

16th-century original sculpture of Hercules and Diomedes wrestling in the nude (wikipedia).

At some point during the festivities, a slightly inebriated Ken Sterling would disappear for a few moments, and then reappear wearing my mom's best cocktail dress (now torn) and a wig. He would remain in drag for the majority of the party. Or at least until us kids went to bed.

I recall a "meditation" box gifted to my dad when we moved into our new home in Eastwood. It was a mid-sized appliance cardboard box with a head and shoulders sized hole cut out at the bottom. If one were to lay on one's back, he could get inside to see a single light bulb which lit up all four walls of the inside. The walls were plastered, of course, with lurid pictures of naked women. As a small child I had not seen such things before, and my curiosity was piqued. It would be a few years later when mom caught my brother and I perusing the pages of those popular men's magazines, scattered on the table in the waiting area at Ulibarri's hair salon. Ah, the seventies ... Much like kids of the 50s flipped through their comics inside of their textbooks, we had wrapped the larger 'hairstyle' books around the magazines and flipped through the Playboys with shocked curiosity. Mom was on to us after we spent too much time picking out our new hairdos.

But the best prank pulled on the Pomeroys was the duck boat incident. Jack Brendlinger goes into greater detail in his book, but I'll hit the high points.

Stirling and Brendlinger borrowed my dad's duck hunting boat for a while. Long story short, they sank it and nearly died. They took a long time to replace it, but when they finally did, it appeared one night in my mom's car (sticking out the back) completely filled with jello. Stuck in the middle of the jello was a large, hand-crank dildo, lovingly nicknamed "The Golden Boy." The end result: Dad got a new boat, it took us a long time to dispose of the jello, and from that point on, mom developed a lifelong hatred of the large black ants that converged on our property for the remainder of eternity. It seems they were attracted to the gelatin.

The gags, pranks, stunts and good-natured ribbings that were so prevalent in my Dad's group of friends would probably raise more than a few eyebrows today. By our current standards, some would probably land a person in jail. Be that as it may, they led rise to many others in the years that followed. In fact, it's possible that Aspen State Teacher's College and other such pranksters owe much of their inspiration to the aforementioned goofballs.

Other antics and stories can be found in *The Days of Stein and Roses*, by Martie Sterling. A beautifully written memoir of the times before our generation, the struggles, the fun and the community that made Aspen what it was at the time, her book illustrates better than I could ever hope to do.

Of course, to mention gags and pranks in Aspen without a nod to Hunter S. Thompson would be an oversight I couldn't live down. While not a close friend of my parents, he did make rounds in many of the same crowds. His haunts, like the Red Onion and Jerome Bar were frequented by our parents and their friends. And in some cases, folks like my mom tended bar at those very water holes.

A few of the more memorable pranks of Thompson's that come to mind, aside from running for sheriff, are as follows:

- Shooting golf balls like skeet with Ed Bradley at the local driving range

- Throwing smoke grenades into the Woody Creek Tavern so he could photograph the "celebrities" running out in terror

- Shooting life-sized photographs of celebrities and politicians and selling them as art

- Shooting George Stranahan with a 12-gauge shotgun full of confetti

- Klieg lighting and firebombing the sky above Jack Nicholson's house as a birthday present

There was rarely a lull when Hunter was alive. Even while I worked at the paper, he was fond of creating drama. "Stop the presses!!!!" He would call in, and follow with something like, "I'm faxing my manifesto!" This was soon to be followed by some crazy rant about giant bats and the local airport.

But while Hunter Thompson achieved National press and worldwide celebrity for his antics, my dad and his friends were content just to mess with each other.

It is my hope that the surviving members of the original "shenanigans crew" know that their legacy lives on in the aspirations of their kids. In fact, I often find myself doing many of the same things. To my closest friends and loved ones, I say now in the same breath, "You're welcome ... and I'm terribly sorry. I blame Ken Sterling."

FIRST THERE WAS
THE "PURPLE BIKE"

MY BROTHER JIMMY, my sister Katie and myself all learned to ride on the "purple" bike. It was a standard 1970s style two-wheeler, and most likely was a hand me down from someone. The purple shade was probably intended to appeal to a girl; however, it was ambiguous enough to serve as a darned good first bike for all of us. It had a low top bar, and a long banana seat. The two large wheels made it fun to jump and to try wheelies for us budding daredevils.

But no sooner than the training wheels came off for me, it was apparent I needed a new bike. At the time, Katie was still a toddler, but had received a "green machine" of the "Big Wheel" variety for Christmas. Jim had his own bike. That left me. It was the year I received my first bike. A standard fare, most likely purchased at the Miner's Building, and I was extremely excited.

That first day, one of the neighbor kids offered to "break it in" by launching off our nearby neighbors' driveway—a good eight to 10 feet off the ground. As he was too big for the bike, and clearly wasn't expecting such a rough ride, he crashed and bent the rims. He calmly brushed off the dirt from his pants and limped away to lick his wounds somewhere else. My bike was more broken than "broken in," but it was mine and I was proud to have it. I made great use of it, though it never rode the same.

Fast forward a few years, I had outgrown the bike, and it was about time for a newer model. One that would last a few more years as I approached the pre-teenage era. One that was durable.

At a couple of points in time, my dad had considered selling bikes at Pomeroy Sports. But likely due to the potential overhead and storage, he opted not to pursue that avenue. Summers for a ski shop offered both opportunities to try new things and struggles to make money from things that didn't necessarily sell well. He'd pondered renting mopeds, a popular offering in beach resorts and elsewhere, but didn't take the plunge. He even tried renting roller skates for a while, but when the fad faded, and with the advent of rollerblades, coupled with the liability, that too ceased to be a viable revenue stream. Bikes, while holding a century-long reign amongst outdoor enthusiasts, never really appealed to him for some reason. I suppose it was a mix of not wanting to compete with the other stores in town, and quite possibly a gentleman's agreement not to pursue that niche.

As it turned out, however, this often presented an opportunity for trade. Dad made many handshake deals and barters throughout town. Often, we were the lucky recipients of whatever he traded. Maybe he picked up a few tricks from Freddie Fischer (Freddy the Fixer), or he was very adept at business, or possibly a mix of both. In any case, deals were made, items traded, and someone's kid walked away with a new pair of skis, and another kid got a new bike.

Behold! The Mongoose. A glorious present for my 13th birthday. Shining chrome, red seat; I could smell the new tires from across the room.

The bike came complete with mag wheels, which I later replaced with much lighter spokes. Sharp jaws that some knew as pedals, the kind that left scars I can still see on my shins today, controlled the brakes, and made the bike go. Much to my mom's chagrin, it had a chain that routinely greased the best of my Sunday pant legs. Call it a design flaw, or a Darwinian test, the gooseneck (a bolt that holds the handlebar in place and allows steering) all but ensured I might never be able to father children. *(My wife and I have two boys — Take that Mongoose!)*

My bike came with matching seat and grips, and a single pad across the top bar, another across the handlebar.

Illustration by Chris Pomeroy.

"That bike definitely won't do until you get a pad for the gooseneck," my brother Jimmy said, "you're gonna wrack yourself." Mom and Dad chided him to withhold his comments from that point, not to tarnish the "newness" of the shiny chrome bike. During the summer months it was my main mode of transportation.

Like many other kids, I was a terror on wheels. With no fear of speed, born from the many years of skiing down steep terrain, rare was a time when I wasn't going fast on that machine. These were the days before helmets, and kids wouldn't be caught dead wearing arm or knee pads unless they were competing professionally. On the myriad of bike trails, pedestrian trails, sidewalks, and after 1976, for a very brief time, the mall, I would blaze through to my destination without looking back, unless I lost my ball cap or popped a tire. Years later they brought in mall bike cops, but they couldn't catch us. Instead, they would chase down unsuspecting tourists with rentals who didn't know they weren't supposed to ride on the mall. The funny thing was, the unique design of the brickwork on the mall made for a BMX paradise: you could jump any number of ditches, and the sloping curbs onto the mall provided particularly good lift off spots, with which you could easily traverse the terrain from asphalt to brickwork.

I couldn't begin to guess how many close calls I had on that bike—a near head-on with an unsuspecting motorist in a parking garage, or a slip on the gravel strewn across asphalt, or by nearly getting crushed by a truck in an alleyway, there were always obstacles to dodge and risks to be avoided. Most close calls were of my own doing. But I never met a kid in Aspen who spent more than an hour a day on a bike, who didn't have similar stories of near-death antics and crazy stunts, that should have left them maimed or with a permanent limp.

Since we lived on the east side of town, getting home was all up hill, albeit at a slight incline. The hill on Hwy 82 was steepest where the Crestahaus was, and on a hot summer day, if I was lucky enough to have spare change in my pocket, I'd stop into the refreshments room and drink a bottle of Coke in seconds flat. Like many buildings in Aspen at the time, The Crestahaus was an inn modeled in the style of a Swiss chalet. In the 1980s the Crestahuas was owned and operated by the Balkes. As I became friends with Stuart, I was lucky enough to stay there from time to time. I always enjoyed spending time with them, a generous and friendly family.

Just past the inn, was the Riverside subdivision, where among others, lived the Simons, the Oates, the Murrays, the Trimbles, the Swantons, the Andersons and the Klanderuds.

Across the highway was McSkimming Road, where you could find the homes of the Taylors, Doremuses, musician Bobby Mason, and the infamous Steven Grabow along with many other families.

McSkimming, and specifically, Bobby Mason's driveway, which met up with Grabow's, made a great shortcut to Eastwood drive where we lived. But once again, this was Aspen. Yes, we were trespassing, but the Masons never seemed to care. And I doubt the Grabows even noticed. The final stretch was mostly bike path, alongside the Aspen Club Condos property next to Crystal Lake.

While one could barely see our house through the Aspen trees on the hill, you could make out a very thin path straight up the embankment, that my siblings and I had carved over the years by traversing it with bikes, sneakers in the summer, and Sorrells and moon boots in the winter. As we got older and more comfortable on our bikes, my brother and I challenged ourselves to be able to ride our bike up the path, no small feat with a 1-speed BMX bike.

The real challenge, however, was not getting killed by oncoming traffic as we crossed Hwy 82, since we crossed on a completely blind curve. Many close calls, complete with blaring horns and skid marks nearly ended it all for me. My brother likely has similar stories. That stretch of road marked the end to numerous pets that didn't quite make it across. My sister Katie's heart broke each time a new kitten came home from the City Market parking lot, where they were frequently being given away, and within months succumbed to "killer 82."

Riding uphill all the way home presented challenges and kept us in good shape during the summer months but going into town via bike was a blast. When traffic on 82 wasn't too heavy, I'd race down Bobby Mason's driveway, to McSkimming, then alongside 82 all the way into town and onto the mall. Often it wouldn't require pedaling at all to make it all the way to Wagner Park; the momentum swift enough to glide me into town.

When traffic was bad, I'd take the bike path behind the Aspen club, through Ute Park and Cemetery, then past the Gant and right to the Aspen Square building at the base of Little Nell where Pomeroy Sports was. There were parts of the trail where I could get a lot of speed, and in the cool mornings, the ride was exhilarating. The trail was so familiar to me that, like a ski run, I could anticipate every turn, every dip, incline and even every pothole. If it remains the same today, I probably still can.

In Aspen we had free transportation throughout the area, provided by Roaring Fork Transit Authority free buses. For a short period of time, we even had double decker buses, courtesy of Michael Hernstadt (later murdered in a drug related incident). They were fun as kids, but sketchy. We always liked to ride on the top level, but you could almost sense how top-heavy they were when they took a tight corner.

While the bus provided timely transport, especially when there were things that needed to be carried, bike was my preferred method of travel. The only drawback was finding somewhere to keep it once in town. Bike racks were available, but bikes frequently were stolen. Often, I'd find a good place to stow it, deftly hidden in an alley, or behind a stairwell. But most of the time, riding the bike was about riding the bike.

Aspen is not very spread out, geographically speaking. However, riding from Eastwood subdivision to Aspen Middle and High School was quite a trek on a one-speed. Yet, in the early 80s one could see me, backpack, and trombone in hand, or on the way to the golf course with clubs slung over my shoulder or handlebars riding from one end of town to the other on my mongoose, sweating and most likely wearing long pants.

The bike allowed freedom from bus schedules, and the ability to beat out any traffic jam. To a twelve-year-old kid, hearing the wind and flying down a hill was vastly superior to the smell of diesel fuel and air brakes on the city bus. Once I outgrew the Mongoose, I had a ten speed for a while, which was eventually stolen. Later I had a budget version of a mountain bike.

Living in the hot South, while I don't ride frequently anymore, I still have a Gary Fischer mountain bike I bought in the 1990s It remains a great bike to this day. But it's no Mongoose. I'm happy to report that both of my boys each have a modern iteration of that same bike I had as a kid. Maybe it's a bit better engineered, lighter, and even more sleek, but it's still the same frame and idea. And though my kids may never know similar experiences as the solitary, quiet and cool air of early morning rides in the mountains, I can only hope they enjoy the bike as much as I did.

COACH KUEHLMAN WAS ALWAYS KNOWN AS A QUIET, AND STOIC AUTHORITY FIGURE

HE WAS RESPECTED AND FEARED as we kids grew into our shoes at Aspen Middle School. In hushed whispers, the kids spread rumors that if he caught you misbehaving, his punishment was severe. It was known by all, that he was able to mete out justice by way of a staunch wooden paddle, kept under his desk in his office, on the side of the gymnasium.

While others knew him as a strict authoritarian, I just knew him as Mr. Kuehlman from church—and my schoolmates, Margo and John's dad.

In short, I had a tough time believing the hype. Naive as I may have been, there came a day when I experienced the true "wrath" of his authority.

While time tends to blur the details, if my memory serves, it was either Scott P., or John "Marky" who broke the cardinal rule in the game of Artillery: "Don't kick the red ball!"

The game was simple. On either side of the gymnasium was a single wooden pin, much like a bowling pin. Each team had guards for the goal. The object was to knock the other team's pin over to score. What ensued resembled absolute chaos, as everyone threw the familiar red, air-filled balls at each other in a frenzy of laughter, adrenaline, and fear. If you got hit, you were out. Once the coach blew the whistle, the balls flew, shoes squeaked, kids laughed and screamed until, once again the whistle blew, only to find out one of the pins had accidentally been felled, usually by the person in charge of protecting the goal.

It was at a slow point in the action when some scoundrel, let's assume it was John "Marky" (the likelier candidate), kicked a ball that was rolling towards him. He kicked it hard. Hard enough in fact, that it shot straight, all the way up to the gymnasium ceiling and knocked loose an asbestos tile.

Now at this point, another lifelong friend and all-around good person, was standing directly underneath. Fenella, the hapless victim stood unaware as the falling object landed squarely on her head, cracked into two even portions, and dropped to the floor. The event left her in tears with a cloud of white asbestos dust settling in her long, red hair.

Being a huge fan of shows like *The Three Stooges* and *Our Gang* (staples in the days before music television and HBO) and due to the sheer happenstance, this was pure slapstick comedy to me. Not the part where Fenella was scared and in pain, mind you. But the randomness of the action and consequence. Larry, Moe and Curly couldn't have pulled off a better choreographed antic.

As I stood laughing for a beat before going over to try to console poor Fenella, Coach Kuehlman grabbed me by the arm and walked me swiftly to a wooden bench outside his office and briskly "invited" me to sit down and wait until after class. I sat in shame, head hung low on the hard wooden bench, until the rest of the kids finished the game. Echoes and shoe squeaks filled the gymnasium as I sat drearily awaiting my punishment. A short while later, Coach Kuehlman and Fenella walked toward me. Neither one looking at me, Coach walked into the office and invited Fenella to follow. While I couldn't hear the conversation, I could see through the open door that it was one of consolation. Shortly thereafter, I witnessed the coach as he handed Fenella a sucker and sent her on her way. She glanced with a quick, concerned look of fear for my turn to talk with the coach.

I waited in pained silence as Coach Kuehlman rolled his chair in close to his desk, and commenced to shuffling papers, writing notes, and arranging items for what seemed like an eternity.

Had he forgotten me hard benching it sitting not 10 feet away? My anxiety and fear rose steadily with each passing second as I watched the clock ticking away. What would my mom and dad think? Would I get expelled? Would everyone at the Catholic Church know I'd laughed? The terror and the shame were unbearable. Just then my heart felt like it was about to jump out of my chest. "The paddle!" My eyes darted in every direction, searching high and low as Coach continued to shuffle papers. Yet, despite my best efforts I couldn't spot the dreaded device.

At about the time I remembered the rumor that he had it under his desk, he casually met my eyes with a perturbed and disdainful stare. Then he flipped another page in his yellow legal pad and continued writing. It was pure psychological torture. For what was probably less than 5 minutes, it seemed like a lifetime of dread rattling my middle school mind. It was a genius move on his part. I could hear the seconds ticking on the clock.

Finally, he pushed the legal pad aside, slid his chair back and reached under his desk. Pure horror filled my mind and assuredly my eyes were popping out of their sockets. He produced the worn wooden paddle and slapped it down on the middle of the desk. My goose was cooked. He turned in his chair, leaned forward with his elbows on his knees and motioned me to approach. Cue the waterworks. All time stopped. I was crying and sniveling like a baby as I left the bench and slowly went in to face the music.

In a calm, but deliberate voice he said, "Mr. Pomeroy, do you know why it is you are in trouble?"

I must have sounded like I had a mouthful of double bubble, as tears streamed down my cheeks and I mumbled something like, "Cuz I laughed when Fenella got hurt?"

"Exactly. It's not nice to laugh at another person's misfortune." To which I replied, "I'm sorry."

He slowly reached over toward the paddle and tapped his fingers on the desk next to it. I must have shrunk five sizes at that moment and turned as white as a sheet.

"What are you going to say to Fenella when you see her next?"

"I tried to tell her, but you ... I ... I'll tell her I'm really sorry."

"That's a good start," he said as he grabbed the paddle and moved it across his knee.

I nearly fell over. The mental torment, coupled with the mere shame of getting in trouble was almost too much to bear.

At just that moment, he raised a finger and said, "Hold on one second ..." and reached under the desk again.

While my greatest fear was that he had some other, unknown torture device, or evil mechanism no middle schooler had ever dreamed up, he proceeded to bring out a small blue bucket.

My dread quickly abated after he reached into the bucket and handed me a sucker. "I think you've learned your lesson," he uttered, and stood up to usher me out. My heartbeat slowed down, I wiped the tears and snot from my face and tried to compose myself. I knew I would hear about this at home, and probably at church too. Not to mention from Margo or John Jr.

Incidentally, he never said a word.

Through the years we had many great teachers and mentors in the school system. Mr. Kuehlman stands as a good example of a teacher who truly cared about the wellbeing of his students, and the lasting moral lessons that could be taught. My parents often lamented their frustration with the Aspen schools, but most of us turned out just fine.

Despite my proclivity to perform poorly in my academics, memories of great teachers abound. Their passion for teaching was evident in the unique ways in which they interacted with all of us. From early on, the kindness exhibited by teachers like Mrs. Grant who's compassion was equal that of her strict code (she once dragged me by the ear to sit in the hall for daydreaming in class), Mrs. Wall, who thrived and continued to expound her knowledge and wisdom, despite going through her own personal tragedies at the time, and of course, Willard Clapper with his quirks and humorous antics that bled into his curriculum in third and then again in seventh grades. Other grand memories easily come to mind, like the time my English teacher, Mr. Christopher, knowing I was a huge Beatles fan, allowed me to listen to his radio instead of attending class the day John Lennon was killed. There was also a weeklong trip to Lake Powell with Mr. Vanian and a small group of students. Mr. Kluchko, the band teacher who would jokingly throw his baton at you to get your attention, stands out, as does the sense of humor of Mr. Larson the automotive teacher. The residuals of the energy Mr. Burson had for history can be seen in my reading selections, which comprise more than 1/3 of all my books. Of course, the many trips we took to see the wonders of Colorado and neighboring states are truly unforgettable.

One special event that often comes to mind, was a day-long trip to Denver in which Dean Jackson, two other students and I were invited to take with Heidi Roupp. Mrs. Roupp had a reputation as a tough teacher, and many feared her. But I couldn't help but like her. As a C student on a good day, I constantly struggled in her social studies class but kept trying. Turns out, I was allergic to homework of any kind. A fond memory is of Dean and I asking her for our grade on a recent paper, she said with a smile to Dean, "You got a B+." He responded triumphantly with a "Woo!" His excitement was infectious.

"What about me Mrs. Roupp? How did I do?" I asked, I was sure I had made a valiant effort.

Her response was as jovial as when she spoke to Dean. Her smile was large, her teeth shined, her eyes squinted, and she almost happily said ... "You failed."

It was a hilarious lesson I learned in accountability. I couldn't be mad at her, despite my wanting to be. Instead, I laughed and convinced myself of the need to do better. It couldn't have been much later in the semester when Dean and I were invited, despite my class ranking, along with two older girls to Mrs. Roupp's Denver field trip to take in some culture. We got up extremely early, piled in the van and headed out towards I-70 east.

Once in Denver, our first stop was a Buddhist temple, gilded and shiny, something I'd never seen in the Catholic Church, in which I was raised. Everything that wasn't walled with rice paper was gleaming with gold. The priest told us a fable of why there were holes poked in one of the rice paper wall separators near the front. It seems a child licked his finger, touched the paper, and melted the first hole through. Then another tried it. So, they put up a sign that said, "Do not poke holes with wetted fingers." As such, the idea became popular, and everyone had to try it. Now the panel more resembled Swiss cheese than a wall. I often think of that study whenever I see a "wet paint" sign.

Our next stop was really a time killer until the third event. We sauntered through the Museum of Natural History and goofed off for a while, likely chiding about potential resemblances of our least favorite classmates with the wax Neandertals on display.

Once it was time, we made our way to the Denver Center for Performing Arts, to take in an Off-Broadway show. The play was *Sugar Babies*, starring Mickey Rooney and Anne Miller. We also enjoyed the opener, which was a popular puppeteer at the time. After the show, we were introduced to the puppeteer and to Anne Murray who graciously talked with us and signed autographs. Mickey Rooney had opted out and left the building.

It was a lot of stuff to pack into one day, and it was a long day indeed. However, I still reap the benefits of the trip, 30+/-years later.

Many of my classmates moved up through the same classes from kindergarten through high school. And despite the transient nature of a resort town, with so many kids and families arriving and leaving over the years, there was a steady group of us that remained through all the formative years. Some of my best and lifelong friends were there at the start. And God willing, will be there in some form or other at the end too.

Many went on to work in Film and TV, like my middle school computer pal, Director Adam, artist Ben, animator Ivan, co-author of this book Andy and of course, documentary producer, Fenella (now Fenell). Some became lawyers or doctors, and quite possibly a rock 'n' roll star or two. Others like my friends Andy and Todd, went on to own their own businesses. Some went on to raise families while others lead somewhat sedentary lives, still in the Roaring Fork Valley. But most of us left to find our own way.

While high school represents a time I often choose not to relive, some of the best friends in my life arrived during that of my schooling. If not for my friends like Todd, Dean, John, Jimmy (Ian), Carl, Marcus, and Ben, and many friends from the Country Day School and neighboring Glenwood Springs, I might not have made it through. Good friends and a sense of humor carried me through the rough times. One need only watch the hazing in the movie *Dazed and Confused* to know what the early years of high school was like. Suffice it to say, I tended to favor the underdog and paid for it in exclusion from the popular crowd.

It was just after the days when it was still okay for the ranchers' kids to bring their guns to school.

They still had the gun racks in the back windows of their trucks, but now they left the actual weapons at home. These were the days before school shootings. The worst thing that happened was when a kid punched the principal in the face. Almost everyone had a pocket knife.

Our school had just over 300 students, and our class (1986) had 88 graduates that year. In contrast, my son's high school has 1500+. It is not the biggest school in the county. He will graduate with more seniors than we had students in the whole school.

If there was a particular activity I'd like to relive, it would be staring at the night sky, searching for UFOs with friends in the park, on a rooftop, or in the woods at a keg party, and just talking about life; learning how to become who we are. Tricia, Carl, Todd, Bonnie, Colleen, Brian, Derek, Rory, Hal, Garrett, Ivan, Gabe, Abel, Julie, Lisa, Karen, John (Nick), Cloud, Lyon, Brandon, Gideon, Terry, Jimmy (Ian), Angel, Theresa, Davian and so many more ...

Our activities were like those of kids everywhere else in many respects. Driving around, looking at girls, listening to music too loud, hanging out at the fast-food joints, playing hacky sack and frisbee, ingesting occasional illicit substances (now mostly legal), and of course, drinking too much cheap beer. In the winter it was similar. When we weren't working, going to school, or skiing on weekends, fun involved finding warm places to hang out, and again, drinking too much cheap beer.

But like any small town, there were good kids, and there were not-so-good kids. There were those that were bullies, and those that got bullied. There were truly exceptional kids, and those who would be lauded as such, yet were not. There were the 'in' kids, and the outsiders. And there were the rest of us, just trying to make it through. The best we can do is to move forward in life and try to raise our kids to be better people.

I feel truly blessed to have known them all, and to have had teachers who devoted their careers to the future successes of their students. Many are gone now, but the tales, the folklore and the memories live on with those of us who choose to remember.

WINTER KILL

ABOUT TEN FEET BACK from the bus stop at McSkimming Road, there was a drainage ditch that was used once upon a time by local ranchers as an irrigation source to water the fields. The ditch itself was about four feet across and at most three feet deep. The Rocky Mountains hosted mostly rocky black dirt with huge boulders. But for some reason the ditches had fine granules of granite that formed a nice blanket of beige sand that was reminiscent of an Egyptian landscape. The water was usually clear and meandered smoothly, quietly throughout the town. During most times of the year, the ditch flowed at a steady but slow pace. Strong enough that you wouldn't want to fall into it, but shallow enough to get out of in a hurry. During the summer you could see giant trout skirt the shadows, tempting the sun's rays to reach down and touch them, which it could almost never do. The slightest movement or sound sent them scurrying for the culvert to hide in the dark.

For the many hundreds of times we tried to catch the trout while the water was high, we never came close. Every year we tried with rods, nets, and firecrackers only to be denied. The fish proved too fast, too smart, and too damned slippery to catch. As the old adage goes, "If you can see the fish, the fish can see you."

That is until the fall. The fall was when the county would cut off the water supply to the drainage ditches. This was to route the runoff to the river, which provided for countless cities down the line for the remainder of the season. This was the time of year all municipalities stocked up on water in their reservoirs to ration out for the long, cold winter ahead.

Come winter, there was but a trickle and giant Ice puddles suspended in midair—inches or a foot above the running stream. But in the fall, these puddles trapped the fish in between sand bars. For about a week before the chilling freeze, the water would pool in what were normally the deepest parts of the stream.

This is where my friends and I would try to catch trophy fish after school by hand. We used to search the larger pools for half-frozen trout. If they were in hibernation, we would grab them. If they were dead, we'd leave them to the elements.

As soon as we'd get off the bus, most of the kids would scatter to their destinations with their book bags and feverish attempts to get home before their parents called out. But for the few of us, and the luckiest of us, our curfew synced up with our parent's work schedules and we'd have a little extra time to tool around before everyone got home.

This was our chance ... Year after year we'd scramble to catch the fish. Mostly unsuccessful, we'd often return home with unbelievable fish tales for our parents and mud-soaked shoes, socks, and pants. One fall I walked the river stones when the water level was low and found a steel rod, possibly used to open sewer lids. An old piece of rebar that not only made for a great walking stick, but also a mighty "sword of retribution!"

I came upon a four-foot pool. Quiet, cool, and calm, the water barely moving in the light breeze. At the bottom I could clearly see several trout of varying size. Out of the corner of my eye I spotted a giant brown trout languishing under a rock. As is always the case in the most amazing events of a life, I of course, bore lone witness. As it was important to be able to prove the sighting, I had to catch this fish. Otherwise, my friends, not to mention my mom, would never believe me. After all, most of the fish we'd caught up 'til then had been smaller than the palm of my hand.

That is ... if we caught any at all. They were elusive. The strategy was simple. Lure it out, but don't scare it into a frenzy in which it could get away. I quietly crept along the shore, trying hard not to let my footsteps crunch in the rocky sand. I slowly lowered myself down on my knees, then placed my palms on the still warm, large rocks and peered my head over the water, my eyes directly above the fish. I could see my reflection in silhouette with my ball cap about to fall off. I waited a silent hunter's eternity until the fish ventured out from under the rock and quietly raised the rod above my head—hand trembling with anticipation—and with a swift, violent swing brought the weapon down.

To my shock, the fish flew onto the shore and flapped and flailed a desperate frenzy until I was able to grab it with both hands, while trying my best not to drop my backpack in the water. I quickly dipped the fish in the stream to wash off the sand and leaves, carefully but firmly squeezing it so it didn't escape. Then, in utter excitement, I ran the quarter mile home, carrying the four-pound brown trout out in front and clear of my best school clothes. But it seems I'd hit it a bit too hard with the rebar because by the time I got to our house, the fish had succumbed to the wound. My mom did not believe me and assumed I had picked up a dead fish from the dry riverbed.

"Get that disgusting thing out of my house!!!!!! And wash your hands when you get inside. It's time to do your homework." The prized trophy of all fishing expeditions—the unbelievable catch of a lifetime, the proverbial "one that didn't get away"... wasted in disbelief. I was told to leave it in the outside trashcan. I went inside and started my homework.

None of my friends believed me either.

ON AFTERNOONS WHEN THE BUS DROPPED US OFF

OFTEN DEAN JACKSON WOULD hang out at "Casa del Pomeroy," or vice versa, I would hang out at Dean's parents' condo. There were days we'd need to stay close to home. So, afternoons were often filled with reruns of Lee Marvin war flicks, *Hogan's Heroes* or other dated content to fill our time. The best viewing almost always consisted of war movies, comedies, or cartoons. But nothing beat the afternoon *Kung Fu* theater hour when it came to creative fuel for our imagination.

Many of the other kids had the luxury of professional training in Tang Soo Do, Tae Kwon Do, or even Tom Crum's Aikido courses. But Dean and I made up our own. It was an amalgam of street-style boxing, various kicks we tried to emulate and a few flips and leg sweeps, etc. We might as well have been Bruce Lee in our own minds. We believed we could withstand attacks from some of the most formidable foes. In reality, we were flailing around like a couple of idiots. We likely looked like we were having spasms. Bruises from failed nunchuck attacks and accidental backwards falls showed the truth. Dorks. Well maybe not Dean, but I can surely say I was a complete dork in the awkward years that lasted until my mid-20s. (*Fun fact. Dean eventually did train in Aikido with Tom Crum. But I bet I could still "kick his ass" Wapah!!!*)

Days when TV reruns didn't take center stage, we would explore. Around my neighborhood, it was either near and around the Aspen Club and Crystal Lake, or up towards the Mountain Valley subdivision. There we would make routine trips to climb the water tower. It was the "height" of excitement and provided one of the best views imaginable of the span of the valley below.

At Dean's subdivision in Silver King, we explored everything at the base of the mountain. Wherever there was pavement, and wherever there wasn't, we were poking our noses into anything that caught our eye.

Our hikes were full of attacks, not unlike Cato in Blake Edwards' *Pink Panther* movies. We would ply our skills and defend from all manner of spastic punches, surprise kicks or even tackles and flips. One might wonder what passers-by thought of the spectacle. (They probably never noticed.)

One favorite exploration spot of ours was at the mine dumps at the base of Smuggler Mountain. There was all manner of dumped machinery, concrete, railroad ties, tires, and such. Endless gadgets and imaginary war landscapes occupied our time and our minds. When Bruce Lee antics were sidelined, we could easily slip back into a Lee Marvin inspired battle scene. Hiding from oncoming trucks, pretending they were halftracks or tanks, we were always evading imaginary Nazis.

It's a wonder we never contracted tetanus from the myriad of sharp metal objects. Or that we never broke an ankle traversing old conveyor belts or lost a limb on a loose piece of sheet metal jumping from garbage heap to junk pile. There was nary a day we didn't go home exhausted and covered in filth.

One fine day, Dean and I discovered an old Photo Booth or two, rusted and mangled amongst the scrap metal. We unscrewed the lenses and messed around with them as magnifying glasses in the sun until we grew tired of trying to light dirt on fire. Just then I spotted a huge square, concrete enclosure. Excited, we both climbed up, and peered through the square hole at the top.

"Dude! It's like a German bunker in *The Dirty Dozen*!" I started to descend the rebar ladder to the bottom of the huge cement box.

"Um ..." Dean stuttered as I explained my strategy to booby trap the bunker for when the Nazis surely would return.

"We'll blow the lid off of this diabolical scheme, and put an end to this damned war, once and for all!!!" I continued.

"Um ..." he tried again to interject.

"Those bastards will pay when they come back! Take that!" I added emphatically.

"Chris! I think I know what this thing is ..." again he attempted to break through my imaginative interlude.

"They'll never know what hit 'em! ... what?" I asked as I scoured the bottom of the concrete tank for treasures.

"I think it's an old septic tank," he stated hesitantly.

"Those freakin' Nazis! A what?" I spoke.

"A septic tank. They use it to hold raw sewage," he finished.

Reality set in almost as quickly as I was able to climb the ladder and jump clear. I was out of there faster than lightning.

We both looked at each other in sort of a state of shock. And then burst out in laughter as we started back towards Dean's parents' place.

"Betcha can't dodge this punch," I lunged at him.

"I'm not even gonna get near you until you wash your hands!" He ducked and started running faster than I thought he was capable.

A few years later the landscape changed drastically when it became an EPA Superfund Cleanup site. There's no telling if the imaginary Nazis finally got their comeuppance.

"ASS, GAS OR GRASS ... "

"NO ONE RIDES FOR FREE." The bumper sticker could be found at many points throughout the town adorning the bumpers of a myriad of vans, on picture boards in the local bars and of course, at the thumbing station on the 200 block of Main Street.

The hippies didn't care much at all about anything. The ski bums didn't care much for the hippies, and the old timers didn't care much for any of them. Yet it somehow worked, and the town became a tight-knit community.

These were the days of no area code and a single phone in the house. Everyone had a 925 prefix and most still had ZG plates adorning their VW's, Scouts, and Willy's Jeeps. It was the second year that the Aspen Police drove Saabs, and a few years before the brand Subaru would become synonymous with mountain living.

Hitchhiking was a prevalent thing. Even in Catechism class, Sister Sylvia once told us a parable about how she injured the tip of her middle finger. As the story went, she had stuck out her thumb to catch a ride. A car swiftly blew past her and yelled out something nasty. So, she had shown the other finger in addition to her thumb, in a gesture of ill will and degradation. Just then, another car came by too quickly and the mirror nicked the tip of her finger. It was a small allegorical tale, with three inherent lessons: 1. Foul language is crass and base 2. Foul gestures don't accomplish anything positive and 3. Don't hitchhike or hell will surely await your earthly demise.

TV was in every home, but channels were limited, and some of us ... gasp ... still had "black and white" sets. Local news came from *The Aspen Times* weekly, radio and of course, word of mouth. There was a local broadcast station, but Grassroots focused mainly on the arts and the local community and remained on a continual loop of old content.

National news came in print, and cop shops throughout the country wouldn't invade each other's "beat." As such, there was little cooperation between precincts, and connected crimes could happen in two parts of the country, but no one would be the wiser.

January 1975 marks the loss of innocence for our small town. Prior to then, we were a community of friends, trust, amicable acquaintances, and "generations of unlocked doors."

That year, we kids were snug in our beds and dreaming of our recently unwrapped Christmas gifts when the world changed, unbeknownst to us.

Somewhere in the night. there lurked a monster. And although in those days, Snowmass seemed like a thousand miles away, it was way too close for comfort.

I remember the smell when our electric heat would kick on. Our world was cozy. Aspenauts (Ski School), snow forts, and sledding down our neighborhood's steepest hill presented some of the best entertainment for us in those days. But when toes started to hurt and fingers turned blue, we always knew there would be hot chocolate and warmth in the house at 244 Eastwood Road. We were blissfully unaware of the deviance lurking in the shadows.

Suffice it to say, by today's standards, someone like Ted Bundy would have a much harder time plying his sick trade without garnering much, much more attention. A month later, the papers would report the discovery of the body of Caryn Campbell, a nurse from Michigan who was visiting in January for a conference. As memory serves, the community treated it as an oddity, and not much else. Nonetheless, the hair on our necks went up, and the women in my family, along with those we knew, had a newfound sense of dread.

Life went on as though nothing happened in the valley. But as time went on, there grew equal parts paranoia and disbelief throughout the community, depending on who you asked. Most guys and old-timers were more interested in their next paycheck, party or day-off to hit the slopes. Most women, on the other hand, were afraid. Not so much of a specific threat, as the crime in Snowmass was still unsolved. But more of a general feeling of dread. "Someone" had done it. And he might still be here, looking for another opportunity to try again.

Approximately six months later, and a long distance away, Bundy was caught. In 1977, after matching a sample of the victim's hair to evidence in Utah, Bundy was brought back to our fair community. Although this time not as a tourist, but in chains. That's when things started to get interesting around town. With the media attention and Bundy's undeniable charisma, there came to be a schism in the opinions of our town's people.

As crazy as it sounds in modern day times, many people believed there was "no way" Bundy was a killer. Most notable among the swayed were many of the local police, including the Sheriff, a lifelong friend of our family and one-time neighbor. In fact, they were so cavalier about it, they gave Bundy free rein of the courthouse library so he could "prepare" for his case. It is no surprise now that with little oversight and a dash of hubris on the part of his caretakers, he was able to jump from the second story window of the courthouse—and escape.

For the first time in generations or possibly ever, doors were dead-bolted shut that day. Cops were everywhere, along with civil servants and the occasional "posse" of rednecks. Our town temporarily became locked down, and nervousness and fear gripped us all. His escape roused the community to host a fruitless manhunt for a few days. It turned out he was not very well versed in wilderness survival and ended up turning himself in ... his injury from the jump proved too painful to continue his flight from justice.

But while he roamed free, despite the terror of our community, there were those who thought it was a joke. I remember the

"I saw Ted Bundy at the (fill in the blank)" T-shirts and commenting, "that's funny" to my mom, to which she replied with gentle scorn, "that's tacky." And after thinking about how a victim's family might feel, I realized that she was right.

Later on, Bundy was again able to escape incarceration in Garfield County, and the paranoia again ensued. This time he fled the state. But the towns were shaken. Eventually he was caught, detained for good, and executed. Nowadays the subculture of serial killer worship exists, and news of mass shootings happen daily, it can seem as if the age of innocence is lost. Still, a fading memory of the days when Aspen was quiet in the off-season, and safety was never a question, barely lives on like a fading legacy. The idyllic days of unlocked doors exist only in nostalgia.

Time passed. History was slowly written in the jaded stone of notorious misdeeds and miscreants, and Aspen gradually recovered. Fear and revulsion dissipated, despite the national news coverage and the subsequent grisly details that came out about Bundy's actions. But as the world quickly became aware of the atrocities Bundy committed, and what a monster he truly was, so did our town. Like the fact that he confessed to killing thirty victims, and that some of his victims were children, that his spree spanned multiple states ... and how he would often pick up hitchhikers.

And just like that, it seems as though the thumbing stations came down.

CHURCH

SUNDAY MORNINGS WERE devoted to revelry at the Catholic Church. This was a huge part of our upbringing. While mass was usually only an hour, we'd pile into the old building and listen to the moral lessons. Communal prayers, creaking pews, tithings, and genuflections became routine over the years. I'd be lying if I were to say church didn't seem a lot longer than an hour. However, after church we'd enjoy "coffee and donuts" with the other congregants. We'd often go to lunch with our closer friends.

Those that know me best from that time might be less shocked to know I was once an altar boy.

For many years we spent time at the church in Catechism class with Sister Sylvia, and later Confirmation classes that did more to solidify my desire to *leave* the church, than to become a lifelong parishioner.

Mom remained a devout Catholic for the entirety of her life. Aside from a few recent introductory masses in attempts to imprint moral fortitude into my children, church has been largely avoided in my adult life.

While Catholicism provided the world with a template for weighing the differences between right and wrong, it also provided the world with examples of hypocrisy I could not tolerate.

Aspen was not spared the stain of sexual assault and molestation by members of the clergy. Our demon was gifted to us with the name of Robert White, after he was cast out of a previous community for crimes against young boys. He continued to ply his trade in yet another community after similar reports from our parish began to make too much noise for the comfort of the regional diocese.

After seeing this play out in our community, I had enough of the hypocrisy, and decided my search for meaning would be better suited in reading the Bible on my own. The abuse got too close to too many people I know too well.

While the church still maintains a valuable institution for teaching the works of the Bible, my take is simple:

> If the only thing keeping you from theft, rape, adultery, and murder, are the words of a potential pedophile at the pulpit on a Sunday morning, there may be a disconnect with the true teachings of Christ. Consider therapy instead.

The church failed the kids and failed the parents too. Our parents were tasked with keeping us out of danger, and unwittingly placed us directly into the belly of the beast.

I try not to preach and will leave it at this. I'm glad I had the opportunity to know the wonderful families we shared our time with at the church. I appreciate and still value many of the lessons I learned in that environment. I know the church is still important to many, and I would never tell anyone what they should or should not believe. I am also saddened that the church allowed good people in the clergy to be lumped in with the bad, by not weeding out the demons from within their own ranks.

Nonetheless, my search for meaning and moral learnings now come from books and from within. And my heart goes out to the victims and their families.

Rev. Harold Robert White – Assignment Record (article).

WAR GAMES

WE WERE RUNNING DOWN the road playing imaginary war games again. Like most days after school, we all squatted behind the sheds and planned the missions. Usually, the enemies were Nazis. After all, our only other points of reference were Korea and Vietnam. None of us knew anything about Korea, and nobody—and I mean *nobody*, talked about Vietnam in those days. Everything else we knew about World War II was either from a textbook, a Time Life Series Book, or from the endless Lee Marvin and John Wayne movies that were on replay on TV.

It was about the time when the pieces of the Space Station were on their way back down to earth. Although it was probable that the parts would all burn up in the atmosphere or land in the middle of the ocean, we all imagined large chunks landing in our backyards.

"Maybe we can make a fort out of the command console!"

"Don't be crazy—you'd burn up from all the radiation."

"Maybe it would make a huge fiery crater—we could use it as a dugout. Like a foxhole!"

"C'mon dude. That would never happen. I heard they used actual GOLD on the reflectors"

"Awesome! We'll be rich!"

"… watch out! Nazis!"

We would all duck and throw "potato mashers" or, in our case dirt clods, over the hedges and wait for the imaginary "BOOM!"

On most days our arsenal was a ragtag assortment of broken hand-me down toys, but with a little imagination we were an elite squad of the best of the best. One kid had a plastic Tommy gun that made noises when you pulled the trigger—at least sort of. It was mostly broken, but sometimes it would sound realistic. There were cowboy cap guns (without caps—none of us could afford them), makeshift pistols fashioned out of scrap wood and nails and of course many, many ordinary sticks that resembled the shapes of the rifles we saw in the old movies on TV. One kid had a broken squirt gun he had painted black, and I had a busted BB gun I traded for a box of baseball cards and an old matchbook collection.

But this day was different. It was different in that I had finally brought out my new CO2 pellet gun I had been saving up for two years to buy. All the penny jars, the birthday and Christmas money and the proceeds for a year and a half of chores put together was just enough to buy the toy gun. As such I didn't bring it out until this day as I had no ammo or gas to make it work until then.

It was a replica of a 357 Magnum of the day. But it really looked like the 44 Magnum from the *Dirty Harry* movies. The handgun that'll "blow your head clean off ..." Fake wood grain handle, with a flat black polished body and realistic sights—it had a revolving chamber and dual trigger action. These were the days that toy guns looked real. No orange plugs or painted blue handles—this baby could almost pass for the real thing.

Some of my friends had seen the gun and got to pull the trigger, but none had a chance to see it work. Not until this day. Another two weeks of savings and pulling extra chores, I was able to buy a small tin of fifty pellets and a box of five CO2 cartridges. I was so excited I was shaking. I think my friends were too, as they were antsy as a bunch of puppies needing to pee. My friends watched on as I put the CO2 cartridge into the handle of the gun—I turned it too slowly and the gas pshewwwwwwwwwd out the sides in a huge hiss. My friends laughed maniacally and scoffed a bit too loudly.

"Shut the hell up!!!!!!!!!!!" and then lower in tone, "don't let my mom hear us."

We all shifted out the basement door and worked our way around the house underneath the windows around to the driveway and eventually to the road. All the while we were being careful not to be seen by my mom. Try #2 was successful—I turned the nut more quickly and the gas sealed.

Then I loaded the six pellets into the round cartridge and seated in the chamber. With a quick snap the gun folded up and was ready for action. "Take the safety off!" one of my accomplices shouted. After I clicked off the first six shots, my friends both screeched with excitement and quickly got bored as they got to squeeze off their turns.

We shot at sticks, rocks and an old rusty can. Soon, boredom struck for those who had to resort back to their pointed sticks and broken squirt guns, and the war games began again.

But the buzz was not gone for me, or my friend Marcus. Marcus was a twin. His brother lived in another county with his mom, while Marcus lived with his dad in the next neighborhood over. While I can't be sure, I suspect we first met on the way home on the school bus.

He was about my size and stature, but Marcus was by far the toughest kid I had ever met. He always outmatched even the biggest kids at school in a fight, and never backed down from anything life threw in his face. I not only looked up to him as a role model, but also instinctively knew that he would defend me, should the need arise (and many times he did). In those early days he was my best friend.

As our small entourage regrouped and started their master military plans, Marcus and I plotted to break out on our own and shoot off some more pellets. We quickly moved our way out into the road and spied potential targets. The first few were no more than ten feet in front of us. We'd shoot at a grasshopper or a katydid, a tree, or a rock. Then we'd shoot an occasional piece of trash or a dandelion until we found a puddle which made incredible waves when the pellet would disappear into the mud.

After a while we looked back, and all the other guys had dispersed into the woods, making occasional "pshoo, pshoo" sounds to imitate their gunfire. They would cry out "Cover me!" and "Medic!" just like in the movies. But now, for Marcus and

I, something was a bit more real. We figured out the pellet gun had amazing range. No more "make believe," we could shoot this thing a long way away. I sighted in a what looked like a metal bell on top of a telephone pole, squeezed off a couple of shots and heard one hit. Marcus and I looked at each other in amazement and shock.

"Holy shit dude! Let me try that."

I loaded a new CO_2 cartridge and handed Marcus the ring for the six pellets for him to load, then handed him the gun. We both scanned the horizon for something to aim at. In an instant, Marcus stopped scanning and aimed the gun up at a 25-degree angle, at a small black dot at the top of a tree approximately 200 yards away.

We both sucked our breaths in as he steadied his hand and squeezed the trigger. You could hear the calm wind and a very distant car driving up the neighborhood on a slow trek home from work, in what seemed like an eternity of near silence that ensued before we heard the snap. We watched quietly for what seemed like a minute until the black dot fell from the high branch of the tree and landed on the ground.

Once again, we looked at each other in amazement and shock. We both said, "Whoa!!!!!!!!!! No way!!!!!!!!" in excitement as we started running to the tree, Marcus nearly dropping the pellet gun in his furious gallop.

Marcus was always a faster runner than me. Actually, he was a better athlete all around than most of the kids at school, but like me, he had no interest in sports in general. He ran ahead and beat me to the spot by a good 20 seconds.

As I ran up to the spot out of breath, I spied a scene that I will never forget. Marcus stood with the gun swinging limply in one hand and a small bird in the other lying flat out for inspection by his head which was hanging low.

I looked at the bird and said, "Wow. Looks like a small finch."

The body was no more than three inches long and had a beautiful plumage of black, yellow, and white with a small wide beak. There was a small dot of blood just above the shoulder of its wing. I looked at Marcus's face—a single tear fell from his eye.

While I marveled at the amazing accuracy of the impossible shot, Marcus realized the implications of life he took. He looked up, composed himself and said, "Let's go find the rest of the guys ..."

―――――

Many years later, and the only other time I ever saw Marcus in a moment of vulnerability, I sat silently in his apartment with a group of punks in our pathetic attempt at understanding and consolation. We stared on as Marcus cracked and downed a cheap beer and walked into his bedroom.

Moments later he emerged with a gun belt with two Colt six shooters ...

This time they were the real thing. He gently hung the belt on the door handle, guns resting against the flat of the door and said, "My dad left those to me."

To which we all awkwardly replied something resembling a consolation but sounded more like, "Dang man ..."

He had lost his father that day.

Marcus cracked another beer. He switched gears, grabbed a record off the shelf and placed it on the stereo.

"Check out this song by Samhain. Freakin' Danzig man!"

I could swear I saw another tear in his eye. But to this day I can never be sure.

THE CASE FOR
A POCKET KNIFE

IN MY MANY TRAVELS and trips to the river to fish for trout, I often found things that others left behind, dropped, ditched, or tried to hide in the river, or on the shores.

It was not uncommon to find fishing gear, clothing, rafting accessories, and other random items. For example, I once found a minibike submerged in the muck just off the edge of the river. It took a few trips and the help of some friends to pull it out. The hundred or so pounds it weighed ensured that it would be so augured in the mud that a mere tug would not loosen it from its otherwise watery grave. We used ropes and sticks in the mud to pull it out.

Once it was free, we watched the muddy sludge drop off the fins of the two-stroke motor and gradually we could see the color of the tires and the rotted fabric of the seat. In the end it proved to be a total loss as the bike was so waterlogged that there was no way to get it running. I considered using parts from the relic to fix up my working minibike, but alas, the parts were all in metric threading, whereas my bike was of standard American craftsmanship. I ditched the bike not 5 feet from where we dragged it from the water. There's no telling what eventually happened to it. Only God truly knows.

By far the most bizarre item I found floating in the river while I was fishing was a standard-sized pickle bucket full of climbing gear, slightly submerged and snagged on a branch that was wedged between two rocks in the middle of the river.

As the runoff from the great divide makes its way down the mountains and ravines of the landscape, settlers of the "land of old" found more and more uses for it. Over the years, everyone near or downstream from the trickles that grew into streams found their own uses for the water that grew into rivers and eventually flowed to the lowest part of the land and disappeared into the sea. Inevitably, almost every drop is siphoned off into the hands of farmers, reservoirs and giant cisterns that served the early agrarian culture that was the West. As such, the once and mighty rivers of the early spring and summers in the Rocky Mountains were now reduced to but a trickle of their former selves.

Today, the water is largely "owned" or earmarked for cities way down-the-line. Metropolises like Phoenix, Las Vegas and even Los Angeles have dibs on the water that starts out as snowpack in the high cliffs and mountains of the Rockies. In the end the rivers once named for their aggression, had been tamed and now flowed calmly down the valleys and provided a nice respite for onlookers and anglers. No longer did the rivers wield the fury of a once freer time, save for a few days in the spring.

As was often the case, the best fishing spots I found were in the middle of the river, under the massive round rocks that made the river sing. I would hop from rock to rock until I was out in the middle, settle down and rig up my best lure, get ready for the long haul and wait to get my first bite of the day.

I had a lucky spinner rod, a lucky spinner reel and of course, a lucky spinner. The Red Devil was the greatest tool in my arsenal as it somehow infuriated the largest and strongest of the fish in the river. If there was an alpha in the water within 15 feet of where I cast, it would elicit a fight of epic proportions. And I would pull in trophy fish more often than I should have been able to. This was all due to my lucky spinner.

In my attempts at catching the behemoth of the summer, one cast landed just over another boulder. I tried to let the spinner "roll" around the rock and then float under the small rapid to elicit the attention of a king Brown or Native Brooke trout only to get snagged in a major way on something just out of view. I knew

I would lose my rig if I tried to yank it free. It was, after all, strung over a rock and out of sight. Since it was my luckiest lure, and it cost over $3, I decided my only choice was to navigate the slippery rocks and find it at its source and pull it out by hand. This was not out of the ordinary. I suspect I saved this very lure in a similar fashion twenty or thirty times by now. At times I would be in the river neck deep trying to untangle the lure from all manner of sticks, muck and more often than not, someone else's tangled mess from a previously lost battle and similar fate. I gently packed up my green tackle box, my backpack and all my other belongings and with fishing pole in one hand I began jumping further out into the middle of the river.

Now I should say at this time, that although the river was not the mighty force of nature it might once have been, the waters were swift, dangerous, and very, very cold. While it wasn't likely I would die from a quick dip, it was no picnic falling in. Especially in the middle of the river. Every year, the newspapers were happy to report the victims of the flow and remind the public of their mortality in the face of Mother Nature's wrath. In short, it was best to stay dry, if at all possible.

As I reached the rock my lucky lure was wrapped around, and reeled in the final slack in my reel, I set down my stuff and began the hard work of reaching into the murky depths to follow the line with my fingertips until I felt the lure. But now, my hand felt something odd at the end of the hook. It felt like the netting from a basketball hoop but seemed to weigh a ton. Feeling around I was able to find a plastic handle atop a wire-like ring.

With all my strength I slowly pulled the object out of the water. Sloshing off the rim of the white ring I began to recognize the shape of the object at hand. It was a standard construction barrel, otherwise known as a "Pickle Bucket." This five-gallon white container had a nest of orange nylon cord, tangled in the bottom. Atop the mess were two items of note: One was a nice climbing carabiner, the other was my three-pronged red and white spinner, the lucky Red Devil – impossibly snagged amidst the ropes.

The origin of the bucket full of nylon cord was and continues to be a mystery. I often wondered if somewhere upriver of the spot I found it, someone dropped the bucket from a high cliff as they were climbing to an unknown summit. As it flipped and flopped down the rocky crag, the rope and carabiner stayed intact. Eventually the bucket found its way to the cold, fluid creek, floating and bobbing in the water only to get caught in an undertow and inevitably to be found by an 11 year-old boy on summer break.

Being a kid of limited financial resources, I not only wanted to salvage my lure, but had an eye for that carabiner. By God, I wanted that thing. Oh yeah and the bucket was kinda cool too. So, picture if you will a 5-gallon pickle bucket filled about a third of the way up with a nest of waterlogged and rotting Nylon cord, with a carabiner hooked through the hoops and my lucky lure snagged in a three-pronged puzzle.

Let's go back two or three years from the current dilemma. As a Leo, my birthday falls in the summer which is prime time to fish and hunt. My Dad is an avid outdoorsman and because of the lack of interest from my older Brother, the legacy of hunting and fishing passed down to his middle child, me. My parents were split when I was seven, so even though Dad had no issue with the sharper edges in adolescent life, Mom refused to allow me to own a pocket knife as she was sure I would injure myself.

Because I would fish nearly every waking moment I could in the summers, and since that often requires a sharp knife, I was forced to improvise. Over the course of a few years, I managed to salvage a pair of broken needle-nosed pliers and a very dull butter knife that I was sure would not be missed. I hid them in the avocado green tin tackle box my grandfather gave my dad, and my dad gave to me. Dented, scratched, and flawed as it was, it proved to be a perfect carryall for my tools and my fishing gear.

Now in my 11th year on this earth and mere weeks from my 12th birthday, I sat on a rock, in the middle of a river with my lucky lure stuck in a mess of nylon cord and no knife. Ok. Full disclosure … so I had the dull butter knife. This brings me to a key event in the story.

I easily unhooked the carabiner with its simple mechanism and placed it in the bottom section of the tackle box. At this point

I began to pull the nylon cord up and out of the bucket to displace the weight of the water enough to try to free the lure. However, I was denied in many attempts to get it loose. The barbs dug in as they were designed to do and began to fray the cord into a further mess of strings reminiscent of a black widow's web. The harder I tried, the worse the tangle got.

I tried the butter knife and soon gave up. It was utterly futile. This is when I grabbed the rusty needle nose pliers and began pulling at the individual smaller strings to free the lure. It was working relatively well for a while, and I managed to free two of the three barbs. Then it happened. As I was pulling at the threads, the cord slipped and drew in close to my chest. The handle of the pliers wracked my lower ribs. As I tried to reclaim my breath, I looked down to what felt like a bee sting and saw a red bead of blood forming at the base of one of the barbs of the lure which had now hooked itself into the center of my thigh.

I recall wincing with pain as the hook worked itself into my flesh. But I weathered it like a boss. My dad had taught me well. I refused to let it bring me down. The only trouble was that the other barb of the hook was still embedded in the mess of nylon cord, which was wrapped around the pickle bucket handle which was still halfway submerged underwater and weighed what seemed to be 6,000 lbs by the standards of an impossible situation.

This meant I was going nowhere until I unhooked the lure from my leg, or the chord from the bucket. Now I realize this sounds ridiculous, and like most things that happen in real life, it was—in hindsight. But the reality of the situation was, I was stuck to a bucket of waterlogged cord which was submerged in the middle of a river with no way to set myself free but for a dull butter knife and a broken pair of pliers.

The knife proved to be worthless, and I may have even thrown it into the depths in disgust and frustration. So, my only tools were the broken pliers and other sharp hooks I had in the tackle. In all it took about an hour to fray the lines into small enough threads to pull apart with the pliers. I remember thinking

"There's no way I can walk all the way home with a 5 lb bucket full of water attached to my leg." Not to mention that I was on a rock in the middle of the river.

By the time I finally cut the nylon cord down to approximately 4 inches from the lure thoroughly lodged into my flesh, it turned out that my leg had swelled up to just slightly smaller than the size of a watermelon. And it was stiff as hell too. I grabbed my backpack and hurled it as hard as I could to the shore of the river. Then buckled the latch on the tackle box and wrapped it with a couple free lines of the nylon cord and threw it as far as I could to the shore. It rattled with intensity as my prized belongings flailed around with the new-found carabiner in the metal box.

Struggling across the rocks, it turned out to be a lot harder to get back to shore than when I casually hopped the rocks out to the middle. My stiff leg stood straight out and more than once I ended up nearly horizontal, stretching my body across the stones to pull myself across. Eventually I made it to shore and gathered my things. As it turns out the lighter backpack came within mere inches of ending up in the river and making its final trek to the ends of the earth courtesy of the relentless current. I hiked back through the woods, past the millionaires' houses and onto the bike path about 1/2 mile from the river. Limping the whole way and crying the "tough kid" cry, I made it to the highway and home was in sight.

After crossing the highway, climbing the steep hill to the short trail to my house, I learned that the last part of the journey is always the hardest. It was at that point I started to think of how the hell I was going to explain this to my mom. I slammed my way through the front door, dropped all my gear and screamed, "Mom!"

Fast forward an hour or so later, to a somewhat comical scene as my mom, brother, and sister all stood in horror as I sat nearly horizontal with my stiff, swollen leg straight out and the familiar Red Devil hook sticking out with a 4-inch orange nylon cord frayed at the end. There may have been a neighbor or two in the mix too, I can't be sure. It was a small town at the time.

Mom grabbed the good pliers and began to pull. It's possible the trenches of the Civil War and the medical tents of WWI saw trauma that elicited a greater auditory response from their victims. But I doubt it. The drama was thick enough for my jaded mother to call her ex-husband to oversee the situation. While the wait seemed eternal to me, he probably took fewer than 10 minutes to arrive.

I'll never forget the event that changed my dad from a strict authoritarian and stalwart figure of great strength and stature to a shaken man of empathy and gentleness. As Dad tried to pull the hook from my leg, I had been reduced to a puddle of pain and sorrow. He quickly gave up, only to suggest a quick trip to the local emergency room.

Finally, it took the advice of a doctor to explain the intricacies of a barbed hook and the laws of physics to us. As it turns out, there is a way to pull a hook from flesh by applying downward pressure to the hook while pulling it out horizontally. While it may make a little area of the skin sore, the hook comes out easily and can be reused with little effort. This was not the case with my lucky Red Devil. In the bizarre turn of events the hook had caused so much swelling that the only effective way to rid my thigh of the metallic, barbed blight was to poke the sharp end through and cut it off—much like the cowboys and settlers of the old days when greeted with an arrow from a native American (that's how it was in the movies anyway).

A chipper doctor quickly washed the leg down, slathered it in Iodine and slapped a Band-Aid on it. He smiled, sent us on our way and was quick to mention to me personally, "The good news is you get to keep your lucky lure!"

Mom and dad were not as pleased as I. The hospital bill was enough to buy a hundred of them.

A few weeks later for my twelfth birthday, I tore into a tightly wrapped, small box from my mom approximately 3 ½ inches long by about an inch. It was a Swiss army knife.

A GOOD DAY

WE WOULD SIT IN QUIETUDE with lines in the water. Watching the refraction of a stick near the bank. Listening to the subtle wind. I would watch as the pollen clouds would lift off the tops of the majestic pine trees and drift aimlessly into the wind, dispersing their fecundity and disappearing into the blue, cloud spotted sky. I matched my breathing to the wind.

From our youngest days, Dad would take my brother and I to the high mountain lakes. They were days of solitude and peace when you would rarely see another person.

Our ritual would begin early in the morning before we would leave the house. It consisted of arranging the gear, cleaning, and threading line through the old fishing poles his father gave him. He would tell us to roll the ends on the side of our nose, so that the "nose grease" would keep the rods properly oiled. In retrospect, it was possibly a ploy to have us walk around all day with black smudges on our faces.

A good day would consist of spending time fishing or hunting with dad, learning the unspoken lessons of nature, respecting and experiencing the magic of everything she offers. It was time well-spent, developing the critical understanding of how life and death are intertwined, and that food didn't originate in a sterilized vacuum sealed package. Quietude and understanding in nature, stamped like an invisible tattoo, are a bond only my dad and his son could know.

Hikes back seemed to take less time. Backpacks filled to the limit with fresh trout. And lungs purified with clean mountain air—these were the marks of a good day.

FUN TIMES IN FAT CITY

DENVER HAD WAX TRAX, California had Tower Records, London had Rough Trade and Aspen had Alan.

The first time I walked into Fat City Records, the smell hit me. It was a small, cramped space on the corner of Monarch and Main. Alan Holland had recently arrived in Aspen with a truckload of ephemera and a mind to escape the heat and drug scene he hailed from in Texas. It resembled the room of a hoarder and I'm pretty sure he lived in the small shop for a time. It's also possible he didn't bathe for a while. Nonetheless, the curiosities he had in that small, cramped space were worthy of a more detailed look. And as such I found myself spending more and more time at his shop every chance I got.

The record shop was a few doors down from the Great Divide Music store, which is likely how I discovered it. On many occasions, I would visit Sandy Munro's store to try out and dream about new guitars. And keep Sandy on edge while 'test driving' some of his finer instruments, which I *definitely* could not afford to replace.

Fat City Records was a small room with posters of bands I'd never heard of, and walls of record racks, jam-packed with the strangest collection of music, both shocking and surreal. At first the shop was almost like "by appointment only" as there would often be a "be right back" note or sign scrawled in pen, taped to the door. Alan would disappear for hours at a time in the middle of the day. But it was always worth the wait when he came back.

When he wasn't playing records at volumes too loud for the neighboring businesses, he would play VHS tapes of movies like *The Forbidden Zone*, and *Eraser Head*, anything by Russ Meyers or John Waters and lots of music videos that would never grace the airwaves of MTV. You could expect to see footage of the band The Residents, alongside deconstructions by artist Mark Pauline. Or a casual live concert of New Order backed up by *The Greatest Rock 'n' Roll Swindle*, a movie about the Sex Pistols. He would rent the tapes out, but his face would show a true sense of dread as he bagged them up in a used grocery sack. He knew there was a good chance that the tape would come back damaged, or not at all. This was less a business transaction, more like loaning out a piece of his personal collection.

Later on, Fat City Records, named after one of Hunter S. Thompson's campaign promises for sheriff, moved to the mall, across from the Wheeler Opera House. For a music lover and enthusiast of the weird, it was glorious. For Alan, it was a space big enough to spread out all his items, and for racks large enough to organize the records by category. Plus, it was a location that allowed Alan to grow his business, and one would assume, make a living. For us kids, it was a great hangout. Decisions were tough to make, whether to spend the week's take from peddling *The Aspen Times* on a new record, or on a Haagen Daas treat just down the stairs. I still think Haagen Daas is some of the best ice cream out there, however I'm glad to report most of my purchases were for new music.

By now, America had worn out the entire catalog of every well-known artist from Bruce Springsteen and the Eagles ad nauseam. There was a scattering of brilliance from folks like the Cars, Blondie, Lou Reed, the Ramones and Pat Benatar, but by and large, the youth was thirsty for something new.

Bands like Joy Division, Killing Joke, Bauhaus, the Clash, Can, Siouxsie and the Banshees, Tones on Tail, and Flipper were always playing just a little too loud for browsing customers' pleasure. But I don't think Alan cared. His ideal was creating a scene and indoctrinating the younger kids with a strong sense of appreciation for the counterculture happening in the arts. And if I had to guess, it was his own way of finding and collecting the coolest, weirdest things available at the time. His favorites seemed to be Flipper, PIL, the Stooges and Joy Division. But it was never odd to hear the likes of The Dead Kennedys, Skinny Puppy, Jesus and Mary Chain, Christian Death, Virgin Prunes, Einstürzende Neubauten, the Residents, and of course the Sex Pistols.

I've pored over the available footage of the Sex Pistol shows in Dallas and San Antonio in 1978 and have yet to find it. But I remember Alan showing me a video of a kid with a red mohawk getting kicked in the head by a band member. Alan swore it was him. And I have no reason to doubt it. He'd gladly show you the scar.

Often, he seemed to be in his own world, either poring over receipts or desperately counting money for the UPS truck. Unfortunately, this made him an easy mark for kids who wanted to line their pockets with the latest "Ratt" tape or some other crap. He stocked the shelves with similar such pap, with the intent to keep the lights on by selling items he would never care to listen to himself. As such, the kids would steal his very bread and butter right from under his nose. But it didn't seem to faze him.

Being a regular in the store, I would consider it a badge of honor to watch the shop as Alan would don his trench coat and round buggy-eyed, red glasses to literally chase down the UPS truck and count wadded-up dollar bills to pay for the days' shipment COD (Cash On Delivery). Suffice it to say, Alan had little luck obtaining credit from his suppliers) He would often come back dejected if he missed it, or worse yet, if he didn't have enough money to rescue the day's treasure-trove of new vinyl or underground comix. If he was gone long, he would sometimes pay me with a choice pick of something I'd never heard of or heard before.

Around 1984, the American punk music scene began to catch up with Europe, and Alan's store started stocking bands from the West Coast, DC and more titles from New York. He also started selling parts for skateboards, which was convenient for those of us who picked that habit up as well. Now on my walls

I replaced posters of Billy Idol and the Cars with those of bands like the Clash, the Sex Pistols and Siouxsie. My skateboards and guitar amplifiers now donned stickers from Black Flag, the Meat Puppets and Hüsker Dü. In fact, I still have the old amp with the SST sticker "CORPORATE ROCK STILL SUCKS" (guess what: it still does).

About this time, a group of friends and I decided to become "rock stars" and started a punk band. Alan wanted to be a part of it. The basement at our house in Eastwood was large enough to spread out, and conveniently had a closet big enough to store everyone's instruments, except for Dean's drums which were on permanent display. They were too hard to take apart easily. John's keyboards weighed in at just under 1500 lbs. And Alan had a bass amp that was as tall as I was, and very much louder.

Although, other than Alan and Marcus, none of us could really play, we tried our best to cover some of the era's edgier tunes and a few oldies too. If you were to walk by the house, you could hear us attempting songs by Joy Division, The Stooges and my mom's least favorite, Suicidal Tendencies—with Marcus belting out guttural bellows, with all the signs of an overblown case of teenage angst. We thought we were great. The neighbors would likely have a different take.

It was about this time that Alan began to change a bit. He was less interested in what the youth was up to, or his customers. Instead, he turned his attention to a special lady who quickly became a fixture at the store. Sharon and Alan were spending more and more time together. She would often tend to the store and was equally cool in her own way. Shortly thereafter, the couple were expecting ... twins.

Nine months later, it was more frequent to see them walking the baby stroller to and from their A-Frame on the west end of town to the store. It was a touching transformation to see him become a husband and a father. Sharon was the yin to his yang. When I left for college, I'm not sure how long Fat City remained in business. One day, when I came back it was gone. As were Alan and his new family.

At college, there was a radio station that entertained and played a diverse selection of new tunes. Many of which I was already accustomed to, thanks to Alan. But it was no replacement for Fat City. Of the many tastes I've acquired throughout my adult life, I owe a debt of gratitude to Alan Holland and his dream of Fat City Records. His little slice of weirdness influences me to this day. Without him, I might still be listening to Springsteen and reading Superman comics instead of Echo & the Bunnymen and R. Crumb. I will likely never meet a more unique individual as Alan, or to find a similar store as Fat City Records. I've never found another record store with similar offerings, and to this very day, I often awake from dreams of poring through the newest vinyl in the racks at Fat City with a deep sense of excitement and nostalgia.

And shocking as some might find it, I say sarcastically, we never made it to the "big time" with our band.

LOST MAN
RESERVOIR.

ONE LATE SUMMER AFTERNOON, my friend Gideon and I were listening to some LPs on the record player, beating on an old minibike with a rusted wrench. Echo and the Bunnymen's B-side "Do it Clean" blasted through the speakers. Almost in sync, the two of us decided that the next day, we would go fishing instead of sitting around further contemplating and discussing how important the "new" English invasion in rock truly was. And that "Zen and the art of minibike maintenance," could wait until another day.

Since we were teenagers and had already experienced everything there was to experience in our immediate surroundings, we decided on a fishing spot a bit farther than our feet could carry us. We headed to Lost Man Reservoir, a place that held a special place in my memory. My dad had taken me many times in my past to the high mountain lake to catch native cutthroat and brook trout. In truth it was one of my favorite places to go, yet I had only gone with my dad. Going without him seemed altogether bold and undeniably independent. I was excited and scared. If Gideon felt the same way, he hid it well.

Although we both were old enough to drive and had our licenses, only Gideon had access to a vehicle, so the decision was obvious who would drive up the pass to the lake. Gideon's dad had an old Jeep. No doors, no electric windows, no radio, no tape deck, no airbags, no anti-lock brakes, no air conditioning, and hell, probably no heat either. It was your run of the mill, basic white Jeep with a soft top and it was freakin' awesome.

We woke up early and I hurriedly rode my bike down the hill to Gideon's with my backpack full of gear and my fishing rod held out like a jousting lance over the handlebars. Within what should be minutes, but felt like seconds, I rang the doorbell and Gideon opened and emerged ready to go. We packed up the Jeep and Gideon ran back inside to emerge minutes later with a single key on a small metal ring.

With a quick twist of the wrist, the Jeep fired up and we were on our way. Fourteen miles later up a winding, treacherous road, otherwise known as "the Deadly Independence Pass," we pulled off the road to the small, nondescript "parking" lot for the reservoir. Truth be told you could park one, maybe two cars total in the dirt pull off that offered respite for many a weary, white knuckled traveler descending from the heights of the pass.

As we unloaded and packed up our gear, I held the fishing poles from falling while Gideon pulled on his pack. He then told me, "Don't let me forget where I put this. My dad lost the other key." He slipped the key on its ring into his top shirt pocket and grabbed his fishing rod. We were ready to go. The hike from the Jeep was about 10 minutes to the dam. But loaded down with backpacks full of water, sandwiches, warm clothes, a bunch of worms and other fishing gear slowed us down a bit. Winded but excited, we were ready to fish.

We set up rigs and fished off the dam for a bit, but aside from an occasional brookie slowly sauntering by our lines, we didn't get so much as a bite on the bait. Things got boring. Quickly (in fishing terms: 45 minutes), we decided to work our way up the bank toward the giant granite rock at the north end of the lake. At each of the stops we made, Gideon and I allowed enough space between us to fish without snagging each other's lines. The day was quiet, and the weather proved to be perfect. There was not another soul there. I could hear the wind blowing through the top of the pines and watch the ripples in the lake while mudskippers traipsed across the water, to wherever it is that mudskippers go.

Somehow there is nothing quite as peaceful as being left alone with your thoughts, miles from anywhere, at one with nature. The tranquility of the silence can be equaled only with the silence of one's own mind. Both elements combined open the secrets of the universe. As profound as it is, the moment is fleeting. All it takes is the quick chirp of a chipmunk or the fluttering of a camp robin sifting through the crumbs, and cigarette butts left by a previous visitor, to break the silence and bring one back around.

As it was, the familiar zzzzzzzzzttttttttttttttt of a fishing reel brought me back to reality. Gideon had hooked a good one and the line from his cast was swiftly halted with his jerky attempts at controlling the surprise. As he flailed his arms in attempts to pull in the bounty, in as quick an instant as he hooked it, the fish was gone. "Shiiiiiiit!" echoed through the landscape. Then a quieter "shit" when he realized his voice could carry as far as it did. I grabbed my gear and met up with Gideon 25 yards or so up the muddy trail, he had packed his stuff and in a matter of frustration announced, "The best spot is on that huge rock." Whether or not the fishing would be rich, we decided it was the best place to eat our lunch before we moved on.

After we packed up our cheese sandwich crusts and Fritos baggies, we moved along up the trail. It would be very easy to break an ankle in the beaver holes in the trail that filled up with water just inches below the surface of the dirt walls. Side by side, the brambles and thorns tugged relentlessly at the fishing line and pack straps that blew in the wind. While it was but a few short yards to our destination, utmost attention had to be paid to the trail as it was treacherous, in its own small way. Mother Nature has a funny way of reminding us how unimportant we really are. Together with a cold breeze, a million gnats and the threat of a light rain, we were happy to find the sun-baked rock to warm our soaking wet trousers and floppy tennis shoes. Standing on the giant granite surface, in hushed tones, we discussed our plans. Gideon would cast to the right along the shore and bring his line in slowly past the well-known snags. I would throw mine to the left.

On the first cast, and to both of our great surprise, I had a hit. Zzzzzzzzzzzzzzzzzzzzzzzzzzzzzzzttttt. My line was nearly depleted in seconds. As I almost lost the fish, Gideon quickly stowed his gear and tried to help. We both knew the drag on my reel was too loose.

"Quick tighten the drag, dude!"

"Ok! Yeah, yeah! Just a sec ..."

I spun the drag as fast as I could. Only thing is ... it shouldn't spin freely. The cap for the drag quickly spun off the reel and hit the rock two or three times ... ptttt ... ptttt ... plorp. And into the water. Incidentally, we both knew the fish was gone. While the plastic cap floated on the surface the metal nut itself had landed in the water. We watched, annoyed as a small cloud of dust plumed up in the water and slowly dissipated. Gideon looked straight at me and said, "I got this. Hold on man. You hold my legs ..." He then proceeded to lie flat on the large granite boulder. With me holding his legs, and he "levitating" his upper torso over the surface of the lake, he reached out to try to grab the metal nut, barely burrowed into the mud. The further out he reached, the harder it was to hold his weight. Inch by inch, through teamwork and willpower, his fingers came closer and closer to the object.

As he grabbed the nut and began to recoil, he held it high above his shoulder and held up his fist in a moment of victory, "YESSSS!!!!!!!!!"

But as I helped lift him up and he began to regain his composure, the pocket on his shirt, where he had kept the Jeep key, opened against the rock and in an instant, we once again heard the familiar sound of metal bouncing against the granite: ... ptttt ... ptttt ... plorp.

We both watched in horror as the Jeep key landed in the same murky water, we had just stirred up looking for the pieces of my reel that had fallen before. It was almost in slow motion.

"Shiiiiiiit." We both said in unison. Gideon dropped the nut. It again plopped into the water—poit!

By this point we both abandoned all hopes of keeping our pantlegs dry and inched our way down the rock and gently eased into the water. A fruitless attempt to keep the mud from swirling up and completely clouding the water.

While the metal key likely landed in almost the same spot as the nut, we tried for about 45 minutes to find the key. Squeezing the mud in our fingers and dredging the waters in every way we thought we could, our efforts proved to be futile. Every movement we made, no matter how subtle, stirred up even more mud into the already murky water. The sun slowly entered the high point in the sky.

We continued to try to find the key—with marked measures of letting the mud settle, as well as a controlled panic, delving into the water in frenzies to find the lost treasure. All attempts proved to be futile. Looking up into the late afternoon sky, we knew we had to try to get home before the sun entered the west quadrant and the beginnings of night would be upon us.

We packed up our stuff and hiked back to the car, pant legs pulled up past our knees and our socks and shoes turned black in the mud. We waddled up the trail like two defeated soldiers in the battle for our sanity.

It's always funny, but the easiest of walks in the wilderness can become seemingly endless journeys back to civilization, when one has been beaten by Mother Nature. Our 30 minute hike into the rock seemed like hours going back with chapped legs and an increasingly apparent cold breeze and thousands of mosquitoes. We finally made it back to the Jeep and after packing everything up, we decided to try to hitchhike down the pass. But not before turning over every single piece of floormat, or seat cushion in hopes of finding a hidden spare key.

Defeated, we decided to appeal to our fellow man and tried to flag down a car, truck or 4x4 on its way to the small town we called home. As is often the case, our beloved human counterparts all felt we were "some kind" of threat and decided to drive on. Clearly it was the safe choice for them. Occasional cars careened down the pass and slowly, cautiously passed us by. It seemed the time of day, the time of year in the season and apparently the situation at hand had conspired against us. After about an hour of pleading with the few cars that passed us, we had no alternative but to go it on our own.

At the elevation we were at, we decided it would take us days to hike the distance to the closest semblance of civilization. A plight we certainly would not survive, both due to the elements and likely starvation as our packs held only remnants of the light lunch we packed for the day. We had gorged ourselves on all our Cheetos and cokes earlier.

Then, Gideon had an idea. It was simple really.

"We'll coast the Jeep down the pass …"

"You're crazy! What about the cliffs?"

"C'mon man. Brakes!"

"But you don't have power brakes. They work … but it'll be tough to stop. Yet alone steer."

"Got any better ideas? We could go back up and swim for the key again … wanna freeze to death?"

"I guess you're right. You get in and drive, I'll push," I said.

"We'll be home for hotdogs and beer before you know it."

Gideon got behind the wheel, and in an ironic moment, we watched "both ways" on the highway to make sure no one was coming. Of course, no cars were coming, nor had they for almost an hour. We stared straight ahead before moving forward. We had about 200 feet before the first hairpin turn. Then … what? We both could only guess. "Winding" was an understatement. The road this high up, made snakes below appear stick-like. For each sharp turn there was a drop-off of potentially thousands of feet down to the river below.

There were many stories of people who had died on the pass, but the actual experience was far more threatening than anything you could recall from the papers and local folklore. The corners of the pass had remnants of the original construction still intact. Sometimes all that kept us from plummeting off the edge was an array of small concrete walls dotting the edge—that and a steady hand on a steering wheel, coupled with a clear conscience. Death seemed to be stalking anyone brave enough to drive the route. No car was safe in the minds of anyone with a healthy fear of heights.

I shoved as hard as I could to get the Jeep moving to no avail. The first bump would prove too much for one person. Gideon then put the Jeep in neutral and joined me in pushing. The Jeep rocked back and forth a few times and soon pushed over the asphalt lip. The Jeep began to pick up speed … and moved closer and closer to

Illustration by Chris Pomeroy.

the precipice. Gideon and I ran like the wind and swung in the open-door frames. Gideon frantically steered with all his weight and both of his hands to right the vehicle with one leg hanging outside of the vehicle as he tried to gain his seating. We slowly turned the curve and around the first bend. The Jeep picked up enough speed to roll at about 15 mph for about another 500 yards.

Gideon used his whole body and strength to steer the Jeep until it finally came to a rest on a flat part of the highway.

We switched spots and both grabbed hold of the Jeep frame at the front window. We pushed and pushed for 100s of yards at a top speed of maybe 2 mph until we found another hill. Then again, the Jeep picked up almost more speed than we could match. We both ran and jumped in the seats as I too struggled with the heavy steering wheel only to keep the vehicle from once again veering off a cliff. We coasted for a good 300 yards or so only to slow to a dead halt.

We both got out of the Jeep and looked at the terrain ahead of us. It seemed like a mile of flat road. Luckily, we both had enough energy to push. At nearly 45-degree angles, Gideon and I pushed forward with our hands in the most advantageous spots with the most leverage. We pushed until we couldn't breathe. We took a small break and then started again.

After a while we were able to get back on a decline and thus continued the cycle for about 12 miles down the pass. Eventually we passed a few houses and the terrain started to look familiar. We were "close" to home. Unfortunately, we had also run out of hills. Now we were undeniably on the flats. It was time to try hitchhiking again, and just as before, it proved unsuccessful. As the late afternoon crept upon us, we hiked along the side of the road about two more miles, past my house and past the bus stop all the way to Gideon's place.

"I think I can find the spare key. Wait here."

Gideon went around the back of the house and opened the back door. A few minutes later he showed up at the garage door where I was waiting, and he let me in.

Once inside, Gideon opened a few cupboards in the kitchen and finally found a couple of old coffee cans. He rattled them and we heard what sounded like loose change. We sat at the table, and he poured them both out. To my shock and amazement, what I was sure were pennies, turned out to be hundreds, if not thousands of keys. As it turns out, Gideon's sister had collected keys from all corners of the earth for almost 20 years and somehow included the family keys of actual importance, with those found in ditches, trashcans and "lost and founds" all around the County. Gideon's Dad never had the heart to get rid of them, and kept them "just in case," as Gideon recalls.

We both dug through for what seemed like days until Gideon found one or two keys that "looked" like the Jeep key. We packed them all up and put the coffee cans back.

"Are you sure one of those will fit?" I asked.

"No. But we need to try," Gideon stated optimistically.

At this point we both jumped on the back of Gideon's older brother's minibike and made the slow, two-mile trek up the road to the parked Jeep. Slow-moving as it was, it was a relief that we were actually motor driven this time. The plan was, we'd ride back down if the keys didn't fit and call it a day.

As it turns out, Gideon's intuition was right and one of the keys did turn the starter motor. There was a sigh of relief from both of us as the Jeep started up and Gideon ground the gears to make sure the Jeep would move. I drove the Jeep back as Gideon rode his brother's minibike. I beat him back by a few minutes which allowed me to pack up my fishing gear and get my pack in order. I set it all by my bike.

Gideon rolled into the gravel carport and parked the minibike where he found it. He had a certain reverence when it came to the vehicles in his household. Sort of like a secret respect for the owners ... imbued with a certain anxiety and fear that his brother would kill him for taking his minibike. He was careful to position the bike as if it were never moved.

Very soon after, Gideon's dad drove up, parked, and slowly sauntered to the garage door. His coat hung over his arm and his briefcase weighing him down like a lifetime of regrets, he casually looked at me and then Gideon and asked, "How was the lake?"

"Good Dad. I'll tell you about it later."

We both breathed a sigh of relief as Gideon walked inside and I started pedaling my bike back up what was soon to seem like the longest uphill ride imaginable.

Gideon called out, "Maybe we should fish the stream behind the house."

"Good plan," I replied. "See you tomorrow dude."

SIGN BOY,
THE POTHOLE LACKEY

As I NEARED GRADUATION from one of Aspen's finest institutions of knowledge, it appeared I had one last summer to go before college. As it turns out, my plans were somewhat vague, and my future uncertain.

It was high time I took a decent job. No more under the table kitchen work, no more retail, no more grocery stores or construction sites, and no more paychecks paid in cash. It was time to take on something that might have some benefits and decent pay.

Through some connections my mom had through the Eagles Club, I was able to get an interview at the city streets department, in the old building underneath the Castle Creek Bridge. It seems they needed a hand with maintaining the city's inventory of signs. In short, my job was twofold. One, replace and exchange any/all faded or otherwise unreadable signs within the city limits, and two, create and maintain all the wooden street signs unique to the town. A third responsibility, as it were, was to do any of the other odd jobs around the property and help with the rest of the guys on bigger projects.

To say the job was easy would be an understatement. But it allowed me to work outside, and to make some decent money while I figured out what to do with my life. I'd work through the summer, then take a job on the ski slope for the winter. I figured I'd live a year as a ski bum.

After that first year, I ended up working at the Merry-Go-Round restaurant at the top of Aspen Highlands for exactly three days. Excited as I was to get a ski pass, on my first day off, I ran down the stairs at home to catch the free shuttle and proceeded to tear out all the ligaments in my right ankle. "The best laid plans ..." so they say. Sitting around in a cast for an extended time, bored to tears, and not skiing, made me rethink going to college. I enrolled the next spring. In the following summer of that year, I went back to work for the city again, and I continued to work there for several summers, through college.

Aspen has always been unique. There is a certain small-town charm that sets it apart from other tourist destinations. Many of the features borrowed from its mining past, others from the "western" ways of life, and still others from the early influence of the Scandinavian transplants during the budding ski days of the late 40s and early 50s.

Familiar sights in the 70s and 80s included Swiss architecture and embellishments, old west barrels used as trash cans and of course the city street name signs. At the time, the signs were carved out of wood and painted a familiar brown, with white lettering. It was my charge to rout out, and hand paint each and every one of them during the summers. Rare was a summer day when I wasn't routing signs in the side building, rife with asbestos and mice, where we stored the wood, tools, and stencils.

The next step was to prime and then coat the beautiful redwood planks with acrylic, all weather outdoor, brown paint. And finally, I would layer in the white lettering in very thick coats, so the letters could withstand the harsh winters and dry climate. When it came to replacing old signs, I would first inspect the old ones or bring them back to the shop if they had fallen off, so as not to misspell the replacement signs. Plus, I had a map at the handy, just to be sure. Once the signs were done, I'd make a trip and unbolt the old ones, drill, and bolt the new ones in their place and calmly go about my business.

I know what you're thinking at this point in the story. "Hoo boy! Excitement abounds in the life of a sign boy!" You're not wrong.

Occasionally signs would get stolen, most likely to adorn the mantle of someone's college dorm room. This was somewhat frustrating, as we often had a limited stock of boards, and there were a lot of very old signs in disrepair. This was the case when I had finally made the rounds to the far west neighborhoods near Red Butte and the golf course. I replaced all of the signs for Snowbunny Lane multiple times. This seemed to be a favorite for thieves. As it turned out I had only six planks left. There were four Snowbunnies missing.

Then I came to Cemetery Lane. It seemed that these particular signs were ancient, and in bad shape. And on second glance, misspelled. Someone, many years prior had routed the signs to say, "Cemetary Lane." An easy mistake, but a good one, as it turns out.

Back at the shop, I went to my boss with the dilemma.

"Problem. We have four missing signs for Snowbunny, and four misspelled signs for Cemetery. Only thing is, we only have 6 planks. How long will it take to get shipment on the next batch?" I asked him.

"I don't see the problem," came his reply. "Just replace the ones you have wood for. But make sure Snowbunny gets all new ones. They keep getting stolen."

I replied, "Don't you think people will notice two different spellings of Cemetery Lane?"

"Hmmm. Well, if they haven't noticed it in all these years, who's gonna see it now?" was his reasoning.

Well, who was I to question it? Executive decision made. " ... Yours is not to question why ..." I went about my way, routed the new signs, and installed them. As one might guess, within a week of the new mismatched signs being in place, the newspapers wrote it up with the blame placed solely on me. Working in a job of mostly blue-collar people, a college kid makes a good target for ridicule in any way possible. I walked around for days dodging jabs suggesting my stupidity and ignorance. I heard it from the cops, the parks people, the city electric, sewer, gas, water folks, and even the bigwigs down at City Hall.

I was also the lucky recipient of several dictionaries via the US postal service. As it turned out, the incident was to be yet another of *many* reasons to finish college. Despite a misplaced public shellacking, ironically, spelling was not one of those reasons.

WORKER BEE
"MORONS"

WHILE EMPLOYED BY THE CITY, through the few years I worked there, the changes in Aspen were becoming very apparent. Some in subtle ways, others not.

My first day on the job was a wakeup call to this phenomenon. Our boss, Elbert "Eb" Tacker, who had replaced the inimitable Harold "Puppy" Smith Sr., as the street superintendent, sent me, the new kid, out with Harold Smith Jr. to drill holes and put-up parking signs on a street corner near the old downtown post office.

Harold Smith Jr, a quiet, mellow man, and a man of few words showed me what to prepare, which tools to grab and told me we needed gloves. As it was my first day, and very early in the morning, I was cold and nervous; A skinny clueless kid, with no idea what lay ahead of me, nor what I would be tasked with doing. Harold moved slowly. Not in a lazy way, but deliberate, calm.

After we hitched up a huge gas-powered compressor, and loaded hoses, jacks, steel signposts, spray paint, shovels, a pick and a gigantic 75 lb pneumatic drill, we gassed up the truck and headed on our way. Our conversation was minimal. Again, Harold, a man of few words, sort of mumbled when he spoke. We arrived at the spot and began unpacking the heavy objects, crashing on the pavement. It was still early, so it made me nervous to make so much noise right outside of someone's home. This would not be the last time this would happen, and it never got easier.

Our task was simple. Plot out, mark and drill holes for three new "no parking" signs to go on the sidewalk. And then put the signs up. The trouble was the owner of the house on that particular corner had torn up and replaced the concrete with bricks similar to what the mall was constructed with. And he likely took down the old signs that were mysteriously no longer there.

When we fired up the drill, a seriously loud operation, and began drilling through the brick, a noticeably irritable man emerged from the house and stood in front of Harold, waving his hands, and screaming something.

We turned off the drill. When it was quieter with only the generator exclaimed, "Do you morons have any idea how much those bricks cost?"

To which Harold calmly replied, "I'd say about 50¢ like they did in the mall."

Infuriated now, the man yelled, "Those bricks were imported from MEXICO! They're worth a lot more than that. I'm calling the city!" He ran back into his house. In the days before modern trade and ease of access via the internet, apparently "Hecho en Mexico" meant something "exotic".

Nervously I asked what we should do—first day and all. Harold shrugged, grabbed a pry bar and pulled a couple bricks out instead of drilling through them. "Grab one of them stobs, the heavy thing you put on top of it, and a sledge." A stob is a short post. Once it was pounded into the ground you could attach a longer post and extend the height of the sign. I had to figure this out from Harold's limited instructions.

With the sledgehammer, Harold then began pounding the stob into the ground where the bricks were removed. Faster than lightning, the man returned from inside the house and screamed, "Stop! You're ruining my sidewalk!"

"It ain't your sidewalk, the city owns it," Harold returned to positioning the stob.

"You will stop, or I'll call the Police!" came the reply.

Harold ignored him and kept pounding. This made the man furious. His face red with rage, he grabbed the sledgehammer and tried to take it from Harold. Now again, Harold moved slowly, but with deliberation. Within seconds, I stared in disbelief as the two men struggled with the sledgehammer, now above both of their heads. They wrestled with it for a few seconds until the man let go and ran back into his house to dial 911.

My mind went straight to the worst, "What the hell did I get myself into with this job?"

Harold radioed the shop and said, "Got a problem, we're a comin' back."

We hurriedly packed everything back into the truck. We grabbed the stob and replaced the now broken bricks in their spaces and climbed back into the truck. After a few minutes, I broke the silence. "That was weird. Does that happen a lot?"

Harold's reply was something to the effect of, "It ain't never happened to me before. Must be a helluva first day."

A few days later after the dust had settled a bit, and the city's easement and legal discussions with the man ensued, we went back and casually put up the three signs as originally planned. This time not drilling through the exquisitely designed, and extravagantly expensive bricks from Mexico, the very same ones that definitely did not look exactly like the cheap imitations used on the mall. (Sarcasm)

I drove by a few weeks later only to notice that the man had removed the signs and erected them behind his fence, barely visible from the street. The city's response was to turn a blind eye.

I bring up this story not just because it makes me chuckle, but also because the event marked a sea change in my perception of the people, we now shared our community with, and how easily the city acquiesced to the desires of one person over the values of the common good. From that point forward I began to pay attention to the entitlement many newcomers seemed to exhibit. This was not just a disparity of the haves and the have nots. We were used to that, and as a kid it never really phased me. Some of my friends lived in mansions, others lived in trailers. We fit somewhere in between. This was different. This was a new group of people that were not only determined to have the biggest home with the best view and the desire to let everyone else know they couldn't have the same thing. In fact, as I analyze my own behavior in business, it's very apparent to me that one of my weaknesses has been that since that time, I will give the shirt off of my back, and go above and beyond to help someone, but if they treat me as though I'm somehow "beneath" them, or that I somehow owe them because of their supposed superiority, we're probably not gonna get along.

Similar instances cropped up from time-to-time after then. Like the time I was tasked to spread gravel to the sides of the brand-new asphalt to keep it from breaking off and eroding. Driving the dump truck and laying down the gravel took many trips, and we were able to do it with little resistance, except for one house on the west end. By the time I came around for a second look, a man had washed ALL of the gravel down the storm drain with his garden hose. So, we replaced the gravel. The next day he had done the same thing. We redid it again. And again, he washed it down the storm drain, which was likely 3/4 full by now. When reported to our boss, the response was to "just leave it alone." The man had called in and "requested" an exception.

While still another instance was installing "Dangerous Curve" signs on a bend in the Aspen Meadows. This time I was called an "inbreeded idiot" because our sign obstructed the man's view from his toilet. I suspect that sign no longer exists or has been otherwise obscured today. All manner of safety precautions be damned. At the time, when he complained to the city, again they acquiesced. My only hope for it is that no one has driven off the side, while this man enjoyed the view from his commode.

My perception had changed, but the true nature of the newcomers was already well underway. Today, the town is unrecognizable.

... AND IN THE DARKEST DEPTHS OF MORDOR ...

IN THE LATE EIGHTIES and early nineties, the city decided to build a parking structure large enough to handle the increase in cars, both local and from out of town. Anyone who remembers, knows that Aspen had a parking problem. Like many publicly funded projects, they tried to plan so that every possible contingency would be in order, and everyone would get something out of it. For the most part, they were successful. However, as they began to dig out the hole for a mostly underground structure, they hit a snag in the form of massive amounts of water.

Whether it was the water table, or possibly runoff from an underground mine, I can't recall. But the short and long of it was that they couldn't make the structure as deep as they intended. When they poured the concrete and started building up from the bottom of the pit, there ended up being a massive void on the lowest level.

The powers that be decided the void would be a great place to store equipment, tools, and street signs earmarked to replace faded and damaged ones around town and within city limits. It made sense, as the city was rapidly outgrowing its space at the city streets shop under the Castle Creek bridge.

The void became a huge storage space for the city, on par with that of a small supermarket, but was only just tall enough near its double door entrance to stand up. Most of the remaining area required you to hunch over or crawl as you got further back.

Hardly any vehicles ventured down to the lower level. Such were the greater parts of my responsibilities as the seasonal sign jockey and pothole filler. Among the other chores I was tasked with, maintaining the metal signs was a daily thing. And after we drilled holes in the cinder block walls to hang the myriad of surplus instructional metal signs, I made daily treks to and from the bottom level of the deck throughout the days of the summer.

"The Nord" was a beat up, rusty old Dodge truck that veered to the right whenever you hit the brakes. It was on loan from the Nordic Cross Country Center which had little use for it during the summer. As The Nord was mostly reserved for my use, I couldn't have been happier. I routinely drove The Nord all over town, replacing and repairing city signs wherever they proved unsightly. And when I spotted unreadable signs, I'd take a note and go back to the city garage to find replacements.

The Nord made a satisfyingly deep rumble when following the spiral drive down to the lowest level. Very few cars parked below. All would be quiet except for the clang of an echo when the door of The Nord slammed. The screech of the hinges in desperate need of some WD-40, would creak and end with a thump that likely shook the windows in the public library a few levels up.

I would unlock the storage area's padlocked doors. Like the gates of Mordor, they would open up to reveal a dank, musty space complete with spiderwebs and all manner of as-yet-unidentified mold and mildew cultures.

With the light of a single bulb, I would pore over inventory, and if there was a replacement, I'd pull it down, load up with the proper nuts and bolts, lock the door and head back up to the surface and on to wherever the unsightly sign hung in town.

I'd be lying if I said I didn't explore the underground expanse myself, just to see how far back it went. There were all manner of city objects stored throughout. Folded up event tents, barricades, posts, and ropes with flags written in multiple languages for

Winternational—bienvenuto, wilkommen, bienvenue, etc. Poles for slalom, old desks, and a few filing cabinets. And the spare Zamboni for smoothing the city Ice Garden skating rink.

Ordinarily I made only one trek to the bowels of city storage in the Nord. But once, I made the mistake of forgetting something and headed back.

When I got to the lower level, a strange situation presented itself. An Aspen Police Saab was parked where the Nord usually staked its claim. Stranger still, the steel city storage doors were open and the light was on. A two-way walkie-talkie hung from one of the cop car door handles, emitting a host of chatter and random beeps that echoed off the cement walls.

The two steel doors were open, the light on, and oddly, no one around.

I thought nothing of it, walked in, grabbed my sign and tools, and loaded up the "Nord." I yelled a few times "Helloooo! Anyone in here? I'm locking up." Total silence.

No one answered so I loaded up The Nord. Before leaving I went back and flicked the room lights. I called out a couple more times. Still nothing. So, I padlocked the doors but left the walkie-talkie where the police had left it and went about my merry way.

About 40 minutes later, I decided to wrap up for the day and headed back down the garage. Only this time, I spotted a disheveled couple of Aspen Police officers (a man and a woman) driving out of the garage in a hurry. They wore distraught, angry expressions.

"Hmmmmm," I thought, continuing down to the lower level.

Once again on the lower level, the patrol car was now gone, only in its place were two steel doors lying flattened underneath the spare Zamboni.

The light was on.

Now I've not been called the world's most romantic guy. But there has never been a time where I looked at a dank, underground crawl space and thought, "What a great place to take a date!" Be that as it may, I guess when the opportunity arises, hell, who knows?

Illustration by Chris Pomeroy.

When I returned to the shop I promptly let my boss know that the doors were down, the Zamboni parked as some sort of getaway vehicle and that the contents of the underground dungeon were open to the world.

Amidst chuckles of disbelief and all manner of prurient jokes, the Street Superintendent had only one thing to say. "Well, I guess we know what you'll be fixing tomorrow."

I PULLED
"SHIT DETAIL"
THEY TOLD ME.

IT WAS EARLY SUMMER or late spring that year. I had started my summer job a month earlier than usual, and there was little to do at this time for the "college kid" who took a year off to fulfill my algebra requirement.

I had been at school for two years now, one year at Mesa College, and another at Colorado State University, where many of my friends from high school had ended up. Todd, my pal and roommate had gone to Australia for a study abroad program, so I booked a stay in the dorms that year, as it was too late to find another roommate before school started.

As it turned out, Colorado State University (CSU) had an experimental math curriculum where there were no *actual teachers* (don't ask). Instead, you had to pass a series of tests at a math center to fulfill their requirement. Each module counted as one credit, and you needed four. As I'd graduated largely ignorant of math at Aspen High, I could only pass one. Thus, with three credits to go before CSU would let me re-enroll, I was "invited" to look elsewhere to continue my education until my math requirement was completed.

So, I enrolled at Colorado Mountain College (CMC—or "See Me Ski") for a year—and lo and behold they had math teachers—people who *actually taught* the discipline of algebra! At the end of it, I made an A and was able to get back into CSU where my friends were. Ironically, the use of math and logic are prominent in my career. I'm thankful to that small college for providing the mathematical foundation I missed in the Aspen Schools.

The City of Aspen Streets Department hired me back for the summer, although the season had not yet picked up. It was still a month early and a month colder, which meant a month of quiet at work with not much to do.

Early one Monday morning I was at the city facility under Castle Creek Bridge when my boss caught me up. "Sorry kid," Jack said with a grin, "you drew the lucky straw and got today's 'shit detail.'"

"Uh—what exactly does that entail?" (My vocabulary did not make me popular amongst my coworkers at the time.)

"You'll see when you get there," he said, stifling a snicker. "Take the blue truck and drive to the gate at the foot of Independence pass. You'll need to wait for the State guys to come unlock it."

"Okay. Anything I need to take with me? Tools, etcetera?" I inquired.

"Just your lunch. Oh, and before you get on the road you need to pick up a guy named Bob Lewis. He's waiting for you at City Hall. Bob's an old guy. Very … unique."

I started for the blue truck with a good amount of skepticism and my early morning Pepsi in hand, only to hear Jack say, almost out of earshot, "Oh! Just be warned … the state guys hate Bob." I heard the rest of the shop guys laughing uncontrollably as I drove out from the giant garage doors.

Shortly after I'd picked up Bob, I realized I knew him. He lived on our side of town. I'd first been introduced to him as an elementary student during a field trip to Braille Trail, a dirt trail loop he'd engineered. Be that as it may, I was scratching my head why this was all a big joke to the guys at the shop.

Then it hit me. Among the ranks of Aspen's old-timers, particularly those from mining, agriculture and blue-collar families in the area, there can be found a certain disdain for people who are college educated and passionate about the environment. I'd noticed it on many occasions throughout the years. While not a complete ideology against intellectualism, there is a side that comes out at times. Those who didn't go on to further their education after high school tended to find fault in those who did. Like a flipped paradigm, the belief is that an educated person is somehow unintelligent, uninitiated, or uninformed when contrasted with someone whose career consists mostly of working with their hands.

As we drove to the pass, our conversation was jovial. It was immediately apparent that Bob was indeed unique, and very focused. Our conversation was mostly about environmental projects he'd worked on and Bob's past as an Aspenite. That and the biology films he and my science teacher, Mr. Beer had produced in the sixties. It was also clear he had a personal, solid connection to the area.

Eventually I turned the topic to the day's tasks at hand. "What exactly are we doing up on the pass?"

His reply was on par with a university lecture on the environment and conservation, and then, "we're working on a long-term project to prevent further erosion. We'll be meeting Tyler once we get there. He'll show you what to do."

We reached the locked gate. It spanned both lanes; on either end were ten-foot berms meant to prevent skirting the gate. Both were massive heaps of dirt, junk, and concrete fill. One blocked entry from the base of the mountain, the other from the road's cliff edge.

Bob and I got out and waited around, kicking pinecones, and watching birds and squirrels do their thing. Twenty minutes later the guys from the State Highway Department showed up. After a nod to me, they unlocked the gate, and that was all. It was clear by the lack of congeniality there was animosity towards Bob. If he noticed, it didn't seem to faze him in the least.

They left after giving me a stern warning. "We close this gate at 4 p.m. Best be back on this side of it before then."

Bob and I made our way up to where the landscape of the pass changes, where walls of snow give way to crags and rocky outcrops. There was a clear path where plows had parted the glacial flows and started the process of melting the drifts away, now approximately 40 feet back from the highway on most sides. It was mostly dry pavement with trickles and streams from the year's runoff coming from under the ice.

Suddenly Bob raised his voice, "STOP the truck!!!!"

The sudden shock had me laying on the brake, leaving black skid marks on the pavement, going uphill. Adrenaline pumped as Bob flew out of the vehicle leaving his door wide open. He commenced to cross in front, jump onto a craggy spire, and climb 25 feet up from the truck. He began pulling and tugging at the very rock face he was hanging onto.

"What in God's name?" escaped my lips as I stared, and gently let the truck reverse, rolling away by another 20 feet.

Suddenly, the spire cracked and began to fall, with Bob halfway attached. It came crashing down, leaving a huge hole in the asphalt and a giant mess of crumbled rocks and dirt. I saw Bob hanging by one hand. He swung himself over and climbed down; an impressive feat for anyone, much less a man in his seventies. As he made his way over to the boulder and debris, it was immediately evident that that rock was going to stay right where it was, in the middle of the road, with a gigantic hole crushed beneath it. And suddenly I realized why the state guys weren't too fond of Bob.

Another reason became evident when we reached our job site—a huge field on the side of a hill being secured so it wouldn't erode. It was a project that not only served an environmentally sound purpose but kept the state guys from going about their normal jobs. Thanks to Bob, they were not allowed to just "dig up" anything they wanted to anymore. They now had to first obtain approval from Bob, the "environ-*mental*" guy.

Bob waved at a guy stowing things in the back of a truck, introduced me to Tyler, and gave me clear instructions, "Do whatever Tyler asks you to help with." Almost immediately, Bob inquired, "Could I get a lift back into town?" to the guy with the truck, to which the man replied, "Uh ... sure?"

And just like that, Bob was off to his next task.

I looked at Tyler and asked, "How can I help?"

"Well, uh, there's not really anything to do. I guess we can move some dirt." He handed me a shovel.

We checked some netting that held the grass seed down, tied a few things and then mostly just chit-chatted. After a few more hours I inquired if Bob would be back. With a shrug, Tyler's answer was quick. "Who knows?!?"

As the day waned, I realized how late it was getting. Tyler and I hurried to pack everything up and I followed him and his Jeep in the city's blue work truck. When we arrived at the gate it was well-past 4 o'clock and as promised, it was now locked.

Had this been a Hollywood movie there would've been a suspenseful "GONG" as the weight of our predicament sank in. No doubt the state guys had ditched us to get back at Bob. I looked at Tyler. He shrugged, jumped back in his Jeep, and drove his rig right over the berm like he'd done it a million times.

It was my turn, only I was in a truck with a long bed. I put it in 4-wheel drive and proceeded to drive up the berm. As I approached the top, a sudden change in my sense of gravity happened as the truck high-centered. My wheels spun, the truck gently rocking at the apex of the berm—all 4 wheels turning in mid-air.

For some dumb reason I put it in Park before opening the door. Tyler was laughing and shaking his head. "Hang on—I've got a winch."

As we hooked his cable to the city truck, a sudden realization made a cold sweat break on the back of my neck. It was now 4:30 p.m, otherwise known as, "Quittin' Time." A bunch of the guys back at the shop would be waiting to pile into the truck for a ride home downvalley. The city's truck, however, was currently performing a balancing act on top of a state barricade at the foot of Independence Pass. Even if it weren't stuck, which it was, it'd still take 30 minutes or more on a *good* day to get there.

As Tyler worked on taking up the slack on the winch, I sat in the truck, fruitlessly trying to reach the shop via the CB radio, which was proving to be just out of range.

"Ready?" bellowed Tyler.

I gave him a thumbs-up and shouted, "Go for it!"

His Jeep tires smoked, the engine revved, emitting a high pitch, and gravel shot in every direction.

The city truck rocked lazily back and forth on the berm like a coin slot pony, almost mocking us.

We must have tried four or five times before the truck started to pitch downward. I looked out the windshield to see the Jeep pulling with the 2 rear wheels, again gravel flying everywhere. It was just then it registered that the Jeep's front wheels were not even touching the ground. The truck was pulling the Jeep as much as the Jeep was pulling the truck.

Tyler let the winch out, and suddenly the truck nose flung back up as the winch fell off. And just as fast as I had gotten it stuck, it began rolling backwards off the berm.

Heaven surely tired of the profanities and blasphemy spewed forth that day. When the dust settled, Tyler was standing at the other side of the gate. "Uh ... I need to get going." My forlorn expression must have concerned him because he quickly followed with, "But I'll tell you what ... I'll see if I can stop by the state shack and let them know you're up here. Or ... or I guess I can call someone when I get back to town. Hang in there." He drove away as the sun had just barely begun to hide itself behind the peaks. The air took on a slight chill.

Downtime in a stressful situation has a way of spinning dark thoughts of dread. *The guys are pissed. What happens if no one comes to let me out? I'm gonna get fired.*

Finally, after what seemed like decades, but was probably only 20 minutes or so, a lone yellow state truck pulled up with his single yellow beacon flashing at the top.

A man jumped out and commenced to unlock the gate and swing it wide open for me. The whole time, he didn't say a single word.

I drove through and looked back to give him a nod of thanks as he closed the gate behind me. He was shaking his head and laughing.

My coworkers had already taken a different truck home.

The next morning, the guys, chortling one and all, unsurprisingly asked, "How was 'shit detail?'"

PROTECT US FROM THE DREADED HANTAVIRUS

WHILE WORKING MY SUMMER JOB, making street signs for the city of Aspen, I was sitting in the asbestos-lined shack to the side of the building. I was busy stenciling signs prior to routing the lettering for a few replacements. I heard skittering. Ignoring it as a potential hangover hallucination, I went on about the business of making wooden street signs. Then I heard it again. A critter was definitely sharing the space.

Meanwhile ... everywhere on the news, was the threat of the pestilence of the year—Hantavirus!!!!!!!!

In the ensuing paranoia, everyone in Colorado and surrounding states was using all available methods to systematically eradicate the spreaders of the disease ... rats. In reality, it wasn't the rat that was the threat but the poop. People were dying from sweeping it up; throwing it away, burning it, etc. and the entire West was scared shitless (... literally).

As I was the one to notify my boss of said potential critters, it was an agreed upon detail that I would find a way to rid the place of unwanted vermin. So, my boss, Jack, sent me to the local True Value, to purchase some rat poison. What to choose. What to choose. Well, as it turned out, there's really only one name-brand of note in a small-town hardware store. For the purposes of ambiguity, I'll call it "D-Kill." The choice turned out to be easier than the task at hand.

Now D-Kill, for those not "in the know," is a small box, approximately three by four inches, and one inch deep, full of poison-laced food pellets that are simply irresistible to the furry little critters. In other words, it's evil stuff. The worst thing about D-Kill is the delayed demise of the victim. In other words, little mousey-mouse eats a bit of it and then crawls off to a corner to die—only to stink horribly a day or two later. The hardest part is finding, and subsequently disposing of the creature. But alas, someone must do it. And it was usually me.

See, my job at the time was something between a paid internship in government bureaucracy, and an unnoticed, anonymous lackey tapped for the worst tasks no one else wanted to do. So, when I arrived back at the shop, it was nearing lunch time. Nonetheless I wanted to take care of the rat problem sooner, rather than later, so I cracked the box open, set it in a corner ... and went to lunch.

While at lunch, the topic of conversation was of the rat problem and its many social implications: humor, anxiety, fear, and outright animosity. Picture 10 old-timers and a college kid grinding mouthfuls of bologna sandwiches like "mules chewing garlic," musing over the current scourge that had the country in a constant state of fear and denial. So, it wasn't a surprise my curiosity was piqued at the success rate of my one-man battle against the dreaded disease, and its chosen carrier.

After lunch I immediately went to check the trap only to find... to my horror and amazement ... the box was completely empty ... and moved about a foot and a half from where I had placed it. What followed was a huge, confused moment, coupled with slight paranoia about the potential deadly virus. I frantically searched for a facemask and realized they were all sitting "face up." Meaning, they all had the potential deadly virus strain *in* the mask, thereby negating any preventative benefit. Nonetheless, my curiosity took over and I closely inspected the room.

Indeed, the box was empty, and it was nowhere near where I originally placed it. My only thought was, *"That's one huge freakin' rat. I gotta get more D-Kill."*

So off to the hardware store I went. I fired up the "Nord" and zipped down to the store only to find that I had previously bought the only single serving of the poison on my last trip. Meaning, I had only the choice of the 12-pak case or an all-out pallet of the stuff.

As it turned out, the 12-pak was about enough.

...back at the shop. I had a combination of two thoughts: 1) I need to take those suckers out and 2) What the hell kind of rat can eat that much poison and still be alive?

So in between my other duties, I planned my next attack. *"Unleash the D-Kill—package number two."* I placed it just about the time we checked out to go home for the day.

The next day, the team sat, drank coffee, and wasted tax-dollars telling jokes about nothing, and discussing the latest episode of Roseanne. Needless to mention, I eagerly ducked out to actually "work" while the team giggled incessantly about how inept the boss was and told jokes that by today's standards would not only get you fired, but bar you from employment just about anywhere.

As I walked back into the side room, I instinctively looked toward the spot where I put the D-Kill. To my shock and awe, the box was once again moved... and empty. Now I was visibly concerned.

Once again ... *"That's one huge freakin' rat!"*

Of course, I set the next trap, thinking *"There's no way even a small dog can live through this"* and proceeded to pour an extra box worth of pellets into the new box. I gently slid it into the corner, while laughing a sadistic, muted, and kinda sad, little maniacal giggle.

Back at work digging holes, filling cracks in the sidewalks and generally finding ways to kill the day until lunch, I couldn't help but wonder what the inevitable outcome of my trap would bring. At last! 11:20—10 minutes before "legal" lunch—(the rest of the guys have been sitting there for at least 20 minutes already), I headed back into the shop via the garage—tossed the tools back into the corner and pulled my gloves off. Immediately I inspected the box.

Yep.

Again, the poison was gone.

I don't give up that easily. I decided to forgo the off-color jokes and "Joe college kid" chidings and take my lunch in the sign room. By God, I planned to see just what the hell kind of beast was capable of downing 4–5 boxes of D-Kill and still come back for more—*"Must be some kind of hound from hell, skunk, raccoon or wild boar, no doubt."*

The plan was simple really: place a new box and wait. No matter how long it took.

And it didn't take long. Regrettably.

You see, here's the thing: when it comes to odd and funny happenings in this world, sometimes life has a way of trumping all. Sometimes you just can't make this stuff up.

All was quiet; I was silently chewing a peanut butter sandwich. As I turned to grab and drink my Pepsi, I heard a small scurrying in a distant corner. I looked over and spied a small hole in the steel siding wall. In snuck a tiny, yet formidable chipmunk. With a couple of sideways glances and "deer in the headlights" flashes, he skittered over and, with both hands, packed his cheeks full of D-Kill. He then peered both ways again and darted like lightning back to the hole from whence he'd come.

As I hurriedly grabbed my lunch and headed toward the lunchroom, I was spitting Pepsi out of my nose in laughter–with a slight turn in my gut at the reality of my deed. With a mix of dread and absolute hilarity I shared the news with the "boys":

"Check this out! That freakin' huge rat ..." The room was silent for one of the only times in bureaucratic history. "... all this time it was a cute little chipmunk."

The room erupted in boisterous laughter.

Then suddenly, from the other room, in walked the elderly secretary with a forlorn and truly sullen face, "You killed CHIPPY?!?"

The room again fell silent. And then muffled laughter.

It turned out she'd been feeding the little bugger for years.

Guilt and sorrow hit me, yet situational irony was still fresh in my mind.

Chippy? Well, yes. Yes, I suppose I did.

THE BARKING PIG
SUMMIT

Aug 5, 1990

Not all jobs leave you satisfied at the end of the day. The city job was no different in this regard. But the money was good, and there was limited oversight. I had a decent amount of autonomy. Yet, whatever the day's menial tasks, or often strange requests were, you could almost always find me sweeping the shop floor as the last task of the day.

As previously mentioned, I was issued a crappy truck nicknamed "The Nord." It came equipped with a 2-way radio as one of my tools of the trade. The brakes were shot, the gears were stripped, and the clutch required serious effort to engage. In short, it was a complete POS. I loved driving it.

For the short-range radio, the street department had its own frequency, so we used it to get in touch with anyone out on a job. My "handle" was "Seven One Nine," which was certainly more official-sounding than "f*ing college boy," or just plain old "Chris." So it went that when I was driving around town on odd chores, I'd often hear something to the effect of "701 to 719, over." Which, in layman's terms meant "Chris, the shop is calling." To which I would promptly respond "719 to 701, copy." Again, in layman's terms: "Yes?"

Soon thereafter, the dispatcher would switch over to plain English and execute a normal conversation. Usually something like, "The boss wants you to pick up an order at Ace Hardware."

Or, "Come on back to the shop, the guys need the pry bar from the back of the truck." In other words, the airwaves were sacred only to a point, but not to be abused—like when an employee once read his grocery list off to his wife who worked at City Hall. You know. Big City stuff.

Occasionally, however, I was called on for something of actual importance. Like to assist at a water main break, an errand for city hall, or someone needing assistance with a trapped porcupine. Odd jobs.

On the morning of August 5, 1990, a call came over to assist the guys in putting up barricades to block traffic for a motorcade. While not totally out of the ordinary for Aspen, this one was for President George H. W. Bush, and for then Prime Minister of Great Britain, Margaret Thatcher. They were to meet at the Aspen Institute for a summit of sorts. Or, a meeting of the minds, if you will.

Meanwhile, as a testament to the craziness that happened in Aspen in those days, just down the road at the Woody Creek Tavern, Hunter S. Thompson and his cronies were throwing a party in their honor which they aptly named, "the Barking Pig Summit." Complete with T-shirts, a splattering of local media types and sycophants (and many illicit substances), the gang imbibed while the bigwigs at the institute spoke to the elites of the age.

While we had strategically positioned the unassembled barricades around town the previous day, the call on this day was to unceremoniously set them up and begin to close off Main Street for the arrival of the VIPs.

"701 to 719, over."

"719 to 701, copy."

"Meet Tony at 4th and Main. They need you to help keep traffic from busting through."

"Roger. On my way." (Layman's terms: OK)

As I pulled up in The Nord, it was clear that traffic was backed up for most of Main Street and we continued to position barricades so no one could pass. As time dragged on, many of the drivers got out of their cars to ask what was going on. Some were visibly irate. I recall one man screaming at me, "Moron! You need to let me through, or I'll miss my flight!"

Aspen's airport at the time was slightly smaller than a suburban Walmart. I calmly said, "I hate to be the one to tell you this, but no one's flying in or out of Aspen Scareways but the head honcho."

Now, I don't believe the event was heavily publicized, but all the locals knew what was going on. This poor sap had no idea. He growled, "I don't care if the President of the United States himself is flying in, you *inbred*. I need to get to the airport."

To which I replied, "Well maybe you'll get to tell him that yourself. He should be coming along any moment now."

Shocked, his response was, "Well I ... wait, *THE* president?"

"Yep," I said, "head honcho himself."

I'll never understand why entitled people try to throw their weight around and yell at others for trying to do their jobs. Yet in Aspen, it happens more often than one would think.

After "king yo-yo" had calmed his jets, the waiting game continued for what seemed to be an eternity. All the way up Main Street to the curve by the old Hickory House on 8th, every lane was cleared. The main artery into town was blocked off and summarily "cleared" by the Secret Service. All the other roads were also blocked for security purposes. There wasn't so much as a parked car for blocks, much less a moving one.

As the crowd grew more antsy on one side of the barricade, there was dead silence on the other. It was possibly one of the only times Main Street was that quiet in the middle of the day since its unpaved days in the 50s. Literally, NO vehicles were moving. And NO vehicles were supposed to be.

That was until ... we spotted a burgundy rental car meandering down the lanes. At first glance we thought it was a drunk tourist. They were going the wrong way and headed toward us. Tony and I began to wave them down to direct them out of the path of the supposed motorcade that still hadn't arrived.

Until recent events, I'd always admired the job the Secret Service is able to do. Like some sort of Magic Eightball of predictive avoidance and prescient force, they are somehow able to thwart catastrophe 99.9 percent of the time.

As the car drew closer, the driver-side window rolled down. Without coming to a complete stop, one of the Agents flashed his badge and said, "Have a nice day, Tony and Chris." They turned on 4th and continued on toward the music tent and the institute.

Tony's face went white as a ghost. And I'm sure mine was a similar shade. The Secret Service had known who we were, despite the randomness of our being posted at that location. Shortly thereafter, the motorcade made its way down the middle of Main faster than I'd thought it would, then took the same route as the Secret Service agents. And that was it. Hours of waiting to see the most important people in the world, and they whizzed on by without even a hint of fanfare. We waited maybe 10 more minutes or so and then let the traffic go on their way.

———

Back at the truck, "701 to 719, over."

"719 to 701, copy."

"Head on over to Rubey Park bus station and pick up Curtis. He needs to come back to the shop."

"Roger. On my way."

Hans Gramiger, an Aspen transplant from Switzerland was known for his antics. While Hunter and his crew partied in their own form of protest, Gramiger had bigger, more audacious plans to make his voice of disagreement heard. In the 1970s, Gramiger had grandiose plans to build a massive restaurant on the top of Shadow Mountain. The plan included a cable car that could transport 50+ people at a time to the restaurant for a spectacular view of the small town to go along with their meal.

His plans were continually ruined by overrides from the City Council, the State authority, the Ski Company, and possibly God himself. So, Hans would routinely light off sticks of dynamite on top of the mountain to make a statement of how angry he was.

Margaret Thatcher's speech was apparently worthy of one of his signature blasts. I drove over to pick up my coworker and had started back to the shop via Durant Street toward the Ice Garden skating rink when we heard the trademark "BOOM," seemingly right above us, it was as if we were under attack! I was so startled I nearly crashed The Nord pulling to the side of the street to see what the hell was going on. We could see a tiny puff of smoke atop the hill, contrasting against the clear blue sky.

Being that two of the world's foremost leaders were in town—the leaders of the free world as it were—the casual pranks of the local townsfolk were not taken as lightly as they might be normally. Within seconds, a Blackhawk helicopter, armed with missiles on both sides, swooped in and faced off with the culprit at the top of the mountain.

All was quiet except for the chopping of the helicopter's blades. You could have heard a pin drop throughout the valley. Gromiger's protest statement took precedence over all the others. Hunter's party suddenly seemed insignificant. Even with custom-printed T-shirts. The picketers on Hwy 82, who'd greeted the motorcade, seemed trite. Even the naked ladies who'd dropped their fur coats for George Bush were forgotten for these tense few moments.

The face-off, though it probably only lasted for about a minute, seemed like an hour. The copter hovered and swayed, ready to fire as many missiles as it would take, to wipe out the threat and potentially level the rock outcropping.

After a little while, the copter swerved to the right and quickly disappeared from whence it came. As we headed back to the shop and thoughts began to clear, for a split second I thought we were going to get a new ski run on the face of Aspen Mountain. And most assuredly, Hans Gramiger required a swift change of his lederhosen.

SHENANIGANS

THERE ARE SO MANY SHENANIGANS to recall, that it would take a whole chapter to index them all. Still, I feel I should mention a few for context. After all, this is a book about growing up largely unsupervised.

During the years as a younger kid, there were incidents when we were caught lighting matches. I know this is no grand shocker, and by most accounts, plenty of kids got in trouble for that. But this one time was different. A pal and I decided it would be a great idea to light the funny pages on fire in an old, abandoned dog house behind our friend Eric's house. We took careful time and effort to catch the papers aflame and soon realized they were burning out of control. Like good Boy Scouts, we stomped it out and poured water on the embers to make sure the fire was properly extinguished ...

Just kidding. Like a lot of other brilliant kids, we freaked out and ran. By the time we got back to my pal's house, his parents were waiting for us with hands on hips.

With a stern look his dad asked us, "Boys? Were you lighting matches?"

Our reply was almost in unison, "Who us?!? No! Why would you think that?"

Little did we know that our eyebrows and bangs were singed until almost completely gone, our faces covered in ash, and we smelled of smoke.

"But what happened to the doghouse?" you may be asking.

Turns out, our friend's mother watched the whole ordeal from her kitchen window. She immediately hosed the fire down once we skedaddled, thus narrowly averting a would-be catastrophe. She then called my friend's parents. It turns out, Eric's dad had the entire backyard littered with coffee cans half-full of gasoline. He was a mechanic for Skico and was cleaning engine parts.

Now, despite the premise and concept of the book, I should say that we were in fact, at times, supervised. But not by today's standards of helicopter parents, or overbearing law enforcement. These were the 1970s and 80s. Instead, our community pulled together. After all, it "takes a village" to raise an idiot. That and I think my dad may be psychic.

The other time I got caught lighting matches was with a different friend, far off in the woods. It ended up being the last time. Aspen was a small, yet tight-knit community. Everyone knew everyone. If someone saw something going on, there was a good chance everyone else would know soon enough. My dad was well connected and had many friends in town, which meant he always knew what we kids were up to, and often "appeared" as though seemingly out of nowhere.

Dad had a penchant for catching me and my friends when we were up to no good. Like when Danny and I tried lighting cap gun caps with giant wooden matches we'd nabbed from Mom's kitchen. We were hiding behind a giant boulder we'd found, hoping to be well out of sight from nosey neighbors. The first match blew out. And there was my dad, standing quietly, tapping his fingers, watching intently. Nothing puts the fear of God into you faster than having your dad "materialize" at just the right (or wrong) time.

Before he moved to Arizona in the early 1980s, he caught up to me on more than one occasion in town.

On days when nothing was going on, Marcus and I, and later Dean, were always in need of quarters to spend on candy, records, or to pop into a video game. Before any of us had jobs, we would sell baseball cards, records, or really anything we thought we could trade for a dollar. We'd check under chairlifts, or vending machines for change. We checked all the coin returns in paper racks, video games, washing machines and pay phones. We even tried putting gum on the end of yardsticks to grab change from the sidewalk grates. On several occasions, I recall seeing a local kingpin drug dealer, Steven Grabow, pumping hundreds of quarters into pay phones to make his calls in attempts to remain untraceable. I'd wait for him to leave and then pick up all the quarters he'd dropped.

One fateful day, Marcus had an idea to sit on the backs of my legs while I reached out to pluck silver dollars out of the fountain at the mall. As the budding masterminds and petty thieves, we were that day, getting caught was not something we even considered. My mom would have lost her mind and committed me to a lifelong servitude at the Catholic Church had it been her that caught us. Morals be damned, we went for it. And there again, as if in a puff of smoke, no sooner had my fingers hit the water than a foot gently pushed my face into the water, then fully dunked me. When I scrambled up and shook off, my dad was standing there with his hands on his hips. He quickly grabbed me by the arm and shuffled me away for a stern talking to. Thus ended Marcus and my great crime spree, further cementing the concept that wishing wells are indeed sacred.

But, of the many shenanigans, few raised the question, "How did we survive?" more often than those Dean Jackson and I pulled over the span of approximately five years. Before I paint Dean as some sort of "bad influence," I'll try to set the record straight by pointing out that the Pomeroy kids were more than capable of finding trouble on our own. Careening through the woods and across our road in front of moving cars on ski-dos (a bike with skis instead of wheels) and sleds come to mind as an easy example.

Dean and I and others, be it from thrill-seeking or just trying to cure boredom, were always exploring—and often, probably trespassing too. There were jumps across the rooftops of the city's taller buildings. Before the advent of snowboards, there were the skis we nailed together and tried to steer down Ajax with rope and no way to stop. There were the scavenging excursions at the mine dumps and the real dump for that matter. There were fireworks, exploring mine shafts, fording creeks, and pole vaulting down steep mountainsides. There was climbing, jumping, and crashing bikes. Catching Black Widows in crawl spaces with my buddy Steven, driving 100+ mph in fast cars on McClain Flats or Maroon Creek Road with Brian and Rhett, and there was of course, reckless skiing.

There were so many shenanigans growing up in Aspen, it boggles the mind how we survived some of them. Or that we managed to stay out of jail for others.

But of the more dangerous stunts, by far the riskiest usually involved sharp objects.

In the late 1980s, a certain toy caused the death of three children and was summarily banned in the United States. Lawn darts are deemed too dangerous for people to own, and not safe for kids to play with anymore, anywhere in the nation. Dean Jackson and I, and a kid named Del, put that to the test—on more than one occasion. (See Fig A.)

Fig. A: Fun™

Today, you *can* buy Lawn Darts, but sadly, they are bereft of much entertainment value. Contrasted with the original, which had a 2-inch spike on the end and were crafted from pot metal, the new ones are plastic and have a bulbous end. Instead of sticking into the ground, they just kinda go "whomp." The originals were about 12 inches long, including said spike, and were of considerable weight. Like many other kids across the land in the 1980s, we already had the real Lawn Darts and quickly tired of the rules. We decided to go for distance.

One of us asked, "How far do you think they'll fly?"

And somebody said, "Only one way to find out ..."

Shortly after testing them out, the three of us fashioned a crude version of the game Mumblety Peg, whereby participants throw their pocketknives at each other's feet and not move out of the way. Yep. We did it with Lawn Darts. When we tired of riding bikes, or meandering around, we'd resort to hurling the weapons of death towards each other until it too, became mundane.

My memory is slightly hazy these days, but there was one time when Dean and I were throwing the Lawn Darts in one of the grassy areas by the Silver King condos. One of us was on top of the hill, the other a few feet from the side of the building, near the downspout. The dart whizzed past and buried its 2-inch point all the way in the wood of the wall. In recollection, it was likely we'd dodged more than a kid's toy. We'd also dodged becoming the fourth American kid to succumb to the unregulated adolescent pastime of the era. We didn't end up on the nightly news, but I can honestly say that it took Dean and I considerable effort to remove that dart from the wall. And we promised one another we'd never try that again.

Probably.

THE ASPEN CENTER
FOR PHYSICS

ON THE GROUNDS of the Aspen Center for Physics, and throughout the Aspen Institute (Aspen Meadows) is a series of shallow creeks no more than six to eight inches wide. Many a weary meanderer has sprained or even broken an ankle "discovering" them the hard way. But we kids knew all about them. Each year the Center for Physics hosted their annual family picnics to which spouses, children, and even friends were welcome to join in.

My mom helped Sally Mencimer in the office of the Aspen Center in the early years and as a result came to know many of the physicists. We became involved over the years, not only with the picnics and other events, but with many of the physicists and their families as well. Part of the fun for us kids at the picnics, were the balsa boat races. Each year, we would design what we thought would be the fastest balsa boat, and with an initial kickoff, kids would start the boats and chase them through the winding creeks to just before they could disappear down a storm drain never to be seen again. I'd like to say that my boats placed well, but no. After all, these kids were the children of geniuses, and in turn, many of them were also brilliant. My boats held their own, but I hadn't taken into account many of the things the other kids had. Like weight, buoyancy, current, aerodynamics, gravity, fluid dynamics, and atmospheric changes. Nope. Mine was just painted to look neat, so I lost most of the time. And I lost more than one boat down the storm drain by not being quick enough to pluck it out before it would disappear forever. What I gained, however, were great friendships with a lot of kids from all over the country, and a few from distant places elsewhere in the world.

The institution, started in the early sixties, was founded by Michael Cohen, Robert Craig, and George Stranahan. Over the years, many of the world's most influential physicists, lecturers, and professors came to Aspen (and still do) for the program. We were fortunate to become friends with many of the families. My summer friends included the children of the Cohen family, the Durands, the Fishbanes, and the Gell-Mans among others.

The Pomeroys became close with one such family. The Durands visited each year, and like many of the returning physicists, they purchased a summer home in the west end, not far from where our first home was. Later, Bernice and Loyal "Randy" Durand were married at my parents' house in the 1970s.

When they would come to our house, Mr. Durand, being a man of tall stature, would hold us upside down so we could "walk" on the ceiling as toddlers, at the house on Fourth and North and again later when we moved to Eastwood. This left an indelible impression on my mind. I can still visualize the shadows of my feet cast from a lamp, as I walked "on the moon," courtesy of Mr. Durand's support.

The house in Eastwood was built for entertaining. While our parents were together, there were countless parties at the home, with all manner of locals and crazies in attendance. I would wager to guess that if the Durands were in town at the time of any of those parties, they were there too.

After my folks split up, mom still enjoyed entertaining, albeit for a much more subdued crowd, and in smaller, more quaint get-togethers. The Durands frequently joined us, both at our parents' parties, and casually for dinners or just to hang out. By the mid-1970s/ early 80s, Tim, Travis, and Chris, Mr. Durand's children from a previous marriage had, for the most part, grown up. When they came, they mostly hung out with the adults, but were good role models for my siblings and I. Us kids mostly stayed out of sight, downstairs in the TV room. But Bernice Durand always made a point to ask all three of us what we were studying. She would reinforce that computers were particularly important and that I should keep learning about them. On previous visits, I had shown her some programming projects I had completed. Her kindness and support were always a welcome conversation. It was many years later that I realized Physicists *are* the main reason computers are so prevalent now. The innovations they came up with and the discoveries they made, were the building blocks for modern day chips and processors. Without physicists, computers would still be nothing but wires and tubes. And, well, without physicists, those likely wouldn't have come into being either.

A few years later, when Mom needed extra income to cover bills, she rented the basement of the house out at various times. One summer she rented a room to Travis's fiance, Kathy, who later became his wife.

Many times, groups of physicists in a caravan of Jeeps, Scouts, Broncos, and Land Cruisers would stop off at our house in Eastwood to plan, and later seek out the best mushroom hunting grounds towards Independence Pass. Countless adventures would find us tromping through the woods like hordes of marauders, lifting logs, rolling over boulders, and wreaking general havoc upon the flora and fauna in search of a trove of chanterelles, morels or even oyster mushrooms.

Many of the best hunting grounds were remote. My dad, being an avid outdoorsman, had collections of 10th Mtn Division topo maps and previous knowledge on how to get to some of the coolest places. So, his old Willy's Jeep could often be seen halfway over a cliff, with only three wheels touching the ground, navigating around an old pass—or mostly unsurpassable dirt road. I say we would see him doing it, because Mom, being somewhat afraid of heights, and more-so afraid of an early demise, would summarily remove us kids and make us all walk. Once Dad made it across whatever bottomless chasm he was attempting, the rest would follow, and we'd calmly get back into the Jeep.

When all was done, nary a shroom was left in its place. We would all reconvene at the house in Eastwood to dry them out on screens and in the oven. And of course, a few would hit the pan and be consumed then and there; a worthy trophy fo a successful hunt.

Looking back, it's clear to me that we were fortunate to live in a place and time that was a melting pot of intellectual thought and artistic innovation. We had access to some of the world's most innovative and influential minds of the latter half of the 20th century. And yet, they were just people around our town; people who hung around with our parents and frequented our favorite places. Why would the topic of Einstein's Unified Field theory, the Heisenberg Uncertainty Principle, or the concept of a quark come up at a pizza lunch with the Gell-Mans, the Cohens, the Fishbanes and the Durands, for example? It didn't. Why would it? Instead, discussions were of family life, popular culture, and entertainment. Heady discussions of particle physics, and quantum worlds were rare. Instead, we talked about who wanted what toppings on their pizza. We were all just family friends having lunch.

These days, while helping my youngest son make and prepare his cars for the Pinebox Derbies for Boy Scouts, I thought back to the boat races. Our modern efforts were much more precise. However, our decorations were still prominent, but we also accounted for aerodynamics and weight. Precise measurements and paint, a team-up of science and art, we took all into account to ensure a strong finish. Alas, as was the case with the boats, we still came in pretty much last. But they looked cool.

My memories of the times we spent with the physicists have instilled in me a lifelong curiosity and thirst for knowledge. And a penchant for tinkering, which drives my wife insane. Our garage is half-filled with projects in mid-completion, burned or broken crucibles, wires, pulleys, switches, transistors, capacitors, lenses, motors, transformers, diodes, fans, powdered ferrite, copper wire, crushed silicon, boats that don't float, vehicles that don't drive, flying machines that don't fly and hundreds, if not thousands of magnets.

THE PAEPKE DREAM

BEFORE I WAS FOUR, my parents lived in a meager home on 4th and North Street. Although we moved to the east side of town while we were still little, our ties to the west side were still strong. In fact, they remained that way all the way up until we moved Down Valley in the late 1980s. Names like Kienast, Blakesley, Markalunas, Larson, Henry, Caparella and Moyes were common amongst our playmates on that side of town. My memories of that time are sparse, mostly due to my age. However, we never really stopped spending time on the west end of town, because summertime was when many of our other family friends would come to Aspen for the season. It was also when the Music Association of Aspen (MAA) music school was in session, and the music tent hosted fantastic classical music concerts.

There's something magical, possibly supernatural about listening to live classical music on an overcast or rainy afternoon. The sounds drift intentionally through the air, while fog and clouds take a more ambiguous path. Somewhere in between, the two meet and send electricity through the atmosphere. The goosebumps on the back of your neck and arms wake and fill you with anticipation. The sounds commingle with the silence of the air until a distant thunderclap joins in chorus. At a truly exceptional performance at the Aspen Music Tent, you knew you were in the presence of greatness, when the audience didn't take a breath during a pause or during a changeover within a piece. Even babies stopped what they were doing. And then, once the performance came to an end, thunderous applause filled the atmosphere—you could almost feel the ground moving underfoot.

Many of the world's foremost musicians and accomplished composers frequent the valley. It's been that way since before I was born. It was the original dream of the Paepckes and their vision of Aspen as a center for arts, innovation and thought.

My mom always loved the music of Aaron Copland. I grew up listening to it, and from my earliest memories, the melody from Appalachian Spring comes easily to the forefront of my mind's soundtrack. The leitmotif is borrowed from a Shaker song and gently makes its way through the piece. From my earliest memories, my grandfather heard me playing the melody, one key at a time on his piano and inquired of my mom, "Where did he learn to play that?" I was probably not older than five. The answer was, I didn't. It is a constant melody stored in the depths of my long-term memory.

While she loved most classical music, the more modern composers also appealed to her. In fact, I think she preferred them. But it is certain that my mom introduced me to the brilliant art form, which transcends the ages. Many modern music genres hold their own, but I wonder if, say, disco will hold up as long as do the works of Bach, written in the early 1700s.

The beauty of it was that in Aspen, we had the opportunity to see the performances live, often with the composers in-house. The orchestra, of course, was second to none and was composed of many of the finest musicians in the world. The performances were flawless, worthy of being recorded. Whether we sat inside the tent, or outside on the lawn, classical music was a huge part of my upbringing.

In the 1980s Mom worked with Nancy Oden at the lemonade stand outside the tent. It was one of the many ways she gave back to the community. She often recruited us kids to help along with Lisbeth, Nancy's daughter, and my classmate. In retrospect, I think it may have been a way to have access to the goings on, as events there became increasingly prestigious, and expensive. It was the beginning of when the locals were no longer considered part of the community, in my mind. Now we were there merely to serve.

While in high school, our commencements were at the music tent. Since I was in the band, we would perform the Pomp and Circumstance Marches on the stage while our classmates walked up to receive their diplomas. The ability of sound to reverberate through that amphitheater remains a marvel of the genius of its builders. It's truly an incredible space.

A few years ago, I watched a "documentary" on television where a group of metal detectors went to unearth the time capsule buried at one of the Design Conferences in the 1980s. I couldn't help but laugh as the show tried to build up anticipation and suspense as they tried to find the "uncertain" location. My wife often rolls her eyes when I yell at the TV, but it was funnier this time because I'd been there when they buried it. "Not there, you yo-yos. Over to the right."

I was always excited to see the first music students of the year walking in town or back towards the music tent. Like a dormant chrysalis, the town was reborn each year with new art, fresh faces, and beautiful music.

At one point, the Music Associates of Aspen (MAA) partnered with our local music program and offered summer music lessons for us kids. We would be paired with a music student or faculty with the same instrument and arrive at their residence for lessons. I rode my bike with my trombone in one hand down the hill and into town to go to these lessons. To my shame, though I participated, my enthusiasm lacked, and I considered it to be a hassle in my youth. So, I didn't end up going to more than one or two lessons before drifting off each summer to do other things.

My passion for being a trombone player was lackluster at best. When the band leaders visited us in 5th grade, and had us all try out for different instruments, I had expressed interest in playing the bagpipes. Parades in Aspen always featured the fife and drum corps from around the state. As a kid I was always in awe when they would come by and aspired to someday play that music. Alas, they told me that there were no openings in the band for bagpipes, but I would make a great candidate for trombone. With a bait and switch like that, is it any wonder I vowed never to talk to army recruiters, cellphone hawkers or timeshare salesmen?

My parents then set forth to save enough money to purchase the instrument, and I was enlisted to have band as my main elective until I graduated high school. At first, carrying the heavy instrument seemed like a point of pride, and I wore it like a badge of honor. Eight years later, it was more like an albatross. For the entirety of middle and high school, I was not able to take any other electives, like art (which later became my major in college). While I liked band, made some great friends, and learned a lot about music, I really didn't want to continue with it, but for the investment my parents made in obtaining the instrument. I would later pick up guitar with the mistaken belief that the girls would be impressed. I still play guitar today. Incidentally, my wife is duly unimpressed.

Having squandered the opportunity to learn from some of the greatest musicians in the world, I found many excuses of why I couldn't attend my lessons. Furthermore, when I wasn't working, with fishing, bike riding, skateboarding and tourist girls, my time was spent in endeavors that didn't revolve around learning the finer nuances of a brass instrument, or the self-discipline of practicing over the summer months. I think back with regret in not taking more advantage, the opportunity for private lessons from some of the more accomplished musicians in the world.

The Paepckes' vision was to have a place where ideas and the arts were open to all, and that the best talents and minds in the world could congregate. It seems that only half of that dream is still alive these days, as the center has become less available to locals and people with meager finances.

Nonetheless, I'm thankful for the opportunities we had. To this day, I am spoiled in that the Aspen performances I was lucky enough to take in, stand out and above some of the better orchestras in cities where I've lived. In comparison to the sounds and music I've seen in Aspen in the 70s through the 90s, I've come to expect a lot. One thing is certain, by growing up around the happenings at the music tent, I have a lifelong appreciation and love of classical music. It is truly a lasting gift of the Paepkes.

THE ASPEN TIMES

ALONGSIDE THE BRICK-COLORED building of Aspen Elementary School was a well-used path we all knew about, despite being partly private property.

On Thursdays, as soon as class got out, it was a mad dash for paperboys (and girls) to get down that path as quickly as possible, without breaking an ankle. Towards the bottom, if there was still snow, you could get lucky and slide a good 15 yards to the concrete pad abutting the shopping center, home to Clark's Market.

At that point, kids would nearly climb over each other to dart through the parking lot and out to the sidewalk to get around to the back of *The Aspen Times*. If a kid was fortunate, the building owner sometimes left the stairwell doors unlocked in the middle of the building, which meant you could leap down, four steps at a time, and come out the other side ahead of most of the other kids. However, it was a gamble. If it was locked, you lost precious time and invariably ended up five or six kids back when you made it around the building.

If you were lucky enough to be one of the first in line, the smell of fresh ink wafting in your face, you could be sure it was a Thursday, and it would be a mere matter of moments until the first issues were pulled off the press and bound for release.

Our first lessons in capitalism could be gleaned from this ritual. A stack of ten papers cost a dollar for us hawkers, and the cover price was 20¢. Cheap at half the price! You were guaranteed to double your money if you were fast, deliberate, and ambitious enough to sell them all. Customers rarely carried two dimes for correct change, so our pockets were made heavier with their quarters, and a familiar knowing nod confirming their tip.

The idea was to buy as many stacks of ten that you could carry and hit the streets running. Small dirty hands would unfurl crumpled one-dollar bills or a small stack of quarters from last week's earnings to purchase a stack. The luckier, and more experienced kids had sling bags branded with the paper's logo. This provided an extra sense of credibility and a great place to store papers, candy, and change for potential buyers. The rest of us managed with what we had. And we hoped our first few customers paid in quarters, so we'd have change for the next person who paid with a dollar bill, and didn't say the blessed phrase, "Keep the change kid!"

Typically, after accosting literally everyone at Clark's Market and the neighboring businesses, most of us would shoot straight up Mill Street on the side of the Hotel Jerome and hit up everyone we saw. Starting with George Lapin at his shop Three Balls on the Mountain, where magician Ricky Jay would often try to trick Dean and I with seemingly impossible card tricks. Once at the top of Mill and Main, only a brave soul would go to the right, past *The Aspen Times* offices to the corner where Carl's Pharmacy was. It was known that past that point potential customers were few and that time spent on that venture would set you behind compared to the better-trafficked areas near the outside mall.

"*Aspen Times*?!" was the familiar call. "Paper?!"

Unless you were one of the first kids up the hill, most people had already bought one. Many were nice about it, but there were a few people who grew tired of being pestered. But as most of us knew the most saturated areas, it was up to us kids to form a strategy. One that had us selling out of copies, and if it was early enough, to go back for a second or third batch.

Some kids would venture into the local businesses until they were not-so-politely asked to leave. Others would roam aimlessly back and forth on the same stretch of sidewalk, asking literally everyone two or three times. Some would have "routes" where they were welcomed in business offices and apartment buildings. Still, others would find highly trafficked spots in front of grocery and liquor stores. These spots were like mining for gold. In almost a mobster frame of mind, kids were prone to hissing at other kids to flee their turf when other hawkers walked by.

Dean Jackson and I had a strategy to go to the bars, where the happy, go-lucky drunks were looser with their pocket change. Occasionally we'd split a five or even a ten-dollar tip from some hapless fellow, three or more sheets to the wind.

Sad was the lonely kid, still stuck with five or more papers as the sun began to set, and the cold wind of the evening started to crisp the air and make cheeks uncomfortably rosy. Sometimes you'd see a kid counting out the change on a waist-high brick wall, and just throwing the remaining papers into a nearby trash can. Then they would dejectedly walk home, slipping on newly frozen slush puddles, in Moon Boots, with the plastic peeling off the sides.

On a good day, you could make ten to fifteen dollars, especially during the tourist season. Seven or eight dollars during the off-season. Most weeks I made just enough to buy a Beatles cassette at Aspen Stereo. Or, if they didn't have one, I'd trek over to the basement of the Miners Building. Then, with enough money left over, I'd buy some Double Bubble gum, a Coke, and enough Willy Wonka Everlasting Gobstoppers to stuff into my mouth to make my cheeks puff out. But I would always be sure to save at least one dollar for the seed money to buy a stack of ten of next week's edition.

———

Hawking the Times is a shared common experience amongst the now-grown youth of Aspen. This book boasts several examples of similar experiences.

ASPEN TIMES
PART TWO

A FEW YEARS LATER, my friend Carl and I would make a similar trek to the press building on Thursdays, not to sell papers, but to "jog" them, otherwise known as sorting, stacking, and binding.

Much easier money, this paid a fresh $20 bill for just under an hour of work. This time around, we were with the folks selling stacks to the kids. At the time, Carl had "heavy metal" hair, I looked like a homogenized version of a "punk rocker" with a flat top (otherwise known as a dork), and both of us had shredded jeans and a shared enthusiasm for the absurd.

"Grab a smock," Hilary would bellow. There was an assortment of ink-stained aprons to choose from. Getting dirty, while expected, could be largely avoided if you were careful. Carl had to tie his hair back, so as not to be sucked up into the machine. As it were, the sorting machine wasn't very consistent. In fact, it seemed to break down often. We would hear the bell, the press would spin up and pull the raw paper through from a giant roll, and like a miracle of the 1800s, a printed sheet would come out the other side. Through a matter of twists, turns, and cuts, a nearly completed section of the paper would end up on the conveyor belt that sent them to us, standing in line ready to stack and count them.

Inevitably, there would be a problem. Something would jam, something else would snap, or the press would run out of ink or paper. The bell would ring, and the sounds would all grind to a halt, at which point Hilary, Arlan, and team would kick into high gear and start us hand sorting and stacking. While this almost always signaled a delay, Carl and I could watch with irony as the kids waiting to buy papers started getting antsy, stomping around in their Moon Boots and Sorels, as we awaited instruction on what task we would need to do to help keep it all moving.

At the end of the run, there were always jokes and giggles, but it would become immediately apparent that we were no longer needed for the task anymore. Now was when the actual employees had work to do. At that point, we would just be in the way. We would saunter to the sink and lather up with the industrial-grade soap/paste, likely made up of engine grease and granulated glass with a dash of orange food coloring for aesthetics. The stuff could remove tar from a bad attitude, if need be, and did surprisingly well with newspaper ink on human skin.

After that, we'd collect our $20 bill and head toward the mall, most likely to hang out with friends and spend it on cheeseburgers and cheap, 3.2 beer—the necessary fuel for "mall laps," an activity many of us teenagers did to languidly waste our time away. At the time, it was common to find many of our friends loitering outside of the freshly renovated building that housed McDonald's, the dreaded corporate chain that drew the ire of many a local. Ronnie's joint was the place we all loved to hate, but secretly ate there daily.

On any afternoon, especially toward the weekend, you could expect to find a few buddies joking around or looking for a pal to play hacky sack. Or maybe just to "people watch" in league with a fellow-minded kid not afraid to miss curfew. It was here that Carl, our mutual friend Todd, and I regularly ran into Andy Collen and his brother. If they hadn't just come from selling newspapers, they were usually strapped with pine-colored, fat boards on their backs. As usual, the two were way ahead of their time, in trying to sell us kids some of the first prototypes of the modern-day snowboard. Being a child of a prior ski shop owner, I thought I had seen it all from the myriad of strange innovations reps were constantly trying to sell my dad. Reps brought in ski-dos, ski wings, day-glo everything, and of course, the "monoboard," which had both bindings side-by-side and came with a guarantee of broken bones and/or sprained ligaments. At the time, if Andy or Mark were around with their snowboards, they probably heard me say what most people at the time were saying, "What the hell is that?!?" Meanwhile, Carl and I would nod and wave at Arlan, or some of the others filling the racks on the mall with the freshly minted edition of the Times. By this time, barely an hour later, the broken $20 was largely spent.

ASPEN TIMES
PART THREE

FAST FORWARD ABOUT TEN YEARS. I had been to college, lived in two mid-sized cities, and moved back to the valley after a failed attempt at a new start in Colorado Springs, and a close call with matrimony to the wrong person, for all the wrong reasons. For a short time in the nineties, while regrouping and regaining my wits, I seriously considered staying in the valley. The temptation to stay was strong. My friends from *The Aspen Times* were a huge factor. Despite being the third or fifth wheel for most of our escapades, I truly felt like I'd found my tribe again.

For a spell, I worked as a Graphic Design lackey at the century-old newspaper.

While at the Times, I was only ever alerted to two mandates. The first is a drug policy: Inasmuch as drug policies go, Arlan, our head pressman introduced himself to me and proclaimed, "We have a strict drug policy here. If you're not willing to share, it's just not going to work out ..." While I had met him years prior, said policy may have blurred a few memories.

The second mandate was an open policy on bringing your dog to work. Aka ... if you had a dog, it was almost mandatory that you bring it to the office so it could roam with the rest of the pack. If you didn't, too bad—"deal with it."

The Aspen Times had to have been one of the most liberal work environments, not to mention publications, I've ever experienced. I applaud it and often think back in awe at the liberties we were allowed. It was my first real foray into the free press; our invisible 4th estate, and a decent introduction to design, advertising, and the printing industry. I guess that makes up for the porridge and whippings we regularly received in lieu of actual compensation. After all, these were the days before the internet was anything more than email, and career benefits consisted of ... a discounted ski pass.

Notwithstanding, we worked hard and produced a paper on par with a larger metro, both in editorial content and design. The Times continually won awards for editorial, columns, coverage, design, and photography despite the endless budgets of the larger papers we competed with. Our publisher at the time was a Pulitzer Prize winner and a pal with George Stranahan, the paper's then-owner. In short, the Times was (and still is) awesome.

We accomplished this with a staff of 30+/- people, including those in charge of the press and postproduction.

... And with a pack of wild dogs running rampant through the facilities.

Literally.

On many occasions, employees escaped a mob of canines, hungry for blood, by closing an office door or hiding behind a group of humans snarling and yelping at decibels higher than the pack. My favorite was a dog named Shiloh, who I affectionately (or otherwise) nicknamed Cujo. Shiloh required a tether in his owners' office due to frequent near-death experiences reported by well-meaning coworkers of said dog's owner. There were dogs that were never bathed, there were dogs that were never trained, there were dogs that would bite, and there were dogs that would fight. All underfoot, no matter how delicate the work was around them. In a sense, the dogs ruled.

It's hard not to look back and laugh at the look on our art director Brian's face, as he swirled paper towels around his hand, wadded them into a ball and took three huge steps to the advertising level, to scoop up, and summarily dispose of in a large trash can, a pile of steaming poop, which everyone else ignored for too much time. Brian's face resembled a disappointed mother cleaning up after a messy toddler.

I recall with horror a day when one of Su Lum's wiener dogs took a bite out of my sandwich. It was still in my hand. Not only did the pup refuse to let go of my $7 sub, neither did she want to unclench her jaw from my fingers holding it, and the dog, several feet in the air.

But I digress. Despite the chaos of a wild pack of dogs, and the publisher's occasional attempt to literally strangle a customer, working at the times provided me with the experience to kickstart a career. I later went on to work at two more newspapers; one, a property in the multinational company, Gannett, and the other a family-owned chain that brought my wife and I to the town where we live now, the Athens Banner-Herald in Athens, Georgia. While many of my friends were writers and editors, I was never in the editorial department. Instead, my career took the route via design, marketing, online and management.

The job at *The Aspen Times* also afforded me the real benefit of working for the more than 140-year-old voice and vessel of the First Amendment liberties. It was there that I met a great group of ragtag clowns, whom I proudly refer to as friends, and still cherish to this day, nearly 30 years later. Cameron, Bob, Brian, John K, Stewart (RIP), Dave, and columnist Barry Smith among many others went on to do other things, but those times still make me chuckle.

———

Just a couple of quick anecdotes about one of my favorite lunatics:

Cam's antics are as unique as his personality, which always makes for an interesting and entertaining happening when he is around.

Often, we would hang out in Basalt before heading up to Aspen for some nightlife. I recall an evening when, as a group, we took in French food at Café Bernard. While memory eludes me on the exact number of us in the group, I can easily say it was more than six, but fewer than twelve.

As the waitress arrived at our oversized table, handed us single-sheet dinner menus, and asked if we wanted to see "Zee wine leest." Cameron immediately insisted on a pitcher of their finest *American* beer. Perturbed, she frowned and took a few other drink orders elsewhere before making her way to the bar.

When she returned to take our orders, she naturally skipped over Cam and made sure to get his order last. "And for you, sir? What would you like to eat?"

"Do you have any *Italian* food?" he asked without skipping a beat.

"Sir, zees ees a *French* restaurant. We specialize in French food," she attempted with congeniality.

"Oh. Sorry. I'll just take some lasagna then," he stated.

Somewhat confused, she retorted, "Zat ees not on the menu. Perhaps some mussels?"

With a wry smile, Cam again "apologized" before stating, "A Caesar salad then."

"SIR," almost loudly this time, "we do not serve Italian food. Zees ees a French establishmont."

Cam finally gave in with, "Sorry. I'll just take the spaghetti ... er I mean noodles."

She stomped off to the kitchen. I vaguely remember chiding and admonishing him for messing with her. My years of kitchen work have softened me when it comes to that trade.

Cam responded with, "You're right. I should go easy on her," and hurriedly followed up with, "quick—trade places with me!"

Not fully understanding why, I reluctantly agreed, and we swapped seats. Before the waitress returned with our food, he reached into his pocket, produced a curly-haired wig, and donned it. It was a brown, Greg Brady style wig from the popular seventies TV show.

Minutes later the waitress arrived with our food and became visibly confused. She asked me, "What happened to that annoying man?" I shrugged, told her what I'd ordered, and watched the continued confusion as she eventually made her way to Cameron. A spark of recognition crossed her face as she handed him his food and, shocked, deftly took her leave. Cam looked at his dinner with his most sarcastic smile as the rest of us burst with laughter.

Before I paint Cam as some kind of deviant (and I assure you he is), I should say that, when necessary, he is a consummate professional and a damned good writer. Cam is well known in the outdoors industry and has a heart of gold. He is also one of the most hilarious people I have ever met. His energy is infectious, and his sense of humor is as boisterous as it is bizarre.

But after the dinner at Café Bernard, I felt the need to throw in a few extra bucks for the tip for our very patient waitress.

A few months later, again in Basalt, I had driven to Cam and Ann's place. The plan was to leave my car there and take the bus back for *The Aspen Times*' employee party at the Flying Dog Brewpub, another of George Stranahan's businesses. The rest of the crew had gone ahead, and Ann planned to meet up with us there after she got off work.

Cam and I had a beer at his place, waiting to go to the bus stop and head into town. While talking, Cam suddenly commented on my collared shirt. "Wait ... you're dressed nice. I feel underdressed. Do you think I should change?" He looked disapprovingly at his own clothes—jeans and a T-shirt.

The bus would be there in around 5 minutes, so it was really time we left so as not to miss our ride. In the interest of time and trying to dissuade him I replied, "No Cam, you look fine. We have to go."

"I'll be right back! It'll only take a minute," he said. "I really don't want to be an embarrassment. After all, this is a company party."

He disappeared up the stairs. I looked at my watch. We were cutting it close. About 2 minutes later I yelled up, "Dude we're gonna miss the bus!"

His reply expressed concern but sounded oddly suspicious. "How much time do we have?" he asked from above, "I'm almost ready."

Nearly one minute before the bus was due to arrive, Cam bolted down the stairs. "Do I look okay?"

He had changed into a skintight black turtleneck and giant bell bottoms—also unnervingly skintight. A large Peace sign medallion swung around his neck and again, his favorite Greg Brady wig adorned his head.

Dumbfounded, and knowing full well there was no time for him to change yet again, I shook my head and laughed. What else could I do?

Just before we left the condo, he grabbed something from the downstairs closet. As we ran toward the bus stop, he pulled out from under his coat a 3-foot beer bong, upon which he had drawn a face and the words 'Mr. Ugly' in marker.

As we climbed aboard the bus, Cam proceeded to accost the other riders and ask if they wanted … "To meet Mr. Ugly." Short of exposing himself, I doubt the other bus riders could have been more alarmed. And hell, at that point there was no guarantee that he wouldn't do that too.

Suffice it to say, it was a long 15-minute ride into downtown Aspen.

I don't remember much of what went on at the party. It was held in the old space that used to be Pinocchio's. Now the Flying Dog Brewpub, George Stranahan who owned both the pub and the Times, had opened a running tab at the bar for all the employees of the paper. The budget was huge. However, due to long hours and paltry wages, the employees were able to burn through the per diem in just under an hour. Many chose top-shelf tequila as their drink of choice, grumbling that it was owed to them. After that, we were all pretty lit up, but the rest of the libations were up to us.

I recall, at one point in the evening, spotting Cam from across the pub. He was dancing like a lunatic in his bell bottoms. He'd picked up—no *literally picked up* Mary Eshbaugh Hayes, the well-known and respected Society Editor, now in her late sixties. He was swinging her around wildly and holding her a bit too close. I thought for sure she would have felt violated and wary of danger. Instead, she grinned the largest smile I'd ever seen, and let out a laugh as crazy as Cam's outfit.

It was truly a special bunch of people.

Our crew mostly consisted of writers living downvalley. And a few of us designers and ad people who shared the love of libations and laughter. When not in crunch time trying to meet stringent deadlines, we could be found haunting the local eateries or warming the stools at the bars and clubs. Or for the more economical option, we'd meet at one of their houses, apartments, or condos. Our off-time excursions were the normal sort in the valley, mostly consisting of mountain biking, hiking, sometimes fishing, and in the winter, snowmobiling, snowshoeing, and of course skiing.

After a few scrapes with the local wildlife and a few with other cars on the commute, I eventually took a job in Glenwood Springs as a designer at the Rocky Mountain Printer, next to "Drugs & Guns" (the former Center Drug), a position held until I eventually moved to the Front Range. There, together with my good friend Dave Evenson, whose parents owned and ran the print shop, we designed and prepared brochures, posters, books, and more for many Aspen customers, including the Ritz Carlton, the Luxury Collection, and many other local and national customers.

The final straw came in the realization that I would probably never make more than $12 per hour, coupled with a face-to-face meeting with an adult mule deer, at approximately 70 mph one morning on my daily drive between Carbondale and Glenwood.

During my time at the Rocky Mountain Printer, Barry Smith, the humor columnist, wrote a silly book of poems and asked me to illustrate some of the pieces. *Ode to Mustard* was one of his fun projects that generated more laughs than dollars.

Ode to Mustard by Barry Smith (store link)

Hunter S. Thompson added his take by way of a review on its back cover, "Good luck, shit-eyes. I told you not to write this horrible, morbid swill. Now you will have to live with it."

Barry summed it up with the following: "This book changed my life like nothing I've ever read. Still … I'm glad I waited for the paperback."

———

I left newspapers in the early 2000s, as it was apparent to me the industry was in sharp decline. My experiences in the newspaper industry brought me to places all over this country. I once proudly boasted that within two days' time, I'd dipped my feet in both the Pacific and Atlantic oceans with work-related travels. Of course, I probably would have jumped all the way in if it hadn't been February. The Gannett company had sent me to the Pacific Northwest, where I split my time between newspaper executive leadership training and animating commercials with Andy and Amy Collen.

My career in newspapers, not counting hawking, lasted the better part of ten years. I look back with fond memories of the people I worked with at *The Aspen Times*. The little local paper started me on a journey from newsboy to a seat at the executive table. And it's where I met some of the best friends of my life.

IN BETWEEN GEORGETOWN AND IDAHO SPRINGS

THERE WAS A SMALL gas station/convenience store on frontage road off I-70. Just like most convenience stores of the time, they stocked the usual assortment of snacks, drinks, various common auto supplies, and slickie mags for homesick truckers. Otherwise, it probably wasn't notable in any other way. Millions of people drove by it without ever noticing. These days it's probably a Starbucks.

In high school in the mid-to-late-80s, the crowd I mostly hung out with would have been labeled "stoners." But the irony was, at that time in that place, it was more likely kids would buy drugs from the so-called "jocks" who stole them from their parents, than the other way around. Really, what it was all about was general teenage angst, and a crew of outsiders who found each other standing on the sidelines. That, and a shared love of what was considered hard rock music. Many of us were listening to heavy metal bands, while others were listening to punk and new wave. In somewhat desperate attempts to claim our own identities, we often emulated our rock heroes in style and attitude. I was somewhere in between. Suffice to say, we weren't dancing to disco pop at the Tippler, or clapping hands along with the "Parrotheads" or Bruce Springsteen fans. And many of us were not fans of the Grateful Dead, either.

It was likely you would see us playing hacky sack and frisbee with the homeless people at Wagner Park. Or skateboarding on the mall. Most likely, we were wearing too many clothes for the heat of the summer, or too few for the cold of the winter.

Occasionally, some of the bigger bands of the time would play concerts in Denver. Since this music was rare in the valley, and bands like that never played in Aspen, we would often make the 4-hour drive to catch a show in the mile-high city. The 1988 Monsters of Rock was one such show.

Jim (Ian M), his girlfriend Angel, Justin, another friend of ours, piled into Ian's late seventies, run-down Oldsmobile Cutlass Supreme, aka "The Gutless." We braved the passes and headed over the mountains toward "the big city."

The opening band, not worth mentioning, was a Zeppelin rip off which proved to be good background noise while we found our seats. We were really there to see Metallica and the Scorpions. But for added bonus, a band called Dokken also opened up for the latest iteration of Van Halen—sans David Lee Roth.

Standard attire for a rock concert of this sort in the 1980s consisted of shredded jeans, long hair (mine was always short) and a genre-appropriate T-shirt, although definitely NOT of the band you were going to see.

When the show was over, we dropped Angel off at a hotel near the airport. She was flying out the next day, likely to visit her father in Alaska. Justin stayed behind with his dad, who lived in Denver. Jim and I got back on the road to Aspen just before dusk.

The Gutless may have been run down but it had made many trips to shows like this before. One to Iron Maiden, where a friend's big mouth got him in trouble with a Denver street gang, another to see Ozzy and Anthrax. Still, one other road trip when we all went to see Megadeth open for Ozzy. A friend of ours, we'll call him Lance, because that was really his name, decided to smuggle the remains of a joint into the show. We tried talking him out of it. But he was determined. He put the tiny "roach" into a film canister and stuffed it down the front of his skinny jeans.

As we approached, security guards were searching everyone, mostly looking in bags and lightly lifting or patting people's coats for liquor bottles or weapons. Lance's face turned ghostly white.

Suddenly he lurched forward, reached into his pants, threw the film canister into a nearby trash can, and shoved between two burly biker types, trying to run in.

Of *course*, they caught him. After an exhaustive interrogation and humiliating strip search, Lance was ejected. He took in the concert from the front seat of The Gutless, out in the parking lot.

Moments after we took our seats, discussing Lance's fate, a group of teens in front of us pulled a three-foot bong out of a coat, lit up, and enjoyed the show in a way that would have made poor Lance green with envy. Such was rock in the 1980s.

During the ride home from the Monsters of Rock concert, still reveling in the highlights of the show, the Cutlass began to have troubles with the steep hills. We noticed there was a lack of power not evident prior. Nonetheless, we thought nothing of it and continued the trek.

Just past Georgetown, the gauge indicated that the car was overheating. As is the case for much of the Colorado mountain terrain, there really weren't many places to stop, so we kept going. We made it about another nine miles, until white smoke began billowing out from under the hood. We pulled off at a tiny place called Downieville, stopping about a mile from the gas station on frontage road. We began walking to buy antifreeze. Once we made it back to the car, we poured the entire gallon into the radiator which created more smoke and left a gallon sized puddle of antifreeze on the pavement. We knew that meant trouble.

We chanced it and drove on and parked at the gas station. Once inside, we inquired with the staff about local mechanics or if the station itself did diagnostic work. After a few calls, and talking with a mechanic, we learned the car was a goner. We'd blown a head gasket. And now, we were stranded in Downieville, Colorado.

We spent the next couple of hours trying to catch a ride back to Aspen. Since we'd just come from a rock concert, our clothes likely made us the least appealing candidates for a free ride over the Rockies. At one point, a family friend pulled into the station to gas up his truck. Mr. Mencimer, who'd just come from a fair somewhere nearby. He was towing the famous calliope often seen at parades in town. Unfortunately for us, he had no room in his rig for a couple of smelly teens dressed like idiots.

We decided to call Justin, even though he'd be back at his dad's in Denver by then. They graciously agreed to come and take us back to his place for the night. That gave us about an hour to kill. Realizing the sad fate of The Gutless was still unanswered, Ian resolved to abandon it, as no local mechanic or regular at any of the gas stops had an interest in acquiring the "classic" car. Jim drove The Gutless around the side of the station where it would have to stay for a while. We spent the rest of the time packing every item Jim wanted to keep from the car into two large trash bags. Then we popped the trunk.

Jim (Ian M) had forgotten he'd left the tools of this summer's trade in the back—an industrial electric weed wacker and approximately 100 feet of cord. Since they were the property of his boss, we were left with no choice but to bring them with us. As we sat and waited, Ian became agitated.

"I just remembered. I just paid a ton of money on new tires and a battery for this piece of shit," he bellowed.

I grimaced and replied with, "Bummer man."

"We're taking 'em," he announced.

I tried to reason with him. "How the hell are we gonna get the tires?"

"Good point," he said, halfway defeated. "We can get the battery, though." We pried the battery connectors loose and used the handy plastic handle to carry it away from the now lifeless Cutlass.

When our ride showed up in a big black suburban, we piled the belongings in the back. Justin's father had a penthouse suite in a tall building with views of much of the city. On any other occasion, this would have seemed like an incredible turn of events. In this case, we were just happy for a place to crash.

The next morning, we expressed our gratitude to our gracious guests and made our way down to the greyhound bus station, passing business commuters and street people alike.

For that long walk, we were a spectacle to behold; two scruffy teenagers dressed in ratty clothing and rock T-shirts shouldering large trash bags full of clothes, with a weed whacker, a 100 ft extension cord, and a brand-new car battery. We patiently entertained the jealous questions put to us by numerous street people. "Where'd you find that awesome stuff?!?"

Having barely slept, we collapsed into chairs at the station and waited for hours. There were people who looked like they'd spent the night in the very chair they were in. There were sketchy junkies and a man who argued incessantly with himself at the top of his lungs until the station staff told him to quiet down, at which point he merely continued in a whisper.

The bus finally arrived. We piled all our junk in the luggage compartment and sat back in the tall seats. In the end, we made it home, the adventure behind us.

Sadly, when we later drove to college at CSU, The Gutless still sat by the side of the building in Downieville. In fact, it remained there for more than a year.

NIGHT NIGHT, JOHN BOY

WHEN WE WERE ABOUT 16, my friend Todd had asked me to help him move some furniture into an apartment his mother had been renting out. The tenants had painstakingly cleaned and emptied the apartment when they moved out, except for a few items left behind, either for lack of interest or from the mistaken idea that somebody might actually have a use for them.

There was a couch, a broken lamp, a small end table, TV, VCR, and some Tupperware containers. Other than these few items, the apartment was bereft of any human belongings ... except for what had us reeling and joking: a single VHS videotape with no label in a *Teenage Mutant Ninja Turtles* case. What was truly strange was that the tape appeared to have been deliberately hidden. We'd found it behind a loose board in the storage locker.

Now, in following the prurient avenues of the teenage mind, one might easily gesture a guess as to what we thought might be recorded on the tape. As the jokes went, "Debbie Does Something or other" and to that order, our imaginations got away from us. We *had* to see what was on the tape!

So, after an hour of back-breaking labor moving the couch, we found the VCR and popped the tape in. No power. OK, so we then spent about 15 minutes finding the breaker switch. Still nothing. The TV, it seemed, had taken a bit of a beating in the move and would need some minor repairs in the near future. So then, we took the tape to another friend's house, and after two more hours of waiting for his mom to leave the house for a weekend trip, we raided the snack cabinet, and the refrigerator for 3.2 Budweiser beer and plopped down to see the *TAPE*.

Our eyes bulged—our mouths dropped open in repulsion for the utter filth we were subjected to. One can imagine our horror when we realized that what was actually recorded on the tape was not "Debbie Does Something or other," but rather, six hours of *Little House on the Prairie* back to back with *The Waltons* recorded on extended play.

FIFTEEN MILES FROM NOWHERE

SOMETIME IN THE MID-90S while working at *The Aspen Times* a friend of mine decided to buy a house above Reudi Reservoir, 15 miles up the Frying Pan River from Basalt. He needed roommates, so his brother and I signed up. Out of respect for his privacy and for comedic purposes, let's call him "Spalding," and his younger brother will henceforth be referred to as, "Chet."

Spalding's realtor was the husband of Bland Nesbit, one of my mom's good friends and an all-around great person. Bland and I also worked on many design projects together at the time. Bland's husband, the legendary Mike Cooper, had taken Spalding out to a house up by Reudi Reservoir.

Cooper said, "I have to tell you, winters up here are long and harsh, but summer is absolutely gorgeous. Just make sure you schedule those two weeks off." Then, to demonstrate the utter remoteness of the subdivision, and as a brilliant sales tactic, Cooper walked around the back of his vehicle, loaded a sawed-off shotgun, fired it in the air, and grinned his trademark smile. (See Fig. B)

Within a matter of days, the property had its new owner. The house was small, but the property was vast enough to ride snowmobiles in winter

Fig B: Mike Cooper's trademark smile.

and still not be a nuisance to the nearest neighbor. And apparently remote enough to discharge a sawed-off shotgun without attracting any ire for that either.

All three of us moved into the house early that spring. I loved the area, having fished the reservoir for many years with my dad, and later on with friends. Reudi Reservoir was large and accessible, but it was rare to see many people on the lake. In short, it was an ideal place to get away and recharge spiritually.

There was still ice on parts of the lake, and there were continual snow storms which often made for a treacherous commute. While its curving dirt road and winding highway could be idyllic, it was no picnic. On certain days I would see majestic Bighorn sheep standing on a sheer rock face no more than ten feet above the road, other days I'd be stuck behind a guy in a Winnebago hugging the curves at 4 mph in fear of driving into a mountain, or off a cliff into the river. The irony is, the width of a road is the same whether one is driving 70 mph in big city traffic, or on a mountain road in Colorado. I'd wager that the true danger is not on the remote roads of the mountains, but in contending with the inadequacies of other drivers in more populated places. However, having nearly slid off the cliff myself one particularly icy morning, I did have frequent concerns about ice, and of colliding with wildlife. Routinely I would see deer, elk, Bighorn sheep, dogs, bears, moose, Bigfoot, and an occasional tourist, bike rider, or angler in the road.

As Cooper predicted, it wasn't long before our first decent snowstorm. The dirt road to the house was very curved, and steep in parts. My poor little Saturn SL1 didn't stand a chance of getting up the hill which was sloppy with mostly frozen mud. So, I parked it, along with a few other unlucky neighbors' cars at the bottom of the hill. A few moments later Spalding drove up in his mid-80s Jeep CJ, complete with chains on the studded snow tires, sandbags weighing hundreds of pounds, mad power in the engine, and a chassis built just for this type of thing, so I hopped in. We made it about halfway up the steepest part, toward the top of the drive, and started sliding back down. Thinking we needed more weight on the front tires, I jumped on the hood as we struggled to get the Jeep up the hill. For about 20 minutes, we sloshed this way and that which spun the tires, and kicked up mud and snow, with little to no progress at all.

Just then, Spalding's brother Chet came putt-putting up the bend in his late-60s VW Bug with no snow tires. Shaking our heads in disbelief, we watched as Chet drove around the Jeep and passed us with no effort at all. It took us another 10 minutes or so to get up the hill, into the driveway, and parked next to Chet's VW Bug. Seems those crafty Germans were on to something when they designed a tin can of a car with no extras.

After the first snow melted, and we began to explore, not wanting to make the drive to Basalt for some entertainment, we often opted to pull up a stool at a distant bar toward the inlet of the reservoir. As it was so remote from anywhere, there really weren't many customers aside from the regulars that frequented the place. They gradually got to know us, but there was hesitancy on their part, likely for good reason. After all, it takes a certain type of person to want to live that far from anywhere. They were the type of folks that, for one reason or another, are hiding from something, or someone.

Of the colorful characters we met there, only a few remain as stand-outs in my mind. There was Militia Mike, a skinhead missing his front top teeth, whose bottom incisors stuck out like those of a bulldog, there was Stonewash Slim who weighed in at under 95 lbs. and wore all denim jeans and a jacket, his girlfriend "One-Eyed Toothless Madge" with an eyepatch, and most notable of the lot, "Deuce" th' Cowboy, who raised cattle and allegedly cultivated "contraband" in his basement for supplemental income.

We were outsiders to the regulars, yet oddly welcome. Conversations were to be had by all and were only broken up by an occasional Bob Seger tune blaring out of the antiquated jukebox. Like the bar itself, the selections on the jukebox seemed to be trapped in time, never going past the super hits of the "golden seventies." Whenever Bob Seger came on, the bar fell silent as everyone set to watching the shameless, somewhat eerie sight of Slim and Madge on the dance floor, grinding out post-disco moves as well as their patent tribute to *Dirty Dancing*.

The silence broke after the song and dance ended. The bar had gone uncomfortably quiet. Deuce th' Cowboy asked, "You remember Russell?"

Nearly all of them responded in unison, "Oh yeah."

Deuce continued, "Now I ain't no rocket scientist ..." Guffaws filled the room. "... but you don't come out of the closet in a bar full of cowboys. We had no choice," he continued, as if on a comedy club stage, "we took him in the field and beat him."

Be it hyperbole or some other form of fabrication but knowing that every fable sprouts from a kernel of truth, it became apparent at that point in time, there was a good chance that we were in fact, not ... in the presence of a rocket scientist. Of course, as so often happens in the Aspen area, he might have been at one time. You just never know. Still, I remain skeptical. In truth, Bruce was a typical example of toxic ignorance and intolerance. But let's go with Rocket Scientist. It's got a catchier ring. ...

Such was the standard scene from then on. Every visit to the small bar was a mix of surreal banter, alcohol, and hilarity. We just never knew what to expect. Mostly we were there to play pool, drink beer and experience a small semblance of civilization. But the activities of the regulars were never dull. At any point in time, the jukebox would fire up, seemingly at random, and the frisky couple would spin and grind out a slow dance to Boston, Supertramp, or even Seals & Crofts. Meanwhile, Militia Mike, dreaming up mercurial machinations or reeling in conspiracies someone else wouldn't even conjure, would corner some hapless tourist, and confide in hushed tones, "I couldn't help but overhear you saying somethin' about ... the govermint ..." Deuce would be sharing his wisdom with the whole bar, and we would chuckle at the whole scene.

On a different night, sitting at that bar while Spalding and Chet played pool, a ruckus ensued when the front door swung wildly open to an entourage of cowboys carrying a short noose. They spied the rafters.

"Who should we hang?!?"

The bar burst out in laughter once again. Apparently, this was a common occurrence. The cowboys sauntered up to the bar, ordered beers, and one of them threw the noose around my neck. Nervously laughing I didn't know what to expect.

"$20 bucks, and I'll hang this guy!"

In a sudden flash of nervous inspiration, I said the first thing that came to mind, "Hell! $50 bucks and I'll hang myself!"

Just like that they burst out laughing, the noose came off, and they bought me a beer. Not knowing how crazy the evening might get once they got properly liquored up, we decided to leave shortly thereafter. But not before buying a round for the regulars. Just in case.

Days spent at the reservoir were always great. Access was within minutes from where the house was. Oddly, while living there it was truly strange how few people frequented the lake. It really felt like we were alone up there. So, whenever we saw someone, we always knew that within a matter of time, we'd end up talking with them.

One day, near the dam, we spied a park ranger who wanted a word. After we showed our fishing licenses, the conversation moved on to water rights and maintenance.

"How much of this water is used by the local communities?" I asked in hopes of educating myself.

The man replied, "Well truthfully, they just sold a whole lot of it off. Now instead of all of it going to the local area," he began unzipping his fly, "this water meets up with the Crystal, then flows into the Colorado River." He began urinating into the reservoir and continued, "which means eventually … it goes on out, all the way out to California. They get to drink up." Finished, he zipped up his fly, said goodbye, and left us to ponder.

There really weren't many signs of civilization there at the time. I remember fondly working on an animation while staring out of the back windows of the house. It backed up to a field where the closest neighbor was about two acres distant. As I punched away at the computer, I spied movement and looked up to see a beautiful fox stalking field mice. He suddenly pounced, more like a bounce really, swooped his head down, then trounced away with a mouse in his mouth. This became an almost daily ritual—a moment of Zen in solitude, where I could focus on the beauty of nature, virtually unsullied by man.

In fact, probably the only time I met one of the neighbors was when one showed up pounding furiously on the front door. I opened it to an irate middle-aged man who bellowed, "Quit feeding my goddamned dog!"

Despite the distance to this man's house, we were fortunate enough to get a daily visit from his Labrador. The first few times he showed up, he was skinny and puppy-like. But as the months went on, he grew fat and slow. We had thought his owner was overfeeding him.

"He's getting fat, slobbers everywhere and shits out all manner of nasty grease all over my living room!"

As I tried to calm him down and reassure him that we were not feeding him, the man grew weary and quieted a bit. It was at about that moment it dawned on me.

Chet is a conscious-minded nice guy, who cares about the environment and nature, almost more than he cares about people. He had decided to try to do the right thing by making a compost pile out of the various foodstuff that went uneaten. Egg shells, rotten meat, bacon grease, vegetable ends, dead plants, and other vegan matter. For months we had thought he had attracted a bear. Or possibly the fox we saw daily was absconding with the trash. We were always shocked and concerned when by morning the compost was mostly gone. Every day.

I explained this to the man. He left slightly less infuriated when we assured him that we would no longer be doing "the right thing." He agreed to lock up his dog. We agreed not to pursue the compost pile any longer. Compromise. We slept a little better knowing the compost thief wasn't a giant bear, with a taste for eggshells and rotten food.

Most of the time I spent in that house was in complete solitude. Chet, a professional animator, would commute to California to see his girlfriend and work on projects, so we would only see him every few weeks. Spalding was ambitiously working both at the local paper and as a computer consultant. He mostly stayed with his girlfriend. When I wasn't working downvalley I was completely alone with my books, my music, and my thoughts. While it was spiritually refreshing, it also proved to be alienating. My only recourse was to pay closer attention to the quietude of nature, and my job search for a professional position, somewhere else. The quiet was deafening, but beautiful. I spent countless hours just listening to bees, birds, and an occasional deer or fox making its way through the tall grass.

But this too, soon ended as winter neared. It was obvious that my daily commute was taking its toll not only on me but on my 2-wheeled drive car, which would surely prove no match for snow and ice.

For anyone who has not experienced driving on a high mountain pass, picture a 2-lane road. Now picture that same road with little, or no shoulder. This makes the road appear not to be very wide. On one side, there may be a rock wall that goes hundreds of feet up, with an occasional waterfall, but you can't spend too much time looking, because the road curves. And if you're not careful, you'll go off the other side—a rock wall that slopes 100s of feet down to a river.

Now picture that prospect going on for a mile or two, or possibly ten. Occasionally there is a succession of "S" curves, and you are forced to slow to about 25 mph. Behind you is a jackass who likes to tailgate, and in front of you are varying pieces of rock and dirt that have tumbled loose from above and landed on the road. At some point, you come to a curve in the road so tight it goes almost a full 180-degrees by the time you straighten out again, and you're forced to go 15 mph or slower.

In winter, the drive is identical, only then there is snow, ice, and occasional fauna—dead or alive—on or alongside the road. The drive made for an impossible commute in the snowy months.

What seemed like a lifetime was only a few short months. I landed a job in Fort Collins that was to start in October so I temporarily moved home to Carbondale with my mom while I prepared to finally leave the valley for good.

As fate would have it, my first collision with wildlife occurred not on Frying Pan Road, but on good old Killer 82, after I moved back to Carbondale.

"THE JUICE"

WHEN I WAS A TEENAGER, our mom bought a second car we called, "The Tank." A lime-green, late seventies Jeep Wagoneer, complete with dents, cracks, scratches, and smells. It had seemingly been through hell before we got it.

She managed to buy it while working herself nearly to death on 2+ jobs to feed and clothe three kids in a giant house, with electricity bills topping $1000 per month in the winter. The sacrifices she made were not unappreciated. Not in the least.

Again, having grown up in Aspen, it is often assumed that our family had a lot of money. I'll not give some sob story that we were destitute, or that we were starving or underprivileged in any way. But I will say, even though our family had greater access than most to sporting goods, more than one season saw me wearing hand-me-down shoes held together with duct tape. We were not rich, but we weren't poor either. I consider myself to be truly fortunate with the things I was given.

The Tank was no exception. Our mom let the three of us share the car, provided we paid for our own insurance and gas. It got approximately six miles to the gallon and weighed in just slightly under what a school bus or "tank" might. And as anyone who's owned a similar piece of used Americana such as an 8-cylinder piece of angry steel knows, "yes" you could see light through the floorboards. Mom bought it for around $1,000 and the three of us fought constantly for the opportunity to "drive" to school or downtown—or anywhere, really.

The Tank turned out to be a good blank canvas as an automotive project for me. Throughout high school, with band taking my main elective spot in school, I was unable to take part in other "hobby" classes, like art and woodworking. Ironically, those two activities are some of my greatest passions. Consequently, I dropped trombone the day I graduated. But while in school, vocational auto was an elective that for some reason, was available. So, I signed up. It was of interest, as I had worked on small engines for years, keeping the minibike I bought from Scott Mars for $50 running, despite its never-ending desire to "just let go." That being said, the mini bike provided a great opportunity to learn how things work and our Wagoneer provided many chances to fix a vehicle and keep it running.

On one occasion, Dean and I took The Tank for a spin up the road toward Maroon Bells. On the way back, I got that old hunk of steel up to 115 mph around the curves and small stretches of straight road. Despite our attempts to win a Darwin Award, the highlight of the speed run was when I hit a pothole and the spare tire, stored in the back, flipped like a pancake, and Dean bounced so high that he smacked his head on the ceiling of the cabin. Of course, we weren't wearing seatbelts.

In the end, Mom sold The Tank for just about what she paid for it, and the three of us said a hard goodbye to our indestructible driving classroom. I bring up The Tank because it would almost qualify as my first car but for two things. One, I didn't buy it and two, it wasn't solely "mine."

Now "The Juice," or "Da Jeuce!"... well that's another story entirely.

With a little help on the down payment, I bought The Juice, a Saturn SL1, for around $11,000 or monthly payments of $249. Now, before someone once again casts a glance of judgment, yes, this was a lot of money for a "first" car in the 90s, but it's important to know that I was 25 years old when I bought it.

You may be asking yourself, "Why did he wait until he was 25 to buy a car?" Well, there were a few reasons, really. First, I was broke. I had no money and no way of getting any prior to my first "real" job.

I had always been taught to "live within my means," but until recent years, my means had always been meager. Second, my friend Tad's dad, Walt, once told me that, "A car was the worst thing I could spend my money on as a 16-year-old." Of course, I didn't realize he meant it was okay to buy one at age 18, or 21, etc. And third, and most important, I flat out got tired of bumming rides from my best friends. And not surprisingly, so did they.

However, to me, driving my first car might have well as made me Mario Andretti. The Saturn was green and made to look like the disposable equivalent of a late 1970s Jaguar mixed with a Corvette or something. One that would also work well to transport groceries and diapers. A friend's elderly neighbor once commented "Whose fancy sports car is that out there?!?" Apparently, they didn't let her off the farm very often. The nickname itself came from a random conversation with my friend Jim, while we were casually ripping on the ridiculousness of pride and identity in the form of a car. Ironically, I was proud to own it.

The Juice, to modern car enthusiasts, was about as generic a car as one could imagine.

Complete with hand crank windows, 4-cylinder engine, manual transmission, and floormats included, this car was anything but basic. After all, it had FM radio and an antenna. (Sarcasm) You could say it was a glorified go-cart.

Now I don't plan on blathering on about how awesome the car was or how enamored I was of it—it wasn't like I was cleaning the wheel wells with a toothbrush or something. The reason I chose to write about The Juice is because, over the course of 4 years' time, it almost became my coffin on more occasions than I care to mention. Yet somehow ... I feel compelled to mention it anyway.

Allow me to explain. It is rumored that the color of a car, statistically, can sometimes affect the potential to be involved in a major accident. Whatever those colors may be, that green death-can was flat-out jinxed.

My first wreck happened on the way home from my job at *The Aspen Times* in about 1995. I was rear-ended in traffic by a woman who was changing the radio station. It was mutually agreed that the damage was so minimal that we didn't even exchange numbers. Ho hum. I know. BORING.

Now ... at some point between wreck #1 and wreck #2, I was gifted with and installed a used 6-CD changer in the back trunk of the car which skipped incessantly. On cold days especially, I was driven nearly mad trying to get my favorite music to play without skipping, or at all for that matter. Music is supposed to have a calming effect, yet when it becomes a challenge to be able to enjoy it without interruption, it can have the opposite outcome. In short, it nearly drove me freaking MAD. Every time the tunes would start playing, I'd get about 2 to 3 minutes of enjoyment, only to be dragged through the gutter with what sounded like a dog humping a fax machine. "Giant steps are what you take ... walking on the moon ... I hope my legs don't grrrrrrrrrrrrrdddd sssssssss ssgdssssss sssssssssbnn nnnn nnnnn nnyyyyytttt tttttzzzzzz."

Ok, that brings us to accident number two. This time on the way to work in a winter storm, while stopped on a bridge, the 17-year-old kid behind me decided he didn't need to slow down and took off the back end of my car, all the way up to the 6-disc changer.

Approximately 1/3 of my car lay in shattered fiberglass pieces on the highway, meanwhile snow and ice was blowing into my car while we awaited the Keystone Cop who showed up and issued the kid a *warning*. After all, my car only bumped the car ahead of me, which in turn started a 7-car chain reaction. I can't, for the life of me, see how the kid behind all of us might have been at fault in *any* way. Pardon my sarcasm.

The result of accident #2 was a four-month stint in the body shop for The Juice. But not before a visit from the insurance adjuster, a strait-laced goon, complete with pleather satchel and spittle in the corners of his mouth.

Back to the 6-disc changer responsible for many a day of dismay and aggravation, yet rare segments of joy—my hope was that it would have played its last tune. Literally. On a good day, the player wouldn't play if there was the slightest amount of condensation on the discs. The car at this point had sat out in the elements for a good two weeks of snow, sleet, and rain. The adjuster asked to start it up to see if it worked and if it should be included in the assessment. I was, of course, elated to do so; crossing fingers I could get a new, working player. And ... as you surely guessed, with the turn of the key, the player spun up like a champ ... "Giant steps are what you take ..." Needless to mention, the adjustment did not include a new player. By the way, that was the last time the player ever functioned. At all.

After the first two accidents resulting from a near hour-long commute to my job at the newspaper, I decided to start the job search anew. After all, many a night shift ended with me driving home at 3 am, dodging deer on Hwy 82. Despite that I had developed keen senses that allowed me to spot a deer from 700 yards off, by spotting my headlight reflections in the eyes of the psychotic mammals prior to their suicidal jumps in front of ongoing traffic; the risk was too great for the pittance I earned at the paper.

I then took a job a little closer to home—that is to say, a mere 20 miles away, in nearby Glenwood Springs, Colorado—home of the hot springs, a train station, and the supposed final resting place of none other than Doc Holliday, of OK Corral and Val Kilmer fame (the folks in Griffin, GA say otherwise).

The commute, while considerably less stressful, was also unfortunately less scenic. That said, accident #3 involved a bit of nature that came a little too close for comfort. Colorado, during the 80s and 90s, became a hotbed of real estate development. Nary a parcel larger than could hold a trailer was marketed, inflated, and inevitably doled out to the highest bidder. As such the parcel of land that was split by Hwy 82 between Carbondale and Glenwood not only served as an enclave for the wealthy but also had an adverse effect on the local wildlife. That is to say, the area of land that once served as a watering hole and migration path for the area's deer and elk for thousands of years was now host to $1–2 million dollar "economy" second homes, and an enclave for folks who moved downvalley.

The result was mass confusion for the area's fauna, and inevitably, my brush with death on Killer 82. I hit the deer square on, at approximately 75 mph about ½ mile from the turnoff to the community college between Carbondale and Glenwood. The irony of it is that I barely saw the deer at all before he jumped into my windshield, yet I can, to this day, see a still-frame of his eye staring me in the face a millisecond from its demise. A look of true fear—and that inevitable, "Oh Shit" moment we all dread.

In a split second The Juice became temporarily nicknamed "The Deer Jump." I'm told that the deer flew almost straight up approximately 300 feet or so and landed in what appeared to be nothing more than a bag of skin and bones, flopping like a ragdoll. The deer's hind legs hit my driver's side window, while the core of its body smashed the windshield and roof of the car. As the roof was crushed down and resting on my white knuckles holding the wheel, the shattered glass from the side window had shredded not only the side of my face but the seatbelt as well. I'll always remember the full can of Pepsi sitting wedged in the front seat with a glass shard that had penetrated the entire can like a bullet, both sides, and spilled the contents across the rest of the car.

I remember gripping the steering wheel, bleeding, and screaming at the top of my lungs, for what seemed like 2 or 3 total seconds. In reality, it was approximately 1 minute. I heard a voice. I looked right to see a somewhat shaken woman standing next to my now-stopped car, staring at me, and asking me something at the same time. I stopped screaming and realized that not only was I alive, but that I had managed to stop the car and remain in the same lane. That—and I was covered in deer urine and blood. It seems that when the deer's legs nearly kicked me in the face from the driver's side window, the impact had squeezed out the contents of the animal's bladder.

As luck would have it, a co-worker was a few cars behind me. He helped me move the car to the side of the road and drove me to the hospital. That and he told my boss I might be a little "late." I remember saying, "I'm glad the woman in the pink car was okay."

Jay, my co-worker, questioned me. "What 'pink' car?"

My Reply: "The pink car right behind me." At about that time, he realized what car I was talking about, and I realized the car was pink due to being coated in a nice shade of red—from my friend the deer. It was a white Toyota sedan, just prior to the accident.

Eventually, my wounds healed and despite a few glass shards working their way to the surface over the years, the memory faded, and the shock mellowed.

Now, The Juice had a bit of a rougher recovery. The car sat on the side of the road, along with the deer, for weeks. When it was finally towed to the repair shop, it had truly earned the nickname "The Deer Jump." The roof line was flush with the hood. The car resembled a ramp.

I have met many people over the years whose cars were marked "totaled" after a small fender bender, or maybe a hail storm. If the value of the car's replacement is more than the potential repairs, or if the integrity of the frame is compromised, the insurance company cuts a check for the bluebook value. But if this was truly the case, I must have been driving a Maserati.

Again, the insurance company deemed it recoverable, and The Juice spent a few months more in the same body shop. The advice from my mom, "Get rid of it! That car is cursed," was solid, yet I had little money to get a different vehicle.

A mere matter of days after I got the car back from the shop, and before the insurance checks had cleared the bank, wreck #4 happened and I was on the phone yet again with my insurance agent, by this time on a first name basis.

"You can't be serious?!? What was it this time?" John exclaimed with a hint of sarcasm in his voice.

"Cows, John. Cows," was my defeated response.

Despite months of driving back and forth to Fort Collins on weekends to work on an animation project, and the daily commute which, as previously noted, was undeniably treacherous, the question "what else could possibly happen," could be answered with one word. Cows. Cows happened.

During one of the few weekends I spent at home, driving back to Carbondale from Redstone one day, a local ranch was running cattle along Hwy 133. I was one of the lucky drivers who were forced to stop so the stampede could make its way past a small bridge. Of course, my car was on the bridge.

The cows began to bottleneck and surround my small car. I stared with terror through the windshield and new side window as cows began to rock my vehicle, bellowing and surging ahead. I was in the middle of the stampede.

Small dogs surrounded the cows as the ranch hands on horseback whistled commands in an attempt to control the herd. I watched in horror as my side mirrors broke off and were scraped along the sides of my car, pressed tightly between the fresh paint job and cows' behinds. Then, a rather large cow suddenly reared back and put its front hooves on my hood.

I don't know a lot about livestock or animal behavior in a herd mentality, but it was pretty obvious to me that if that cow decided to walk over my car, others would follow, and that the roof surely would not be able to hold the weight. I quickly assumed the fetal position in the front seat and waited it out until the car stopped rocking. Luckily the cows stayed to the side and didn't go over the roof. After a few seconds, I looked out the rear-view window and saw that the cows were now dispersing into the range land. I got out and inspected the damage.

A single ranch hand was following up the cows. I screamed out, "Hey!!!!" She turned in her saddle to look at me. "What about my car?!?" I yelled.

She yelled back, "Call the (unintelligible) Ranch." Then she spouted a phone number, which I immediately forgot, and rode off into the sunset. Literally.

Cars slowly drove around me as I searched for a pen and paper. I finally gave up and drove home.

Aside from the "hopelessly marred" paint job, my missing mirrors in crushed-up pieces, and a mix of cow dung and dents on the actual metal panels on the car, there was a single, perfect impression of the hoof of a cow in the middle of my hood.

About a year later, I'd moved to Fort Collins and begun working for the newspaper there, tasked with creating and maintaining an online presence. It seemed that this whole "internet thing" might actually become something. With a real paycheck and a steady income, I could afford a better car. I traded The Juice and finally closed the book on that woe-begotten car.

They say, "The best two days in a person's life are the day you buy your boat, and the day you sell your boat." While The Juice was not a boat, the day I sold it was a pretty good day, a damned good day indeed.

NAKED
BRUNCH

STANDING IN LINE AT A LOCAL coffee shop recently, I spied a 1959 edition of Allen Ginsberg's "Howl." It spawned a delightful memory.

At the time of my recollection, my interest in the Beatnik writers had started to wane. The escapades and liaisons of the often prurient and crass group of authors were intriguing to my innocent, onlooker perspective at that earlier period of my life.

I had developed a taste for Kerouac's adventures in his first two, and most famous works, "On the Road" and the "Dharma Bums." I had begun to read, and subsequently collect signed versions of all three authors.

Their lore outside of their novels was legendary. From the "William Tell" incident to drug use to jazz and trysts of all imaginable combinations, the authors were seminal in culture from the 1950s to the present day. The free love of the 1960s, for instance, would not have been possible were it not for these authors' brazen affronts to authority, or to Puritan ideals on sexuality and "polite society" in general. In fact, "Howl" was litigated on "obscenity" charges and further cemented America's First Amendment rights, the pillar of free speech, when the case was overturned.

Throughout the years, my mom would often tell us that she was related to Ivy Ledbetter Lee, the publicist, and personal public relations handler for the Rockefeller family. In researching facts about the key three authors of the "beats": Kerouac, Burroughs, and Ginsberg, there was mention that Burroughs was also related to Ivy Lee. When I pieced together the connection within her lineage, I could not contain my excitement. In conversation with Mom later that day, I mentioned it and received a slightly disinterested, cursory "Huh. How about that," I thought, "I need to do something about that." This man was a legend, and he even sorta looked like my grandpa.

It was 1992, with the release on VHS of *Naked Lunch*, the movie adaptation of the book by William S. Burroughs, I rented a copy from the neighborhood video store. I had good intentions of impressing my mom by showcasing the talents and notoriety of a famous member of her extended family.

Like many old-timer Aspenites, we had moved "downvalley". Although by this time, my brother, sister, and I had moved away for college, Carbondale was for our family a home away from home—just like the other neighboring communities were to other families who did not want to completely leave the valley but decided to leave Aspen proper. I was living at home temporarily, while back from CSU.

I had a handful of small jobs while in town, one of which was as part-time cashier at Mr. C's liquor store, which was next to the supermarket, and a mere quarter mile from mom's house. As such, my reliable transportation was my handy mountain bike, which was fitted with screws in the tires during winter commutes for better traction. The only drawback was carrying items that wouldn't fit in my old school backpack. After nearly dropping the tape from my handlebars, I rode home with it, a six-pack of beer, and a new book I'd purchased from a used bookstore on Main Street, Carbondale. Carefully avoiding potholes, curbs, and ice, the trek was short but not done without considerable effort.

Back at home, Mom was sitting in her reading chair at her spot by the old clawfoot, oak dining table we brought from the house on Eastwood Road in Aspen. There were the customary items one would normally see adorning her on either side. A newspaper opened to the crossword puzzle, a stack of books she had recently read, her cup of tea, and her "no smoking" ashtray, filled with butts. "Smokin' Joan" was habitual in her rituals.

Excitedly, I told her I had rented *Naked Lunch*, had a short conversation with her about her famous relative, and asked if she wanted to watch it with me. She politely declined, only to focus intently on the last few squares of the crossword.

The house in Carbondale is a tri-level, with the kitchen and dining room on the middle floor. The staircase to the upper level was open and provided an airy, high ceiling which allowed you to view the kitchen downstairs from above. As such, little sound escaped the attention of someone in either room.

I trudged upstairs to watch the movie on the upstairs TV and settled in the lazy boy for a two-hour escape into the Hollywood machinations of a William S. Burroughs hallucination. Not to critique the movie, suffice it to say, it is an abridged snapshot into the drug-addled mind of a privileged lunatic—a Kafkaesque, B-grade movie that tried its best to adapt a nearly unadaptable novel. With that being said, it did have its moments.

As the movie droned on, and it *is* a weird movie, I could only imagine what my mom was thinking downstairs. It was nearly impossible for her not to hear snippets of the film. She must have been shaking her head listening to the dialogue.

Fig C: From the WEIRD side of the family.

About halfway through the movie, a somewhat quiet scene came up, and in narrative form, Burroughs said the following:

"A curse. Been in our family for generations. The Lees have always been perverts ... I would have destroyed myself—But a wise old queen—Bobo, we called her—taught me that I had a duty ... to live and to bear my burden proudly for all to see. Poor Bobo came to a sticky end. He was riding in the Duc de Ventre's Hispano-Suiza ... when his falling hemorrhoids blew out of the car ... and wrapped around the rear wheel. He was completely gutted, leaving an empty shell ... sitting there on the giraffe-skin upholstery. Even the eyes and the brain went ... with a horrible 'schlupping' sound. The duke says he will carry that ghastly schlup with him to his mausoleum."

Just then, Mom's voice boomed up from the lower level, so I paused the movie only to hear:

"HE'S NO RELATION OF MINE!!!" and then quietly, "they were always the WEIRD side of the family."

After my boisterous guffaw, and a slightly audible chuckle from Mom, I resumed the movie at a reduced volume. And never brought it up again.

SKIS

LIKE MANY OF OUR FRIENDS and classmates growing up, my siblings and I were virtually brought up on skis. Again, it was as if we were born to ski.

Christmas was always a special time. And more so when we knew we'd be getting new skis. My dad owned a ski shop, and as such we were all but guaranteed to get the latest skis that fit us as we grew taller each year. Additionally, he had worked out deals each year with Mr. Tribolet, who owned the Hobby Shop toy store to ensure his kids got new skis and we got cool toys too.

Some of my earliest memories were of visits from overly inebriated Santas carrying pillowcases full of ski gear and the newest toys. Together with the Mencimers, we would stare wide-eyed as Santa would make his rounds. Assuredly Santa was one of Dad's friends, much to Mom's chagrin.

Skiing was such a large part of our lives there were times I would simply opt-out if the weather wasn't ideal. I began to drift away from my passion for the slopes. In short, skiing for us was just "what you do." However, a new pair of skis was *always* worth more than gold. Just before I moved to Fort Collins, I received the new Lange skis at Christmas. I was able to ski them only a few times before the sport became essentially out of reach for me in my pastime.

Fast forward to 2003, the day before we moved to Georgia, was literally and figuratively the end of an era for me.

It was mid-winter, and we had packed all our earthly belongings into a Ryder moving truck bound for the East Coast.

I had been living in Fort Collins for the past four years, had recently married my wife, and bought my first home from some great friends. As fate would have it, my wife and I had just been hired by the *Athens Banner-Herald* newspaper and were ready for our new adventure.

For everything we weren't taking with us, there were yard sales, schlock-a-archons, donations, and eventually trash. However, there was one item I really didn't want to part with but would have absolutely no need for in the new climate.

My skis were nearly new. However, when I got them, I had already almost totally quit skiing. But they were glorious. By far the nicest and best skis I had ever had. They were 205 cm tall, which was perfect for my height and stood as a badge of honor for my so-called prowess as a skier.

After asking around and placing a classified ad to sell them, there were no takers. By this time "parabolics" were in style and long skis had become a thing of the past. I asked everyone I knew if they wanted them. But still no takers. It reminded me of the old wooden skis we'd see around town—mostly decorations for nostalgic purposes. My beautiful, shiny new skis were relegated to the annals of days gone by.

In a last-ditch effort, I sharpied a slab of cardboard and hung it from the skis, and placed them in a snowbank at the end of my driveway, where they would sit untouched, and marked "Free" for nearly a week.

After having packed the last of anything we thought was *something*, we set the alarm for early in the morning and went to bed. Before the clock could go off, however, I was awakened by the sounds of the trash truck crushing something, grinding up metal, and snapping wood.

It seemed someone took my skis after all.

The day itself was a blur, but we scurried to finish cleaning the home before the realtor showed up and to corral our three beloved pets into the car before it started snowing. Three cats, 4,000 lbs. of schlock mart crap, furniture, skateboards, and clothes weighed down the moving truck, along with our fans, computers, and expired spices. We took the plunge and made the

Illustration by Chris Pomeroy.

trek. My wife took the car, and I drove the truck as we took off for our brand-new life chapter. We made it barely five miles due to the weather, and we ended up staying with Angie, an old Aspen friend who lived in Fort Collins. Having slept, and with a small clearing in the weather, we left the next day.

Driving into the mountains has the uncanny power to take one's breath away. Driving out of them can have the same effect, but for the opposite reason. Bereft of the majestic views and scenery, driving east on I-70 is somewhat anticlimactic. In this case, more so as the sky grew darker, and the snow made it harder to see in front of us. We only made it a few hours before deciding we needed to stop for the night.

We stayed in a motel in Russell, Kansas. Though we had barely made it over the border from Colorado, we were on our way but needed a safe place to recharge. After smuggling the cats into the hotel room bathroom, and breathing a few deep breaths from exhaustion, we slept hard with the hopes of reinitiating our journey, first thing in the morning.

Our new adventure was just starting. No more mountains, no more snow. By tomorrow, we would be well on our way to a new reality. The fate of my skis, as did my ambition to use them, faded in the rear-view mirror until sadly, they were out of sight for good.

I began thinking about life in Colorado, of the years growing up in the mountains, the people, my family, my friends. And thoughts of my youth spent skiing, sledding, and skitching as fast as humanly possible, fishing, hunting, golf, racquetball, tennis, riding bikes, ice skating with celebrities' kids at the Ice Garden, exploring old mine shafts, jumping on giant, loose boulders up Independence Pass, and spending afternoons up to my neck in the deepest parts of the rivers. Past visions of jumping the gaps between building rooftops, climbing the water towers, skidding to stop on a minibike with only shoes for breaks, pole vaulting down the summer mountain with bamboo slalom gates, and staring into the night sky with friends on cheap beer and flawed philosophical meanderings, became simple thoughts and memories of good times, and times I probably shouldn't have survived.

The next day, storms continued. About 30 miles outside of Russell, on the Dwight D. Eisenhower Interstate, I drove the moving truck cautiously across the black-iced roads of middle Kansas, going east towards Georgia at approximately 25 mph. Conditions were worse than bad. Yet, through the snow flurries and icy wind, I spotted a strange road sign. Eyes squinted and slowly coming into view, the sign indeed said what I thought it had. "Last chance … turn now for the Garden of Eden."

Had it all been real? It literally seemed like a lifetime ago.

Putting curiosity aside, and focusing instead on the road that lay ahead, now it was way too late to stop or to turn back.

Instead, I directed my eyes back on the road, and just kept on going.

ACKNOWLEDGMENTS

Special thanks to all who helped make this possible:

Joan Pomeroy, Jim Pomeroy, Courtney Alford Pomeroy for endless amounts of patience, Katie Pomeroy, Jim Pomeroy and Libette Mathias for helping me remember, George Burson, Bland Nesbit, Cameron Burns for keeping me honest (for the most part), Andy Collen, and of course, Amy Collen whose efforts made my portion more readable. Also, to Adriana Oberto, who came to Aspen as an exchange student in the 80s, for pulling together and writing the feature on the Upham Bigelows in Rome, for GiroInfoto magazine. I would also like to posthumously thank Nick DeWolf for his donation of several PMC 80 computers to the school. Were it not for his generosity and vision, I might not be where I am today, in a successful career using a technology that is now solidly embedded into the fabric of everyday life. I feel we had a leg up on the competition due to his gift and I am grateful.

With apologies to the many friends who were not mentioned in my stories. Perhaps some day there will be a follow-up.

And with gratitude to whom this material was written to begin with: My boys, Nicolas and Zachary, thank you.

SUGGESTED READING

- *The Days of Stein and Roses* by Martie Sterling
- *Aspen, the Quiet Years* by Gaylord T. Guenin and Kathleen Krieger Daily
- *Whiteout, Lost in Aspen* by Ted Conover
- *Don't Get Mad, Get Even* by Jack Brendlinger
- *Aspen Unstrung* by Sandy Munro
- *Ode to Mustard* by Barry Smith, illustrated by Chris Pomeroy
- *Shoes of Kilimanjaro* by Cameron Burns
- *Aspen: Then and Now: Reflections of a Native* by Tony Vagneur
- *Compass American Guides: Colorado* by John Klusmire
- *Generation of Swine* by Hunter S. Thompson
- *Stories I Tell Myself: Growing Up with Hunter S. Thompson* by Juan Thompson
- *The Magic of Conflict* by Tom Crum

CAST: Tom Alpern, David Burson, Jenny Carlini, Sam ... ...ularz, Mark Mitchell, Heidi Roupp, Hina Schramel, Lisa Shuldener, Kimberly ... Jamie Cotton, Nathalie Gerschel, Brian Kelcher, Beth MacCarthy ... ...ahn, Piper Stapleton, Dasha Stapleton, and Gab...

In recognition of ... affixed seal

Aspen

DRAMA

"... Wendy Las...

MARCH 15, 16, 17, 1984.

Under Milkwood

Dylan Thoma...

ASPEN COMMUNITY THEATRE
NOVEMBER, 1983

KISS ME KATE

Aspen Community School presents

eugene o'...
"Desire Un...

...RESE... OF ...
THE District...
HELD ON Janua...
EVENT: Drama
Martin ... DIRE...

Aspen Community Theatre presents

AS YOU LIKE IT

CONTRIBUTOR:
DEAN JACKSON

IN ANOTHER LIFE, Dean Jackson was a professional actor, voice-over artist, and puppeteer. While living the life of a starving artist in New York City was an adventure, that life transitioned into a more traditional career once he got married and discovered that Ramen was not a lifestyle choice.

Dean and his lovely wife, Kyra, now live in the San Francisco Bay Area. He has managed high-rise buildings and since applying those skills to create the project management division of a local community management company, is the point-person for managing their team and a multitude of community living challenges. He wrote for an industry magazine for sixteen years, and wrote the travel blog, "So I Married a Tour Guide." He has begun dabbling in voice work and acting once again.

In their spare time, Dean and Kyra enjoy traveling, gardening, reading, listening to Jazz, and slow dancing in the kitchen.

DEDICATION

I dedicate this book to my parents,
I love you with all my heart.

I also dedicate this book
to the memory of my grandparents,
Ana and Norman Shapiro,
my uncle (brother) Marc Shapiro,
and to Meyer Ruthenberg.

NEW JERSEY

MY COLORADO STORY started in New Jersey. I was born to a single teenage mother at St. Barnabas Hospital, Livingston NJ in the Spring of 1968. I was at least a month premature, weighed fewer than three pounds, and had a cleft lip and palate. Fortunately, St. Barnabas had, and still has, one of the premier cleft palate centers in the country, and I received (many) state-of-the-art surgeries there as a child, and again as a college student.

My mother unexpectedly got pregnant with her boyfriend at the time, Stuart. When he offered to take care of me and her, she decided against it. From as early as I can remember, my mother would show me pictures of Stu and tell me about him. She let me know that, if I ever wanted to meet him, she would facilitate the meeting. The fact that he offered to do right by us, and that he was a class act, made me interested in eventually meeting him.

Instead of staying with Stu, my mother married her high school boyfriend, Doug. The marriage was short-lived. Because he was abusive to her, and even hit my grandmother, my mother made the decision to leave him before I was born and save me from violence. I appreciate the bravery that it took for her to willingly be on her own with a special needs child, while still in her teens. She did it to protect me, herself, and her family. By the time I was two years old, my mother had met and moved in with a young, bearded man with hair down to the middle of his back. He would end up raising me as his son and eventually adopted me.

My father-to-be worked for NYC Mayor John Lindsey, while my mom worked as a hairstylist. During this period my folks had two sets of friends who had kids around my age. Kathy, my mother's childhood friend, had a son named Tommy and a daughter named Kim. Tony and Linda, our neighbors, had daughters Diana and Lori. I had a built-in set of playmates. My earliest memories involve exploring the woods with Tommy while tolerating his younger sister, or playing in the sprinklers with Diana while tolerating her younger sister. When Tony and Linda decided to move to Colorado's Roaring Fork Valley around 1975 my parents soon decided to uproot us and move there as well. My mom and I arrived several weeks before my father, who had scheduled a sabbatical from the mayor's office. It wasn't long before Kathy, her boyfriend Doug and Tommy and Kim followed in their Airstream. It was a bit like a prolonged caravan.

Upon arriving in the Roaring Fork Valley, in the Summer of 1975, my mom and I went to stay with Tony, Linda, Diana and Lori at Wingo Junction Ranch, near the small town of Basalt. The ranch had a big house, where the folks in charge stayed, while we stayed in one of the trailers designated for the workers. During the days us kids would explore. We found caves in the nearby hills, antique cars and trucks, fruit trees, and a wide variety of animals. It being summer vacation, and me not yet being enrolled in school, gave us the freedom to just be kids. We played volleyball, took care of a litter of puppies, and ate big bowls of cereal from boxes festooned with Independence Day decorations, containing flags and other patriotic items. We marched around waving our flags and called the game the 1776 School.

I slept in the trailer's living room, on a foldout bed. This was a simple space, off of the kitchen, with decorative tapestries hanging from the ceiling. There were always mice around, and it was not unusual to hear the snap of a mousetrap at mealtime. One night the mice came inside, by the hundreds. I have no idea how they got there, but they ran all over the living room, up my blanket, and over me—I freaked out. I have no memory of how this resolved itself, but to this day I am repulsed by mice.

I was fortunate to have parents who loved classic rock music, which at the time was simply called rock music. I listened to it with them. I was introduced to The Beatles (still an obsession today), The Doors, The Band, and The Rolling Stones, to name a few. While we were at Wingo Junction Ranch, the Stones were on tour. They stopped in Fort Collins (July 20, 1975) My mother decided to go to the concert, with me in tow. Though I'm told that I went to concerts earlier than this, this is the first one I have any memories of. Those memories, while including Mick Jagger doing his rooster thing on stage, are mostly of how we got to the concert. Having no car, we hitchhiked to the show and back. This was a several-hour journey, and it took several different vehicles to get there. I remember sitting in the back of a Ford Bronco, of the same vintage as me, rolling over unpaved roads, to a small ramshackle cabin. These strangers invited us inside to rest, have a snack, and get my mother fortified with a (then) illegal substance. I don't remember how we got to the show, but I do remember the ride back towards our temporary home in a Winnebago. Unfortunately, my mom left the Stones LP she had purchased in the camper. I hope those fine folks enjoyed it.

Volleyball at Wingo Junction

A couple of months later my father arrived, having driven across country in our 1974 Audi Fox. Though ostensibly on a sabbatical, he was given an ultimatum by my mother. She was staying in Colorado, he could stay or he could return to the East Coast without us. I'm told that it nearly went the other way, but he ultimately decided to stay. With his arrival, the little trailer at Wingo Junction became too crowded. We now had a car, and we rambled on down the road a bit to an area called Old Snowmass. At the foot of the road up to Old Snowmass there was a Conoco station on one side of the two-lane Highway 82, and a motel, consisting of one-room log cabins on the other. The innkeepers allowed us to stay in their cabin while they were away, my parents having befriended them at the ranch.

Old Snowmass was a quaint little town, fairly unknown, but near enough to its more famous Pitkin County sibling, Aspen, Colorado, to elicit thoughts of a winter wonderland. That winter the names of two skiers, Spider Sabisch and Franz Klammer were all over the local news whenever I turned on the radio, the former for his tragic death earlier in the year, and the latter for the skills he showed at that year's World Cup.

I lived with my parents, in a tiny one-room log cabin, which was part of a motel lodge. We borrowed this room from friends and made our home there as the recipients of their generosity. We had a small table, a hot plate, two chairs, a bed, a radio, and a space heater. When it was my bedtime, my parents unfolded an Army surplus cot. I'd like to think of this cabin as cozy and romanticize it in my memory, but in retrospect it was utilitarian. The warmth of the cabin came from the space heater, the radiator, and my family.

Each evening we would gather around the radio and listen to a vintage radio show which chronicled the adventures of the *Cinnamon Bear* as he made his way to the North Pole to meet Santa Claus. At dinner time we listened together to tales of narrow escapes, of hot-air balloon journeys, and evil curmudgeons. We anticipated each evening, and the ways in which the Christmas spirit would prevail against overwhelming odds as the innocent hero made his way to meet Santa. He was on a quest to prove that Christmas is important, and the generous spirit is necessary for everyone. This program was not *A Christmas Carol*; it was a somewhat amateur, endeavor, but an endeavor that stripped off any pretense about the holidays. Each evening I learned that it was important to give, and that family was as valuable as any gift could ever be.

The snow enveloped the landscape around our cabin, the vista in certain areas only broken by a wooden fence and the footprints of small animals. I would take morning walks (not too far from my parents' eyes), cherishing the chance to follow the animal tracks and try to mimic the tracks with my own small feet. Bundled in my parka, I took full advantage of the idyllic and unmarred area, peacefully unaware of the financial hardships facing my young parents.

I was never hungry, I was always clothed, and we were together. Having no television, we all looked forward to those evenings around the radio. Having no cartoons, I had those Christmas journeys of the imagination. Having little money, we had each other. I don't know why I didn't expect a gift that Christmas; the thought just didn't seem important enough to occupy me for any length of time. The only time that I recall thinking about gifts was when I asked my parents how Santa Claus could get into our cabin if we didn't have a fireplace or a chimney. I was relieved when my father told me that he could make his way into a room through the radiator. Apparently, any heating source would do. Not having that detail to worry about, I went about my business and didn't focus on toys.

I will never forget waking up in that chilly cabin on Christmas morning. I could see my breath in front of me and, unlike most children, I was awake after my parents (throughout my life this pattern has often reasserted itself). My parents were waiting with an unexpected gift. Seeing the gadgets kids can get for Christmas nowadays, gadgets and games that rival the arcades of my youth, I sometimes think that it might have been nice to have had some of those things as a child. I have only to think back on that early Christmas and those envious thoughts are vanquished. That morning I received a single Matchbox car and a spring-loaded contraption that would launch it across the floor to bounce off of walls, and my parents' feet. To this day that is my most cherished Christmas gift. It came wrapped in family. I was able to share it with my friend, the Cinnamon Bear, who taught me a life-long lesson: obstacles are made to be overcome, curmudgeons are made to be transformed, and money only makes the gift bigger. The heart has to learn to grow on its own.

OLD SNOWMASS

OUR SHORT STAY AT THE MOTEL ended when we moved into a tiny two room apartment which was attached to a larger rustic house in Old Snowmass. This house was at the top of a long dirt driveway, about two or three miles up the hill from the Conoco station on Hwy 82. There was a smattering of houses up and down Old Snowmass Road, and at least one trailer park. The house was close to a mountain stream, and there was a teepee frame on the property. This place was an adventure waiting to happen, so our small accommodations didn't really phase me, I was outside more often than in.

My young parents, having a child who needed periodic surgeries, and who had low-paying jobs, registered for welfare and had my medical needs met through a program called "Handicapped Children." This care included orthodontics, which continued through college, surgeries to repair the cleft palate and lip, to improve my crooked nose, and other items. The surgeries started months after I was born premature. I spent the first few months in an incubator, and the surgeries started shortly after my mother brought me home, and they continued into adulthood (most recently six months ago). When welfare visits happened, my mom would send me out of the house, and I would visit Noah at the Shores' solar house. This was one of the early solar homes in the Aspen area and built by Ron Shore. I was always welcome to come over and play in their VERY open floor-plan home. The entrance opened onto a large ground-floor room with a kitchen and living area. The second level consisted of a catwalk overlooking the ground floor room. The second level included the sleeping areas and the bathroom, which was entirely unenclosed. The toilet was pretty much in the center of the catwalk and looked straight out over the living room to a spectacular mountain view. Having grown up as a hippy kid and seen communes this was, perhaps, not as jarring to me as it should have been. I will say that the view moved me, more than once.

Eventually, we moved into the larger part of the Old Snowmass house. We had a large kitchen, a large living room and I had my own private bedroom. This added space supplied room for some pets. George, the hermit crab, lived in a terrarium in the living room, Cosmic Cat and I were inseparable, and Buddy the rabbit had lived at first in a crate, and then outside around and under our house. He and Cosmic actually got along well. My parents were by this time both working at a disco called The Paragon, 30+ miles away in Aspen. They worked into the wee hours, leaving me as a latchkey kid. From the late afternoon until bed time I had the place to myself. This time was often spent playing with the pets or watching TV. I was fond of *Three's Company*, and *Happy Days*, and I would watch *Dark Shadows* until the National Anthem played and the color bars came on the screen.

I wasn't alone in the house when my parents were at work. Early on in our Old Snowmass residency, my parents took me to a house a short distance away where the family cat had just had a large litter of kittens. A passel of tiny striped kittens were falling all over each other, playing in the grass. I was distracted from the entertainment by a buff-colored puff of fur and determination. This kitten, larger than the others, without stripes, and with different coloring, didn't appear to be a part of the same litter, though we were assured that he was. While his brothers and sister were all youthful play and energy, he was stillness. A grasshopper was bouncing its way obliviously around the lawn and the kitten carefully watched it, eyes moving but body immobile, until he struck with deadly accuracy and caught the grasshopper.

I pointed to the predator and said, "I want that one." My parents had to convince the family to part with the kitten that they had intended to keep, but he came home with us. Initially named Sam, I called him a cosmic cat, and the name stuck. Coz was my constant companion from then on.

Timothy lived down the road from us in a large house where he and his parents raised rabbits. I would often spend time there, watching Disney movies like *The Computer Wore Tennis Shoes*. Tim and I would go frogging at a nearby pond and fish for trout in the creek behind his house. I became fascinated by the family's rabbits, which unbeknownst to me were being raised for food. I wanted another pet and convinced Tim's family to part with one. Tim and I built a chicken wire coop, and I took Buddy the rabbit home. He soon outgrew the coop and my parents let him out and he proceeded to live under the house and frequently played with Cosmic, who could have chosen to make him a meal rather than a friend. My trio of pets was rounded out by George, the hermit crab, who happily lived in a terrarium and whom I could watch tunneling around for hours. One day Buddy disappeared. To my dismay, I was told that he had run away. It wasn't until nearly twenty years later that my mom slipped and mentioned that my dad had accidentally backed over Buddy when getting ready to drive to work. I like to think that, having spared him from the dinner table, he had a good if short life.

My parents didn't always leave me at home. A friend had an apartment above The Paragon and sometimes I would be deposited there for the evening to snack and watch TV while my parents worked downstairs. In August of 1978 it was in this apartment that I: 1) learned who Elvis was and 2) learned that he had died. When my parents brought me to The Paragon I would sometimes eat at the bar as my mother set up. They served escargots, so I would usually order a "snail sandwich" and a shot of coke. Later, when we moved into Aspen, I would continue to grab meals at The Paragon, and later at Taka Sushi, where my father would eventually work as a bartender.

Disco Mom!

The Paragon was a cavernous space, with several bars and a large dance floor. My mom had started as a cocktail waitress and quickly became a bartender, with a sideline teaching The Hustle to would-be disco divas. She was in charge of a small bar at the far end of the room, next to the dance floor, and the door to the alley. This is where I would sit for my snail sandwiches. It was a cozy space with five or six bar stools, and intimate enough to make one forget the much larger and crowded areas around it. Perhaps this is why well-known people tended to gravitate to the small bar and my mom. She was often unimpressed with celebrity. Later, when selling clothing at Tom Mix, which would later become Curious George's Collectables, Jack Nicholson came in and the sales staff swarmed around him. Mom stayed back, apparently uninterested, and he gravitated towards her, and she made the sale. It was an unspoken rule amongst locals that famous folks were to be treated well, but not fawned over, the sales staff broke that rule, and my mother didn't, BINGO! Teddy Kennedy took up residence at the bar and engaged my mother in conversation while downing glass after glass of expensive champagne. She describes him as charming and inebriated. He was, however, civic-minded. Having polished off the bottle he exited to the alley and proceeded to recite the Gettysburg Address at the top of his lungs. He didn't miss a word.

Christmas Eve, my father, his childhood friend, and our house guest, Steven, my mother, and I were in our Audi. Having just picked up my mom after her bartending shift, it was about 2 a.m. and bitterly cold. Driving the thirty or so miles between Aspen and Old Snowmass was a tricky thing even during the daytime. The two-lane Hwy 82 was twisty and often had a mountain on one side and a sheer cliff or steep hillside on the other. One had to pay attention to avoid hitting a speeding vehicle head-on, crashing into the mountain, or going over the cliff, which in some places would have resulted in a drop of hundreds of feet. In the back seat, I dozed a bit but was awakened by the sensation of a dizzying spin. From my perspective, I could see through the windshield the dim, outlines of mountain / trees / mountain / trees / mountain / trees / and then stars—then trees on either side as the black ice we'd spun out on slid us *over* the side of the road and we made a steep backwards descent towards the river.

I was yelling, "What's happening? What's happening?!" Then we abruptly *stopped*, having hit a tree or boulder, just feet from the icy Roaring Fork River. After a stunned silence, everyone was all-at-once asking if I was okay. Thankfully none of us was injured, but we were at the bottom of a steep incline, at 2 a.m., in 10-degrees below zero weather.

We slowly climbed the hill, leaving the car and a trunk full of Christmas gifts to be dealt with at another time, and set off walking towards home. We flagged down one of the rare cars on the road at that hour and were dropped off at the Conoco station at the base of Old Snowmass Road. We had a couple of miles to walk before getting home. We began our trek, ill-prepared for the cold, and

I was soon crying in pain while being alternately carried by each of the adults. About halfway between the highway and home was a trailer where a friend, Leslie lived with her daughter Sophie. My father led us there, but we found the trailer empty, with Leslie and Sophie away. Al broke into the trailer and lit a fire to thaw us out. We stayed for an hour or so and were able to make it the rest of the way home, a bit of breaking and entering now on our resumes. Remarkably the 1974 Audi survived the accident, and I inherited it a few years later.

SCHOOL DAYS

THE CLOSEST TOWN TO US was still Basalt, and that's where my parents registered me for the second grade, in Ms. Evans' class. Basalt was a tiny, charming town, and the school was small but surprisingly modern. I'll never forget the day that my parents took me to register for school. Basalt was a community comprised of working-class and farming/ranching families. My father had hair down to the middle of his back and dressed very much like he walked out of Woodstock (and he had been there). I had white-blonde hair down to my shoulders. It would be an understatement to say that our young family appeared a bit out of place in a town where cowboy hats and caps with the CAT logo printed on them were the norm. As we walked the sidewalk through the large courtyard/play area, through a valley of shoveled snow, a chorus of children's voices could be heard. "A hippy! Another hippy! Look at the hippies!"

It was at the Basalt School that I met one of my first friends in the area. Dmitri was another long-haired kid with a cleft palate, and he looked as out of place as I did at the school. He enjoyed the school more than I did, however. I was painfully shy, very small, different, and a good target for bullies. While the other kids would go sledding at lunchtime, I would hang back in the lunch building (mind you, not a lunch room, a building). With the exception of Dmitri, I don't recall making any other friends there. It wasn't misery all the time, but it wasn't joy either. Ms. Evans didn't even know where I belonged. Though she participated in my parent's interview, and I was small for my age, she consistently thought that I was an older kid who was kept back in her class. She also insisted that my name was spelled Deen and that I kept spelling it incorrectly. When I left that school, after the second grade, the only thing I kept was my friendship with Dmitri.

It turns out Dmitri and I were practically neighbors in Old Snowmass! At least we were walking distance from each other if I didn't mind walking through the woods. He and his mother, and her sometimes boyfriend, lived in a duplex on the other side of a large shale hill (or a short shale mountain). He and I would play on that hill, or in the woods around it, between his house and mine, and I would walk around the hill and through the woods to his house every Saturday morning for cartoons. We were fans of the *Super Friends*, *Grape Ape*, and *Magilla Gorilla*. Dmitri and I didn't want to miss a second of any show, so I would often bundle up and make the trek as the sun was rising. It was on one of these mornings that I found myself of interest to a mountain lion. I was walking around the shale hill, on a relatively narrow path with several outcroppings of rock above me, and thick trees to my right. I came around a bend and the rising sun glinted off of the cat's eyes, as they stared down at me. I knew that I was in danger, but for some reason, I didn't run. If I had run I have no doubt that the mountain lion would have given chase. Dmitri's house was close, so I continued to walk purposefully in the direction I was going, looking straight ahead, and walking directly under that rock outcropping. I didn't look back, and I made it in time for the *Wonder Twins*' powers to activate.

THE ASPEN COMMUNITY SCHOOL

Larger view of the Aspen Community School lookout tower with us kids up on the roof.

ONCE WE MOVED INTO the larger part of the Old Snowmass house, I made some more friends, and in 1976 my parents enrolled me in another school which changed my life. The Aspen Community School is a private school located in Woody Creek. At the time there were classes for kids from K–8. I was not part of the conversation that

*Aspen Community School lookout tower with us kids up on the roof.
For a larger, full-color version, scan the QR code above.*

precipitated this move, but I am so grateful that it happened. This school was not free. My parents, when working at the Paragon, and as housekeepers for a company called Vilcore, also worked at the school as janitors, cleaning bathrooms and more, to pay my tuition. I still experience the benefits of their sacrifice to this day.

From the third through the sixth grade (1976–1980) my school experience was as adventurous, and unique as they come. The school was housed in a quaint log building, Circa 1969, with a lookout tower, Circa the Middle Ages.

The teachers had more in common with the denizens of a commune than with the teachers at the Basalt School. Whereas Ms. Evans was at least in her 60s, focused heavily on cursive, and couldn't keep my name or age straight, the Community School staff were young and unconventional, they got to know students personally and encouraged them to ask questions, to explore nature, to read, and to immerse themselves in the arts. Many were hippies, many were artists, and to my memory, they were all supportive, creative, and kind. This school was a different world from the Basalt School. Long-haired hippy kids (and parents) were not gawked at, they were embraced … or in charge.

The school was unique, in that there was a heavy focus on theater, music, the arts, and nature. Subjects such as literature and math were taught at a very high level. Between grades three and six, I went from barely reading at all to reading *The Hardy Boys* to reading *The Grapes of Wrath* and *The Scarlet Letter*. During the same period, I learned about and wrote a paper on The Alhambra (the visiting of which became a bucket list item fulfilled in 2019). I had a math class in which we studied geometry and made three-dimensional paper and wax containers in order to measure liquid volume. John Katzenburger, math teacher extraordinaire, even had about half the school collaborate to build an early desktop computer, which took up a pretty large table. I don't remember much of what that computer could accomplish at the time, but I remember soldering the circuit boards, putting various items together, and the rush when the thing actually worked when we switched it on (I also nearly soldered an electrical outlet, so there's that too).

Wonderful teachers, such as Annie Teague, who allowed me to beat her at basketball on our first meeting when I was eight, was as sweet and nurturing to the younger kids as Rhett Harper was passionate about literature and grammar ("*When* is NOT spelled wene!"). Paul Lieblich, John Katzenburger, and Diane Burton rounded out the faculty that I can remember, though I am sure that there are some that I should be mentioning.

The architecture of the school and its grounds was a large part of the education to be had there. The log structure encouraged community learning and interaction between all ages of children and all of the teachers. Everybody knew if only at a distance, everybody else. At the very center of the school was a cement floored common area, with classrooms up a short series of steps, on either side, a stage, and a small gathering area, used alternately as a music room or arts/crafts area, at the far end of the building, opposite the entrance. The classrooms, in many cases, were open to the common area and the other classrooms, the kids gathered in the center common area or on the adjacent stage and steps, to eat lunch and socialize. The school "office" area sat at one end of the space. It made for a cacophony and a community.

The school grounds consisted of the main building, as well as some domes, one of which served as the gym, and another as a solar greenhouse, which we built using coffee cans, painted black and full of water, to gather the heat of the sun and supply warmth for the plants there. The neighboring property was owned by the father of one of my schoolmates, Juan Thompson. His father, Hunter Thompson, about whom Juan would write a wonderful book, would often fire guns on his property. It was not uncommon to be in class and to hear the crack of a rifle echoing off of the hills.

It was in that common area cacophony that I first met my dear friend Andy Collen. In my recollection, it was during one of those break times in which kids were playing, conversations were happening in surround sound, and some things could be easily missed. Andy and I met near the bulletin board. He was new to the school, though I hadn't been there long myself. Although he is a couple of years my senior I mistakenly thought he was younger. I went to him because he appeared to me to be alone and unsure of where to go. We struck up a short conversation, and then I got distracted, turned, and started talking to somebody else. When I turned back Andy was convulsing on the floor, as somebody

nearby asked "does he always do that?" I bent and said his name a few times, and when nothing changed I ran to a teacher for help. That moment was the first of many times, over forty-five years, that our lives have intersected and brought us to the friendship that we, and our wives, have today. As I write this I am sitting in Andy's living room with my wife, as she studies for her degree, and as he does something creative on the other side of the wall. I'm glad I could help.

Felicity (Flicka) Huffman on the cover of Aspen Magazine.

Though now in my mid-fifties, I can look back at those young years and see some of the most formative times of my life. My love of music was encouraged both at home and at school. At home, I listened to Lambert Hendricks and Ross, The Beatles, Lord Buckley, and Led Zeppelin. At school, we were introduced to Blue Grass music by local music guru Sandy Munro, founder of The Great Divide Music Store, cornerstone of the local music scene and local music historian (see his book *Aspen Unstrung*), and a wonderful influence on mini-me. Jimmy Ibbotson, of the Nitty Gritty Dirt Band, even stopped by with his guitar, to teach us the Kenny Loggins classic "Return to Pooh Corner." School camping trips, of which there were many, always included songs around the fire and kids did at least one musical theater show a year.

Sandy Munro's encore memoir, Aspen Unstrung (website) ©Sandy Munro

Early on at the Community School, I was one of the three stars of a silent movie which took place in the old west and may still have a home at the Aspen Historical Society. Notably, Felicity (Flicka) Huffman was also at the school and was in the film. That experience, and the other plays that I did there, were the beginning of my love for acting.

Silent movie cast. I'm the guy.

Silent movie cast photo. I'm in the front right row, kneeling.

The Community School encouraged a love of theater in its young students, and each year we did one drama and one musical. The musicals were the usual suspects, *Annie*, *Camelot*, *Oliver*, and others. The dramas were another matter entirely. I credit the Community School with fostering a love for theater which shaped much of my adulthood, but in retrospect, I think that we were thrown into the deep end a bit too early.

Paul Rubin, our neighbor in Old Snowmass, had built a log cabin with his wife Missy, which was very close to the home that we rented. Like the Shores' home just up the hill, their cabin was one of the early solar homes in the area and boasted a chemical toilet, and the hodgepodge architecture of the 70s self-built "close enough" Aspen homes of the era. (Close enough, nail it together.) Paul's son Joshua and I were friends and both students at The Community School. In the absence of a school bus, Paul was my ride to school, as he was the director of the school dramas. On winter days I would trudge through the snow to their cabin, Paul would scrape the ice off of a remarkably small section of the windshield of his old pickup, and, peering through the six-inch section of clear glass, he would drive us from Old Snowmass to Woody Creek and the larger log cabin that was our school.

When I was in third grade, a year before my first school play, I remember watching rehearsals for *A Streetcar Named Desire*. Paul was the director, and the actors were in grades four to eight. One of the stars was a very young Felicity Huffman, who had recently done her first ABC After School Special and was, as I mentioned, one of the stars of the silent film that we had done in 1976, she would go on to become one of the stars of *Desperate Housewives,* and an Oscar nominee. I had no frame of reference for age-appropriate theater, and I don't remember any of the parents sounding any alarms.

My first drama was *One Flew Over the Cuckoo's Nest*. I played Scanlon, Andy played a very convincing Martini. The show opened on March 11, 1978, my tenth birthday. Subsequently, under Paul's direction, I performed roles in *Blues for Mr. Charlie*, and *Desire Under the Elms*. When I exited the stage after

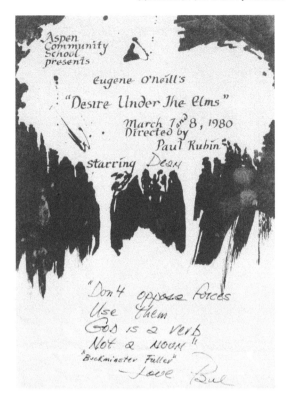

Aspen Community School presents

Eugene O'Neill's

"Desire Under The Elms"

March 7 & 8, 1980
Directed by
Paul Rubin

starring Dean

"Don't oppose forces
Use them
God is a verb
Not a noun"
"Buckminster Fuller"
— Love Paul

Blues for Mister
Charlie, ACS
1979 program.

Desire Under
the Elms, AHS
– The Aspen
Times article.

a big scene as Peter in Desire, in which I managed to get some laughs, Paul lifted me up into a bear hug and congratulated me on my performance. That moment, at 12 years old, was when I decided to pursue a career in acting. When the show closed Paul presented me with a poster from the show on which he wrote this quote from Buckminster Fuller, "Don't oppose forces, use them. God is a verb, not a noun." (Pictured above.) I took this advice to heart as I pursued a career in the arts.

Paul was a mercurial person, varying between explosive anger (never physical), introspection, encouragement, and what appeared to be depression. If there was ever an example of the tortured artist, at least to my rudimentary understanding, it was him. I believe that he had a deep desire to direct these plays with adult actors, but he only had us kids. Now, 44 years on, none of the shows that he chose for us youngsters would pass the PC test. I would never agree to have my 10-year-old explore the themes

One Flew Over the Cuckoo's Nest, 1978. Crazy kids. For a larger image, scan the QR code that follows..

of any of those plays, in retrospect though, I benefitted and learned a love of the theater. I sincerely hope that the other students were as fortunate as I was and that none were harmed. It's a tricky thing to think back on that time, as I have so much gratitude to Paul for what he taught me, and at the same time, I know that much of the material was not appropriate for our age group.

The Community School was a special and unique experience. I entered that school as a fearful and quiet kid. I did not know how to stand up for myself and I did not have any particular areas of interest. Several experiences, in addition to theater, supplied me a foundation upon which my confidence and joy grew. While theater brought me out of my shell, the camping and rafting trips helped me to learn to collaborate with other people, to enjoy cooking, and to love the outdoors. I am not exactly sure in what order these trips were taken, but several memories do stand out.

Larger view of the One Flew Over the Cuckoo's Nest cast photo.

We were always to have several things: A frame backpack, hiking boots, wool pants and socks, sweaters, parkas, a flashlight, a canteen, a pocket knife, and a mess kit. My gear was almost entirely Army surplus. We would generally leave from the school in an old school bus and arrive at our setting off destination anywhere from an hour to six hours later. There was a 10-day hike over Conundrum Pass during which Rhett would do her "Julia Child's Cooking in the Wild" contests. We learned to make pizzas cooked in the coals of a fire, baked goods, soups, pancakes, and many other things. On one trip we camped by a stocked stream and lake. There were so many trout that we were catching them by hand. We cooked over 40 fish over the fire and had a feast. This was also the trip during which everyone, students and teachers alike, went skinny dipping. The hippy vibe shared by the teachers, the kids, and the parents alike fostered a trusting atmosphere which apparently raised no red flags. To my knowledge, other than the nudity, nothing untoward or abusive happened, and nobody, to my knowledge, complained.

We had a long rafting trip on the Yampa River. We took turns on the different rafts, paddling as a team, riding the pontoon which carried our baggage, riding on inner tubes, and enjoying the spectacular canyons. At night, around a campfire, we would have singalongs guided by local musicians and teachers such as Dan Sadowsky (Dr. Sadistic and the Silverking Crybabies among other bands) and Sandy Munro (Easy Pickins, The Salad Boys, and many more).

Camping with the Community School.

Before the Community School, I was an easy target for bullies. There was one kid, David, who had mercilessly bullied Tommy Wells, the friend whose family followed us from New Jersey, at the public school. He got in so much trouble that they kicked him out, and he came to the Community School. He was much bigger than me, and he almost immediately started taunting me and other smaller kids. I don't remember him beating anyone up, but he so got under my skin that one day, as he was picking on another kid I came up behind him, tapped him on the shoulder, and cold-cocked him as he turned around. He then gave me a black eye. Then there was an incident where he picked on me on the school bus and I wouldn't

Apparently I had class schedules on my mind.

back down, we ended up jumping over the seats to get to each other and we had to be pulled apart. After that, he never picked on me again. I had much the same experience with a kid who called himself "Twinkie." He picked on me, I fought back, he stopped. This is a pattern that was repeated several times in different schools over the years. I would get picked on, I would hit back, they would stop. Rinse and repeat.

Having, since I was an infant, had surgeries to address the various complications that come with a cleft lip and palate, it was no surprise that these would continue once we got to Colorado. Handicapped Children, a federal program associated with Medicaid, had paid for my hospital care since my infancy in New Jersey. They continued to do so in Colorado, on my too-frequent trips to Denver to see what seemed like an endless parade of doctors. There were surgeries to address a crooked nose, a deviated septum, a cleft lip, gauze implants to address my profile, and removal of said gauze once it got infected. These trips to Denver, usually over the Thanksgiving holiday so I didn't miss school, continued from about fourth grade, through high school, and meant that it wasn't until I was in college that I enjoyed a good Thanksgiving dinner. Dry turkey, powdered potatoes and niblets of corn do not a holiday celebration make. We would usually travel from Aspen to Denver on Rocky Mountain Airways (aka Scareways). Puddle jumpers are fine, but when your puddles are 8,000 feet above sea level, and between jagged peaks, quality matters. On the best of days, I have read, that landing or taking off from Aspen Airport, with a short runway, wicked wind, and in a valley, is a harrowing prospect. Aspen's public bus system consisted, at the time, of military surplus olive green busses held together by tape and chewing gum. Aspen Airways seemed to subscribe to the same supplier. Their planes, with two cramped rows of seats at either side of an aisle, were basic. The bag storage was minimal, and the flight attendant would offer, if we could find no storage space, to "show you where to stow it."

We were supposed to be on a flight for one of my appointments when my mother switched our flight to the next plane. Shortly after take-off, the plane returned, having lost its windshield. My Mom said she "had a feeling." These planes were unpressurized. Denver is called the "Mile High City," and Aspen is even higher. On another flight, with the cabin unpressurized, once we rose into the air the pressure on my eardrums was so intense that I began to cry. No amount of yawning or blowing my nose was going to help with this severe ear pop, so the flight attendant gave me an oxygen mask and I waited it out with tears. The other local airline, Aspen Airways, was more expensive, but also more modern. If only for the pressurization, they would become our go-to service for those Denver outings. The thing about Rocky Mountain Airways, as retro as their equipment was. They never once let my parents pay for our flights. They were all heart and duct tape.

Though usually at Thanksgiving, these surgery trips would sometimes come unexpectedly. One week we took a trip to Denver for yet another appointment. My mom and I dropped into a record shop and she bought me the David Bowie's double LP, *The Rise and Fall of Ziggy Stardust and the Spiders from Mars*. I loved that album, but didn't get much time to enjoy it before, about a week later, my parents informed me that I would be leaving for Denver and having surgery the following morning. I broke into tears, this was disrupting to life, school, and just plain scary for a child not yet ten.

The day prior to my OR visit, my mom requested that my doctor, when taking a blood test, also check for my blood type. Doctor Dean was no phlebotomist, and he had the bedside manner of a lamp post. He began taking my blood at a station set aside for that purpose. For some reason, he attached a tube to the needle in my arm and ran that to the syringe. He proceeded to take multiple vials of blood when the tube became disconnected and my blood went everywhere, and I nearly passed out. Dr. Dean walked away unconcerned, my mother left shaken and dealing with my situation.

We got back to my room and, as was her custom, my mother slept in a chair beside my bed. After we had been asleep for some time, the door opened, letting in brief light from the nurse's station. In stepped, not so quietly, Dr. Dean. He turned on the light, syringe in hand, and was startled to see my mother sitting up, also startled. He tripped over his words, explaining that the blood he had taken earlier in the day had been put in for the wrong tests, and he would need to take blood again. Mom was going red in the face, but I, at nine, beat her to the punch. "You won't take my blood again, you're an awful doctor. You're a disgrace to the name Dean!" To this day, over 45 years later, I have never come up with a zinger like that again.

Closer to Aspen one could turn off the highway and drive along a beautiful stretch of road whose gentle incline would bring the driver to Snowmass (not to be confused with Old Snowmass), and its ski resort, village, and its high-end houses. One of these was owned by a former boss of my mother, Gaye, and she needed house sitters for a couple of months. My parents got the gig and were spared from paying rent. It was around this time that Kathy, Doug, Tommy, and Kim arrived in with their Airstream trailer and their Great Dane, Luke. To round out the bunch of us, my teenaged Uncle, Marc, arrived from New Jersey to spend the school year with us. He was having trouble in school and my grandparents thought a change in scenery would do him good. I idolized Marc, who

Uncle Marc

at only eight years older than I was, was like more of a brother to me than an uncle. The house was large enough for all of us.

It was a remarkable time. Tommy and Kim, both towhead blondes like myself, were very close to me in age, Tommy was a year older and Kim a year younger. I had my best friend Tommy right there all the time, and Kim was usually game to hang out and not make too much trouble unless that was our plan.

My uncle often supervised us when the parents were busy, and he seemed to relish his mentorship role. I did, however, suffer from a lack of supervision. Tommy and I would often

float firewood down the stream behind the house, both divesting Gaye of her supply, clogging the stream at other homes, and causing flooding. We called it logging, the angry neighbor had more colorful words for us.

Tommy and Kim

I would wander into the huge living room late at night, and read *Time* magazine, or watch movies. Two memories stick with me, a *Time* magazine article showing beheadings by the Viet Cong in Vietnam, and watching *Fearless Vampire Killers*, directed by Roman Polanski. Neither experience was healthy for a kid under ten years of age, and both linger in my memory. For that brief time, it felt as though my family had been expanded, our small clan and large dog worked together, (mostly) behaved, and took care of each other. Slowly but surely, we were moving closer to Aspen. The next stop would be at the base of Smuggler Mountain.

EVENTS IN AND AROUND SILVER KING

WHILE ASPEN, COLORADO MAY bring to mind fur coats, mansions, celebrities, and MONEY, many of us who grew up there were children of parents that made their living as small business owners, blue-collar workers, or working in the various service industries fueled by tourism. In those days many local families could afford modest homes, some had not-so-modest homes, and as in my case, they could afford to live in employee housing. Among those bastions of the ordinary was Silver King.

Silver King was a hodgepodge of apartment buildings, built in different phases from the 60s through the late 70s. The earlier phases were brick buildings with dank basement storage areas and laundry rooms, another of the phases were stucco monstrosities with open courtyards on the ground floor, and the final phase was made of wood and was markedly more attractive. Though the Big Bad Wolf would have had more success with that final phase, I feel fortunate that our apartment was in one of those buildings, near the pool and the sand playground. During the mid-80s through the early 90s the middle phase was turned into "affordable housing" and afterward I understand that the complex is now condominiums, and I'm not sure whether or not the buildings have been razed or remodeled. I am pretty sure that I couldn't afford to live there now.

We moved in about 1977, while I was still at the Aspen Community School. As with our original cross-country convoy, we followed friends Kathy and Doug, and my childhood friends, Tommy and Kim to Silver King after Doug got a job there as a maintenance man (with free housing). Us kids had the run of the place, there were so many buildings that we could explore, there were nearby woods where we built forts, and there were the stairways down to the dank laundry rooms (more on that later). Tommy and I would explore and play games. We made friends with Adam, who lived in another of the wooden buildings with his father, a cab driver, and his grandparents. We spent a lot of time there, listening to music, playing with Adam's ferret, and hanging out in the apartment whose walls were darkened by the smoke of his grandfather's cigars.

The sand playground next to our building was where we usually hung out. We would fly off of the swings at the apex of their swing, we would find hundred-plus-year-old mining tools beneath the sand when the area was renovated. We once found a stash of pot in a Band-Aid tin buried in the sandbox (yes, a sandbox in the middle of a sand playground). We had rock fights, played with cap guns, and miraculously survived.

There are times that I wonder that I didn't die amidst those apartments. Silver King is built on a mountainside with the older phases at the lower elevation and the newer ones on the higher elevation. The perfect spot for helmet-less skateboarding down the steep driveway and through the parking lots. We also had a cart which, without working brakes, coasted on skateboard wheels and was steered by leaning. This thing sat three inches from the ground, and its profile was perhaps two feet high. While short people skateboarding through traffic is dangerous enough, on those same hills we managed to find a way to make ourselves even less visible to drivers.

Then there was the motorcycle. Tommy had received a 125 CC Indian "Enduro" motorcycle, circa 1972 or so. It was a small bike and not the image of the Indian road cruisers everyone knows. My understanding at the time was this was made by an

Italian company licensing the Indian name. My folks soon bought that same motorcycle for me (no idea why Tommy wasn't able to keep it). The bike was small and sprightly. I had no idea how to ride it. My father, having met my mother while they both rode motorcycles, thought he could teach me. I did get the hang of some things and could ride around on straight alleys and the dirt roads near Silver King. I never made it up to the Mine Dumps, just above the complex, where riders much more skilled than I would ride the rough terrain and jump and speed to their hearts' content. I wouldn't have survived the first 15 minutes.

My short motorcycle adventure ended just outside of Tommy's apartment. I took off up the dirt hill and towards the parking lot above. Two-thirds of the way up the hill I hit a large rock, went into an uncontrolled wheelie and collided with a car parked at the top of the hill. My left leg was sandwiched between the bike and the car. Failing to either let go or release the gas, I was then pulled over the trunk of the car and landed on the same sandwiched knee. I'm glad I was wearing a helmet and knee pads. I got up, proceeded to walk towards my horrified mother, then collapsed when my knee wouldn't hold me. I was ok after the application of ice and aspirin. The Indian, having had the gear shift impale the gearbox, was the more injured of the two of us. After that it languished, chained to a telephone pole until it was removed. I hope it got a better home than I provided.

As I said, we had the run of the apartment complex. The "Old Hospital" was nearby, having been phased out when the new one was built. This building eventually became the Aspen Community Center, but for the time it was vacant we were always able to find a way to enter and explore. At this point in time, my parents had a friend who was living on-site at the old hospital as the caretaker. One evening we were over there and my parents, with the caretaker, having found a tank of laughing gas, decided to inhale and skateboard through the halls. I'm not the only one who could have died near Silver King. Apple, tree, and all that. Yeah.

I also nearly burnt a building down. As Johnny Cash sang in Folsom Prison Blues the narrator "shot a man just to see him die,"

I threw a lit book of matches into the trash can in the laundry room just to see what would happen. I honestly, at nine or so, didn't realize the implications of what I'd done. The trash went up like the fire fuel it was and in seconds flames were two feet over the trash can's rim, and the plastic can was beginning to melt. I first froze, then I calmly walked out of the laundry room as if nothing had happened, as tendrils of smoke started to drift out of the vent in the door. I. Did. Not. Tell. Anyone. I walked briskly away, trying not to draw attention to myself. Before I got too far, one of the maintenance men ran past me in the direction of the fire. Thankfully nobody was hurt, and the quick response limited the damage to one melted garbage can, a sooty circle on the floor, and perhaps some clothes that smelled worse when they came out of the laundry room than when they went in.

Around Silver King I also found a new source of income. While other kids were selling *The Aspen Times* (as did I from time to time), Tommy and I discovered that someone had left all of the coin vaults, in all of the laundry machines, in every building, unlocked. Though Tommy lived in the same apartment as the maintenance supervisor, to my knowledge he never told. For at least one or two weeks we had access to quarters upon quarters and made our home at either The Pinball Palace or Holy Shirt, where we could throw the quarters into the Asteroids or Defender machines as quickly as we could "acquire" them. I once even brought David Burson on one of our acquisition journeys. One day the jig was nearly up when a resident caught me with my hand in the cookie jar. I thought he would turn me in. Instead, he asked for the quarters that he had put into the machines, saying, "I'm not mad at you, but I'd like to do my laundry for free today."

Another Silver King friend, Robbie, and I spent a good deal of time together. He was maybe two years older than I and, even at that age, he was quite flamboyant. While he loved talking about Halston's new fashions, and musical theater, he was great company, but he had few friends. Robbie and I would create little plays and perform them in the courtyard areas of the wooden buildings. In one of those dank phase one basement stairways

Robbie created the RA Gallery where us kids could display art. While mine was rudimentary, Robbie's was quite good and our friend Ivan Dewolf (son of Nick) displayed some great, if creepy, clay sculptures. These art shows actually went on for a couple of summers until Robbie rented (I don't know how) a space in downtown Aspen and brought in at least one photographer who either was or was reminiscent of Robert Mapplethorpe. Robert Mapplethorpe-type subject matter was not something that kids would normally traffic in (I'll leave you to Google it), but Robbie was not a normal kid. He played by his own rules and was picked on because of it.

Robbie was a kind and sensitive kid, and we were instant friends, and remained close starting when I was 10 years old, and through the first two years at Aspen High School. I would later, in my 20s, work at the Guggenheim Museum as a security guard. When they presented a Mapplethorpe exhibit I requested not to be posted in that gallery. I write this having heard that recently Robbie had passed away. While I haven't seen him since high school, the messages of condolence that were sent to his mother paint a picture of a kind, generous, and wonderfully talented man. I still have a painting of his that he gave me when we were kids. I'm glad that I kept it. I miss him.

Robbie Appleton, The Aspen Times news article from June, 1982.

Robbie Appleton obituary in The Putnam County News & Recorder from May, 2022

THE
DEAF CAMP
PICNIC

MUCH OF MY SILVER KING TIME was spent at the Aspen Community School, but at the age of 12 I went to Aspen Middle School. This is where I became friends with Chris Pomeroy, though we had met a year earlier at the Deaf Camp Picnic. The Picnic began in the 1970s as a benefit concert for the Aspen Camp School for The Deaf. Pioneered by, among many others, John Denver, it became an annual event. It was a party for the locals that many looked forward to. A large meadow, with a gradual incline, surrounded by woods and mountains was transformed annually by the addition of a modestly sized stage, some porta potties, and hundreds of locals sitting on their blankets eating, drinking and ... partaking of other substances.

I went to the picnic several times when I was young, so after a while they all run together, but the partial memories formed an indelible impression on me. In those days, while parents enjoyed the music and their libations, us kids were free to play and to roam. It was during one of those roaming sessions that I first met Chris Pomeroy. It was approximately 1979 and I was still at the Aspen Community School, in the fifth or sixth grade. I found my way to a marshy area behind the stage and, as wonderful music played behind me, I wondered and began using my pocket knife to playfully slice down cat tails. It was a foldable Opinel knife which

I bought, without my parent's consent, from a local sporting goods store. The knife was wickedly sharp and well enough balanced that, a couple of years later, I would be able to throw it at my dart board and get a bullseye. As noted from our later adventure with Lawn Darts, my game was of interest to Chris. I lent him the knife and he proceeded to slice, slice, slice. And so began a lifelong friendship, as well as a fascination with sharp objects which continues to this day (I collect antique swords and knives). As I have stated previously, Chris and I are lucky to still be alive.

The music was glorious. My memories include John Denver singing "Grandma's Feather Bed," "Rocky Mountain High," and "Thank God I'm a Country Boy." Charlie Daniels sang about the time when "The Devil Went Down to Georgia" and his fiddle was amazing. The Nitty Gritty Dirt Band regaled us with "Mr. Bojangles" among many others. Less famous local musicians also heated up the stage. This being a benefit for the deaf, all songs were translated by signers at either side of the stage.

Jimmy Buffet, who had a home in the area, as did John Denver and members of the Dirt Band, was also a staple at these concerts. In 1980, just after Mount St. Helens erupted he sang "When the Volcano Blows" which seemed prescient considering the fact that he released it prior to that event. I recall him performing many of his hits and some lesser-known songs like "Pencil Thin Mustache." His performance of one particular song stands out. My mother reminded me of it recently and it came right back to me. As the first verse started, with many in the audience singing along, the signers were dutifully and happily translating along. And then came the words that make up the title. The signers looked confused, and a bit taken aback, they looked across the stage at each other, shrugged, and then using the gestures that one might expect, signed "Why Don't We Get Drunk and Screw."

Chris and I had many dangerous adventures through middle and high school. We liked throwing knives and ninja stars at pretty much any inanimate object. When a knife handle broke, some twine would turn the blade into a whirling dervish of death. We, with the help of superglue and strike-anywhere matches, created exploding pellets which we would fire from a pellet gun and obliterate our clay targets (we were not dumb enough at that time to shoot at each other). We would explore construction sites, jump our bicycles while not wearing helmets, jump across rooftops, and Chris would occasionally take the Wagoneer for a spin way before having a driver's license.

Then there was the time I nearly killed my best friend.

Back in the days before we had to wear helmets, when the bottom of the boardslide spit you out onto asphalt, and kids often had all day to make trouble while Mom and Dad worked, we had access to dangerous toys. I had a BB gun and shot out the window of our Silver King apartment, Chris and I had the aforementioned throwing knives, our toy guns looked real enough to get us shot today, and we had ... Lawn Darts. When we would hang out, Chris and I would toss regular darts in the other's general direction and dodge them. Why not try something like *that* with a dart 30 times the size? All innocent fun ... what could go wrong?

The idea behind the game of Lawn Darts was to throw one so it arched high and to land it in a series of concentric rings. Nowadays the game is played with a 12-inch dart comprised of plastic feathers and a weighted front so that when it lands it stands upright. In those days we had a 12-inch ballistic missile of destruction. While the plastic feathers were the same, the weighted end consisted of a 3-inch steel spike. Really? These things could be thrown great distances and quite accurately.

One day, at another community near to Silver King, Chris and I, and another friend, were playing Lawn Darts. We were playing by the rules of the game, and all was as safe as a game like that could ever be. As boredom gradually set in, the darts started inching in just a bit closer to each of us.

Throw number one to Chris: Swish, Thunk, landing 4 feet from him. He was able to make the stretch and collect the dart. Throw number two: Swishhhh, Thunk! The dart sank in the ground just 3-1/2 feet from our friend, an easy stretch for him to reach it. Throw number three to me: Swisssh, Thunk! I stretched and easily reached the dart.

Another series: Swisshhh, Thunk! Chris easily made the stretch; Swishhh, Thunk! Our friend barely had to take a step to retrieve the dart; Swishhhh, Thunk! I could swing my leg and tap the dart with my foot. Another round: Swish Thunk, Swish Thunk, Swish Thunk, and we were all laughing giddily—we barely had to move to touch the darts after they'd landed. As the game progressed the darts would nearly soundlessly thunk into the sod at our feet. We moved further and further away from each other. Accuracy at a distance wasn't a consideration—we were on a roll and laughing all the way. Swish … Thunk. Take a step back. Swish … Thunk! Step back.

It was my turn and I wound up to make an extra-strong throw for distance. Swishhhh … the dart flew about 30 feet in a straight line. THUNK! Chris and I stood motionless for a moment until he turned his head to the left and eyed the dart that was now embedded in the fibrous T1-11 plywood siding, not six inches from his head. It took both of us tugging and pulling on it for about 10 minutes to remove it from the wall.

For our stupidity alone they should have banned the toy, but that didn't happen until, tragically, several children were killed. While Chris and I remain friends to this day, if Darwin had had his way, one or both of us would probably have shuffled off to the great beyond much earlier. That Silver King area holds many memories; I'm fortunate that I'm still here to share them.

THE PASSION,
THE PLAYS,
THE POOL TABLES,
AND THE PARTIES

WHILE MY PASSION FOR THE THEATER began in the Aspen Community School under the mercurial direction of Paul Ruben, it only grew as I moved into the Aspen Public School system in the seventh grade, and then through high school. Through those years there were several constants; school plays in both middle and high school, The Aspen Community Theater, and The Theater Under the Jerome. Another constant were parties, house parties, cast parties, and parties with only two or three participants. We were adept at partying, why wouldn't we be? Many of us learned from our parents.

I thought I'd made the decision to leave the Community School and attend the Aspen Middle School. I remember making the announcement to my parents. My best friends at the time, Tommy and Adam, were there (the Silver King crowd), and I thought it would be a good move. I loved the Community School, but I announced that this would be a positive change. In retrospect, my parents were neither shocked nor saddened by "my" decision. They actually appeared relieved. I think now that there were probably many subtle hints thrown my way that the middle school was the path to take. I likely saved them a difficult conversation in which they would have told me that they were withdrawing me from the

Community School. They were both working as bartenders, I think that they just couldn't afford the tuition anymore. I'm so grateful to them for that experience.

The Aspen Middle School was housed in a nondescript brick building, with a commons that had a stage, and a catwalk/balcony above the room. The Community School once had a class trip in which we visited the middle school to see a production of Peter Pan, they made great use of the catwalk and a zip line to make Peter fly. I would do two plays on that stage, *Oliver* and *Sleeping Beauty*. Both of these plays repeated experiences that I'd had at The Community School. I had done a production of *Oliver* there a couple of years before, and at the tender age of thirteen I did my second play in drag. Perhaps a year and a half after I had done *Desire Under the Elms* in which I had played the lead Peter in one cast, while my friend Dmitri played the same role in the other cast, and we both, being very small, filled out the party scene playing girls, and wearing Felicity Huffman's (fellow ACS student and future celebrity) dress.

While I had played the minor role of Mr. Brownlow in the Community School version of *Oliver*, I was cast as one of the leads, Fagin, this time around. The Aspen Middle School repeated the Community School practice of double casting, with different groups of kids playing leads one night and another group the next. My Fagin counterpart was Bruce Johnson. I'm sure I looked as silly in a beard as he did. This show was my first experience in which the teacher/director was supportive and sought to teach performance rather than to demand results. I don't remember who directed it, but I was able to achieve a much better understanding of blocking, of beats, and of connecting with an audience. If I wasn't hooked before then, I was now. This show also brought me back together with my once and future friend, Chris Pomeroy. He played the constable who, using a starter pistol, was to eventually shoot Bill Sykes. That scene did not play out exactly as planned. As Bill Sykes climbed up scaffolding to the catwalk above the stage, Chris the constable was to yell "Halt!" and then fire. When the time came, he yelled "Halt!", but his pistol went click, click on an empty chamber, so he yelled, "BANG!" There was a brief moment of silence, then Mr. Sykes went limp on the scaffold. Though Chris would later become a pretty good musician, and a wonderful artist, animator, and woodworker, I think that the episode of the starter pistol perhaps ended his acting career before it began.

Drama Award from Aspen Middle School

Certificate of Award from Aspen Middle School for the Oliver Award.

Snow White was my eighth-grade production. It was directed by Don Dillon III and it was a blast. The cast all came out of his acting class, and he was the most gracious and supportive acting and music teacher we could have hoped for. He really took time to teach us and gave us individual attention. I really wanted to play the role of the sentient mirror, and I thought it was a lock until I cackled. Some of the girls were preparing for their auditions for the Wicked Queen and at some point, I discovered I had a talent for cackling. Naturally, I was trying to help the girls prepare by teaching them how to cackle too.

Unbeknownst to me, Don overheard one of these sessions. He approached me gingerly as if about to impart a whispered secret. "How would you feel about playing the Wicked Queen?"

I was somewhat speechless. Don knew I wanted to play the Mirror, and I repeated that preference. He asked me to think about it and told me that he thought I would be great. We went back and forth, and at one point I asked him if the role could be changed to a male. He tried but couldn't make it work. Ultimately

I jumped in with both stockinged feet, with false eyelashes, and with lipstick.

Don and I even wrote a song for the show: "Mirror Mirror on the wall, watching kingdoms far below, Mirror Mirror on the wall, who's the fairest of them all?"

At a Q&A with a class from another school one of the kids called me out, "Are you a boy?" I removed the eyelashes to a stunned silence followed by a chorus of applause led by Don Dillon III, who would, at middle school graduation, give me a special award for bravery.

During my two years at Aspen Middle School Robbie and I continued to be friends but drifted slowly apart until we were more than acquaintances but less than buddies in high school. We still hung out together, but with less frequency, and never with my other friends. We shared a love for theater, but at that time, in the early 80s, homosexuality

Snow White newspaper article.

was a stigma which in small-town America was hard to overcome. While he wasn't "out" he was flamboyant, and proudly so. I never shunned him or shut him off, but peer pressure likely set me on a path toward more socially acceptable friends. He was truly one of a kind, and KIND is the word that comes to me as I write this. He felt everything deeply, even when sad he focused on bringing joy and humor to others.

One memory of that time is when he and I were at the corner of Main Street and Mill Street, outside the Hotel Jerome. We were at the light, waiting to cross the street, when Patsy, his mom, waved at us and with her companion crossed the street in our direction. A car ran the red light and struck Patsy and her friend, launching them forward about ten feet. Robbie stood stunned and collapsed into me sobbing. Heedless of traffic we all rushed towards the middle of Main Street where the two who had just been hit were shakily getting up, with little more than bruises. The car had driven off, and the situation could have been far more catastrophic. What stands out to me is how Robbie and Patsy threw themselves into each other's arms, the love was so obvious, as was the relief. Robbie went away a short time after this, but that moment is a fitting memory and memorial.

Also, on Mill and Main Street was the Hotel Jerome. This Aspen landmark's doors, which opened in 1889 housed the Jerome Bar. A favorite of Hunter S. Thompson, the basement held the former Rocking Horse Saloon and future Theater Under the Jerome. The Mill Street side held a little shop called Three Balls on a Mountain. So much happened within one or two square blocks of this place. The Miners Building, just across Main, held the hardware store and hobby shop where I bought BB and pellet guns, lawn darts, and so many other things that should have caused more damage than they did. Carl's Pharmacy was one block down, on Main and Monarch Streets, and back in the day you could sit at the soda fountain having a milkshake, ice cream, or saccharine-sweetened water, which those of us without cash would drink as an excuse to sit at the counter. Upstairs was a toy shop, where I bought many Matchbox cars and several explosives. Their poppers were operated by pulling a string, then BOOM! These listed for 5¢ apiece, and no tax was levied on purchases up to $1. I figured out, at a preteen age, that if I had $1, I could buy about eight poppers, because the tax would nix the purchase if I added more. If, however, I made separate purchases I could get some extras. This led to me driving the cashier crazy with *multiple* purchases of two or three.

Things got crazier when I had extra funds from selling *The Aspen Times*, printed just down the block. Wholesale bought ten papers for $1, and their 20¢ sale price guaranteed doubling one's investment, or tripling it—or more, if one knew where to sell the papers. Turf was everything, and competition was fierce. Chris and I are still in business together today because of a prowess which at that time brought us to the inebriated people at the bars who would pay up to $5 or even more, per paper. On those Thursdays, when I returned to Carl's, I'm convinced the cashier wanted to kill me when I neatly set out my multiple purchases and asked, "What will $15 buy me?"

Three Balls on the Mountain was a tiny collectible store owned by a former New Yorker with a handlebar mustache named George. Chris and I wandered into the store during the eighth grade, and through high school and the store's several incarnations we became fixtures there. It began with coins. Chris and I were fascinated by them, and George sold them. Soon much of our *Aspen Times* income was transformed from dimes and quarters into Buffalo Nickels, Mercury Dimes, Morgan Dollars and more. Chris and I would spend hours at his house comparing our collections, mounting them in coin holders, cataloging them, and putting them in binders or purpose-built wooden boxes. George more than tolerated us—he engaged us and taught us, and of course, took our money. To his credit, he once sold me a 1858 Flying Eagle Cent for about $9.

Immediately after the transaction he paused thoughtfully and asked if he could take another look at the coin. He took out a jeweler's loupe, looked closely at the coin, sighed, and put the loupe and coin back on the glass counter. "You got yourself a good deal kid," he said, "that's a 1858 (8 Over 7) Flying Eagle Cent, pretty rare. I should have charged you a bit more for that." It turns out that he took a loss on the transaction of at least $100 at the time, and much more now. I still have the coin and the eclectic collection around it, neatly in the binder that I put together in my living room and Chris' basement. Around this time my family bid farewell to Silver King (aka Hunter Creek Properties) and moved to affordable housing at Castleridge Apartments, near the "new" hospital.

Immediately after I graduated eighth grade I went to a summer theater program at Brigham Young University. My first extended time away from home. Having immersed myself in theater over the past couple of school years I was ready to learn more and to have an away-from-home adventure, or so I thought. The classes, kids, and teachers were great, but we were in the middle of Provo, Utah, at a Mormon school. I had no background with religious teaching, and everyone there was happy to give me my freedom and never pushed religion on me. I was offered rides if I wanted to attend another church or synagogue and wasn't judged when I stayed in the dorm while their services took place. Still, I felt like

At home at the Castle Ridge Apartmen. Circa 1984.

an outsider, not understanding the lives of the other kids and the staff, and I became homesick. This came to a head when we were working on a production of *Godspell* and the reference to wine in one of the songs was cut. I just didn't understand, I felt like I didn't belong, and I missed Cosmic Cat back home.

I lasted about three of the six-week program and asked my parents to pick me up. I'm grateful that I did because shortly before I left BYU, Cosmic got sick. By this time he was about six or seven years old and we were inseparable. He was an outdoor/indoor cat who spent a lot of time around Silver King, hunting, playing, and doing his cat thing. I once saw him jump off of our third-floor walkway and catch a mouse in the courtyard below. He would often bestow his gifts upon us.

Imagine trying to get a live and terrified gopher out of your living room. When another cat somehow ended up on our balcony, there was a short-lived confrontation, and Coz would walk in from the now-empty balcony. Though he was always out and about, I had only to jingle my keys to call him, and he would come running.

The contrast between Coz the healthy and vibrant cat and Coz the sick cat was not striking. He still looked the same, but he was slower, preferring to sit on my lap rather than play, and eating less. One morning I woke up to find Cosmic lying on the living room floor, breathing heavily, and not moving. I sat down next to him and, when I started softly petting him, he began purring, and then his breathing stopped. Had I stayed at BYU I wouldn't have seen him again. I woke my parents to tell them the news, and my father took my friend to be buried in the woods near a friend's cabin.

Later that day, after a good deal of crying, I rode my bike to George's store, Curious George Collectables. I don't know why that was the first place I went, but George made it feel like home. At this location, and his next in the old location of the Tom Mix clothing store, where my mother had once worked, Curious George's Collectables thrived. He sold more than coins, having graduated to leather goods, antique guns, and other collectibles.

I was interested in the knives and swords. While I still collect antique swords today, at that time switchblades fascinated me. Though illegal to sell and own then, and now, George had some, and I bought more than one and stupidly carried them (never used them). I once bought some brass knuckles from him for $10 and sold them for $20 to another kid. A small-time arms dealer, whose career was cut short when the other kid hit a schoolmate in the arm, dimed me out, and I dimed George, whose brother was a local police officer. I thought I was in trouble when I was told at school that a parent and I would have to meet with the police youth liaison officer. I told my mom and she kept it secret from my father, who would have gone ballistic. It turned out that I only got a severe warning, and George a talking-to, but nothing more. Amazingly, once I showed up and apologized to him, aside from occasionally ribbing me about it, he never seemed to hold the incident against me. Throughout my high school career, I continued to be a denizen of his store.

When I was 14 I performed my first and only wedding. My mother and the man who raised me from two years old, and would later adopt me as his son, had been living together but had never gotten married. While I wasn't ordained or licensed to officiate, they wanted to formalize their common-law marriage. Several of my parents' friends joined us as we hiked to the cabin we sometimes shared with friends. The cabin was on unused public land, near a stream. It was another of those "close enough" buildings, when the boards were close enough to where they should be they were nailed together. There was a teepee and an outhouse on the property, and the cabin had a small kitchen, a loft, and always had a supply of alcohol. In these picturesque woods, my parents stood on the porch, and I read from a page that I had written, talking of love and summer, asking them to join hands and kiss, and pronouncing them married. I like to think that Cosmic Cat, buried in those woods, was looking down on us, and purring.

Aspen High School had an annual selection of Experiential Education trips and local activities for those who could not afford to travel. Freshman year I selected a program close to home, video filmmaking. The object was for the team to make a collage of videos and edit them into a whole. In 1982 the camera equipment used at Aspen High was circa 1977. The camera was huge and connected by a series of cables to the recorder, which weighed about 40 pounds. Chris was in on this adventure as well and directed a video to the tune of "Cross Town Traffic" by Jimi Hendrix. His project included a slow-motion hit-and-run accident in which one student feigned being hit by a slow-moving car and actually landed on the hood and rolled off, and into the street. We were doing stunt work at age fourteen.

My feature was shot at the arcade called Holy Shirt, with the theme that playing video games all day was a dead end. Little did I know that the world of video games would bring with it lucrative competitions and careers centered around playing the games. At the time, though I loved playing Asteroids and Defender, I didn't see a future in it. I had one girl dress as Mario, complete with a mustache, and play Donkey Kong in a robotic fashion. Chris, in my motorcycle helmet, sat in a race car game, wildly steering, as the screen read "Game Over." The end result was a lot of fun.

Sophomore year again had me staying close to home, taking a class in first aid and CPR. Pierre Pelletier and I teamed up and became very proficient in what we were learning. Resusci Anne became a friend. At the height of the Cold War, in 1983, tensions were high and the TV movie, The Day After was released. While learning to patch people up we were all thinking about the looming threat of nuclear war. It was against this backdrop that Pierre and I collaborated on a poem, based on *The Night Before Christmas*.

The Day After Christmas

T'was the day after Christmas
and out in the yard
Everything was blackened, smoking and charred.
Family was packed in the cellar and scared
And Bobby and Amy were losing their hair.
Waldo the dog was up on the porch
Just like the yard, smoking and scorched.
Then out of the sky, coming faster and faster
There were more missiles and more disaster.
Who pushed the button first?
Was it in vain?
Our country is gone.
Is Russia the same?
The world we once knew no longer remains.
The world we once knew had gone up in flames.

Pierre and I spent a good deal of time with our friend Eric. The three of us shared an interest in spy craft, good conversation, and humor. We would explore the town, have contests in which we would go to different locations in a hotel and try to find and ambush and "assassinate" the others. Over time we took to wearing fedoras when spending time together and speaking in mock Russian accents. We called ourselves the Boris Party. It was all fun and games, blowing off steam in a town that could, at times, be exciting and boring. Eastern Winds, a local Chinese restaurant, was our weekly (more or less) gathering place. Fedoras in place, we would ask the host for a table. When it was our turn we would hear "Boris, party of three ... Boris, party of three ... your table is ready."

I didn't do a school play after the eighth-grade production of *Sleeping Beauty*, until my sophomore year in high school. That's not to say I did not act. I had auditioned for the Aspen Community Theater's production of *A Mid Summer Night's Dream* a couple of years before, with my friend Robbie. He was cast and I was not. In my freshman year I auditioned for them again, this time for their production of Dylan Thomas *Under Milkwood*. Though under the auspices of the community theater, this would end up being considered the inaugural production of a new theater company called The Theater Under the Jerome. The play was helmed by Al Lions and introduced me to many members of the Aspen Community Theater family with whom I would work many times. It also introduced me to Brad Moore who became a friend and mentor, with whom I would rarely not be working on a show through high school.

The old Rocking Horse Saloon, under the Jerome Hotel, was converted to a Welsh pub. The space, having been a drinking establishment, was well suited to the transformation. The Rocking Horse could be entered by descending a narrow and dim flight of stairs. Upon entering, the bar was immediately ahead and the tables and dancing were in a large area to the right, the entrance of which was surrounded by ornately carved wood. It was this area that eventually became a black box theater, though when I first saw it it was full of garbage and old tables, ripped-up flooring, and some pretty gross substances.

The basement, which opened into the catacombs of the hotel's basement became our unisex dressing room, with areas masked with costume racks for discreetness. The labyrinth below the hotel, buttressed by huge brick arches, was a place that, at 14 or 15, was ripe for exploration, and I often went there to be alone. I once missed an entrance during a performance because I lost track of time and the voices calling for me were blocked by layers of brick and multiple alcoves.

Once the transformation of the former night spot was complete it appeared as though one could get a pint at the bar (but there was no liquor license), and then walk back in time and across the pond to spend time with the Welsh residents of Milkwood. Simon Peters played First Voice, Brad played Second voice, I was Nogood Boyo, and many characters were portrayed by a variety of locals, including Nancy Oden, who was a mother figure to me on this and

several other productions that we did together. She and Simon, another mentor, are missed. We will not see their like again.

In 1984 I was in the chorus of *Kiss Me Kate*, with Chris' brother Jimmy, for the Aspen Community Theater. This show was performed at the Aspen High School and was again directed by Brad Moore. It was a fun show, followed by

Under Milkwood: a magical journey, article by Andy Stone.

a cast party in which Jimmy and I, with one other kid, received "The Terrific Teen Trio" award. It was also where I had my first taste of whisky, which I did not like.

My sophomore year saw my first high school production, *Grease!* This was the first of many times I would be directed

Cast of Kiss Me Kate.

by Brad Moore. Having taken a break from school productions and dipped my toes into adult productions, I was ready to jump back in. I already knew I couldn't sing and wasn't the T-Bird type, so I auditioned for the role of the nerd Eugene. Not being able to sing didn't mean not singing at the audition, it was required.

As I was about to go on stage for the audition, the first part being Eugene's high school reunion speech, my cheering section emerged. One student handed me a cap, Don Dillon, the music director, gave me his glasses, and another student pulled my pants up to nearly my chest. I walked awkwardly to the stage (the pants helping in this regard) and took my place before the microphone.

Someone shouted, "How does it feel?" I answered, with admittedly good timing, "Painful." When the laughter died down I did an acceptable monologue, followed by my rendition of "Gee Officer Krupke" from *West Side Story*. Being a fan of the movie, during the "The trouble is he's crazy, the trouble is he drinks, the trouble is he's

Larger view of the Kiss Me Kate cast shot.

lazy, the trouble is he stinks ..." section, I did a variety of voices and repeatedly hit myself over the head with a rolled up newspaper, in an imitation of the scene from the film. It worked, I got a standing ovation for my audition, and I got the role, and we created a fun production.

The *Grease!* cast party was held at a house in Mountain Valley. It was March 17, 1984 and I had just turned 16. We piled into his basement where there was alcohol aplenty, beer and other libations, and perhaps some harder substances. I was there with my friend John who intended to sleep over at my apartment several miles away at Castle Ridge apartments, near the new hospital At a folding card table a group of kids, headed by Danny Zuko himself, Mark, was playing quarters. The object of the game was to bounce a quarter off the table and into a shot glass initially filled with beer. If you made the shot you chose who drank the shot. I think I lost. At some point in the game, the beer was colored green in honor of St. Patrick's Day.

When I was chosen I drank the shot. I was chosen frequently. At some point, I was later told, the green beer became green vodka, but I was too blitzed to know. In retrospect, I was to learn that I got sick and literally painted the bathroom green and had somehow pulled one or more towel racks off of the wall. I do remember being tossed outside into a snow bank, then later walking home in the cold with John, slipping on the ice every few yards. I awoke with a scab on my chin and was unbelievably able to make it to my drum lesson the following morning.

That cast party was not the only time that I lost at quarters. One evening three of us were playing a game at Eric's house. Though it was just beer this time, I didn't fare much better than I had at the Alpern's house. It seems that the other two had it in mind to team up against me, so each time a quarter made it into the shot glass, that glass was put in front of me. Bounce, clink, drink, bounce, clink, drink. After a while, it became a blur, and I was blitzed enough that the other two had to get me home. I believe some drunk driving may have been involved.

They got me up the stairs to the front door of our apartment where I turned and heaved over the railing. My parents didn't ask too many questions about my evening behavior, I didn't get in trouble because they didn't see what I was doing; they could conveniently ignore what they may have suspected, but hadn't been confirmed. That evening, my friends, having nearly carried me up the stairs, used my key to unlock the door and pushed me inside. I stumbled from the living room, down the hallway, and into my bedroom, which shared a wall with my parent's bedroom. I stumbled into the room and proceeded to fall over my vintage Ludwig drum kit, Zildjian cymbals crashing to the floor. Drum roll please ... busted (ba-dum-bump).

Those drums got put to use when Chris, Marcus, and I put together a "band." Chris and Marcus could play their guitars, but my drumming was rudimentary. We fancied ourselves a punk band and tried our hand at covers of Suicidal Tendencies, The Stooges, and others.

Alan, proprietor of Fat City Records suggested that we call ourselves Eclectic Blue; we settled on Buckets of Acid. Using a tape deck we recorded "I Wanna Be Your Dog" and "The Rape of Mrs. Goldberg." When I shared it with my uncle he said, "You know on

This Property Is Condemned

that song, 'I Wanna be your dog Mrs. Goldberg,' your friends sound like they are on speed, you sound like you are on quaaludes." We never got a gig, and another friend stole my cymbals and left town.

I was 16 when I did my first professional show, at the newly christened The Theater Under the Jerome, which by this time was a fully functioning theater and no longer resembled a pub. *Three by Tennessee* was directed by Kent Reed, another frequent collaborator and mentor. The play consisted of three one-act plays by Tennessee Williams. I was in *This Property is Condemned*, a two-person show about two young teens meeting on a railroad track and discussing their lives. It was an intimate show, starring Laurel Holstein and co-starring me. This was my first foray into true dramatic acting. We were sharing the stage with two other plays with entirely adult casts. Kent was an excellent teacher,

This Property Is Condemned

a supportive director, and he didn't accept anything less than 100% from us.

Laurel turned in a wonderful performance, and *The Aspen Times* agreed. They apparently thought I did a good job too, as their review called our one-act, "Arguably the best of the three." This cast party took place at a nearby basement restaurant. It was a small affair in which we sat around a large table. No alcohol for us youngsters this time. It was here that Kent handed us each an envelope with $50 inside, our cut of the box office, and my first professional acting gig.

My junior year saw high school productions of *South Pacific* and *Ramshackle Inn*, the latter of which I was cast in without auditioning. I was at the hospital in Denver for another of my many cleft palate surgeries and was unable to audition. Brad cast me as Officer Gilhooly in absentia. When Billy's grades didn't allow him to stay in the show I was upgraded, at the last moment, to the role of Constable Small and John took over my role.

In my absence, while in Denver having one of many surgeries, I was also cast in the small role of Dennis in *Much Ado About Nothing*, performed by The Aspen Community Theater at the newly renovated Wheeler Opera House, a 19th Century theater that had been long neglected and used for a variety of venues, including a movie theater showing *The Rocky Horror Picture Show*. The former show was directed by Brad Moore and the latter was directed by Al Lions, whom I suspect was encouraged by Brad to cast me. These were my first and only experiences being cast in anything, that I was not involved in creating, without an audition. Tom Cruise I am not.

DARK HOUSE

MY SOPHOMORE, JUNIOR, and senior years were difficult at home. My parents increasingly immersed themselves in the local party scene and I increasingly threw myself into theater as an escape. My friends and I also had our own party scene. I refer to this period as "Dark House," because even in the early afternoon I would return to our apartment and the shades would be closed, detritus from the night before's party scattered through the house, and a ten dollar bill on the table for me to get something to eat at McDonald's. Sometimes my mom would be on the couch listening to LPs and smoking a cigarette, still awake even after I had been at school all day.

The drugs were never hidden from me. It was not uncommon to see marijuana seeds on a record cover, or a rolled up bill next to a mirror, or a random razor blade sitting in an ashtray. We lived in a two-bedroom apartment and my parents frequently got into shouting matches during which my mom would lock herself in the bathroom immediately outside my bedroom door as my father yelled and pounded on the door and, at least once, punched a hole in it. The arguments were so loud that I am surprised the neighbors never called the police. The parties were often loud enough that I had to go to the living room in my pajamas and ask them to keep it down because I had school the next day. My father never hit my mother or me, but once I thought he had hit my mom and I hauled off and punched him. He looked bewildered, but didn't hit me, or even yell. I often

CONTRIBUTOR: DEAN JACKSON

spent time at friends' houses rather than at home, I could at least sleep there. I had also learned to party from the best.

———

I wrote this poem a few years after the "Dark House" period:

Dark House

Walk slowly with me, to explore love and hate, in a
world dark with despair, in which light is a memory of
tenderness and a dark house is all that is left of the soul.

Mother's love and kiss that lit a fire to caring memories.
Father's strong touch upon a growing shoulder gave hope
where problems stand in the mind of a growing child.
A child's love in return made a bridge that crossed
the abyss of years and made a family complete.

This was a perfection, where love was the strongest bond
and a parent's hand touched mine. It made the world seem
an eternity away and life made everything beautiful.

A memory clouded with love and pain rests itself upon
my soul, when I recall this time of life where
everything seemed beautiful, and then remember
the shattering change that followed.

On entering the age of responsibility, change overflowed,
and life became a shroud of death. A return home from
a day's encounters with life, while the sun still ignites
the blue sky with the brilliance of life, gave way to
oppression upon entering the door to my home.

The house seemed as though the night had never merged
with the day. Shades were still drawn from the night

before, and the refuse from the party that preceded my
entrance were still strewn about in chaotic order.

The cans lay as though the sea had carefully placed
them before my eyes. The stale air, smelling of smoke
and endless thought, hung in the room like the
reaper, aware that his prey had fallen at his feet.

The taker of love, still in neat, mirrored, piles
about the room, made me aware that mother
and father slept in its wake, restlessly.

An open window would only shed light upon destruction
and anger. So they remained closed in the night of day,
as I took the money, placed in memory of me, on the table.

And thus I ate, again alone, again with tears in my
eyes, but never with the thought of change.

"I love them," my heart pounded.

"I love them."

I loved a love that I couldn't share, I loved and I couldn't
tell, for they were blinded to me and to each other.
We were unseen, unknown.

Thus our lives passed each other, by hours and years.
Growing apart. Loving still and hating my love.

"I love them" to myself the words were poison.

"I love you." I lingered in thought.

"I hate you."

The return home always grew longer.
Home was no longer home.
Home was a cave full of arguments induced by false utopia.

Apart we grew as lightning struck the ground between us.

I once said, "Mom, I need your love."
She gave it to me and kept me alive as she gave me a hug.

To my father I said the same, result was failure as he gave his love as money to me, but still loved me with real love... under glass.

I could look under the cloud of the lie that was their
life and remember a warmer time, and cry for want
of that time, in a house as dark as the soul.

My memories flooded me as my tears.
My voice hung on one phrase as their lives
hung on to poison.

I still cry at that memory, though much has changed.
Love has returned to the world of the living.
The family, now changed, has reunited.
Apart, yet family still, loved and loving.
Changed by the dark house and the light
that came after.

———

During the Dark House period cocaine was a constant presence in our house. It was common for my parents to hold all-night parties while I was trying to get some sleep for school the following days. I would come out of the bedroom to find a local musician, Rooster, playing honkytonk on our untuned upright piano, or find members of other local bands hanging out all night. On one occasion we saw the band the following evening and they apologized for keeping me up and dedicated a song to me.

The drug scene in Aspen was not without its casualties. In 1984 Keith Porter pumped 20 rounds into the body of Michael Hernstadt as he sat in a car on Cemetery Lane. The murder took place after an all-night cocaine fueled party. The news got around, and Chris and I decided to indulge our morbid curiosity and go to the police impound lot to look at the car. The red car, an economy model, was parked next to the fenced-in area behind the courthouse that became famous a few years earlier when serial killer Ted Bundy jumped from a second-story window and escaped. The hood of the car was peppered with many holes, the windshield and side window were blown out. There were holes in the front seats, which like the dashboard, was spattered with blood. Also visible was a pack of Lucky Strikes, covered in blood.

In December of 1985 my friend Eric and I were driving to the parking lot of The Aspen Club to drink some beer. Eric and I would frequently have little two-person parties and I would often stay with him and his mother Carol, in their quaint house in town. On that evening we were seeking a secluded place but we never got to the parking lot. There was a police roadblock, and they turned us away, not even bothering to ask what we were up to. Later we heard that a local drug dealer, and quite a jerk, Steve Grabow, had been killed in his Jeep by a pipe bomb, likely placed by a cartel member. His was a gruesome death. The bomb had been placed under the driver's seat and went off when he started the car. The focused blast went through the seat and directly into his body without damaging the rest of the Jeep. He crawled out onto the pavement and died. Prior to this event I had heard a story that he had put a ski pole into the head of a friend's dog, so I held little sympathy. I don't know if my parents knew either of those guys, but especially in the case of Mr. Grabow, there was danger that came with the drugs.

I continued to dive into theater, and into my own party life, to stay out of the apartment as much as possible. Without parental supervision, and with their tacit approval, I could do what I wanted. I often stayed out all night, I crashed at friend houses, and I still managed to do well in school, on the speech and debate team, and to do as many plays as I could, sometimes more than one at a time.

Keg parties were a thing. I don't recall who threw them, who paid for the alcohol, or who was actually invited. I was not one of the popular kids and wasn't invited, but my friends always heard about the happenings, and I tagged along and was never chased away. One kegger occurred at The Mine Dumps, above Silver King at the location of a long-closed silver mine. There was a bonfire, a lot of beer, other libations, and some pot. We sat around the fire, laughing, drinking, being teens. A very pretty, somewhat shy, girl was at the party. She was a bit older than I was and, I would find out later, came from show biz royalty, and some years later I worked as an extra on her film, *Night Falls on Manhattan*. I would like to say that I engaged her in conversation, but at the party, and at the cinema I was only able to admire Bridget Fonda from afar.

Tom Crum (senior) looked like a surfer. Longish blond hair, muscular, and always with a ready smile, Tom was a cofounder, with John Denver, of the Windstar Foundation. Windstar was dedicated to environmental conservation and continues to this day. Tom was also a martial artist, an Aikido expert, who moonlighted as a bodyguard for John Denver. When he visited Aspen High to demonstrate Aikido I was stunned. He taught the concept of being centered and showed its power. He had the audience perform an exercise in which we put our fingers on a partner's chest and pushed them off balance, and then repeat the push after the partner had centered themselves, the result was that the push had no effect, the pushed partner became immovable. Tom then had two football players lift him, one on each arm, high in the air.

He centered himself and the athletes started to struggle, their arms buckling, and they slowly lowered him to the ground, trembling. I was in Tom's class on the following Saturday. Tom was a nurturing and friendly teacher, but there was no doubt about his power. He would begin the class with a warmup consisting of Aikido rolls, stretching and pushups, then pushups on our finger tips, lifting a finger on each hand at intervals until (some) would be doing pushups on just their thumbs. Once, having injured an arm in a skiing accident, Tom went through the pushup routine with, literally, one arm behind his back. He ended the warmup doing pushups on a single thumb. At times we had classes in a park flanked by a Tang Soo Do class and Hwa Rang Do class. The Tang Soo Do folks were in clean ranks practicing punches and kicks, the Hwa Rang Do students were in neat formation doing incredible kicks.

Our Aikido class was in a circle, asking after each other's well-being, laughing, and then warming up. Though it seemed casual, it was the caring and personal connection that connected with me and others. There was not a person among us who could not throw another, roll, or use a Bo staff. We may have seemed casual, but Tom taught a formidable martial art, always with the goal of diffusing a situation without causing injury. At this point in school bullies were no longer a problem for me. Tom has written several books, all of them worth a read. *The Magic of Conflict, Turning a Life of Work into a Work of Art* still informs my business and personal life today, long after I stopped studying Aikido.

The Cortina motel was a frequent site of our parties. I never knew who rented the room or brought the alcohol, but every couple of months a party would ensue with a lot to drink, including bathtub punch with Everclear. My friend John once took many hits of acid and sat in a snowbank outside the room. I once drank enough punch to make me sick and threw up on a girl I had a crush on. We had "upside down margaritas" where someone would sit on a chair with their head back and the ingredients were poured into their mouths, they shook their heads to mix, and then swallowed. Frequently, if you put your head back for the drink, when your head came back up it would have an extra hole with an earring. It wasn't always about large alcohol fueled parties. One night my friends Eric and Rhett and I stayed at Rhett's immense house and smoked pot all night while listening to the Grateful Dead. We all made it to school the next day and got the three highest grades on a science test.

John, Billy, Mark and I were at an apartment that Mark and Billy shared. We were playing Pente and someone broke out the hits of LSD. I took one. As the effects took hold I found myself laughing a lot and very very interested in the glass beads that served as the Pente pieces. As the night wore on we found ourselves in the middle of a deserted street near the fountain at the mall playing with prisms and flashlights. We spun these "trippy toys" and watched and laughed, and thankfully didn't get hit by a car. We took a car up to Independence Pass (I don't remember who drove or how many near misses we may have had) to watch the sun rise. When I got back home, after dawn, I had a vision of a dove flying into a cloud carrying a roach clip. I was performing in a professional show that same evening.

The Theater Under the Jerome moved to another below ground location, beneath a hot breakfast spot called The Mine Company, whose outdoor area was home to a huge mural depicting Picasso's version of Don Quixote. Below the restaurant stood the former home of The Slope, an apres ski joint where one could lounge on couches on a sunken carpeted floor, or lay down on the carpeted itself, and watch a wide variety of silent films projected on a fairly large screen. Small, and dark, a kid wouldn't draw much notice whilst taking in the black and white shorts, and I often found myself there while my parents were across the hall at Alice's Alley. Drinks could be purchased in this dank subterranean pool hall that, even when I was small, allowed me to play pool under the supervision of my parents, and brought across the hall in time to see Buster Keaton hanging from a clock. Like its last home, The Slope had to be cleaned up and turned into a black box. There was old furniture strewn about, a wooden platform stood about 8 inches off of the floor, where from behind the screen the films would be projected. This area would become our dressing room. Whilst helping to dismantle the platform I found multiple film tins, I wish I knew what became of them.

A Perfect Analysis Given by a Parrot, by Tennessee Williams, among the first of the shows that performed in at at The Theater Under the Jerome (under the Mine Company), as part of an evening of one-act plays. I was playing a small role in the play, directed by Kent Reed, but I was being paid for it. Even as a teen I was making respectable money acting in our local theater companies. Dmitri was playing a larger role in one of the other one-acts. I auditioned for it and was jealous at the time that he got the role, but he hit it out of the park. I had a show on the evening after the "trippy toy" party and didn't realize how long LSD lasts in the system. I did not expect the effects to persist even until the evening performance. I acted like I was feeling under the weather, drank several cokes, lay down on a bench, but as the lights were about to go down I was still very off. I made it through the performance, but it was less than stellar. It was at that point that I decided that I preferred theater over drugs. While I did do drugs at various times after, I never did them prior to a show or a job, and I never went into a situation where I committed myself to do a job or a service while under the influence.

Ecstasy (X) was a big thing while I was in high school. We believed that it acted as an aphrodisiac, making the parties to an amorous encounter. We believed if we took the drug and the girl sitting next to us took the drug, we were gonna get lucky. A very simple view of MDMA, but our teenage selves could be rather simple at times. X was a frequent topic of conversation, though to my knowledge none of my friends had tried it. It was against this background of teen hormones, sexual inexperience, and overconfidence, that I had my first and only experience with Ecstasy. She was beautiful in a cowgirl/party girl kind of way. A younger, blond, less weaponed version of *Yellowstone's* Beth. Long wavy almost white, blond hair, denim everything, and an easy smile. She was about 22 to my 17 and ran in the same party circles as my parents. I had an immediate crush, and during the many parties at our apartment she indulged me in conversation and supplied good company. I think everyone in the room knew I was smitten, even though now her name escapes me. One of our conversations turned to X, I think I pushed the subject, and before long she invited me to go to her place and try it with her. I was stunned, I believed that she had basically just asked me to bed.

About a week or so later the night came for our interlude. Being seventeen, I didn't dress any differently than my T-shirted and jeans norm. I entered the studio apartment, dimly lit, with only a chair and a bed, and a small bathroom to the right. My host was very welcoming, invited me in and gave me a beer. Dressed only in her underwear and an oversized shirt, her presence nearly made me panic, and I could barely keep a thought in my head. Then she emptied two capsules into two different glasses, dissolved the contents in water and we both drank. Our conversation, friendly but unromantic, continued as the drug did its work. I felt a bit dizzy and giddy. I eased more into the conversation, less self conscious, feeling some of the expected effects. By now it was mid-evening, and she received a phone call. She went into the bathroom for the call, returned a few minutes later, sitting a bit closer to me on the edge of the bed. Another call, some laughter, this time from the chair near the bed. Call ended, some smiles, cracked another beer. Another call, long. As the calls continued, a friend stopped by, dropping another six-pack, I remained fully clothed, she remained half-dressed, as she either cluelessly or skillfully, tantalized me. Another call or two and our little party seemed a bit overcrowded.

Slowly, hazily, the picture of beauty who had welcomed me into her studio apartment, became less so in my eyes. Her smile was less welcoming, more sinister. Every conversation was, in my mind, a conspiracy. Any physical contact became suspect. I abruptly got up, said goodbye and walked out. Apparently, this drug, once thought to be the nexus of bliss to my teenage mind, had the opposite effect on me. Instead of romance, great expectations, lesson learned.

For the remainder of high school, I continued to have parties with the other kids, at least once I remember smoking cocaine either in, or crystallized on the outside of a cigarette, or mixing it with baking soda and smoking the dried paste off of aluminum foil and awaking to an alarmingly fast heartbeat. I continued to drink and use drugs with virtually no supervision by my parents. There was one time when some friends came to my apartment. My mother was there, and they became very alarmed, but she was a "cool mom" and they were put enough at ease to break out vials of coke. My mom was alarmed and took it from them, concerned that it would be cut with poison, as kids of our age wouldn't be able to afford uncut cocaine. Much to my friends' horror, she flushed their stash and proceeded to break out a large bag of powder, and shared it with me and my friends. I recalled something my folks told me some time before, "If you want to use drugs ask us first, so we can make sure it's safe." She was a "cool mom," at least my friends thought so from that moment on. I never brought them over again.

The rest of my junior and senior years had me performing in several more shows at *The Theater Un*der the Jerome, the Aspen Community Theater, and at Aspen High School. There was one point where I was doing A Chorus Line at the Community Theater, Mine at The Theater Under the Jerome (under the Mine Company) and another show at the High School. Brad Moore was directing *A Chorus Line* and, as I was being paid for *Mine* and was getting credit for the school play, I dropped out of Brad's production. *Mine* was a small production centering around a coal mine in Appalachia. The one-act play was knitted together with musical interludes performed by Kent and two other musicians. I was the narrator. I introduced the show, and I would make appearances periodically through out. At 17 years old, I was anchoring a show with nearly 20 pages of monologue. One evening, standing in the middle of the stage, about five feet from audience members on three sides of me, I was in the middle of a particularly long section about the religious lives of Appalachian folk and my mind went completely blank. The actor's nightmare. As I stood there, having obviously forgotten my lines, a strange thing happened. I felt the audience rooting for me. I felt them supporting me and willing me to succeed. I don't think I have felt that way before or since. My knees stopped shaking, I took a deep breath and then ad-libbed "Now folks in this area were known for their commitment to their churches, and on a good day you would find at least two or three of them there ..." The audience got the joke (churches were usually packed), they cracked up and I found my place again. Later, when Kent's group lost their place in John Prine's song Paradise, the audience applauded and encouraged them, briefly audience and cast became a family.

I may have immersed myself in the theater, *but I also needed to ke*ep up with school. The school show was a showcase directed by students. I played Mr. Baker in Neil Simon's Come Blow Your Horn. I got laughs at nearly every line, even the non-comedic lines. I couldn't understand why, but I rode the high. I later learned that the powder used in my hair to age me, coupled with the hat I wore and sometimes removed and put back on, had me followed by a talcum cloud whenever I was on stage. Though I was embarrassed, the talcum was the better white powder for me.

In the summer of 1985, I went to a summer acting program at Carnegie Mellon University. We were housed in a dormitory right down the block from Mr. Rodger's house and across from a park where The Society for Creative Anachronisms would often don their armor and beat each other silly with their padded swords. This is the first time away from home that I really enjoyed. It got me out of the difficult home environment and immersed me in creativity. We had classes in movement and monologues, dramatic literature and Shakespeare. I found myself being less shy amongst peers that hadn't known me for most of my life. I came out of my shell and made some great friends. One of these was a girl named Angela. She was beautiful and many of the boys had an immediate crush on her, but she was also very shy. Though I also had a crush, we were fast, platonic, friends. I returned to Aspen with renewed confidence, sporting an earring, in time for my senior year. Angela and I continued to have periodic phone calls and maintain a long-distance friendship. My crush continued from afar.

FUN AND GAMES

My family had kind of a tradition. My grandfather was an expert pool player. He started playing 8-ball and other pocket pool games, but these became too easy for him and he took up snooker, a game dependent upon geometry, accuracy and bank shots. He taught my uncle to play, and together they taught me, and I inherited my grandfathers cue. During high school 8-ball and 9-ball were an obsession to me. Friends would often gather at one of the two local pool halls and put our quarters on the table to wait for a match. Though we were underage we would often find ourselves in the adult section, upstairs at The Cooper Street Pier, and none of the staff seemed to mind. The three tables were often monopolized by high school students pumping in quarters, but spending very little money (the occasional Coke or order of fries notwithstanding). It is against this backdrop that I met Rat. Rat, whose wispy mustache and "beard" certainly had earned him the name. I was alone and just shooting rack after rack of balls. Rat and a rowdy leather-clad group of bikers crowded into the area, took over the tables and ordered many pitchers of beer. Rat politely asked me to play a game, so I set them up. I was a pretty good player, so was Rat. Over the course of an evenly matched game I started to run the table, and the rest of the gang suddenly took a keen interest in the game, cheering Rat, and looking askance at the twerp that was beating him. I was oblivious for a few minutes, until it dawned on me that I had a straight shot, 8-ball in the side pocket. Recognizing the interest that the bikers had in the game, and the interest I had in keeping my knees intact, I realized that it would be best to throw the match. I called the 8-ball in the side pocket, and then I deliberately banked the 8-ball into the other side pocket, as if to say, "I could have won, you know?" After I left it occurred to me that I wasn't necessarily the smartest pool player at the pier.

———

There were a couple of kids who had an affinity for fast cars. Brian, from Booneville, Mississippi, loved his Plymouths. When he moved to Aspen, he was a fish out of water. He came to town senior year to stay with his father, an Aspen Police Officer, at Castle Ridge Apartments, where we lived. He was a building over. With an afro and a fuzzy mustache, Brian stood out with his Southern accent and decidedly un-Aspen like attire. He was friendly, but shy. I don't recall how we met, but we became friends quickly. He showed me photos of the Plymouth that he left at home in Boonville, he missed that car. Shortly after his arrival his father bought Brian a late 50s or early 60s station wagon. It was a tank, its interior ratty, its engine seemingly on its death bed. Brian hated the car but needed it to get around. He was eagerly awaiting his father's purchase of a new muscle car. When the bright orange Plymouth Roadrunner arrived, Brian was jubilant. In celebration, he and I took to the station wagon and drove towards Independence Pass, which was blocked by boulders and snow at that time of year. Stopping once to add oil to the air filter, to produce thick black smoke, we arrived at one of the boulders blocking the pass. Brian proceeded to slowly drove towards the boulder and when the bumper made contact he gunned it, pushing the rock several feet before the front end lifted from the ground. The rear-wheel drive pulled us off of the rock, and we had several more goes, with the car belching black smoke all the while.

Brian's orange Road Runner was a loud beast. The early 70s era muscle car was a statement on the road. Between the throaty growl and the bright orange factory paint job, the car was hard to miss. He, Rhett and I would speed down straight aways at 120 mph with ear-splitting noise, only to slow down before the first turn. The car held to the road, and surprisingly Brian never once lost control, after we graduated and as he was preparing to move back to Mississippi, Brian sold the car for $400 and a set of speakers. I don't think the speakers would have made as impressive a sound as that piece of Detroit muscle.

Rhett had a red Mustang Mach 1 Fastback. This car was beautiful. He doted over it. The three of us would also take this car on the straightaways. I recall the speed ramping up, the car starting to tremble, and then the front end came off of the ground, we started bouncing, the front end acting like a basketball, each bounce getting higher. We dribbled down the road towards the turn, reaching a speed of 155 mph before finally slowing enough to regain control. Shortly thereafter Rhett sold the car, believing he would die in a fiery crash if he kept the Mustang. Years later Rhett located the car in another state, it only had nine additional miles on the odometer. Apparently it was purchased, and parked. Rhett bought it back, at a premium. Its years in the sun necessitated a restoration, but to this day he still has this classic. I wonder how fast he drives it now.

Rhett's red Mustang Mach 1 Fastback.

I pursued parallel passions in senior year. While I continued to act in school plays, and with the Community Theater and Theater Under the Jerome (under the Mine Company), I also pursued leadership of the high school's Thespian Society, and the Speech and Debate Team. True to form I did the acting competition, consisting of two-person scenes and solo story telling. My partner Damon and I did a scene from *The Creation of the World* and *Other Business*, by Arthur Miller. God and Satan are seated on a cloud overlooking creation. Satan is advocating for knowledge, as Adam and Eve hadn't yet discovered how to be fruitful and multiply. "Look," says Satan, "he's kissing a tree." We did quite well with this scene, winning award after award, all the way to the competition to make it to the state finals. We came up against two girls doing our very scene. Both them and us were crushing the competition, and when we came up against each other Damon and I barely brought in a win. Overall, however, the girls tallied with higher scores and they went to state, while we were the first alternates.

My solo story telling was a three-person scene comprised of monologues from three characters in *Blues for Mr. Charlie*, by James Baldwin. I won a few trophies with that one as well. Our team included John, Billy, Damon and myself, Mark, and Wendy and Theresa, twin sisters at the top of the class. After one of the final competitions, the whole team having done exceptionally well, we proceeded to party with some of the other teams. Someone brought the Everclear and made bathtub punch, others brought various spirits, and we partied, all participated, with the exception of Damon, who wisely went to sleep. In the morning we arose late, I made the bus, staggering and made an excuse. Once we were on the bus, the chaperone held up and shook a bag of glass bottles, we were busted. Upon our return to Aspen we were all interviewed, Billy and John copping to bringing the alcohol, John and I copping to partaking. All of us exonerated Damon, and we all covered for the twins. Theresa had at least a 4.0 GPA and Wendy had one nearly as high. We knew that they were slated to be Valedictorian and Salutatorian, and we didn't want that to be

CHSAA – Aspen High "Superior" rating for Duet Acting (Speech and Debate) 1986.

CHSAA – Aspen High "Superior" rating for Drama (Speech and Debate) 1986.

in jeopardy. We all fell on our swords, and that was a good thing, the valedictorian speech at Commencement was worth it.

For much of my senior year I put in applications to acting programs across the country, but I really wanted to go to New York City. I wanted to pursue an acting career and I also wanted to get as far away from Aspen as possible. I would make several trips to Denver to audition for schools such as Juilliard, the American Academy of Dramatic Arts and NYU. While my auditions didn't get me into any of them, my grades got me into NYU. That year one of the Ex. Ed. trips was to New York, and I got my folks to fund me. Knowing I would be attending NYU I lobbied for a trip to the "campus" which is located in the middle of the West Village and is anything but isolated. Sitting around Washington Square Park, the dorms and university buildings were in the middle of the action.

I fell in love at once. We visited museums and saw the Off Broadway production of *Little Shop of Horrors* at the Orpheum Theater. I later married a lovely lady who had workshopped that show prior to its Off Broadway premier. The NYC trip whet my appetite to leave the mountain town that I had called home for the last 11 years. This desire was fueled in equal parts by a sense of adventure, a desire to pursue acting, and the need to excise myself from a very toxic environment.

Just after I was accepted to NYU's Liberal Arts Program (my Denver audition for NYU didn't go well enough to get me in to the Drama program the first time around), I went on a school trip, finally able to depart Aspen for an adventure in New York City. This was my first visit to The East Coast since visiting my grandparents in New Jersey several years before. The student group stayed in a little hotel in Chelsea with a view of a brick wall. It wasn't lost to me that the movie across the street was showing *A Room With a View*. We walked and shopped SoHo, visited museums, hung out in Central Park and even went to Washington Square Park, where the "campus" of NYU was located. A haven for pot dealers at that time and beyond, it was no surprise that many of us were approached with the familiar overtures to purchase their product. The kids were amused, and the teachers were shocked. That week our eyes constantly strayed to the TV screens that seemed to be everywhere. In the window of a Crazy Eddie's in on 6th Avenue we watched with anxiety as the news of the Chernobyl meltdown dominated the coverage. On this trip we took a bus to the West Village to take in the Off-Broadway production of *Little Shop of Horrors*. Having not considered traffic we arrived after the curtain had risen and had to wait about 15–20 minutes before entering. The show was amazing. This was my first Off-Broadway production, and the Orpheum Theater was a small venue, so we enjoyed an up-close and personal production of a very new and innovative play. The Audrey II puppet was mesmerizing and contributed to my love of puppetry, which would become a brief career in the early '90s. Upon our return to Colorado, I was immediately ready to be back in New York. On that short trip my home in Aspen had been replaced. I would be a New Yorker, back on the East Coast, where my journey began.

George Burson and Bob Simons were opposites as teachers. Mr. Burson, a decorated Vietnam veteran with Democratic Socialist views, and Mr. Simons, a veteran of the Korean War with a decidedly right-wing leaning. Mr. Burson's history classes were thoughtful, he encouraged questions, shared his experiences in Vietnam, and his experiences of hearing the jubilant reactions to JFK's assassination while he was a college student in the South. I learned critical thinking in those classes, to view society through a hopeful, but informed, lens. Mr. Simons taught English. What I remember most about his class was his fierce belief that after graduating high school each student should do military service. My draft registration was on the horizon, and the continuing Cold War made me quite averse to that point of view, and I argued it with him, in front of the class. I suggested that two years of military service immediately after graduation would put the graduates at a disadvantage in the job market. Two years focused on the military is two years delay in one's college education, and therefore a two-year delay in joining the job market, and a continued delay in advancement. Those already in the job market and not subject to the service requirement would have an advantage which, my argument stressed, would be difficult to overcome and could increase over time. I must have made my point, because the class erupted in applause, and Mr. Simons got red in the face. It was after this event that my grades in his class would start to suffer. This coincided with my immersion in theater and the difficulties at home, so I don't know if it was retribution or not. I would, however, end up graduating with As and Bs in all classes. I think I got a C in his.

I had never had a date to a school dance, and I was determined to change that. Though I had several female friends in high school, and I'd once had a girlfriend from another school, there was no romance in my life. I decided that I wanted to go out with a bang. I had $1,000 in the bank and decided to give Angela, from Carnegie Mellon, a call.

"Do you want to go to my Senior Prom with me?" I asked, "I'll buy your plane ticket." Much to my surprise and delight she said yes. I flew her out and she stayed with a neighbor for a few days.

I showed her around and introduced her to my friends, and our parties. Though still shy, she got along with everyone. Her prom dress, worn recently for her own prom, matched my tux exactly, through sheer coincidence. When we walked through the of one girl who had, politely, turned me down when I asked her to accompany me. It appeared that nobody expected me to have a date, much less a beautiful mystery woman. As we danced slowly we shared our first kiss. For those brief days what began as platonic became romantic, and I fell in love for the first time.

Prom glamour shot.

That evening, after the dance, Angela, me, and a couple of friends made our way to Brian's apartment where we proceeded to play quarters with champagne, and Angela and I stayed up most of the night alternating between deep conversation and romantic interludes. Though I was smitten, the relationship was short-lived, as she was in Pennsylvania, and I was in Colorado and was very bad at writing letters. The long-distance thing wasn't going to work. I only saw her twice more.

In 1994 I was watching *Pulp Fiction* on the big screen when Bruce Willis' taxi driver, Esmeralda Villalobos, came on the screen. I was stunned. There, two stories high, was the face of my prom date, Angela. I was too stunned to focus on the rest of the movie. When I got home I found her Pennsylvania phone number and called to congratulate her. Her mother answered the phone and informed me that she was in New York to promote the film, and she gave me her hotel phone number.

The very next afternoon we were sitting in her hotel room happily reminiscing, and again platonic. Two years later, when I was visiting my parents in L.A. she invited me to the wrap party for the film *Curdled*, produced by Quentin Tarantino, co-starring Billy Baldwin, and starring my friend and first love, Angela.

Commencement was what one might expect, we all were robed, hat and tassel, and sitting in alphabetical

Decked out for prom.

order. I received a scholarship from Les Dames de Aspen, towards my theater studies. Adam, sitting next to me won a scholarship from the Aspen Community Theater, where he'd done a few more shows than I had. Theresa, valedictorian, took the podium and did a speech which made the newspaper. It seems that she, and A student, and Will, getting Cs or Ds at the time, performed an experiment aimed at their suspicions regarding the grading perimeters employed by English teacher, Mr. Bob Simons.

Theresa turned in a paper, Will turned in an identical paper, down to the comma. She walked us through the story of how she won praise, and an A, while Will got a much lower grade. Their experiment revealed that Mr. Simons graded upon his <u>expectations</u>, rather than on content. A collective gasp went through the audience as Theresa, tassel swinging in front of her eyes, uttered, "That's okay,

AHS Commencement Program (image).

its all just BS anyway." Mr. Simons' initials burned into Aspen High School history, and into the headlines.

"AHS graduation shocks a few" by Mary Eshbaugh Hayes - The Aspen Times (article).

My high school career ended, fittingly, with a keg party. The location was a meadow on a mountainside at Buttermilk. Around dusk we started to arrive, I drove the battered 1974 Audi Fox that we had gone over the cliff in on Christmas Eve several years before. That car had the heart of a lion. We were assured that we would be able to stay at the location until nine a.m. and I paced my drinking so that I would be sober by that time. We sat around the fire, reminisced and had a good time. I wish I remembered more of the party, but I do know that tears flowed, and vows of forever friendship abounded. At least now, with Facebook, a version

Graduation Day: Chris top left, me – upper right, and Brian below.

of that can exist today, though until those reconnections I let many of those friendships lapse in the ensuing years. The party did not go on until 9 a.m. Around dawn a maintenance crew arrived and told us that we needed to leave immediately. I had only put down the beer about two hours before, expecting to drive out around nine, so I was still buzzed. I should have gotten a ride and returned for my car, but I instead opted to drive. On the road down from the mountain the Sheriff's deputies awaited us. I was so nervous when one came to my window that my foot was shaking on the brake pedal. I could not recite the alphabet backwards as he requested, and I even burped in the middle and laughed embarrassedly. He made me promise to drive directly home, only a mile or two away. I agreed and drove slowly away. I made it home without incident, proof again that I must have had an angel on my shoulder. I think that angel sits there still.

———

My last Summer in Aspen consisted of parties with my friends, and a couple of shows at the Theater under the Jerome, including a performance of different scenes in which Dmitri and I did a scene from *True West*. I longed to leave Aspen to pursue my education and my nascent acting career. As summer came to a close I flew to NYC with my mother. She and my father's cousin, Iris, helped me to shop for bedding, school supplies, and other items to make my dorm room homier. That 6th Avenue Crazy Eddie's came in handy for the small TV I wanted and the electronic typewriter that I needed. The night before my orientation, as I settled into my room overlooking Washington Square Park, my mother, true to form, invited me and my roommates to an after hours club called Save the Robots. My roommates politely declined, and I answered "Mom, I love you, but I have school tomorrow."

EPILOGUE

WHILE IN COLLEGE I CONTINUED to act in plays in school and outside of school. In 1988 I played a major role in an art house film, and I got a call from my biological father, Stu. That call started a close relationship with him, and my two half-brothers that is still going strong. I visited Aspen two or three times more during college, and once more, in 1991, the year after graduating from NYU.

There is something magical about the Maroon Bells, fishing in the streams that feed the lake, picnicking in the meadow on the shores of the lake, climbing the shale hills at the foot of the peaks. My last time at Maroon Bells, and in Aspen, was on a trip to visit my farther. I had been away for some time but had decided to return during the summer and the Aspen Music Festival. My dad loaned me the use of his early 70s Toyota Land Cruiser, 3 on the tree. I used this vehicle to explore the formerly familiar streets of Aspen and roads of the outskirts. One evening I happened upon the Rocking Horse. A wonderful local musician, Dan Forde, was playing a lovely set on his Ovation guitar. Sitting in, with her guitar, was my friend from NYU.

I met Talia at NYU, after a drama lecture. I was wearing a shirt from Taka Sushi, an Aspen restaurant where my father worked as a bartender. Talia stopped me and asked me where I had gotten the shirt. Once I had explained that my dad once worked there, we discovered that we had parallel lives in Aspen, running in the same circles, but never having met. We became fast friends and spent a lot of time together while at NYU. We saw movies, had gatherings in her West Village apartment, tried to find her

Talia.

stolen bike in the East Village, climbed on the statues outside of The Plaza Hotel, and just had a grand time. I must admit that I had a crush on Talia, but we were just close, platonic, friends.

When I visited Aspen in 1991 it had been several years since Talia and I had seen each other. She was a natural in her performance with Dan Forde. When she and I reconnected after their set, it was like no time had passed. We reminisced, laughed, cried, and then ended up at Maroon Bells, where she was staying in her pickup truck, with a camper shell.

Even in the summer, snow-capped peaks, overlooked the deep green lake, fed by tributaries and surrounded by lush forests. A flower-laden meadow faced the lake, and provided an ideal spot to camp, take in the spectacular surroundings, and sleep under the stars. It is impossible to put the beauty of this place into words that would do it justice. There is no place more lovely. When the time comes I want my ashes spread on that lake and mountain.

When the hours passed and day turned into night, we sat and looked at the stars, the mountains barely visible, and wrote a song. We sat by a fire, near her pickup, sharing the time with her dog, Shacti. Talia was adrift but trying to find herself. I was finding my way after college, trying to live as an actor, and paying the bills as a puppeteer.

That evening, under the stars, I wrote a poem and, with her guitar, Talia added music to the song. In 2018, upon hearing of her passing, I re-wrote the final verse. Talia was a singular person, a sweet and troubled soul, a wonderful friend, a talented artist, and I am honored to have known her.

The Poetry of Wonder:

When your heart beats with the rhythm of the place
You know where you belong
When your soul sours like a bird aloft
And greets you with a song
In the pillowed clouds you find a place where you can rest your head
Enraptured embrace of angels protect you in God's bed.

In nature bright and friendship warm
In a dark and starry night
The poetry of wonder, love and memories give us light.

Majestic peaks of sculpted rock lend grander to the skies
The wonders of the mountain tops open to our lucky eyes
Together as one we watch the mighty miracle unfold
Heart to heart and hand in hand, a friendship forged in gold.
In nature bright and friendship warm
In a dark and starry night
The poetry of wonder, love and memories give us light.

A deep green lake fed by streams teaming with life
A lasting peace warmed by sun erasing the strife
A little dream grows with years as memories abound
A little smile dries my tears as I remember the sound

Of nature bright
Of friendship warm
Of your singing soul that night
The poetry of wonder and your memory
brings me light

The Poetry of Wonder (audio)

I CHOOSE TO CLOSE MY ASPEN STORY at Maroon Bells, because it is the first thing my mind goes to when I think about the place that so formed me and then transformed me over the course of a brief 11 years. Unspoiled, the mountains and lake, the expansive sky, can make one forget that the Aspen of my childhood has largely vanished, in favor of Prada and Gucci.

Everybody's experiences of Aspen differ, but I am grateful to have shared so many adventures with crazy kids that I still call my friends today. Their craziness has, thankfully, helped me stay sane.

———

Gazing at the snow-capped peaks of Maroon Bells, one can forget even that Aspen itself exists and be transported to that famous Rocky Mountain High.

Maroon Bells photograph © Mark Ronay – markronayphotography.com

CONTRIBUTOR:
LO SEMPLE

Lo ARRIVED IN ASPEN IN 1974 in the
back of his parents green Volvo station
wagon. He currently writes a local
column every Saturday for the Aspen
Daily news, and can be spotted around
town or on the bike trails and ski
mountains of Aspen and Snowmass.

He also helps travelers from all over the world via Suit
Yourself, Aspen's mobile skiwear outfitters—renting skiwear
for over 25 years.

GENTLEMEN OF ASPEN: THE SCRUM OF THE EARTH

ONE THING I LEARNED at a very early age growing up in Aspen was that rugby players are not to be messed with. I arrived at this conclusion after watching my very first Ruggerfest in Wagner Park, as the helmetless bruisers collided with each other with terrible brawn and might. It was like watching big horn sheep square off, or an ongoing, chain-reaction car crash. Suddenly an oddly oversized white football would pop out of the scrum, as one of the brutes would thunder down the field and slam the orb onto the ground in the end zone. If you look closely, you can still see some of the former local rugby stars limping around town with most of their teeth.

Our physical education instructor at Aspen High School, Coach "D," was a rugby player, so he made a noble attempt at teaching us kids the nuts, bolts and nuances of the old-world game. The ironically named "Gentlemen of Aspen" rugby squad shared the Gentlemen of Aspen: The scrum of the earth

The ironically named "Gentlemen of Aspen" rugby squad shared the Aspen Skiers trademark red-and-black uniform colors. It was common to see bumper stickers on cars locally urging fellow motorists, pedestrians and passersby to "Give Blood. Play Rugby." One time we threw a water balloon into an open window of "The Pub" where a bunch of rugby players and other assorted hooligans were gathered after a game—the place erupted like a hornets nest as we sprinted away on our BMX bikes.

While I never really understood the game of rugby, I remain oddly fascinated by it. It's incredible that over the years, rugby has remained a defining sport of my childhood and beyond. Rugby players are in a category of their own: hulking thighs, unapologetically short shorts, gladiator-esque physiques—some held together with various braces, wraps and white athletic tape—fun-loving and jovial, and nary a helmet to be seen. The protective devices you do see remind me of rudimentary road cycling helmets from the days of old. Wagner Rugby Stadium undergoes a magical transformation giving our town park an international sporting vibe that's right up there with the World Cup.

One of my favorite parts of watching games at Wagner Rugby Stadium is when a team kicks an extra point or a field goal towards the Mountain Chalet, and the monster ball comes careening awkwardly down onto an unsuspecting car with a loud thump, setting off the car alarm that inevitably draws a comical reaction. Other times a ball will errantly soar into the mall, landing who knows where.

Does anyone remember the crowd favorite Gentleman of Aspen floats in the Wintersköl parade? The displays create a scene of snow-warfare carnage that every hoodlum kid in Aspen wanted in on. It was a green light to throw snowballs at adults for an hour or so. Behavior like that from us kids usually led to an immediate ass whooping.

Their float was a barbaric scene of excess and carnage, begging brutality. Twenty or so rugby players would pack into the back of a large flatbed truck with sides, a keg of Coors in the middle flowing like wine, each holding trash can lids and wearing goggles to deflect the barrage of frozen projectiles. We would establish higher ground above Aspen Drug and throw chunks of snow we had calved-off of the downtown snowbanks. It was absolutely ruthless.

Local rugby culture introduced me to a whole host of different personalities over the years like Samoans, Brits, Aussies, Kiwis, South Africans, Irish and Scottish players among others. The team rosters from the '70s and '80s read like an Aspen Hall of Fame "local characters" tribute edition.

It came to my attention after digesting bygone accounts that the genesis of the Aspen Ruggerfest was an offer made to the Aspen City Council: essentially, we'll clean up Wagner Park (which at the time was trashed) if you let us host a rugby tournament there. The rest is history. I truly hope that over the past half-century the many returning teams have formed meaningful connections in our community—and forged memorable war stories. It's important to me that the newcomers and old-timers to Aspen Ruggerfest feel genuinely welcome.

Another historical point of interest is that the Gentlemen of Aspen were hired to do security for the Rolling Stones at Folsom Field in Boulder on July 20, 1978. There's a picture in the Aspen Historical Society photo archives of our Gentlemen in their unmistakable trademark red and black striped uniforms standing at the ready down front while Uncle Mick, Cousin Keith and the boys rocked the house. I would've loved to hear the conversation leading up to that gig. Better to hire guards known as "gentlemen" than Hells Angels, one would surmise.

Over the years I've come to look forward to the pageantry of Ruggerfest—the colors, the sportsmanship, the brutality and grunting, the smells of billowing bratwurst smoke, beer and Icy Hot, players on their hands and knees looking for their teeth in the grass, the war horses hobbling through town after games, and the tight-knit community of rugby in Aspen and abroad that coalesces here every year. I like watching the games early in the day, then getting home safe in bed before the players start drinking heavily, fighting and potentially busting up the joint. Lock up your daughters, it's Ruggerfest.

CHRISTMAS IS COMING, THE GOOSE IS GETTING FAT

I'VE REALLY DONE IT THIS TIME. I went and did the unthinkable and bought a one-piece suit as my primary ski outfit for the season. Now comes the real challenge—fitting into it. I'd just as soon get back into some semblance of ski shape post-haste, but there's a hundred miles of bad road between my fitness goals and me. My biggest fear is getting so old and fat I can't bend over to get into a proper tuck on Kleenex Corner.

This time of year is like "Shark Month"—a feeding frenzy consisting of linked holiday parties offering large extravagant meals slathered in rich sauces, and all the shrimp cocktail you can hold down. Moderation is not my middle name. Come to think of it, I don't even have a middle name, only the potential for a nickname with a leftover turkey sandwich in the pocket of my new one-piece.

When your family tree is a pear tree like mine, the shape of your body tends to follow suit. Long stretches of my day are spent thinking about my next meal. As the temperatures plummet, visions of chunky stews, swampy gumbos and toasty garlic bread with melted Parmesan dance in my head like sugarplums.

Remember when ski-conditioning classes were all the rage? "Dry-land" training they called it. What happened? You used to see every single gym and fitness center advertising their specific methodology and ski-specific, fanny-busting workouts in the paper starting in October. The classes would fill with a virtual who's-who of local skiing prowess. Now the overarching notion is "skiing yourself into shape."

I can remember as a kid, the Aspen Club was "the" place to be for ski conditioning. They would hold these brutal workout classes every evening down in the gym that consisted of squats, tucks, jumps, rolls and every other conceivable torturous exercise. The instructors were usually local legends like the Tache/Cooper dynamic duo, or that guy "Quad-Zilla," with a McBride or two thrown in there for good measure. People you knew in public as perfectly reasonable people suddenly took on the air of Eastern-European drill sergeants, yelling commands. You'd wake up the next day cursing them, basically unable to walk.

From what I can tell, Jean Robert's Gym and CMC are the only ones offering ski-conditioning classes now. If you're new to town, they're a fantastic way to get into the spirit and meet people, too. The concept being: Do preseason fitness classes now, hit the ground running, and when the big snow starts falling, leave your friends in the dust. Like the ol' saying goes, "No friends on a powder day"—or in my case, no friends on most days.

The one-piece ski suit is making a comeback. You heard it here first. As far as I'm concerned, it never left. People like me, relatively high-functioning ski bums, are seeking them out with passionate intention. Brazilian tourists call one-pieces a "Maccacao," which I'm told means monkey suit. The styles are new-school, meaning they must take inseam cues from prison fashion, as seemingly all the younger generation of skiers look like some odd sort of wealthy Anglo rappers/gangsters ... kind of how I must've looked 10 years ago in my first-generation Strafe "Sick Bird" onesie. The modern, New Age, Aspen ski bum must adapt or die. For me, wearing a one-piece is part of that amorphous process.

Women's one-piece ski suits also are making a big bang out on the slopes, too. Obermeyer has again reintroduced its longstanding line of ladies getups that are sure to impress out on the slopes. Don't take my word for it, though; their sexy "Katze" suit was featured in Cosmopolitan magazine. All fashion is a reboot, including those shiny silver and gold get-ups people snarkily call "microwaves."

People here in the 1970s will remember "Suzy Chapstick" wearing one, among others.

They tell me serious skiers don't wear onesies. Oh yeah? Don't laugh at someone wearing one, because someday, somebody wearing one may be laughing at you. I'll never forget, one year long ago, when the Aspen Highlands Bowl (when even the ski patrol still called Highlands Bowl, "Highlands Bowl") was in its open-to-the-public infancy stage. I'm talking pre-Deep Temerity lift; when you had to exit on the daring OK Traverse, and the Steeplechase Catwalk all the way back to Midway. I'd hiked to the top on a sleeper midweek snow day. There was no powder panic, or ant-line, or bowlcat, or any of that jive. I was standing atop the "Ghetto" area admiring a virgin un-skied line before me.

As I reached down to make a final equipment tweak, a long, tall, elegant blonde woman wearing a swank Post Card one-piece suit replete with a fur hood murmured something as she came blasting by me with a very European style of skiing—no daylight between the legs, slightly counter-rotating her upper body with each turn. The last thing I saw was her tightly braided, blonde ponytail vanishing into a vapor trail, as she unapologetically purloined the powder I had planned to ski.

And you thought having your line poached by a snowboarder was bad. ...

THE PESSIMIST IN OUR MINDS

THIS IS THE TIME OF YEAR I affectionately like to call "panic season." There's always an undercurrent of anxiety just below the surface of everyone's psyche in the ski industry.

Is it going to snow or not? What can Aspen Skiing Co. possibly get open in time for the impending horde of tourists lurking off in the distance? Will Highlands and Buttermilk open as scheduled, or is our season doomed before it even got started?

The pessimist in our minds runs riot.

The local climate warriors are predictably active in this dialogue when it doesn't snow according to the SkiCo's schedule. They'll blame global warming and fires on private jets, traffic, monster homes, IKON passholders, the X Games and humans in general if the snow report is grim. Let the doomsday predictions begin. Don't blame me—I compost!

Here's an interesting journal entry from Walter Cornell, Aspen's assistant fire chief in the late 1800s, back when "panic season" was in its infancy: "9/28/1898: Warm. Pleasant. Very dry and dusty. Forest fires raging close by to town. Did some writing at Ramsay's ..."

Notice how he was a realist—he didn't fly into a panic. It was the end of September and there were fires burning out of control on our urban wilderness border. The local fire chief's right-hand man responded by going to a bar to "do some writing"—today's version of the poser like me who posts up at the J-Bar with his laptop.

If that happened now, the town would be in a tizzy. The assistant fire chief would be shamed on social media then canned for not caring. (Note of interest: Cornell died by suicide.)

As someone who makes a living from the ski industry, as we all do directly or indirectly, I reserve every right to fly into a panic about the lack of snow this time of year. But over the years I've learned that it always snows eventually, and even if it doesn't, people still come and have the times of their lives. Thanks to the marvels of modern snowmaking, we can always salvage some semblance of a ski season. It's like having a wad of cash stuffed underneath your mattress.

There's a whole contingency of locals who think that snowmaking is pure evil and in some sense it is; the water being used on Aspen Mountain is city water—treated with fluoride—presumably for ski health. The sheer gallons being consumed for us to slide down the mountain on sticks is ghastly and obscene. And that comes right on the heels of a water-devastating irrigation season. It feels like you can see the rivers go down in flow and hear the trout gasping for water when snowmaking starts, and it's always at the most delicate time of year, when the rivers are already stressed. Now that you can blame me for—I'm in the lawn-care industry and the ski industry.

There's another school of thought that teaches water "banking" through snowmaking—the argument being that the snow being made now will be added to the runoff in the spring—effectively setting that water aside now as savings for later. That's a fairly tenuous argument, but if you're a skier you better start buying into that portfolio now like it's Bitcoin.

The snowmaking system at the top of Aspen Mountain is going to prove pivotal. I'm a big fan of experimenting with snowmaking on expert terrain. I haven't been up there yet this year, but one would imagine that we're getting fairly close to being able to ski from the top down to Lift 3. Ajax is an anomaly in the ski industry in the sense that you can ski the top section with a crepe-paper thin coating of snow. The upper mountain has basically been picked clean of rocks by former ski patrol legend Robin Perry.

Well, not quite "clean" according to the bottoms of my skis over the years. I never met a pair of rock skis I didn't like. There's a funny saying, "Nothing drives like a rental" that applies to skiing and rock skis. When you're skiing on rock skis there's an ambivalence to the snow conditions that is downright liberating. People on the gondola who complain about bad snow conditions suddenly turn into monotonous, droning bores. Sometimes you'll see tourists on high-end rental skis with the damage insurance waiver (or not) skiing right down into town on Mill Street, just like the olden days.

I humbly urge our valley residents to celebrate Aspen's 75th "double diamond" anniversary of skiing with me. Whenever I become frustrated with myriad growing pains and presses of development in Aspen, I often find solace in our town's ski history. Framing the present, and glimpsing our future through our past, really works for me.

If you feel like the ski bunny you've been chasing all these years has left you behind—a girl named "Aspen" with an insatiable appetite for powder whose spending and partying are spiraling out of control—train your thoughts toward our history this winter for peace and understanding.

Don't panic, she's still worth chasing. Even if you have to follow her down the manmade "ribbon of death" on Ajax with rock skis.

ENTRANCE TO ASPEN, A SONG THAT NEVER ENDS

BACK WHEN I WORKED for Aspen Skiing Co. and had long brown hair—nary a touch of gray, wore pointy sideburns, a shirt and tie, and passed urine tests with flying colors—I think I may have voted for the "Preferred Alternative" to the fabled Entrance to Aspen. It's been so long I honestly can't remember.

But I do recollect being on opposite sides of the issue with my childhood friend Tom, so I called him to remind me what our arguments over the then-proposed four-lane entrance to Aspen consisted of. He quickly offered to send me an email with his idea; I pleaded, "Don't." The whole subject has become so convoluted and conveniently conflated with other tiresome, bleeding-heart local issues that taking a stand one way or the other feels exhausting. Mere moments into the conversation my plasma pressure began to noticeably notch.

What I've learned over the years as a local columnist is that our political conundrums are often more complex than they seem on the glassy surface, and you never know which camp the people you know and love are going to side with. That being said, I'm generally opposed to a four-lane highway coming into Aspen, but am open to accepting bribes in any form imaginable to sway my fragile eggshell mind.

Double "S" Curves

There are people in town who've fashioned entire unpaid careers on being armchair experts on the Entrance to Aspen dilemma. The highway rant defines them; it consumes them to the point of public avoidance. Aspen will do that to you if you're not careful. Then no one wants to be your friend or invite you to dinner parties. Just look at the letters to the editor in the coming months. It'll baffle you how many experts on small-city, semi-urban traffic flow we're surrounded by. Whenever I read a diatribe on the subject, I think to myself, "I wonder if CDOT is hiring? I bet this person could start as a trash picker-upper, maybe get promoted to snow-plow driver, and ultimately work his way up to designer of our new Entrance to Aspen."

Besides, I would fathom a wild guess that the people writing letters demanding a highway upgrade represent single-person vehicle trips in and out of Aspen. Does Aspen owe you a quicker drive time? If you're driving a car like me, you're part of the problem. I don't feel like Aspen owes me anything. I provide services to locals and tourists alike, I make a comfortable, modest living; I wait in traffic like the next guy. Right now I have major car problems. One of the speakers in my Spicoli van is blown and there's nowhere to get it fixed in a three-state radius until 2024.

Here are the things I've noticed in the 25-plus years since the original Entrance to Aspen dialogue flamed out: The air quality on Main Street is not good, and the street-side dining or socializing experience is not relaxing. The S-curves have become a gauntlet of employee housing. When traffic is stop and go, it's arguably more livable in terms of safety compared to cars whizzing by at speed. Splitting Main Street at 7th Street in and out of town would effectively create an inhabited island of housing to the Aspen Villas and the myriad employee housing complexes within. That's a lot of local voters pooled in one area.

There have been two articles in the papers recently with some insightful observations. CDOT officials basically said, "When you guys are done playing your little game of grab-ass over the entrance to precious Aspen, call us. Oh, and by the way—you're at the bottom of our list." I'd like to think that Aspen is one of the butts of their jokes in state planning meetings whenever our name comes up.

I'm a big fan of CDOT. Frankly I'm still in shock there hasn't been a peep out of anyone about the repaving of the inbound Main Street lanes from 7th to 1st streets. They came in unannounced and banged it out in a single day. Between that little blacktop overlay of the previous dysfunctional pavement-patchwork quilt, and the retiming of the lights on Main Street, my quality of life improved considerably. Thanks CDOT!

Local officials have pointed out correctly that the town has changed since the last Entrance to Aspen vote, and that there needs to be the collective political will to get it done which was absent prior. It looks like the current trajectory we're on points to yet another vote on the entrance, preceded by a contentious, detailed reeducation process of our fussy electorate.

The real X-factor of this vote could be the West End homeowners opposed to the "sneak" and those who live in the potential inner islet of homes within the concept of another bridge coming into town. If all of those voters united—think planetary alignment—it could prove a unifying bloc that sets the tone and potential outcome of the vote.

I try and see all these local political issues through the gauzy, historical lens of the fact that Aspen hasn't yet reached her previous population peak of 12,000 permanent residents during the heralded mining heyday of the late 1800s.

The other day I parked over by 7th Street and stumbled around the area, trying to visualize what a new bridge, Highway 82 and Main Street reconfiguration would look like, and the impact on the current residents. Would the "Fritz-Carlton" I lived in for a year fall victim to eminent domain? What about my buddy who owns a front-row end unit in the Villas? But more importantly, would the new highway solve any of my personal problems?

Apparently I used to think so. Now I'm not so sure.

TAKE THIS JOB
AND SHOVE IT!

MY BOSS IS A JERK. Everyone in town knows it. I've always wanted to quit right when we're slammed at work—a bunch of customers standing around with their mouths open, watching in disbelief at how poorly the business is being run—and making a big dramatic exit to a boisterous round of applause.

It's a fantasy, because I work for myself. I am my own boss. I can never call into work sick or get the satisfaction of telling a manager I'm fed up with this crap. Because the truth is, I'm resigned to people telling me what to do, and I've never met a job that was beneath me.

The latest construct says that America is going through a coming-of-age midlife crisis of sorts it seems, with droves either reevaluating the worthiness of their jobs, changing their careers, or dropping out of the workforce entirely—which seems like a luxury, not a crisis. Maybe I'm ahead of the curve or just plain lazy, but I've been having these feelings before the word "pandemic" was ever in our daily vernacular. I don't get it. And I'm not buying the argument that the government's to blame.

Let's say you have a COVID-spurned, come-to-Jesus moment about how hollow and meaningless your job really is. A ray of sun breaks through heavy clouds, you're standing in a shaft of light, and suddenly you realize how you're as expendable as a Solo cup at a keg party. You storm into work—or sit down and craft an emotive email rife with philosophical platitudes—and quit. Then what?

After working for myself and owning my own businesses for this long, I'm basically unemployable. The thought of trying to reinvent this middle-aged dog and find another line of work is daunting, almost like dating again. Putting out feelers, handing out a resume (having to assemble one first), selling yourself as something better than you actually are. I have an Aspen High School diploma, one foggy year of college and a relatively small skill-set. I cringe at the thought of someone in HR handing me a piss cup and inquiring, "Where do you see yourself in five years?" Answer: Doing the exact same thing I did today, that's where.

I feel callous writing about unemployment because I've never really had to sacrifice or struggle. Ever. Sometimes I'll go into a local business and see someone I know working there for the first time and be taken aback. It makes you wonder what people are going through to end up at jobs you think they're not suited to.

I'm having trouble trying to reconcile the national trend of people dropping out of the workforce, because I live in Aspen. If we had a town song it would be, "We're so busy!" Every time I ask someone how he or she is, the first response is, "busy." A lot of us have the luxury of saying "no" to work. We can pick and choose what work we want to do, when we want to do it and for whom we want to do it. Try calling a local trade provider with a small job and see. Maybe nationwide trends can never find a steady job in Aspen.

Dare I say it's an "employees' market" now for people seeking employment? Especially if you barge into a business looking for help and declare you have a place to live. Soon lift ops will start demanding an Audi, valet parking and a tomahawk rib-eye dinner every Friday at the Nell. There's an air of desperation in some of the help-wanted ads. Scanning them, trying to picture myself in a foreign uniform with a name tag, I thought of what might have been in my life.

The one demographic I haven't heard as much as a peep out of is the robust Latino workforce here. It seems like they are keeping their heads down and working right through the upheaval. It makes me wonder if Americans are lazy. I'd like to think that Americans inherently want to work and be useful. I grew up privileged in Aspen, but I genuinely like to work. I need to work, like a shark that dies when it stops moving. Even if I didn't have to, I'd like to think I still would. Two days of not working and I go absolutely crazy. Case in point: Going on vacation is incongruously more exhausting for me than work.

I'm always suspicious of people who "love" their jobs. When I hear someone say something about how if you love what you do for a living you'll never work another day in your life, I tend to smile and walk slowly backwards away. I have moments of liking what I do for a living, but to me I save my love for things that actually merit receiving what a finite resource my love is. I love to cook, but not professionally. Same for skiing and riding a bike.

The one thing I've learned about work and jobs and making money to live is that there's no easy way. If you're always obsessed about money, Aspen's got to be a terrible place to live—every day having your nose rubbed in exorbitant wealth, like a puppy in potty training that soiled the carpet.

Besides, Aspen has always been famous for people with decorated college degrees punching down into the labor market, working relatively menial jobs as far as societal norms are concerned. Every time I find myself wanting to quit my job, I'm forced to grab myself by the front of the shirt, look in the mirror and say, "Get over yourself, man." Finding a new calling is an interesting concept, but not one I can seriously entertain at this juncture.

EMPLOYEE HOUSING: LIVIN' THE 'UNDERWROTE' DREAM

IF ASPEN HAS PROBLEMS, then the APCHA employee housing program is one of the key solutions. I've lived in a prefabricated government-subsidized development dwelling for nearly 25 years. If you're in one of the factions who hate the employee-housing program, the people who live in it and anything to do with new proposed complexes, all I can do is humbly thank you for your generous subsidy; like a tip you'd rather not leave that's involuntarily been added on at the restaurant much to your dismay. And by the way, you're getting a smokin' deal with me.

"Scrap the whole program, it's rife with trustafarians, scofflaws, loopholes and corruption!" some say. My retort? "Hogwash! I'm living proof the system works. Sure the organization has flaws, but fret not, we have our best people on it!"

I never thought I'd be a middle-class American living in government-subsidized housing. How would you even classify that? "Trickle-up" economics? I epitomize the employee housing program in action. I grew up here, own two businesses, raised two kids under the safety-umbrella (ella-ella-ella-ay-ay, for all you Rihanna fans) and am stealthily planning my exit strategy — retiring in my employee housing — as we speak. You better believe my eye is trained carefully on all of the dialogue about retirement requirements and such. A part of me is scared

I'm going to somehow get kicked out. There, employee-housing haters — I'm living in fear. Are you happy now?

When I do retire, I will be of tangible value to our community. I plan on making myself useful by volunteering all over the place — at the Wheeler, up at the schools, walking dogs, signing up for boards and steering committees, engaging in the community, being an on-snow ambassador and giving back to Aspen, a place that has given me so much.

As a kid, my mind was clouded with visions of grandeur that I would forever be living in my parent's house in the West End. The day would come soon after puberty, I imagined, they would pull me aside and bequeath the three-story, five-bedroom, solar-heated, architectural marvel to its rightful heir, leaving my sisters in a hissy fit to fend for themselves. I could put my Madonna "Boy Toy" poster back up and play KISS on the stereo as loud as I wanted, forever and ever.

Then reality hit. One day I came home and there were the dreaded, tacky "For Sale" signs hammered into the heart of our front yard. The piranha were already circling in their Limited Edition Grand Wagoneers with fake wood paneling, and the trendy new status symbol car kid on the block — the daunting, symbolic Range Rover — all the while talking on their state-of-the-art flip phones. Fine, I thought. If that's the way you're going to treat your 24-year-old son who so graciously moved back into your house with your first grandson, so be it.

I put an ad in the paper actively seeking a permanent caretaking gig. Crickets. The chilly winds of desperation blew over me as I looked at the pitiful state, price and size of apartments to rent in town. I looked around and thought to myself, if all these other people can make it happen here, then so can I.

It just so happened I saw an ad in the Aspen Daily News for a room for rent in the West End, mere blocks away, for $600. My first roommate in Aspen was the mighty Bob Meyers of Meyers & Company — a man nearly three times my age. Bob got married and moved out, then my hoodlum buddy Pete Auster moved in. Our living situation was oddly like that show "Three Men and a Baby." I quickly christened our little carriage house the "Love Shack."

The world turned much faster as a single dad, and soon enough fate found me in love playing the housing lottery. Our number came up and things happened very quickly. People I'd never met were calling me asking if I was going to buy the place. They, too, were circling like piranha. We bought the house. At the time, growing up here, Cemetery Lane felt like down valley. Luckily the people who lived there before us were relatively clean and high-functioning, despite one of them being a "Deadhead."

I cringe at the thought of people buying places in uninhabitable disrepair. If aliens abducted me, and my place came up for sale, buyers would be blown away at how nice and well-maintained the house and grounds are. I also have less than zero respect for people who game the system. I can say with certainty that all of my immediate neighbors are playing by the rules and contributing to our community in deep, meaningful ways. If any of them were doing anything fishy, I would call them out in person and, if things didn't change, I'd narc on them so fast their heads would spin.

Every 10 years or so, a dialogue pops up about lifting price caps and restrictions on employee housing and letting the whole inventory go back into the free market. The free-market of Aspen has proven itself to be a pitiless Terminator with no conscience, feelings or remorse.

A lot of people would probably take the money and run. But to where? Not me. I'd treat my situation as if I were a contestant on the "Price is Right" — where you're holding a briefcase with a known amount of cash and the buxom blonde is tantalizing you with the unknown bounty of what's behind door No. 3. It could be even more cash, or it could be a stuffed animal. I'll keep the cash because it's hard to live and retire as a stuffed animal.

To those locals disenchanted with the housing dilemma in Aspen, I would urge you to be persistent, unwavering in your quest and keep playing the employee housing lottery.

DOCTOR CALL ME CRAZY, SOME SAYS I AM SOME SAYS I AIN'T

THERE ARE TWO TYPES of people in Aspen: those who think they're crazy and those who don't. Generally speaking, the ones who think they're crazy aren't. The ones who don't think they're crazy usually are the ones who are. There are often times I find myself thinking, "Wow — I'm about to have a nervous breakdown." Or that I'm actually having a panic attack.

When we talk about mental health, we need to be blunt. Currently there's a proposal to host two community events at the Wheeler Opera House focusing on suicide awareness and mental health awareness. I'd go to that. I applaud the Aspen City Council for trying to somehow flip the tables on our mental health problem in Aspen. When we assemble our support resources in one place for everyone to see all the options, it will be astounding. What if we put as much emphasis on mental health as we did on our physical fitness and appearance? Social media is another problem. We know it's toxic, but we still ingest it, like eating produce that we know has been sprayed with just a teeny bit of Roundup.

Over the decades I've been to multiple therapists and counselors; I've sought answers through local fellowship organizations. Other times I'm lazy and I find a sort of comfort in self-medicating, overeating and wallowing in my own rut of depression. This time of year gets me every time. There is no shame whatsoever in asking for and getting help. There are awkward times when I'll see one of my psychologists in town.

I always think to myself, "Man, that person definitely thinks I'm crazy." Can you imagine what the front-line workers of mental health and psychology, like therapists and counselors, have been going through lately?

After years of being exposed to the elements at high altitude, all of the docudramas I've endured being in the customer service trenches, and the rest of time doing manual labor, I'm fairly confident that I'm crazy. Living the dream can easily turn into an unmanageable horror show. This town will chew you up and spit you out psychologically and emotionally if you're not careful. I know from both good and bad experience that Aspen is a world-class party town. The highs are high and the lows are bottomless. Yet, I also learned that Aspen's a good place to recover, get sober and heal. There's an undeniable energy here you can tap into that will lift you up. For me, that magic is combination of the people and nature, the sum of which feels greater than its parts.

One of the ways I like to make a positive contribution to the mental well-being of others locally is by letting them know they are loved and that the work they do is of value and appreciated. It's often that I'll tell my friends that I love them. Just because you're not swapping bodily fluids with somebody doesn't mean you can't say, "I love you." Reaching out to others — strangers, tourists, locals and employees; people you've seen around town and always wanted to know who they were — making those connections can make someone's day and rekindle their waning faith in human nature.

Sometimes I feel like I'm Mr. Magoo, blindly bumbling my way through my own life; a series of hopelessly linked sagas, bouncing from guard rail to guard rail across oncoming traffic, one near miss after another. Then I'll swing wildly to the other end of the spectrum, feeling bold and unstoppable.

Other times it's as though I have the "Pampers touch," where everything I insert myself into turns into soupy yellowish baby excrement. The good news is if you need to get your head straight, there are resources in town if you need them. We're lucky. Our resources have resources, and that's a good thing, because our problems have problems.

There's lots of senseless death and mourning now in Aspen. Suicide is a thing here that's affected every single one of us. A friend once told me suicide is a permanent solution for a temporary problem. Men who are going through a divorce seem particularly vulnerable to suicide. I know I was. Suicide scares the crap out of me. Finally last year, I made the decision to have a hard conversation with both of my kids that no one was going to commit suicide on my watch. If they were entertaining the notion of killing themselves, they had to call me and talk about it first. And if they only reach my voicemail — they have to wait. I've since made that same pact with close friends.

Every desperate situation is always at its very worst point and seemingly hopeless right before it gets better. Tell people what your darkest thoughts are. It's never too late to ask for help or start over again. Build structure and routine into your life. Establish a support network before you need it so you always know you have a safety net for mental health to fall back on, much like you'd prepare an evacuation route for a fire.

If only our brains had smoke alarms ... or one of those buttons that pops up when the turkey's done.

HOMELESS IN ASPEN

ASPEN IS BY NO MEANS IMMUNE to any of the unsavory byproducts of the human condition you'd usually associate with a big city. Whether you're talking about crime, murder, rape, suicide, prostitution, drug and alcohol addiction or homelessness, all of these things exist here in their own funky little Aspen way I'm reminded of homelessness in particular most every time I go on a mountain-bike ride.

For the past two years, I've wanted to write about homelessness, as my route has skirted the county-sanctioned Brush Creek Park and Ride homeless encampment complex that's slated to close at midnight, on the morning of Nov. 1. Better late than never (my writing about it, not the closing of the encampment). The inequity of homelessness is jarringly juxtaposed as airplanes nonchalantly whoosh overhead and car, trucks and buses remorselessly speed by, all on their way to get in on our spoils of treasure and greedily suckle at the engorged teat of Aspen.

There was an article by Andre Salvail in the paper last week (and another yesterday) about the homeless outreach program — and a success story, even — I found sobering. When I read that the director, Dr. Vince Savage (big fan of his work) was resigning, it made me wonder what the future holds for our town's homeless population.

Prior to the campsite, a more anarchistic sprawl grew all the way over to the overflow lot, with a fire ring and lots of trash right near a manufactured wetlands. I was the nosy neighbor that called the county urging them to put up a chain and keep the event-parking section closed.

I'll be at home having a tantrum about something relatively trivial — like the internet or the power going out, or no hot water, or an undercooked artichoke — while as the temperature plummets, right across the river basically a little over a quarter-mile away, someone living in their car at a homeless enclave is clinging to what they have left of their life. People have died there, as well as underneath the shale bluffs highway. The ones who actually interface with our town's homeless population are the selfless workers at the shelter and churches, as well as the police and sheriff. I can only imagine what effect that has on you in terms of how you view Aspen and life in general.

Years ago, I wrote a snarky comment about homeless people in Aspen having cellphones that unfortunately snuck past my editor. The very next day in the paper there was a letter to the editor from a local social worker lighting me up like a cheap cigar. The swift response snuffing out my self-perceived cleverness was deserved. I tried to grow from that experience. I was reminded of this when I almost penned a similar tone-deaf, misogynistic misfire about the Monster Girls during X Games.

There's an unusual, nervous feeling I get from donating items to people in need — and seeing them when you do. Those are moments and micro interactions you don't soon forget. It's markedly different from just dropping off items in the alley behind the Aspen Thrift Shop. I've driven over to the penned-up area before to donate clothing items like jackets, pants, hats and gloves in the winter, also up to the Health and Human Service building as well. It makes you feel good inside, but I often wonder why there's an associated guilt, or why it makes me feel better about myself for a short period until the sensation wears off slowly, like Novocain. Maybe it's because I grew up here privileged. The experts always say not to give panhandlers money, but there are times when I still do.

Not infrequently, you'll hear critics of the homeless population: that they're gaming the system, able bodied, straining the system or getting away with one at somebody else's expense. It doesn't look that way to me. Much like folks will say how luxurious the Pitkin County Jail is — comparing it to a spa or a country club — and liken homeless people living in a car, big motor home or sprinter van to glamping. Not from where I'm standing. Homelessness strikes me as something you rarely if ever fully recover from. That's where the hard work of the support systems in place nobly attempts to lift people back up into society, while another faction tries to spitefully cut holes in the social safety net with poultry shears.

Certainly there are varying degrees of homelessness or jail conditions, but arriving at those places doesn't strike me as intentional. You'll also hear -decriers saying homeless people don't want to work. Apparently, from what I've been reading lately, it's not just homeless people who don't want to work — it's reaching epidemic proportions. To me there's a mental illness component, like a deep-seated depression and shame that comes with facing the daunting prospect of having to reinvent yourself.

If homeless people stick around Aspen for long enough and frequent high-visibility areas downtown, they'll reach a creepy celebrity status here. Take "Standing Man" for example, or the poor couple who lived in the blue van. Other vagrants come and go, blowing in and out of town like tumbleweeds, like Jeep the Clown. Who can forget the story about Aspen paying a transient and buying him a bus ticket to leave town?

If you poke around Aspen's urban/wilderness interface buffer zone, you'll see all kinds of people living in the woods all over the place, granted mostly in the summer months. Some sites are more elaborate than others. Just ask any Pitkin County trail ranger if you don't believe me. It's nothing new. When we were kids, we'd often stumble across hobo camps on Shadow Mountain. There also used to be a three-story wooden play structure in Herron Park where we'd constantly find telltale signs of people sleeping there. It was horrifying to read the articles this summer about the homeless camp behind Walmart and the amount of trash and syringes that were removed.

I've tried engaging and conversing with homeless people here in public, never with the intended result of making a meaningful connection. More so, I've been left asking myself, why did I do that? I wish I had answers, I just don't. I try to be empathetic and use these experiences to be more grateful and help frame my own place in society. As we celebrate snowfall and cold temperatures, another faction of humans sees the impending ski season in a whole other light.

ASPEN, HIGHER THAN YOU

THE CONDÉ NAST TRAVELER readers just rated Aspen the "Best Small City" in America. This is a fascinating award that proved two points I've touched on before. The first being that Aspen isn't a town any more; we're a small city. The second is, vacationing in Aspen is arguably better than living here permanently. When you're on vacation here you have no worries other than where your next meal out is going to be.

Who exactly are the Condé Nast Traveler readers that gave us this flattering distinction? The Condé Nast traveler is a high-functioning, affluent beast with discriminating, overindulgent tastes and uncontrollable urges. Singling out demographics is dangerous business, but generally the subject is an upper-class traveler that stays in expensive hotels, sleeps on clean linens and eats in fine-dining establishments. And really, being voted No. 1 by them is the ultimate compliment. We should all be very proud, because from the very top to the very bottom we've all contributed to the accolade in our own unique ways.

The ones really deserving of this award are the front-line workers at our hotels and restaurants. The rest of us just make Aspen look like a cool place to live and be. We're good at that. That's what we inadvertently do all day long.

What the Condé Nast Traveler readers clearly didn't do was look behind the curtain. They left our dance before their carriage turned into a pumpkin. If they stayed longer, they would've heard us complaining about how "unlivable" the town is, and how the latest influx of residents are the "wrong type" of people. Every single day it seems there's yet another letter to the editor from someone who lives here reminding us how awful and dystopian Aspen really is. We may not be a utopia, but that's what we strive for. Private jets, e-bikes, traffic and housing are all to blame as if Aspen is a former lover who left them behind. I'm constantly astonished at how many experts on every topic there are here — myself included!

If there were a valleywide reader poll on Aspen as "Best Small City," we would lose handily because Aspen isn't "real" enough. My Aspen is deadly real. People love to hate Aspen — even some who live here. You'll even hear locals threaten to leave, but bemoan they can't because they're trapped in the "golden cage" of employee housing. Then the ones who do leave either become authorities on Aspen from afar, or attempt to break back into Aspen like a twisted inversion of Snake Plisken's "Escape from New York" character trying to return as opposed to fleeing. I stopped going to those "going away" parties years ago because predictably you'll see the person on the street a year later.

Newcomers to Aspen trying to get a foothold that aren't successful in doing so will often lash out at Aspen and take bitter parting shots, calling us suckers or rich entitled assholes. The whole Aspen thing is a charade, they say; a mirage, an overpriced, overrated, unattainable farce, where the lifestyle being pedaled like a drug isn't even remotely commensurate with the cost of living.

Fair enough. If that's what you're feeling and experiencing, your feelings and experiences are real to you.

I'm fascinated by the amount of whining and complaining that goes on here and the unwillingness to be responsible for any of these perceived Aspen problems. No one is willing to be even remotely accountable. Traffic? If you're sitting in it, you're the problem. Mental un-health? If you're angry all the time, get help — you're a contributor. Aspen has made a lot of people a lot of money and continues to do so, but there's very little if any thankfulness associated with that either.

What about our beef with over-development or the insane amount of construction happening? Who's responsible for that? And what exactly do you do for a living, or how did you make your money to get here? How does that factor into our town's woes? The latest impassioned (laughable even) war cry of "enough is enough" is lacking any leadership, ownership, gratitude or vision whatsoever.

Have you ever heard anyone in the construction industry apologize? No, but you will hear constant grievances about fees and regulations. Have you ever read a county commissioner or city councilmember's quote saying, "Hey, sorry, this is all us and the policies we created?" I've heard locals blame previous councilmembers and commissioners for our "problems."

We're all just trying to make a living like the next guy. Remember, it's the people here like you and me that make this community so special — we got this. Everything is cyclical, and there's an end to every slam.

Our population has ballooned to over 7,500 permanent residents. More than 2 million tourists make their way through our sterling gates annually. The harsh reality brought to the spotlight by the blissfully observant Condé Nast reader is that Aspen isn't a town anymore — we're a quaint "small city" — and that our lives as locals aren't, in fact, better than their vacations. Thank you for the award, and more importantly, the lesson in humility we're silently hungry for, dear Condé Nast readers.

CONFESSIONS OF
A LAWN GUY, PART 6:
FALL CLEANUP

THE LAST FLIES OF SUMMER are getting lethargic, the grasses are lying fallow and the penultimate Saturday farmers market is today. The heat just kicked on inside my house with the acrid smell of burning dust and flambéed mouse droppings.

If you bend your ear toward our town's daily chipper conversations, you hear locals constantly gushing how now is their favorite time of year. Not me. Being in the lawn-care industry, I've grown accustomed to a tedious love-hate relationship with fall, as in every year I'm headed for one. All that oohing and aaahing over the foliage only makes the perennial sinking feeling worse when you're the one who has to rake all the leaves, bend over and pick them up like a parent cleaning up after a mindless toddler, put them into the back of your pickup truck and drive the little decaying buggers out to the landfill for recycling. My back hurts just thinking about it.

I don't know what my problem is, but every autumn there's a primordial mercury switch that flips internally, throwing me into a spiral of depression, irritability and anxiety. I'm like a pinball machine on tilt. The headless horseman in my mind starts galloping around, barking insane commands. There's no consoling me until the very last leaf has been removed from every single one of my lawn accounts, then I can start properly stressing out about the winter. But wait, what about going on a nice, long, relaxing vacation during offseason? With the pandemic, my waning urge to travel silently died inside of me, and I crapped it out one morning before work.

It seems like every year the fall cleanup gets more voluminous. Aspen is a certified "Tree City" and we indisputably benefit from that distinction. I've talked to a city forester about the designation, and my understanding is that the threshold is a certain percentage of treed canopy, as viewed from above. After the leaves turn on the surrounding mountains, there's what I refer to as Fall 2.0 — the valley floor's majestic cottonwoods and artificially acclimatized aspen and fruit trees drunk on city water change next, effectively giving us an encore into Indian summer.

One thing that drives me absolutely crazy is our town's relationship with bears and our love of crabapple trees. If you start at Paepcke Park, and continue down Main Street toward the courthouse, there's a gauntlet of crabapple trees — an all-you-can-eat buffet for bears that gets constantly destroyed by bear attacks. The only rational hypothesis I can come up with is that the city thinks it's "cute" when bears ravage these trees nearly to the point of destruction, and they enjoy the ensuing cleanup. Go ahead. Leave them as is. All you're really doing is encouraging bears into the downtown core, and expediting their senseless euthanization.

It's surprisingly easy to "bear-proof" crabapple trees, simply by pruning them. I have a crabapple tree in my backyard that the bears couldn't care less about. It's not like we don't have the budget, or the manpower, or the equipment, or the collective conscience or the wherewithal to prevent this from taking place every single year. With all the other excellent work the city does around town, this shouldn't be that hard.

I dare you: Pick one crabapple tree on the city right of way and experiment with it this week, like the one in front of Carl's. Same goes for local homeowners who have unpruned crabapple trees. You're begging for a home bear invasion.

All you have to do is aggressively round-sculpt the tops and shape the trees with a hedger twice a year like I do, once in the fall and once in the spring. The process prevents the trees from flowering, they don't produce fruit, and hence, no bear attacks. Remind me again how many tree services and arborists there are in Aspen? I really wish someone from the city forestry department (and anyone with crabapple trees in their yards that get attacked by bears) would swing by the St. Moritz lodge and take a look at what an incredible job Michael has done with his fruit trees. He inspired me.

One thing I will say is that out of all of the different types of animal waste I've grown accustomed to picking up, bear dung is by far my favorite. It's relatively benign in terms of odor, and often times the fruit-filled feces are actually works of natural art. You can discern the dietary trends of bears easily by looking at the gargantuan heaps of scat. The berry-laden lumps will often leave a beautiful purple stain on the pavement, the hues of which are stunningly vibrant. That's much more than I can say for the average pile of dog excrement I inevitably step in.

A man's got to know his place, and for the next 10 years until I retire, it's at the end of a rake every fall equinox doing fall cleanup. I've tried every conceivable technique short of setting them on fire, from mowing them to blowing them, to vacuuming them up, to raking them onto a tarp like the Latino crews do so efficiently. I use my leaf blower sparingly, like a good chef scarcely augments a curry with fish sauce, almost indiscernible to the naked taste buds.

All of this obsessing over leaves and crabapple trees and bears has me wondering if my obsessively compulsive attention to the immaculate yard is somehow overrated? The only way to shift my mindset is by being stoical and flipping the tables on myself, from I "have" to do fall cleanup, to I "get" to do fall cleanup. Every rake I break, an angel gets its wings. There. That's much better now.

IT MAY MEAN A THING IN 100 YEARS

A HUNDRED YEARS FROM NOW, historians, archivists and locals will look back on the period of Aspen we're living in as another heyday, every bit as significant as the silver boom of the late 1800s. It's more than just real estate now, though; there's the incessant whoring of the intangible, the illusory, ever-changing Aspen lifestyle itself. The miners probably did something similar as we locals do now, constantly telling anyone with ears and a pulse how amazing it is here and glamorizing their monotonous routine every chance they had.

Over the years I've learned to embrace change and marvel at it. That's the cool thing about Aspen — the longer you stick around, the more you get to see change. Even so, it seems like when I simultaneously train one eye on the present and the other on our past, I still see the same old people in the same old town doing the same old thing. We're the ones who found our own funky foothold and stayed here. Work is plentiful, we have housing, we know how to ski, we give back to the community; we play the town for all it's worth.

Aspen is all things to all people, but my version of Aspen has transformed very little over the years. My concentric circles and wobbly orbits are largely the same as they've been for a generation. Even among what is often perceived and touted as undesirable change, and an increasingly degraded quality of life, I've found stasis.

The shrill cries of town being overrun and unlivable due to tourism and development have reached a fever pitch this summer. Make up your mind, is Aspen amazing or does it suck? The one refrain that I keep hearing over and over is that there's a huge shortage of housing and employees, and that people in the service industry are burned out. I know after being in restaurant, manual labor and service-related businesses here since eighth grade, I am, too. Is this a turning point, or really any different than it's always been? I'm not so sure. Time will tell.

Each decade, like clockwork, there's a palpable feeling that the town of Aspen is finally ruined. Every generation of Aspenites thinks that the epoch they lived in was the best, and last. Remember when Boogie's restaurant was this big horrible thing that signaled the end of Aspen? It ended up being a focal point of the community. Then the Hard Rock Cafe and Planet Hollywood tried to drive a stake through our heart. Never happened. What about timeshares? When they first came on the scene, Aspen was apparently doomed. Snowboarding on Ajax? Death knell. Then the Aspen Art Museum — that was the final nail in our coffin. There are people still so bitter they'll never even set foot in that place.

But the issues of today, I'm told, are deeper and more dire than ever. Or are they? Housing, employees, traffic, wages, service, gentrification, inflation, mental health, crowding, construction and environment are global issues. We don't have the market cornered on any of these problems. Every resort town's got the same laundry list of pushes, shoves and pinches, impending doom always lurking right around the corner, hiding in the alley with a scythe.

I'm not buying it. I'd actually make an argument that we've done an excellent job of managing our mess. Delegations of officials from other townships would argue the same, and they have.

At some point, we've singled out just about every solitary demographic and sector, then demonized them for the perceived demise. Name a problem in Aspen and I'd say we have our best people on it. I'm a firm believer that our elected officials — and those who work in conjunction with them in and out of city government — are doing meaningful work with everyone's best interest in mind. While I might not always agree on every trajectory or indulgence, my feeling is that the Aspen City Council and Pitkin County commissioners are the ones actually sitting through the meetings, looking at the numbers, digesting all the facts and making hard decisions based on what's actually happening as opposed to the usual knee-jerk reaction from reading the cover of the paper and being an expert on the drama du jour.

One big difference I have noticed in Aspen is the polar shift of a resort focused on high turnover to one focused on selling houses. It used to be: Come to Aspen, bring your family, ski, shop, eat, hang out, do some fun activities, then split." Now, it's "Come to Aspen, buy a piece and stay." Not that there's anything wrong with that. It's a temporary cycle.

Back in the 1990s when the first seedlings of mega real estate were germinating in our petri dish, my dad Lorenzo imagined a super-realtor, a hybrid character capable of selling the ground right out from under your feet, named "Stirling Ritchie," whom we often joked about. I saw his six-million-dollar uber-realtor and upped the ante with him gallantly charging up to each showing on "Starfire," one of Carol Dopkin's horses. This 100-year boom of prosperity that's like a bad episode of that show "Billions" made me think, "What if I became a real estate agent? Would my father be proud of me from his home at the lonely Aspen Grove Cemetery, or would the ground rumble?"

Instead of looking down the handle of a lawnmower and rake every fall, I'd be casually holding the steering wheel of a Range Rover with my manicured hands. I'd have a gold watch, finely brushed teeth, a $150 haircut and a James Perse outfit. I'd reek of exotic cologne. Ever notice how really rich people smell different? When the word got out I'd joined forces and my new picture hit the paper, that might very well be the end of Aspen.

JAZZ ASPEN SNOWMASS' TRIUMPHANT RETURN

WHAT A FASCINATING VERSE of musical history we're witnessing here in Aspen with the celebratory return of Jazz Aspen Snowmass's Labor Day festival. I'm doing my meager part and civic duty to keep the touring concert industry buoyant by having purchased a three-day pass to Aspen's biggest social event of the year. My patchwork party pants are primed to go, glow sticks at the ready and proof of vaccine card saved to my phone.

I feel like I have this festival dialed-in now after all these years — e-bike to and from the show on the bike path, hit the chicken-naan wrap booth, see all my friends and dance the night away.

This weekend is going to be emotional for a swath of gritty locals, suave second-homeowners and starry-eyed tourists alike who've yet to see a live concert since the pandemic started. This will be my third rock concert, so I've already shed those salty tears of joy, danced my legs sore and screamed my throat raw. The bitching and moaning going on surrounding proof of vaccination for concert attendance nationwide is embarrassing.

JAS and Jim Horowitz have been stalwart stewards of the robust live concert scene and vibrant music history in Aspen, with a successful track record of pulling off shows locally, just as Bob Goldberg at Belly Up has. From what I've read, both local concert magnates are working together nicely.

Looking into the crystal ball of JAS' storied past, the memories come rushing over me. There have been so many goose-bump moments, like the proud parent sensation of seeing a red-haired kid crowd-surfing up on the Jumbotron during Steve Miller, and realizing who he was, and screaming out "That's my son! That's my son!"

Or watching Robert Cray perform "It's Because of Me" at a tent in Lot C of Snowmass, where a hulking timeshare now casts its ominous shadow. Or the thrill of seeing James Brown in a tight blue jumpsuit wail "Living in America" up at the on-mountain Burlingame venue. Or Monkey Train playing a set at an upper tent before Willie Nelson hit the main stage, as I danced with my son on my shoulders. Or David Byrne blistering though a 45-minute set of Talking Heads material while snow appeared behind him on the Big Burn. One time after a show I even ended up in Keith Urban's tour bus and caught a ride from backstage to the Intercept lot.

As the festival commences, it feels a little rash to mockingly belt out "Ding-Dong! the Witch is Dead" into the menacing face of the pandemic. I'm reminded of the Broncos playing against Tom Brady and the Patriots. Premature celebrations are dangerous business.

Acts are withdrawing all over the place. Some flat out canceled their entire comeback tours. Last year, Roger Waters rescheduled his Denver show for 2022. Def Leppard, Motley Crue and Poison canceled their stadium tour until next year. Others like Guns N' Roses are charging right into the jaws of the beast, fully vaccinated with a Les Paul in one hand and a bottle of Jack Daniels in the other, stacked Marshall amps turned up to 11.

I've never been in the VIP section of the local Labor Day fest, but the brochure looks nice. I can only imagine the curt conversation backstage between the headliner and promoter before they go onstage: "When you walk out onstage, you're going to see the venue is divided right down the center — VIP on one side, GA on the next — please be so kind as to treat both concertgoers with the same courtesy and attention."

The VIP section doesn't bother me now like it used to. One day I'll be in it. Every major band and festival has one. It essentially subsidizes the whole operation. I see it as a microcosm of the bigger picture in Aspen, a mirror image, and a musical chairs-like metaphor for our current socioeconomic status. We benefit from it, I'm told. It's good people-watching — sometimes better than the talent. There's a lot of "looking at me, looking at you" going on from the GA to the VIP section. Then there's ol' Robin Hood, passing free drinks over the barrier to his hoodlum buddies.

Anyone remember the famed "Cake incident" when the lead singer started a yelling match with a dude in the VIP section? The guy onstage with the microphone generally wins that pissing contest.

People often decry the outrageous prices of local concert tickets. Weighed objectively against the harsh reality of missing two days work and driving to Denver, getting a hotel room, buying food and party favors, risking ruin after the show as you search for an all-night diner or injury-death in a car accident driving to and from Aspen on I-70 and Highway 82, getting home the next day with sound fatigue and brain damage from the concert and struggling to form basic sentences ... suddenly the concept of paying extra to see a band in your hometown and sleep in your own bed afterwards starts to come into better focus.

It's tough being a middle-aged live music fan these days. All the acts of my troubled youth are flirting closely with becoming oldies acts. Last time I saw Jimmy Buffett was at the Aspen Club, with Leon Russell opening for him, and before that was at the Deaf Camp Picnic. I hope Jimmy regales the crowd with funny tales about Aspen. What's the real story behind that song "Gypsies in the Palace" anyway?

NEIGHBORS
WHERE THE SUN
DOES SHINE

IT LOOKS LIKE I'M GETTING a new neighbor: a solar farm. They've been moving in all summer long. Starting at 7 a.m. every morning since June, the trucks, machines and humans hammer away until evening. Between that and the jets ripping overhead every other minute, it's quite the symphony of evolution. Funny isn't it, how you can support something when it's first proposed and then wrestle with your decision like it's a greased pig when you see it physically.

When it was first proposed, many in my government-subsidized employee housing neighborhood and the surrounding neighborhoods objected. Conveniently, I can't see it, but I know exactly what it's like to look out your window and obsess over an inanimate object. It may be TMI, but my ADD has OCD. Let's be clear here: The field where the solar farm is being built was a leach field for human waste, deemed "uninhabitable" — not a pristine, wildflower-infested meadow.

Several people contacted me directly in an effort to get me to write something in the newspaper opposing our new neighbor, the solar farm. After enduring various rants, I assured them in no uncertain terms they were barking up the wrong tree. My response to those inquiries is always, "You write it."

Besides, asking a loose cannon like me to convey their will in a column in the local paper is dangerous business. It could very easily backfire. Columnists aren't journalists. They don't exactly "work for the paper." We're hired guns who often bloviate themselves into their own irrelevant oblivion.

Think about this: We had some eco-warrior lunatics turn off our natural gas supply last winter during Christmas week. After seeing "ExxonMobil change or die" spray-painted on the sidewalk by the post office yet again, I thought to myself, "The people who did it are still here."

I keep circling back to growing up in a solar-heated house in Aspen's West End. The construction was, interestingly enough, also government subsidized by a grant from the Carter administration. The local architects were the clever drafting-board duo of Bill Lipsey and Don Erdman. The houses — which are still standing — were simultaneously marveled at and scorned. I recollect Fabi and Fritz Benedict huddled in our driveway pointing and criticizing the three houses. I felt that was a good time to introduce myself.

Our house at 905 North St. was featured on the cover of Town and Country magazine, with an accompanying picture spread and article highlighting the terra cotta tile, the New England "salt box" roofline and the Doric columns in the plant-filled upstairs living space. It was a marvelous home to grow up in, floor-to-ceiling glass on the south side, sparse high windows on the north, with some cutting-edge technological features like temperature-sensitive automatic drapes and louvers in the ceiling with a Freon-filled chamber that opened and closed automatically as the sun rose and set.

At one point we had black barrels filled with water to absorb heat and then radiate the sun's thermal energy at night. The basement had an intricate valve system with a vast network of copper pipes leading into boilers and such, feeding the radiant floor heating throughout. Interestingly enough, the Aspen airport terminal building was also being remodeled and constructed with fascinating solar features like the same Freon skylights, and Styrofoam bead-filled walls fed with forced air and then vacuumed back out to let the sun in. U.S. Sen. Gary Hart christened it at the public opening ceremony I attended with my family.

Sometimes it feels like the walls of Aspen are closing in around me: on one side, a constant stream of traffic and trucks; on another, "killer" Highway 82 lined with road kill and refuse; on another, a solar farm; on another, the "intercept lot" (now called the Brush Creek Park and Ride) that'll be a major transport hub in the next 50 years; and above, a constant stream of jets ripping overhead. I'm literally boxed in by the luxuries and conveniences of development and the never-ending human rat race. Ah, but the view. ...

Nature's billboards keep screaming for help — wildlife, the rivers, the forests, fires and floods. Even humanity has advertisements of its own, from the pandemic, to sprawling homeless encampments to climate-forced migrations. Throw in a few mass shootings and you have an award-winning ad campaign.

I remember the energy crisis of the late 1970s and driving cross country in our yellow Mazda station wagon, waiting in hours long gasoline lines. I also recall being a kid, wearing my John Thomas Dye school uniform and sitting in the back of our green Volvo on our way to school in a carpool. Every day on Wilshire Boulevard we'd pass by the Veterans Cemetery. The carefully laid-out rows of headstones created a macabre optical marvel as they lined up symmetrically with each other, then morphed into the next row, seemingly infinite. As I turned my head and looked out the other window, it was a haunting mirror image.

Interestingly enough, I had that exact same sensation while riding into town past the new solar farm on my dastardly e-bike. Just then, a tourist couple passed on their energy-sucking e-bikes, presumably on the way to the Woody Creek Tavern for lunch. The guy said to his girlfriend, "Look — are they building an orchard?"

How about them apples?

PANDORA'S BOX: AS THE GONDOLA TURNS

MY GUT — THE SAME GUT that kept popping open the button of my ski pants all last winter — tells me that soon the Pitkin County commissioners are going to vote in favor of the proposed Pandora's ski area expansion. All indicators are pointing that way in terms of the Planning and Zoning Commission review, the U.S. Forest Service approval and the support it's receiving from those whom I've talked to in town. And I honestly feel like I've probed a fairly indicative cross section of people.

I've talked to environmentalists, ski patrol, powder guides, ski instructors, lift mechanics, ski bums, jewelry salesmen, housewives, backcountry enthusiasts, degenerates and upstanding citizens. Hell, I even asked a dog. The vast majority of people are in support of this project. The concerns of the opposition — people I know whose opinions I respect — are valid: the environment, the slow steady drip of overdevelopment and the wildlife that will be impacted. The opponents see a step towards what they call industrial tourism. They want Ajax and Aspen to essentially remain inert, an unalterable hot tub time machine.

Whenever new ski terrain comes online in Aspen, it gives the town an energy, an excitement, a buzz, a vibe, a buoyancy, a shot in the arm that we all could use right about now. That's undeniable. If you're against this project, I better not see you back there on a powder day "whooping" it up when it gets completed.

One of the most interesting components of the Pandora's proposed expansion is the zoning. Zoning has always been a moving goalpost, from what I can tell. It's negotiable, it's malleable. In short, it's ever evolving to suit the needs of various different interests. For example, the property adjacent to where I live is zoned "uninhabitable." (The only zoning that really seems ironclad to me is wilderness area.) As such, there's a concern, even a fear, that Aspen Skiing Co. will start operating its own overnight backcountry cabins in the area. The next logical step from there is ... gasp, roller coasters. Snowmass, it seems, is not zoned "ski rec" and has somewhat of an on-mountain Jurassic Park feel to it in the summer.

From what I can understand the "ski recreation" zoning is how Aspen Mountain, Highlands and Buttermilk are currently zoned, and the Pandora's area will follow suit — that is, it will strictly be for skiing in the winter during operation hours and dormant in the summer.

As someone who's made a modest living in the ski industry, I'm a part of the beast, a cog in the machine; I'm a voice that's not the ski company. The ski industry has always evolved. Stagnation is not an option in Aspen. Not in business, the town or your daily routine. It never has been, and it never will be. Just like the ski bum — a lifestyle that has by no means disappeared, it's just morphed, having adapted — we find our own funky foothold in society, operating on a different level out of necessity. There are forces of humanity at play here much bigger than we can fathom.

It often seems to me like people get possessive of Aspen Mountain. To a fault. Like they become a "check with me first" expert on the day-to-day and future ski operations. It's almost like they feel Aspen Mountain's a girl they used to date and now they see her skiing with other, younger guys.

I try to imagine how the forefathers of skiing in Aspen, like the 10th Mountain Division brigade — Andre Roch, Stein Eriksen, Friedl Pfeifer — would react to this expansion. Another part of me wishes SkiCo would partner with the Forest Service to do a great deal more forest management, like removing any dead standing trees immediately, and ski area expansion. Like into Maroon Bowl, for instance, while I'm still physically able to ski it.

As evident by our existing terrain, the finished products SkiCo offers are top notch. The environmental impacts are reduced to the barest minimum. Wildlife rebounds and thrives in many of these areas.

The other day, I was riding my e-bike up Summer Road over the very ground that our childhood and adult heroes have passed over on skis — like Klaamer, Kidd, Tomba Vonn, Shiffrin — conjuring memories from World Cups gone by. It was like looking through a kaleidoscope, colors and shapes coming in and out of focus. I was thinking of Aspen Mountain's rich history, from the time of the Ute Indians to the mining days to the birth of skiing in Aspen. I was thinking about our place in that timeline.

The backside of Aspen Mountain has always been an enigma to me. Part of its mystery lies in the avalanche history there. One in particular always captivated me: that of Meta Burden in 1972. I knew her son Doug and her daughter Beezy and their uncle, "Big" Doug. Some of you probably remember the Burden family. We were good friends of the Burdens growing up in the West End. Her surviving husband Andy was our school bus driver.

Meta died in Christy's Chutes when it, too, like Pandora's, was an out-of-bounds area of Ajax. Meta's nephew, a wonderful writer named Nick Paumgarten, penned a particularly moving piece in the New Yorker in April 2005 that I feel compelled to revisit every few years. I'm always moved and re-moved by his account of her death. I try to frame that account in context of this current proposal. There's even a brief account from the mighty James Salter. I highly recommend reading it.

HAVE YOUR NEXT AFFAIR IN ASPEN

THERE USED TO BE A bookshop/gift shop downstairs on the Hyman Avenue pedestrian mall where 7908 restaurant is now, and where the Irish joint was before that, and then something else I can't remember before that. As spirited youth, we'd walk into the gift shop and peruse the posters when we hopelessly exhausted our supply of quarters at the video arcade next door.

I'm thinking it was called Timberline Gift Shop. All I know is they had one of those upright poster displays you could flip through, filled with all of the cool, old ski posters that were actually current at the time: the kitten hanging off a chairlift with skis on that said "Keep your tips up!" or the buxom blonde Lange girl; the guy standing on a haystack with a pair of skis on that said "Ski Texas" or the cartoon drawing of a ski area with funky caricatures doing all kinds of wacky stuff on skis. Then there was the holy grail of posters — the "Have your next affair in Aspen" poster, with two dogs fornicating in the middle of the street.

The slogan is blunt, metaphoric, and full of obvious sexual insinuation and allusion. Very meta and Vegas-esque. The archival historic picture begs detailed study. Like the double terminal on Nell Chair, the Walnut House where Rick had those insane posters of Mick Jagger and Bjorn Borg, Crossroads Drug, the Sinclair station, Aspen Drug and Toro's. There's a lot to unpack there, but the real superstars are a copulating canine couple — a white Husky and a black Lab.

I always laugh when I see that poster because we used to have a dog named "Barney," an old mutt we got from the pound. One day my sisters took him for a walk into town, tied him up in front of Tom's Market (where the Ute Mountaineer is now) and accidentally left him there overnight. We had a charge account there and the deli hamburgers were especially delectable. The next morning at the breakfast table my mom asked, "Where's Barney? Has anyone seen Barney?" My sisters looked at each other, did a hard swallow, and scurried away from the table, down Hopkins into town — and there was Barney. Sitting right where they'd left him. I think that incident made them better parents.

Last year during the fall, I felt something was missing. Then I realized one morning the Aspen Skiing Co. hadn't launched an advertising campaign for the ski season. Fair enough; everything was in question. It still is. There are even locals who say that the SkiCo and the town of Aspen should cease to do any advertising whatsoever because Aspen's become "unlivable." Hmmm. Why do an ad campaign when you have thousands of fabulous people from all walks of life unintentionally posting ads on social media? Because, not launching an advertising campaign this year would be another giant missed opportunity. A penalty shot with an open net.

What changes from our tourist base did you notice last year? More domestic visitors, no Brazilians or Australians? Last year, I saw, interacted with and did business with more African-American tourists in Aspen than ever. And rappers. It made me happy. I was flattered to be an Aspenite and host.

I don't know if anyone noticed, but the best advertising campaign for Aspen that SkiCo or the chamber's never done happened right before our very eyes. A mega-rapper named Young Dolph rolled into town with an 18-wheel car-carrier with two matching paint job sport cars, and a four-wheeler with a matching paint scheme, and drove laps through town — "scooping the loop" was what we used to call it in high school — professionally filming every move. They hit the jewelry stores and paid for everything with cash: fat stacks of the stuff, like you only see on TV.

Then they stormed the dispensaries and gutted the places. Then they went back to their rented mega-mansion with chefs, masseuses and chauffeurs catering to their every whim and posted pictures on Instagram of their posse standing in the snow getting high in Aspen.

But Young Dolph didn't stop there. He recorded and filmed a song called "Aspen." They even played it one time during a Cyclebar class I attended in Aspen. I've done my best to interpret the lyrics and it can only be construed as the biggest compliment we've ever had. As a cherry on top, the music video starts with him reading the Aspen Daily News.

To me Young Dolph's presence in Aspen was a direct result of the advertising that SkiCo's been doing over the years in terms of cultivating diversity, inclusion, love and acceptance: ad campaigns that at first are difficult to understand. I'd even trace the origins of Aspen's popularity with the rap crowd back to the Winter X Games and their music offerings. Regardless, it's happening. The knee-jerk mentality is to mock the ads, and us, and start a huge flame war in the comment section with trolls chiming in about virtue signaling and being "woke," and how horrible Aspen and the people who live here are.

"Have your next affair in Aspen" could be just a marketing slogan our town needs right now to plant a flag atop our heap of irreverent, dog-loving, messy vitality. Call and book your vacation today. Operators are standing by.

THE 'WEST END SNEAK'

I'M GUILTY OF DOING THE "West End sneak." That's where you drive through the West End neighborhood in an effort to get out of town faster.

Honestly, it doesn't feel good to me. Maybe I'm in the minority, but I actually feel terrible doing it. The reason for my misgivings about driving through the West End to beat the traffic is because I grew up there — a block away from debatably the worst intersection — and I can empathize with the people who call it home. If 2,000 cars were driving through my neighborhood five days a week, I'd be pissed too.

The West End has been vilified over the years as being a dead spot where no one lives, full of second homes, without families and somewhat exemplary of what is wrong with Aspen. I'm here to tell you that's simply not the case. I know and love people who live in the West End. Frankly, my dream house is in the West End. It's arguably Aspen's best neighborhood. The people who live there are seriously bumming about the traffic cutting through all the time. I don't blame them.

On some level I can commiserate. I live in the flight path. From 7 a.m. to 11 p.m. every single day, the oppressive roar and swoosh of all types of jets and the lawnmower-esque whining of prop planes fills my senses. Now you understand why I'm the way I am. Then when I pull out of my neighborhood onto my extended driveway — McLain Flats Road — it's into a steady stream of commuter traffic that's in a real big hurry to get to Aspen.

The same commuters are in an equally big rush to split. It's like Aspen's a woman everyone wants to have sex with, and right after they orgasm, they can't leave fast enough.

Out of curiosity, would those same commuters be happier working closer to home, or is sucking off of the engorged nipple of Aspen too tempting, too fruitful, too easy, too financially rewarding to let go? Regardless, I see the pattern every single day because I'm a part of it. I have four cars in my driveway — not because I'm rich or greedy, but because I'm a gas addict like all other Americans who aren't living in tipis off the grid. I live in employee housing and own and operate two service-oriented businesses.

I'm the problem. I'm a self-loathing member of what I call the "White Truck Brigade" — one of the hundreds of white trucks that come into Aspen every day to provide services and make the world turn, and I specifically plan my schedule so that I end with my last account of the day in the West End, so that I can exit town via Power Plant Road. My only saving grace, if there even is such a thing, which there isn't, is that I turn right onto Cemetery Lane and head for my "driveway," McLain Flats road. Don't even get me started about all the mini plastic liquor bottles lining the downvalley shoulder.

Every single day without fail I'm either tailgated or passed on a double-yellow line; or someone's drifting into my lane, cutting a blind corner. Calling specific people out besides Roger Marolt in the newspaper is futile for three reasons: 1) it's a bad look 2) people don't read this crap and 3) you're not going to change anyone's minds because everybody's right all the time. It's a one-way, my-way world. The deleted comments from the West End article in the comment section of this paper were really, really disgusting.

Not only is the West End bad, but Cemetery Lane also is an extremely busy road. I've nearly been creamed while mowing lawns on a couple occasions. The people who live there are every bit as dismayed as the West End residents. I shudder at what it'd be like now, had the city not put in that well-used, elevated bike path, the sidewalk and the speed humps. "Locals" actually fought it vociferously at the time.

The recent tack and angle that the West End group has taken to discourage the "sneak," of idling being bad for the environment, misses the mark for me. We blew through that four-way "bad for the environment" stop sign a long time ago. The air quality on Main Street is actually poor. And frankly, the pollution is better now than it used to be here. Remember PM-10 and the brown cloud over Aspen every morning? It's like they're going to have a breakthrough because they're tugging on the heartstrings of environmental warriors on council.

The more important part is that the "sneak" is just plain intrusive — and dangerous. I don't buy the defiant commuter's argument that you can drive anywhere on any road because it's America, and you can't tell me what to do — which seems to be the lowest common denominator of most arguments these days. Traffic, like all the other oft-bemoaned woes of poor downtrodden locals, is a fire hydrant you can't turn off. Redirecting the stream is the best you can do. Aspen is a small but mighty city now. There is no solution other than literally handing out condoms at the entrance to Aspen.

I arrived at the odd place this winter where I intentionally waited in line on Main Street to exit town with everybody else. In retrospect, it was a learning experience to me, and an exercise in patience. It was time to put all that yoga, mediation and lip service to the hippy-dippy mindset we're quick to espouse, but hesitant to actually practice. Frankly, after being holed up with near-delirium-grade cabin fever, I wasn't in any rush to get home. In retrospect, had I not done that, I mightn't have noticed the Shadow Mountain Yeti in late March, first thinking that it was a fugitive scrap piece of white Tyvek housing wrap construction waste, blown by the wind.

I've been heartened by, and applaud the recent efforts of, the Aspen Police Department, which keeps traffic flowing through the West End as best they can, and for opening the downvalley bus lanes past the roundabout to evening commuter traffic.

The other day they were doing the boogie in front of a message board, bringing much-needed levity to the situation. I feel the pain of the West End residents and hope that these efforts help to assuage their feelings of being constantly pinned down by commuter traffic.

The "West End sneak" has been going on for over 25 years. I wonder who the first person to do it was, and how people reacted when they bragged about it from their stool at the J-Bar?

It's going to be fascinating to see how this situation gets addressed. If the residents upset about traffic start clamoring for the four-lane into town, things could get interesting. That's the cool thing about Aspen — the longer you stick around, the more you get to see happen.

LOCAL POLICE
DOING IT 'MY WAY'

ONE TIME A GUY ASKED ME if I'd ever been to jail. It took me by complete surprise. It made me stammer. Was it a trick question?

Upon further reflection, it occurred to me my shock and confusion about the blunt query was a kind of moral flash reckoning of sorts. I probably should've, could've, would've, but didn't.

No such thing as bad publicity you say? Imagine what it's like to end up in the local paper in the police blotter. You'd suffer immensely from the bad publicity alone. This newspaper even threatens the consequences of suspect behavior with its ominous credo. Local law enforcement personnel are the ones who know the real dark and dirty secrets of Aspen — the kind that sink large, reputable ships.

I always get a kick out of Aspen law enforcement's dubious relationship with federal law enforcement agencies. If our local police and sheriff's office had a theme song it would not be "Dragnet." Frank Sinatra's "My Way" would be more fitting.

There was a time in Aspen when police officers wore button-fly 501 Levis and drove baby blue Saabs. Soon they'll be wearing body cameras on their tactical bulletproof vests. Growing up in Aspen, I was friends with both the sheriff's kids and the chief of police's kids. We all were. The Kienast and Hershey kids were well known and liked. I'd say generally, from personal experience, that the Hershey kids were better behaved. I can now say with confidence that I've never been in jail, but I did spend the night in the basement of the Kienast house once after being hauled down to the station.

Knowing the local police and being friends with them is much more important than you think it is. Having those relationships with law enforcement builds a profound sense of community, and you never know when you're going to need a friend. I'm catching myself insinuating that a police officer would let you "slide" because you're acquaintances, like there's a home-team referee component. Who knows, that logic may backfire spectacularly. I can hear it now: "You're the jerk who writes for the paper; book him, Danno!" I've had warnings that in retrospect probably had more impact that a ticket, or worse, might've.

Take the recent news of Jesse Steindler retiring from the Pitkin County Sheriff's Office — there's an example of what quality law enforcement we have here. Our kids grew up together and the interactions I've had with him, however small and far in between, have had a positive impact on my life here, and my perception of local law enforcement.

Or I think about my friend, Officer Jimmy, whom I went to Aspen High School with, and how much I value our conversations in town whenever we run into each other on the bike paths or in town or at an event. Look at local law enforcement's integral presence at our schools as another example.

To me, these interactions highlight the importance of reaching out to law enforcement whenever you get the chance. It usually has the effect of brightening your day. They do tons of outreach, but it's the reciprocation by us that makes it all meaningful. There was a time in my life when I never could have imagined being friends with police, or ski patrol for that matter. Now, I've never been so happy to have a deputy living two houses down from me.

The other spring I found myself participating in a local George Floyd march through the streets I grew up on as a kid. "Defund the Police" was one of the slogans that came parroted out of my mouth. It was an interesting sensation to be confused by what I was saying or doing and about what my role as a guy in little ol'

Aspen had to do with the big picture of policing in America and the turmoil our country was going through. Why are police killing so many people? My only logical conclusion is that they're addicted to violence after seeing so much of it. Seeing your fellow man at their absolute worse all the time must be devastating — like doctors who don't believe in God.

There's a story that pretty much sums up my relationship with local police in Aspen. One day after school in eighth grade, we were getting high with a homeless guy over in the shady northwest corner of Wagner Park. He had horrible psoriasis and was passing around a joint of homegrown with more rolling paper than pot. I was concerned his skin ailment was contagious. Out of nowhere a police officer appeared and busted us. Our first instinct was to run, but he halted us like scared animals.

He took out a spiral notepad and wrote down all of our names and phone numbers. "When you get home, tell your parents I'll be calling this evening to tell them what happened," he said. "It'd probably be a good idea to let them know in advance."

I raced home in a fog of stoned panic. Much to my horror, my mom and dad were having a big dinner party that night. The dining room table was set meticulously for an elaborate meal of curried chicken and all the fixings like toasted coconut, golden raisins and thinly sliced scallions. This news of the their little angel getting high with a homeless guy after school would most certainly curdle the curry.

The damn phone wouldn't stop ringing. Each time it did was like an electric shock, the waves flushing my face, and then coursing throughout my mind and body. But the police officer never called. I slept with the secret. Only one kid told his parents. In retrospect, he was the lone honest punk among us with any integrity. I thought I got lucky, but I can only imagine what's going to happen when my mom reads this.

Then again, one night she sat next to Hunter S. Thompson at a dinner party. He said if you ever get pulled over, "hand the officer this" — it was a get-out-of-jail-free card with his name and logo on it.

OOOOH OOOH THAT SMELL

THERE WAS A SOBERING ARTICLE in the paper a while back about the Pitkin County landfill, and the projections as to when it would be full. Right now there's a project on the northern flank to extend its life for another six years. After that, there's another proposal for a mega southern expansion that gives us another 30–40 years.

All the while, the city of Aspen and Pitkin County are actively trying to implement programs that reduce and divert the "stream" of waste. I'm all for that.

It seems more like a raging river of trash. Ever been up to the Pitkin County landfill?

It should be mandatory for everybody who lives in Aspen to go up there and check out the sights, sounds and odors. Kind of like one of those "Scared Straight" programs for troubled youths, where they go to a jail and have a homicidal, facial tattooed lifer-convict scream at them. From spring to fall, I typically go up to the landfill once a week to sprinkle a few grass clippings on top of the heap like a parsley garnish. It costs me exactly $12.50 to dump my load of compostable yard waste.

The landfill is a popular place. There's always a line to get in.

Want to know what Aspen really smells like? Go up to the landfill and find out. If you're hungover, you had better have a barf bag at the ready, because it can be foul, especially in the stifling afternoon heat. The composting section is particularly putrid. They have these long trenches — some filled with a brackish compost gumbo — that would be unthinkable to swim through.

That's where I'd put the course of one of those "Tough Mudder" events and see what people are really made of.

Every time I'm up there, it seems like the ravens are blatantly mocking me. "Kaw, kaw," they say, over and over. It makes me wonder what they think of my career choice in the water-wasting lawn care business. Is it a means to an end, something of necessity, a valuable local business, or am I just another disposable service provider — a human behaving like an insect — taking piles of this and that from one place to another, all for some great, unknown, yet-to-be-determined 100-years-from-now cause?

It'd be fascinating to see all of the waste I've produced over the years. If you could go out to the Bonneville Salt Flats, and line up your trash shadow from day one — diapers, crib boxes, wrapping paper, greeting cards, food waste — to current trash, like old vehicles, torn down houses, textiles, books, plastic ... what would that look like? You could probably fill a football stadium with my plastic takeout boxes alone.

A few years ago I read an interview with a lady from the Pitkin County landfill and she said, "We can't recycle ourselves out of this mess." I remember when I used to be so gung-ho on recycling that I wouldn't even throw an aluminum can away into a trash can if there wasn't a recycling option available. I'd take it home with me and recycle it there. Now I'm slightly disenchanted with recycling. I'm not so sure that it's even being recycled, or that people even care.

This feeling of uncertainty is amplified when I go out to our neighborhood dumpster and see single-use recyclables sitting mindlessly in the trash can when there's a recycling dumpster right next to it. I'm generally an optimist, as my doom and gloom wrestles internally with blossom and bloom. I still pick up pennies, and other people's trash. But the disregard for recycling really makes me wonder.

The Pitkin County landfill is a bustling place. The burden of going there and the oppressive emotions I harbor from the reality of how much trash Aspen produces are always brightened by the cheerful ladies at the scales' check-in window — the lilies of the landfill: Katie, Marty and Jade. I cherish my homeowner trash voucher book as if they're coupons to Disneyland, being certain to use the "E" ticket rides sparingly.

I can definitely do better with my Zorro-esque trash signature. Our employee-housing neighborhood has a complimentary composting bin that we've been using for a couple of years now. It's incredible how much that cuts down on kitchen and household trash, and smell.

Remember when the pandemic hit? Everyone was commenting on how good it was for the environment. Not only did that ship sail, it sank in the harbor, spilled its haz-mat cargo and killed the crew and all passengers. Entire houses and hotels are slated for burial at the landfill. Roadsides strewn with trash, human waste near trails, traffic jams, private jets swarming like mosquitoes and mountains of cardboard boxes from a daily avalanche of packages: the UPS man worked until 10 o'clock each night delivering them.

As the environmentally contradictory township of Aspen bustles headlong into the future, the rivers slowly dwindle, our skies cast an eerie glow from wildfire smoke. We dodge mudslides from burn scars, beetle-kill trees line the lower reaches of Ajax and the Yeti of Shadow Mountain climbs higher and higher to some semblance of safety. I'm feeling a certain form of climate anxiety that can only be tempered by the fact that I'm getting a new neighbor: a solar farm. The question is, do I run an extension cord out there now for my Christmas lights display this winter?

FOURTH OF JULY PARADE: IRREVERENT OR IRRELEVANT?

WHEN I READ THE PLANS for the Fourth of July "stationary" parade, my thoughts were to make a judgment after seeing it.

Personally I liked it. I liked the fact that it looked, felt, sounded, smelled and tasted like a street party. Town was packed. I dig town when it's crowded. The energy recharges my spirit. In retrospect, had Main Street been closed for a traditional parade, with all the traffic from the I-70 closure rerouted through town, things could've actually gotten ugly — that's according to local police.

What I definitely didn't miss about the traditional parade was the deafening wail of sirens and the obnoxious motorcycle parade. I also didn't miss the repulsive toxic masculinity of people trying to out-America each other, to show everyone who's the bigger patriot. Aspen needs to be more like David Bowie — the original defier of ordinary — and reinvent ourselves out of necessity, like we always have and always will.

The things about the parade I did miss were the vets, the kids, the F-16 flyovers and marching bands. And no Smuggler cannon this year? How do you honor our vets without giving them PTSD with that and fireworks? I went and checked out the laser light show with my son, and we thought it was really cool. The laser light show has serious potential. It reminded me of an old-school "Laserium" show. It was every bit as visually stimulating, colorful and vibrant as a fireworks display without lighting the mountain on fire. A friend of mine reminded me at the Hickory House bar on Monday that one year during Winternational, laser images of skiers were projected onto Aspen Mountain.

Honestly, the parade for the past few years has turned into a big irrelevant advertisement. It sorely lacks the illusive endangered species "irreverence" everyone always bemoans is MIA. It raises the question, what is irreverence, or messy vitality, or weirdness or whatever you want to call it, and how do you engineer it back into the parade? Where's the line of tastefulness? How do we make fun of ourselves without hurting people's feelings?

There are countless funny, interesting, wacky people in Aspen with creative ideas. The Aspen Chamber Resort Association is doing an online survey right now to solicit interesting concepts and constructive criticism for next year's Fourth. I have faith in my fellow imaginative, irreverent Aspenites that this quest will be fruitful. Somebody prove me right.

I keep hearing a common complaint this week that town was too crowded. Stop being so damn fabulous all the time, posting every precious local detail of your life on Instagram, and people won't want to come here, have your life and be like you!

It's dangerous business making fun of people moving here, or bemoaning tourism, when you live in a tourist town. Being a schoolkid and calling the tourists "turkeys" is one thing, but what I'm hearing is next level. Guess who paid for my house and most of my living expenses? Tourists. It's hard for me to disconnect that and be ungrateful. I'm not saying we can't be critical, just be mindful of stepping in your own trap and playing right into everyone's favorite negative stereotype of "Aspen" and all the horrible people here.

Guess what happens when the master critic and arbiter of all things "Aspen" goes somewhere on vacation? There could quite possibly be a "local" sitting on the corner thinking your same thoughts. Who's worse, the locals or the tourists? Personally, my pain threshold is much higher for tourists. Locals should know better.

When we moved here from California, people hated us. Kids called me a spoiled rich Hollywood brat and taunted me with the "Jingle bells, Batman Smells!" song when they found out my dad wrote the 1960s *Batman* movie and TV series. They even hated our solar-heated house. One day I came home on my mini Schwinn Stingray to discover Fritz and Fabi Benedict standing in our driveway critiquing the architecture and saying how outrageously close to each other the houses were. It took me years to process this, and to some extent I still am.

There's definitely a Three Little Bears syndrome going around Aspen right now. Too hot, too crowded, too many e-bikes, too much construction, too many private jets, too much traffic, no parking. Not enough this, not enough that — almost as if we own the rights to these problems. Whenever you catch yourself doing this, ask what's the "just right" amount of everything ... or is that just sentimental fantasy? If you're one of the locals ranting about this stuff, get out a brutally honest personal checklist and ask yourself where you came from and what exactly your role is in all of this?

BOMBS AWAY?

As LONG AS I CAN REMEMBER, there's always been a vocal faction of Aspenites clamoring for an end to the yearly Fourth of July fireworks display over Ajax. Even before the drought and uptick in wildfires. Some say, "Who are these people, communists?" If only it were that simple. It seems to me like a lot of the criticism understandably comes from dog owners who live in the core.

Fireworks scare the crap out of animals — and not just dogs, but wildlife living right on the fringe of our precarious urban/wilderness interface buffer zone, of which we are luckily surrounded by three solid sides. Imagine being a bear here. You somehow narrowly survive the summer without getting euthanized, relocated or run over, eating a paleo-plus diet of fruit, grubs, berries and trash, all the while smelling tantalizing steak and seafood essences belching out of restaurant exhaust fans. When you finally get to sleep in the fall, you're instantly jolted awake by the incessant dumpster lid thumps of avalanche concussion explosives. All winter long. Those bombs aren't going away soon.

What about the menacing four-barrel Fourth of July cannon 6 a.m. wake-up call from the Smuggler mine? The only one sleeping through that is my teenage son Oliver.

I like the fireworks display on the Fourth. I also understand everyone's on edge about fires and freaked out about drought. I am, too. A good, safe, memorable fireworks display takes careful, well-thought-out planning. It reminds me of the time I was a kid messing around with some hoodlums up at the Stern's Residence in Starwood — the one with a retractable roof over the pool. One night, some kids poured kerosene into the pool, lit it on fire, then jumped in from above. I have no idea where the parents were. For all I knew, the kids were test-tube babies.

Later that weekend, perhaps inspired by the swimming pool antics, we put an M-80 into a can of latex paint. Perhaps we thought we were Hunter S. Thompson, Steadman-esque artists: the explosion would pleasantly spray paint all over the wilderness surroundings, like spray painting the Mona Lisa, a gender reveal party or one of those ink blobs you blow with a straw in kindergarten art class. What we didn't realize is that the can of yellow paint we picked was highly combustible. We very nearly lit the whole of Starwood on fire. Our family would've had to literally move out of Aspen.

Let's say that hypothetically, a fire started on Aspen Mountain as a result of the fireworks display on Independence Day. A big munition lands right on Little Nell above the Alps condos and burns all the way up Gentleman's Ridge, parts of 1A, Bell Mountain and the upper portions of Ajax, all the way up to the Sundeck. The Aspen fire department and its trademark "same-day service" is able to effectively push the fire away from any structures, but the Bell chair is burnt beyond recognition and repair. The town is outraged! Lots of finger-pointing ensues, and a healthy portion of "I told ya so" scowls are heaped atop an ever-growing pig pile.

When the smoke clears — and people realize that the skiable acreage on Aspen Mountain has just increased by some 500 acres — there's a big paradigm shift in local know-it-all attitudes. It looks like Ajax of the mining era: vast areas are burned bald as Telly Savalas. They even rename a treeless portion of Bell Mountain "Kojak."

The people who started the fire end up being underground ski bum subculture heroes. Skiing in Aspen has never been better — lines previously un-skiable are now wide open. After all, the "Big Burn" did wonders for Snowmass. Think of what a "Little Burn" could do for Ajax.

Funny thing is, one year the mountain actually did light on fire because of fireworks. I was there, frightfully watching it burn from the top of the water tank on Little Nell. When we went to get off the thing and run for our lives, someone before us had very cleverly laid down the ladder, and you had to do a sketchy hang-and-drop move to get down.

Another year at the International Design Conference of Aspen, a famous Italian family lit off a gargantuan fireworks display in the West End, right next to our house on Eighth Street that could've easily torched the whole neighborhood.

What does a future without fireworks look and sound like in Aspen? If the city does decide to permanently cancel the Fourth of July fireworks for fear of something awesome like this happening, I'd be disappointed, but I'd also understand. We'd seriously need to reinvent ourselves on the Fourth. I'm really interested to see the laser light show. What ever happened to that drone light show they've been threatening us with for the past three years?

Is there an area of compromise — for instance, only having fireworks in the winter for New Year's and Wintersköl? Or do we have fireworks based on a rigorous moisture meter safety threshold number? And how about the guy with the enormous anxiety-triggering fireworks stand on Highway 82? Do you shut him down permanently? Frankly, before the no-fun police pulled up, I was tempted to go buy fireworks and have a small Class C street show — with sparklers and ground flowers and snakes and those mini-tanks that shoot screaming fireballs on the pavement — in front of my house, all while firmly clutching a garden hose. This is the greenest drought I've ever seen.

HIGH COTTON

LEAVE IT TO ME TO TACKLE the provocative topics that other local columnists shudder with fear over, like all the cotton blowing around town right now. "Snow in summer," "Winter in June," whatever you want to call it — it's everywhere. Personally, I kind of like it. I actually look forward to it in a twisted way.

In terms of allergies, the cotton never bothered me. I could snort the stuff and still be unfazed — more energized as a lost-sailor, landlocked Popeye. Other people fly into a panic teetering on a nervous breakdown when they see the cotton blowing around like a tornado vortex of perceived allergens. Here's the funny thing – the cotton itself is benign. It's about as toxic as a T-shirt lying on the ground.

My loose understanding is it's the pollen from the blooms weeks ago that's the real allergen, not to mention the film of green pollen coating the entire valley floor from all the evergreens. When the cotton flies, it means we're nearing the end of the allergy battle. Aspen trees incidentally also produce cotton of their own. Legend has it that locals used to stuff pillows with it and use it as bedding.

The one thing the cotton is, is highly flammable. We discovered this as hoodlum kids in the West End when some local derelict pyromaniac — of which there were several — hipped us to the fact that you could light the piles on fire.

Where others see misery, I find humor and profit centers. I've always thought someone could start a business here called "Cotton Busters" specializing in high-end cotton removal at people's homes and businesses. All you'd need is a spiffy, logo'd Tyvek suit, Pit Vipers, a mask, a shop vac, a few pole feather dusters and you'd be in high cotton. I imagine you could easily charge in the neighborhood of $75 an hour for cotton removal services. It'd be a good summer gig for a couple of Aspen High kids to start — catering to the wealthy's obsessive-compulsive fear of cotton. Imagine the opportunities that could lead to — think pool guy on Red Mountain assuaging the lonely sugar-mama's crippling cotton-complex each week in June and July.

But what to do with all the harvested cotton? Make high-priced women's underwear out of it, that's what. Sell it at Carl's upstairs for an outrageous price. Market it through the chamber and SkiCo with a titillating, "Have your next affair in Aspen!" campaign. Sorry — no men's version, but there's no law that says you can't.

If I were a robin, I'd have the plushest, phat-stacked cotton-condo nest you've ever seen. Females would fly from miles around just to lay their eggs in my plump, overstuffed, cotton-concubine confines.

One of the unspoken reasons that Aspen is so desirable is all of the mature, non-native species cottonwood trees — the deciduous tourists of the tree world — on our valley floor. Because of the cotton they shed, you have people who moved here complaining about trees that moved here before them.

At some point in our fluffy history, someone — probably a woman — had the foresight to create an irrigation ditch network from the base of Shadow Mountain through the West End, and plant cottonwood trees all over Main Street and town. Now a lot of the trees are rotten from the inside, reaching the end of their lifespans.

I remember during one of our daily violent afternoon summer windstorms a mature cottonwood fell squarely onto a parked car over by the Ullr lodge — all four wheels of the flattened Cherokee were splayed flat on the ground like a cartoon. We can always blame the long-gone miners who may or may not have planted them.

If the woodpile up at the Pitkin County landfill is any indication, the local tree-removal/maintenance industry here is a multimillion-dollar venture these days. Bucket trucks, chipper shredders, stump grinders, crews of spidermen with chainsaws, loppers, ropes and harnesses crawling around in the canopies — it's got to be a harrowing occupation. It'd be a good side-hustle for an aspiring mountaineer. Even the city of Aspen has its own salaried "forester."

I love the next phase of the cottonwood docudrama, when the aphids set up shop in the heirloom cottonwood trees and start feasting. They chow on the leaves, and then basically urinate all over everything, misting the surfaces around the trees with a revolting, shiny, aphid shellac — or "honeydew" I've heard it called. Some days you can see the mist raining down from the trees: the Holy Grail being an aphid-piss rainbow.

As someone in the lawncare industry, the cotton is a big mess. Especially when you come in hot with a leaf-blower and kick up clouds of the stuff, then saunter right through it covered in sweat. It clings to you and you look like an abominable snowman — yet another reason why lawn guys like me here in Aspen are so popular.

Good thing Aspen's at the top of the water pyramid, because all these cottonwood trees do is sit around, throw shade, make a mess and drink 'til they fall over — like drunken sailors at the old Cooper Street Pier.

WHO WILL STEP UP TO SAVE THE ISIS?

I'D LIKE TO USHER AN IMPASSIONED, sobbing and tearstained-face cry for help to save the beloved ISIS Theatre. Perhaps there's someone out there in Aspen who has bottomless pockets, and a desire to gallop to the rescue, clad in shining armor and riding a white horse, to have a theater in Aspen under their command — a pet project, if you will, to cement the future of cinema into their local legacy.

I know you're out there. Think, one-of-a-kind concept theater — interior decorators, overstuffed Italian leather recliners for all, F&B service, fresh-cut flowers, film festivals and premieres with A-list stars. Lord knows it wouldn't be the first time something fantastically absurd happened in Aspen.

Based on my loose understanding of who owns what, and owes who how much, current exhibitor Metropolitan Theatres — which has done an excellent job to date, all things considered and as far as I'm concerned — is basically running a pop-up until its lease expires at the end of August. After that, the venue will effectively be thrown to the wolves of local real estate development. Blood is in the water. The piranhas are already circling. This could very possibly be like a bad movie where the guy gets hit by a truck in the end.

Some locals would just assume the ISIS dried up and blew away with the rest of Hollywood, but not I. Admittedly my reasons for wanting to save the ISIS are selfish, and can be reduced in a saucepan of nostalgia down to a thick, rich, brown reduction you'd glaze a steak au poivre with. The mere mention of the ISIS brings a flood of memories. My favorite was seeing "Flash Gordon" there and hearing the crowd cheer when my dad's name ("screenplay by ...") flashed up on the screen.

When we were underage kids, you used to be able to go to an R-rated movie at the ISIS with a note from your parents. Can you imagine? "Dear Dominic, Please allow my 13-year-old son Lo to see 'The Exorcist' tonight. I hope he gets the fecal matter properly scared out of him. Signed, Lorenzo Semple."

Dominic Lindsa was the owner of the ISIS and would be seen at the cash register at the top of the stairs at the entrance every night. He'd then take up his post in the projector booth and announce the coming attractions as well as his brief take on the movie you were just about to see. He was definitely an over-sharer of information. The term "spoiler alert" may have even come about as a result of his notorious pre-show reviews.

His wife Kitty always reminded me of my grandma Dot, as did a fixture behind the snack bar. I've never been able to scrub the image of the pickle jar on the counter from my memory. The only thing strikingly close to the ISIS these days is the Crystal Theatre in Carbondale — one of my favorite rides on the ol' time machine.

The other movie theatre in town was the Playhouse run by Don Swales. When the anticipated monthly schedule came out, X-rated adult films ran once a week much to the delight for all the creepers in town. My friend Mark Kelly and I went to see the sold-out movie "Greased Lightning" starring Richard Pryor one night, and he dropped a full bottle of wine out of his ski parka and it shattered on the floor in the lobby.

The Wheeler Opera House was the third movie theater in town, and they had a regular movie schedule as well, perhaps more on the avant-garde/eclectic side. The Wheeler used to be a dump. There were bench seats in the balcony and they used to show 3-D movies each year — a double feature even — such as "It Came from Outer Space" followed by "Creature of the Black

Lagoon." The mighty John Busch would often take a verbal beating by the raucous, inebriated crowd when he announced the movies with his less-than-booming voice.

We've gone from three theaters to one and almost none. What can be done? Why doesn't Aspen, with its rich movie tradition and strong ties to Hollywood (past and present) have a more robust moviegoing populace? I've heard of saving the ISIS with the swollen Wheeler RETT fund, but there are too many emotional and financial wires crossed there for that to ever happen. We need a local nonprofit war for funding, or another reason for people to judge then hate the city, like a fish needs a bicycle. The best way to save the ISIS is to commence going to movies again, something I've not started doing. Yet. The ISIS is now open. Beat the heat. Go get dinner and see a movie.

The ISIS has survived sharing a name with a notoriously heinous terror organization, but the coronavirus, absurdly high rents and America's fascination with streaming may be its last act. I sure hope not. We need an overly generous movie buff to step up. Who's going to be the next local legend? Imagine the possibilities.

A town without a movie theater just doesn't feel like a town. Besides, if the ISIS shutters, where are all the local middle school and high school kids going to go to make out?

WE LOVE OUR MIGHTY ASPEN HIGH SENIORS

IT'S IMPORTANT FOR ME to start this piece by thanking all of the teachers and staff at the Aspen School District. The general consensus around town is that you've gone well above and beyond the expectations and risen to the occasion of teaching our local kids during the year of the pandemic.

Homecoming, the bell ringing and prom have all been noteworthy, adaptive, improvisational and highly memorable events. Even the aptly named "Silver Queen" yearbook is exceptional. Times like these command deep reflection and honest introspection. Some local parents are still in shock, trying to reconcile the fact that they've had to actually spend this much time with their own kids.

For me the fitting imagery of this year's Aspen High School graduation is stark and metaphoric: from the symbolic march across a bridge, to a high-speed chairlift ride ascending Tiehack, to getting their diplomas with the backdrop of Pyramid Peak with its triangular omnipotent symbol of strength.

I have a lot of emotion invested in the Aspen school system. My emotions have entire portfolios of their own, from my second-grade teacher Carol Hall to my school-appointed speech therapist Paula Bickelhaupt tasked with the daunting challenge of de-lisping me and taming my steady stutter. Then there was the time David Hauer's dad rescued me on a camping trip to Ruedi where I had fallen behind and was sobbing uncontrollably because my pack was too heavy.

My son is graduating from Aspen High this year, and sentiments are running high. Barring any future unexpected pregnancies, his graduation will demarcate a lilting swansong of my career as the parent of local school kids. And I'm gushing with pride that he'll be the third in our family to end up on the school's "Wall of Fame." Take a gander sometime — you'll recognize the names. The old photos in particular paint a fascinating portrait of what Aspen used to be like.

Our school kids are a direct reflection of us. Their behaviors, their attitudes, their preparedness as they head out into the jaws of the beast of the real world. At least they'll all know how to set up a two-man tent when they get there. The kids here are so cool — look for their gleaming pictures posted on banners strategically placed throughout the core. And the funny thing is that a lot of them are considerably more local than the guy we all know who prefaces his epic rant about everything with how many years he's lived here.

The local kids who were born here have a leg up on the Clydesdale already. Whenever I get all high and mighty about my local status, my son happily twists the knife and reminds me of that fact — usually in front of a bunch of people — that he was born at Aspen Valley Hospital and I wasn't.

Everybody's getting thrust back into society by being shot out of the COVID-19 cannon like one of those traveling-circus stuntmen donning a helmet and cape. Lots of parties, lots of events. It feels good. I'm making a lot of long-lost connections with people and the interactions seem genuine and meaningful. There's a palpable buzz I can feel in town surrounding graduation.

The one thing I really missed the past couple years is the rent-a-senior program. I always hire a couple every year to wash cars and such. One year, a girl was vacuuming-out our cars and asked "What kind of dog do you guys have?" Funny thing is, we don't. Just a couple of long-haired AHS Class of 1986-ers. I'm even married to a fellow classmate — of the opposite sex! Apparently we're shedding.

I do some of my best work stuck in the 1980s. For me, they were a higher functioning, more debauched version of the '70s. Whenever the subject of graduation came up in the past, I eventually mentioned that the heralded Class of 1986 graduated at the music tent and how cool it was. Now I'm not so sure. Seeing last year's graduation at Buttermilk, and this year's scheduled ride up the Tiehack Lift, our ceremony is starting to look more like standard graduation rigmarole. Though we did have a kegger with our teachers at West Buttermilk.

When we were seniors, there were bad attitudes as far as the eye could see. We hated Aspen. My senior quote was a permanent swearing-off of Aspen. Perhaps we had listened to "Going to California" one too many times, because that's where we all wanted to go. And many of us did. More than you'd reckon came back and stayed. A funny thing happened when we awkwardly found our way out of the forest — we finally saw the trees.

Volunteering up at Aspen High for the Skier Scribbler for the past couple of years has been one of the most rewarding things in my life. I've also participated in marches from the campus into town that provides you with a totally different perspective on Aspen. I would strongly encourage people to get involved with the local schools if it's something you're interested in and have time for.

They say a child is a product of every personal interaction they have in their town growing up — micro and macro. We all have a role in that. But the ones who make the most difference are our teachers: often underappreciated, but not by me. Their hard work, dedication and desire to make a difference doesn't go unnoticed by me. A big thanks to every teacher and adult in town who's played a role in raising me, and my kids.

MELLOW-DRAMA
AT THE MUSIC TENT

WHEN THE STORY IN THE PAPER first came out about the Music Associates of Aspen charging for coveted, previously free lawn space at the Music Tent this summer, there was only one person whose opinion I was even remotely interested in: my former neighbor in the hood, the delightful Gerri Karetsky. She's heart and soul. Gerri's the one whose idea it was to gift the endowment to the MAA, ensuring complimentary lawn seats in perpetuity to Aspen's great unwashed masses.

I did what any self-respecting, somewhat believable local columnist would do. I called her.

The lowdown behind the free lawn is that it was her idea as a present to the local community. And more importantly, her way of honoring her late husband David, who died far too young on March 12, 1991, in a tragic helicopter accident that rocked the community. The delicate negotiations happened during an MAA heyday — the beloved Robert Hearth (who was also taken from us prematurely) era, a time looked back upon with fondness and reverence.

As it turns out, the MAA has since rethought that decision and will not in fact be charging for lawn space on Fridays and Sundays, but will nonetheless regulate the attendance. It'll be interesting to see how that sonata plays out. My thoughts were to have half-igloo-shaped pods manifesting as Bayer-esque sculptures of an ear that holds up to six people and catches the sound, all by natural design.

If you ask me, I was personally OK with the MAA charging for this one summer to set a tone moving forward. I've witnessed some seriously questionable behavior over the years out on the lawn. At times it can be anything but relaxing, like when the darling couple rolls up next to you with a smorgasbord of the loudest possible food offerings — Doritos, kettle chips and even a blender, with crinkles, crunches, whiz-bangs — and graces everyone with loud, uninteresting conversations throughout the whole performance. It almost makes the private jets, cellphones, barking dogs and screaming babies palatable.

Regardless, being outside the tent during concerts is the equivalent of being out in the parking lot with ticketless deadheads during a rock concert — you're missing out on all the action, man. There's so much to see and lots more to hear. I'm particularly fond of the festival's best-kept secrets, like rehearsals where you can hear the conductor interact with the students. That's where the real fascinations lie for me. If you're so "into" classical music, try buying a ticket for once, you whining freeloaders!

My history with the Music Tent runs deep as a bass cello, with undertones of flute. Ever since I was a kid growing up in Aspen's Wild West end, the soothing sounds of classical music were always in the background of my long, lazy summers — that is, when we weren't listening to Kiss at volume 11 and generally terrorizing the festival grounds on BMX bikes, skateboards and mini bikes.

Our exploits included, but were by no means limited to riding BMX bikes in and around Hill Park, inside the Music Tent when the temporary seasonal canvas roof was down, skateboarding in the empty Aspen Meadows pool, the stage and isles of the tent itself. And then there was the holy grail: skateboarding on the actual roof of the Music Tent, where the brilliant architect Herbert Bayer had inadvertently designed a perfectly suitable skateboard ramp. We spent countless hours of our juvenile delinquent lives stoned to the bejesus, getting sunburnt beyond recognition on the angular bleach-white Bauhaus surfaces.

To make matters even worse for the sacred silence, we had a mini bike track adjacent to the Music Tent on the vacant lot where

Estée Lauder's house now sits. The tent manager would fly into a rage at the incessant, shrill sounds of our two-cycle Yamaha YZ 80s, piloted by rowdy kids like Bob Coakley, Jim Salter, the Kienast brothers, Rishi Grewal and George Parry.

It was all fun and games until we saw the immaculate, fire-engine-red Jeep Cherokee of the mighty King Woodward — or "Woody," as he was dearly known — speeding down Music School Road to royally bust us. We generally evaded his wrath by scattering like cockroaches through the vast surrounding sagebrush fields whenever he approached. Years later in the early '80s, fate and fortune would have it that King Woodward ended up my boss at the neighboring Aspen Institute, where I received my very first formal paycheck at the age of 15, working with the likes of trustee brats like Doug and Phil Adler (Mortimer Adler's kids), under the watchful eye of a guy named Michael Stiller.

For a summer in the early 1990s, I ended up on the Music Tent crew, assembling the tent in the spring, setting up for concerts, cleaning the bathrooms and taking it all down in late August. It was a time in Aspen when you would often hear the trills and flourishes of violins and French horns throughout town, or an occasional opera voice booming from a random open window. As a result, Beethoven posthumously indoctrinated me through melodic osmosis; classical music was systematically embedded into my DNA.

The free-for-all lawn scene at the tent is going to have to be regulated at some point in the future. That's just the way things go. As it's gotten more crowded, I've frequented it less. My thoughts are that this new lawn parameter is a step in prepping the landscape for what that looks like in seasons to come. But the lawn will always be free to the public — perhaps regulated, but open — and that's a good thing. It keeps Aspen's beloved, endangered species, "messy vitality," safer from greed-mongering hunters looking to suck the joy marrow from our bones. Thanks for keeping Aspen real, Gerri.

WELCOME TO THE BOOMTOWN

JUST BY LOOKING AROUND Aspen it seems we have ourselves a good old-fashioned boomtown on our hands right now. Real estate and construction are obviously the big driving factors, with a trickle-down effect adding financial buoyancy to just about every conceivable cottage industry. When I look at the exorbitant prices, I feel a bemused detachment from and indifference to the hundreds of millions of dollars. Nothing in Aspen surprises me anymore.

I'm not amazed at how fast someone can run or bike up Smuggler anymore, or how fast someone can skin up Aspen Mountain or hike the bowl, or do the Power of 4. It's the guy I see out for his first run of the season, pounding along the bike path like an elephant with a beet-red face, or the girl hyperventilating at her first exercise class of the year, trying to get back in shape — those are the people and things that impress me now. People and their everyday struggles with the human condition pique my interest, as opposed to an incomprehensible orbit of wealth that I occasionally graze off like a wayward asteroid.

Perhaps that has something to do with the fact that I own my own employee-housing, free-standing home outright. My tax valuation deed just arrived and my humble abode's overall value is probably less than the yearly landscaping/snowplowing and maintenance bill at most of the big residences. When it comes to the astral cost of real estate here, I'm largely unfazed by it. I'm not planning on leaving or moving ... ever. My strategy all along has been to retire and then die peacefully here in my employee-housing unit, with one of my kids changing my diaper and feeding me canned carrots and fruit cups to the bitter end.

I've never gotten sucked into the money frenzy of Aspen. Whether it's real estate or new cars or flipping houses or buying real estate in other zip codes, I've always been perfectly happy living on the fringes and margins of local society. When I hear people who moved here as adults complain about development and construction I have to chuckle to myself. It's almost as though they feel they are defenders of Aspen on some profound level. Truth is, there are forces of money and power at play here much bigger than we are and well out of our control. It's like trying to hold onto a runaway high-pressure fire hose or putting your foot on the rail in an effort to stop a train.

Then it occurred to me — over the course of my life, toiling away at living the dream in Aspen, I've made a million dollars. Look Mom, I'm a ski-bum millionaire! All I have to show for it though is skin cancer, scars from knee surgery, used cars, a kit house with an addition scabbed-on and a hopelessly new-age Colorado state of mind.

Part of being content in the midst of a boomtown economy is knowing your responsibility in it and being confident in that role. I always liken the economy of Aspen to a giant whale, and me and my businesses one of those pilot-fish that attaches itself to the whale and sucks off of the plankton and microbes stuck to the vast surface area of its sides. As I scour the dermal layer of the giant beast, keeping it barnacle free, we exist together is a state of symbiosis. It's a mostly silent mutual agreement. Kind of like an Old West-style handshake agreement — no legal papers or signatures required.

It makes me wonder what Aspen was really like in its previous heyday of the silver boom of the late 1800s with its whorehouses, opium addicts and whiskey bars. How did the workingman reconcile a place in society with wealthy barons, landowners, developers and mine owners? What was the dynamic back then between the immigrants and the different ethnicities doing the heavy lifting, and the Native Americans struggling to keep a foothold in the valley without literally being killed? What was our real estate and housing like then in the pandemic of the early 1900s?

Living in close proximity to wealth like we see here on a daily basis will afford you some interesting opportunities if you open your eyes to it and aren't so blinded by jealousy and rage about it that you can't see straight. Even so, a man has to know his place. Mine is right here in the middle of it all, going about my business with my head down, watching it all go by: day after day, season by season, year after year, town drama after town drama, adult child after adult child.

OFFSEASON IN ASPEN — WHERE EVERYBODY KNOWS YOUR NAME

THIS TIME OF YEAR, it feels like every person you see, you know. It's a welcome departure from the usual, "Who the hell are all these people?" bewilderment. One of the things that's been thoroughly enjoyable and refreshing about this upbeat offseason are the protracted conversations I've been having with locals around town. There's a renewed sense of community and a relaxed nature that allows for more connection than usual for the nonstop stress factory we call Aspen.

Not to mention cruising around town without a mask feels like you just shaved your beard — or like you're missing your wallet or an item of clothing but can't quite put your finger on which one. It's good to see people's faces again and reestablish those links that have been dormant for so long. It feels like we have our town back. At least on the weekends.

As relaxed as offseason seems, there's still a palpable edge to town on the weekdays. You see it mostly out on the roads and the streets. I don't know what's in the air and the water around here, but I've seen more rude, aggressive drivers around town than ever before. Especially out on the highway: excessive speeding, the guy on a motorcycle trying to break the sonic barrier, people drifting into your lane, cutting blind corners, tailgating, honking, aggressive passes, dirty looks and the like. I guess that's just where we're at now. McLain Flats has speed limits for a reason — you never know when a deer, an elk or a road biker is going to dart out in front of you. I remember when the protocol on that country road was to wave to other drivers. A strategically placed, decommissioned cop car on the straightaway would do wonders.

The news stories about how busy town's going to be this rock concert-esque, "sold out" summer already has people wincing. I've formed a plan of attack. E-bike, hit town during shoulder times — early and late. And no matter how much of a hurry you're in or how lucky you feel, never, ever pull into the City Market parking lot. The parking area at Clark's has gotten to be a crunch as well. Patience and courtesy are key. If someone's in more of a hurry to get to their crap job than you are to get to your crap job, by all means let them play through.

I'm part of the lawn care service industry that I refer to as the "White Truck Brigade." No one is ever happy to see us. Even dogs hate us. Frankly, after mowing lawns since sixth grade, it's an industry I can't wait to get out of. The noise, the dust, the ground-up micro plastics, the water usage, the fertilizers — risking cancer so someone has a dandelion-free yard — is it worth it? The good news is you work outside. The bad news? You work outside. After work, all you want to do is find a rock to crawl underneath.

I spend a lot of time on the local bike paths around town. Once I found out there was an artery behind the post office that bypasses the three-way-stop intersection at the Mill Street Post Office/Clark's Market intersection, I haven't ridden through there in years. The valley floor is covered with a spider web of interlocking trails to get you wherever you need to go. Oftentimes when driving, I'll interface with a bike rider on the road — and not in a calming way — when there's ironically a bike path right next to them. The bike paths to me are my own little private club where membership has its privileges.

As an avid pedal-assist e-bike rider, I'm having a tough time right now having any respect for the people on e-bikes now that aren't even pedaling, like it has a throttle, flying through stop signs and intersections in town. Same on the Rio Grande Trail. Just motoring along without even pedaling. They're in this nebulous grey area of motorcycle/bicycle rider I'm struggling to identify with.

I was happy to see the Thrift Shop open again — it's like a harbinger of our triumphant return to glory. Also, the city of Aspen is doing their generous Spring Cleanup trash pickup again. As the scabby snowpack recedes like a middle-aged man's hairline revealing a tender, damaged scalp, I'm seeing an inordinate amount of trash around town on the roadsides: lots of bottles and a ton of discarded masks everywhere. Kudos to the local trash warriors who actually bend over and pick this stuff up. Posting Earth Day memes on social media apparently didn't work. The whole town needs to be power washed. Rain helps, too.

I have my eye trained on the runoff now. Our only job as a state is to fill up Lake Powell and Lake Mead. It seems like we are having a fairly moist spring so far, and I hope it keeps up. May here is supposed to be miserable. Prepare yourself a tray of mental comfort food; we're at least two more snowstorms away from summer, then hopefully the monsoons will return.

Now that our positivity rate has gone nearly to nil, it's time to flatten the curve — of my waistline. My six-pack abs are hiding behind a pony-keg of lard right now. Halfway through the ski season, I surrendered and stopped buttoning the top button of my ski pants altogether. It's time to get back in shape and clean this town up in the process. "Work-fit," I call the two-fold regiment. I've been planting sunflower seeds at random roadside locations throughout town, so we'll see where they pop up.

Green growth is spreading like a long-awaited disease across the valley floor. The real harbinger of spring? Tom Moore dragged his pastures on McLain Flats, leaving visible artistic striations. The hayfields are his canvas, and the tractor his brush. Spring is in the air. The willow bushes are a vibrant orange and red as they start to bud, and the river is gurgling back to life. My sights are set on a summer of bike riding, jumping in the river, paddleboarding, the farmers market, Snowmass concerts, some big rock shows in Denver and going to eat out at restaurants again. If you see me around town, be sure to say hello. I always like to know what's on people's minds.

OH TO LIVE ON, BUBBLE-MILK MOUNTAIN

IF YOU HAD WALKED INTO the J Bar 20 years ago, sidled up to the bar and proclaimed that Buttermilk would one day be hosting the FIS World Championships of anything other than snow plowing, people would've thought you were the town drunk. Interestingly enough, in retrospect, had SkiCo's upper brass listened to me, probably none of these competitions — or the X Games, for that matter — would be happening either. Guess the joke's back on me now.

Years ago in a sales meeting at the old green admin building at the base of Buttermilk, the VPs put me on the spot and asked what I thought about the X Games. There I was, shirt and tie, telling them it all seemed silly to me. With the snowboarders flopping around in a primitive stunt-ditch and snowmobiles flying through the air landing on each other, it had very little if anything to do with skiing, I told them, and that we should laser-focus our efforts on the World Cup Downhill on Ajax. Incidentally, it looks as if the X Games and now the FIS World Championships at Buttermilk are greasing the rails to get the downhill back in Aspen. All these events are sending a crystal clear message to the FIS: ready when you are.

One of my Aspen Mountain-centric buddies asked me where I'd been skiing, to which I exuberantly responded I'd been "... ripping Buttermilk." After a pregnant pause he replied incredulously in the form of a question dripping with sarcasm, "Ripping Buttermilk. Huh. Is that even possible?" When you're sharing the mountain with the world's best male and female freeskiers and snowboarders, it is. Just watching the way they attack the terrain on their way to the course is dumbfounding. The mind-boggling shapes they throw on snow and in the air are downright extraterrestrial.

This week, I've been skiing and keying into the feverish activity at Buttermilk. I'm drawn to these events like a mosquito to one of those bug-zapper lights. Buttermilk is a vibe, even a state of mind. The snow conditions have been a veritable smorgasbord of corn-uroy and turkey-powder, with all of the spring condition trimmings. I skied Red's Rover, Ptarmigan to Magic Carpet, bombed Savio to the Toilet Bowl rim-to-seat, and even sent it off the Bear jump for good measure. People are often surprised at how often I intentionally ski Buttermilk, with purpose and vigor. I learned to ski there as a kid, so it's a comforting touchstone for me. When life is puzzling, I go to the safe haven of our beloved Buttermilk. Its energy is grounding. You have to keep in contact with where you came from. By knowing your ski past, your ski future stays in better focus.

The international element of the FIS World Championships at Buttermilk makes me giddy. The flamboyant outfits alone are worth the price of admission, let alone the rest of the snow circus. There are by far the most international visitors I've seen in Aspen in over a year. Aspen has operated successfully event-wise this winter in the sense that Buttermilk has hosted the X Games in a COVID bubble. (ESPN made employees wear a company-issued mask because apparently the tattered buff reeking of pot, beer and cigarettes wasn't cutting it.) It's an experiment that has shown we can pull these events off in a pinch, with little notice. I have a funny feeling a lot of that's due to the steadfast acumen of John Rigney at Aspen Skiing Co. — a guy I humorously refer to as the "Jason Bateman" of SkiCo.

They have the venue fairly locked down right now. There's even an on-site COVID test trailer. No spectators, few banners, very little flare. Just the stark contradiction of kids, ski school and beginner skiers mixed with the best skiers and snowboarders in the world.

On one side of the run, you have a sponsored superstar straight-lining. On the other, a snow bunny in an all-white ensemble, losing control and throwing her poles into the air in a last-ditch effort to stop as she's heading for the trees. Just below that, there's a guy in a microwave-silver, Trans-Am jacket with over-the-ear headphones in an aggressive snowplow deliberately skiing without poles. Then a booming voice comes from the woods where a skier is flailing, "Oh, S*%$! I'm stuck!" His girlfriend sits in the snow on a snowboard with body language that screams irritation and defeat. Yes! Beginner skiers! These are my people! These are the ones that go back to from wherever they came and will not shut up about Aspen.

When you triangulate this event with the X Games and the and then the FIS Alpine World Championships at Aspen Highlands this April, you could make a pretty good argument that we're sitting in the catbird seat right now to reacquire a regular stop for the men's and women's World Cup downhill, aka "America's Downhill," back on Aspen Mountain. I can't wait to see what course they set for the downhill on Highlands — perhaps Mousetrap to Olympic to Moment of Truth, or maybe they even run the downhill on Aspen Mountain? It's slurry bar talk like this that makes me want to see a triumphant reprise of the "24 Hours of Aspen" event. The FIS is watching closely. I want everybody on his or her best behavior. Don't screw this one up, Aspen.

'THE NAKED APE'

When I was a senior at Aspen High, I won a spot on the coveted Desolation/Grey Canyon spring rafting trip for what was then called Spree Week. The prerequisite reading was a book called "The Naked Ape," but there was a major catch, and a grim one at that — a mixed written and multiple-choice test before the trip.

Whoever tanked the test the worst would become the one in charge of the "groover," the gruesome receptacle for our human feces.

I never read the book or even bothered skimming the CliffsNotes. I failed the test miserably, but fate or dumb luck or karma or coincidence — whichever conspiracy you subscribe to — would have it that I landed in the penultimate position on the proverbial totem pole, narrowly escaping the No. 2 crew.

My classmate Craig Melville, on the other hand, wasn't so lucky.

The premise of the book, I surmised from the cover, was how we evolved from apes yet are stuck wallowing in a profound sense of denial of the fact that we're animals — a concept to which I wholeheartedly subscribe. Like I said, I never read the book and have resisted my better, commonsensical urges to look it up on the internet for the sake of writing an educated and informed column about it. I'm leaving the door open here to one of my former teachers to write a scathing op-ed in response.

The pandemic we're in has me wondering how, as naked apes, we're navigating our way through the fog using our primordial compasses. How are our animal instincts manifesting themselves, or are we too disconnected from that rarely admitted reality to see it happening? We're constantly trying to deny the elephant-in-the-room fact that we're just high-functioning apes, whether it's by manscaping, getting lost in our smartphones, correcting our posture, denying our connectivity to nature and the heavens or admitting how seasonal changes affect us. Sometimes I think we're more like insects than apes.

When the threat of death makes itself known, how do our instincts manifest in today's tech-driven society? One of the animalistic byproducts I see here locally is the surge in real estate. You can make a cogent argument that this is essentially reflective of the basic instinctual urge and need for shelter. It just so happens that the people doing the purchasing are wealthy — like squirrels that have an overabundance of acorns.

Or are our needs embarrassingly simplistic, like hoarding toilet paper and food? You could say that the amassing of local real estate is essentially shelter mongering. I recently paid my house off. When times were good, I continuously threw money at my mortgage, more than required, in an effort to own my own shelter. One could reason that paying down your mortgage — contrary to the anti-ape corporate mindset of constantly borrowing on your investment — is a prehistoric manifestation of securing your shelter.

I'm seeing a reckoning of sorts happening in Aspen right now. Our town has been bustling during the pandemic, busier than we were anticipating — maybe even more so than we were emotionally prepared for. We're often torn by the relationship we have as a resort town and as a community, and where those two concepts intersect.

The thought of more people living here full time is daunting to many of the transplants that live here now. I see this as the confluence of two rivers: kinetically similar entities seeking a destination, yet originating at different places.

Another way the pandemic has been manifesting itself in a primordial sense is the locals' figurative circling of the wagons and trying to protect what we have, and for good reason.

It's a form of protectionism — dare I say nationalism, in some respect — arguably a tribal instinct to defend the nest we've made.

When I was young and angry, I subscribed to these notions, often railing against monster homes, expensive lift tickets and what I felt was the gentrification of Aspen. As I've aged, it seems the bigger picture has come into clearer focus. Wallowing in the quagmire of local issues and harboring resentment has become counterproductive to me. I've come to see myself more as a parasite attached to the whale that is Aspen.

Sometimes I find myself feeling jealous of new arrivals: trendy, carefree tourists and exorbitant wealth. Authenticity is the one thing that can't be bought, but you can rent it for an hour or two. I'm viewing the influx of new people in town as a positive that will ultimately challenge us and spur personal growth. Cue the Eagles' "New Kid in Town" and press play.

These next months will really define who we are as a community. How we react as a collective entity, how we choose to assimilate or alienate our newly arrived naked apes from other tribes. Our kids — and we — might actually benefit from meeting some new people. Making new friends is one of life's simple pleasures. While I never did read the "Naked Ape," I've seen "Planet of the Apes" multiple times and have taken those lessons from the silver screen to hominoid heart.

GETTING SCHOOLED
BY A LEGEND

It'd been a while since I'd been called out like that, and honestly it felt refreshing. For once, instead of going around judging everyone like we all do all the time, I was the one taking the brunt of the criticism, my glass house was taking a direct hit with the business end of the omnipotent, shaming hammer. Guess what my infraction was? Carrying my skis the wrong way. In a ski town, for someone who calls himself a local, that's a yellow-flag-worthy offense. A 15-yard penalty from the spot of the foul, and loss of down.

I'd just pulled into the lot at Highlands on a busy powder-day weekend morning and miraculously managed to find a teeny parking spot between a Sprinter van and a rental Suburban. After putting on my boots and getting all the maddening bits and pieces organized, putting the keys in the special hiding place, it was time to make my move; get ahead and stay ahead of all the weekend warriors. There was definitely a sense of urgency. Powder days can easily be screwed up by a series of self-inflicted bad decisions.

Just as I was getting the skis off the roof of my Mini Cooper, you know the poser one in town with "ZG MINI" vanity plates, I saw her out of the corner of my eye. Fan boy alert! She's a living local legend in my mind. One of those fast women in Aspen who can ski better than all of the guys who think they're the best skier on Aspen Mountain. She's already forgotten more about skiing than I'll ever be able to learn in a lifetime of lessons, Aspenauts, racing, hiking the bowl and countless hours of freeskiing with hoodlum buddies reeking of pot.

I absentmindedly grabbed my skis and made a hasty break for it, just to be in her mere presence, to see if her skiing prowess would somehow rub off on me like an inexplicable case of osmosis. She was walking briskly toward the entrance of the ski area, and I followed her like a kid who chases a fire truck would. As I cheerily said "Hi!" she looked at me like I had the plague; she sped up and delivered a sobering criticism that shook me to my core. I had it coming, I deserved it. That's what made it so devastating.

"Dude. Seriously?! Tails first?" she said, and picked up her pace to get out ahead of me, so as to not be associated with anyone who would intentionally carry their skis over their shoulder, tails first. I blushed and swallowed hard. As a cherry on top of my Screw-up Sundae, the ski brakes were such that the ski on top had slid nearly a foot in front of the other so it really looked like I was, gulp, not necessarily from around these parts. The real clincher would've been my dangling power straps and rear-entry ski boots.

Mea culpa: In my defense, 99.9 percent of the time I always carry my skis the "right" way; on my left shoulder (because I'm right handed), tips first, with the toe binding behind the shoulder and both my ski poles in my right hand. This tails-first debacle was a hasty exception just to be near someone who has done the daunting all day and all night, top to bottom, in a tuck, 24 Hours of Aspen event and won it, thrice.

It cracks me up to see all the different ways people carry their skis now. One of my favorite pastimes is to sit somewhere near the gondola and watch the various techniques, and refer to them by their clever names like "the offering," "the bazooka," "the try-hard," "the dragger" or perhaps the most clever in my opinion, "the suitcase," each one of which boils down to a psychological case study in what a pain in the ass skiing and all of the equipment can be at times, especially for people here on vacation, new to the sport. You sometimes see families having China-Syndrome nuclear meltdowns simply trying to get their kids to carry their own equipment from the rental shop back to the hotel.

Not us locals. We know better. Whenever we see someone doing something wrong, we either help them, or shame them into doing it how we feel is the right way. I promise, I'll never carry my skis the wrong way again. Look at the bright side: Basically all there is left to do is ski now, so everyone's going to have plenty of time to work on their ski-carrying technique this spring.

GONNA
HITCH A RIDE

"HEY MOM, CAN I PLEASE have some money to go see a movie tonight at the Isis?!" If only I had any real intention of going to see a movie. That's usually how my weekends began in the West End over by the Aspen Ice Garden during the winter months. The main objectives were to go skitching, get a heaving slice of deep dish supreme pizza, then finish the night out at the Pinball Palace playing Space Invaders until I ran out of quarters. It was a time in Aspen, incidentally, that a grade-schooler could go see an R-rated movie — unaccompanied by an adult, with hand-written note from your parents.

You know what the problem with local Aspen kids is these days? You never see them skitching anymore. I know they have it in them. I see them prowling around town in small mischievous wolf-like packs. What exactly is skitching? It's the pinnacle of thrill, excitement and danger in degenerate winter sports: hanging onto the back of a car's bumper and being pulled around town over icy and snow-packed streets, undetected. Skitching was an early renegade form of ridesharing. Some drivers would let you grab on and hitch a ride, then intentionally tried to whip you off their bumper by speeding around corners, like trying to flick a booger off a finger.

There were some spectacular wipeouts, but as far as I can recollect, no one ever got hurt. (Editor's note: Skitching is a horrible idea, should not be tried by anyone and is potentially fatal under any circumstance.) Probably the most dangerous was skitching behind a RFTA bus. When you hit a dip at an intersection, if you were too close and slid too far under, the rear bumper could come down and crush your legs like a Dixie cup. The Holy Grail of skitching, that we always talked about but no one ever obtained, was the ultimate defiant act of skitching behind a cop car. Our oh-so convenient excuse was usually that Saabs had crappy bumpers for skitching, anyways.

There was more to it than just grabbing a hold of the bumper and getting dragged around. It was like cross training for skiing and hockey. Style, form and where you placed yourself on the bumper were key. Too close to the exhaust, or right behind the wheel for example, were not sweet spots. You could hit a pothole, or a manhole cover. Footwear was crucial — Moon Boots were my choice. Another key component? Knowing when to let go of the bumper and run from the local police.

It was one of the biggest kid-scandals that I can remember. It all happened at the hallowed corner of Bleeker and Garmisch in plain daylight, was captured on film, and ended up on the cover of Thursday's Aspen Times. Skitching had caught the attention of a number of parents and teachers around town, and they were generally unimpressed. One day when school let out, a huge, honking, 1970s-style land-yacht of a car with an enormous chrome bumper stopped in front of the lower-elementary school now known as the Yellow Brick.

What looked like a baker's dozen of Aspen school kids latched onto the back of that thing, like adorable little ticks, all of them wearing backpacks and pom-pom hats. The car started moving and the photographer snapped a picture. Busted. Cover of the paper. When we picked up our stacks of Aspen Times to sell that Thursday in the alley behind Carl's and saw the cover, our stomachs sank. Shock waves of punishment rippled through town that night. Kids were grounded; some still are, others were scared straight. Skitching was officially outlawed. It was like a big drug bust in the sense that after a couple weeks of discretion and laying low, normal skitching operations inevitably resumed again.

Skitching was mostly done by boys, but a couple of girls got in on the action, like my mini-bike-riding tomboy heartthrob who lived up the street on Hopkins, right across from the Parlor Car restaurant, Beth Madsen. She could skitch with the best of them.

You know how you can tell the local adults that used to skitch as kids? They boot-ski whenever they get the chance; that's the slowly dying art of sliding across a surface with ski boots on. Next time you see a group of Aspen kids standing awkwardly around a stop sign in the middle of a neighborhood, check your rear mirror after you pass and see if you have any devious skitchers stuck to your bumper.

CHAIRLIFT STORIES

IS THERE SOME OTHER SPORT or activity I'm unaware of where one of the pre-requisites is being copasetic with sitting in a chair that's hanging on a moving wire 40 feet above the ground? It's astonishing to me that there aren't more chairlift accidents, or that I've never fallen from a lift. If you've ever seen a chairlift malfunction and "rollback," that would make you jump off for your life. I've always wanted to jump off of a chairlift for kicks, but the sun may be soon setting on that ill-advised bucket list item as every time I get the urge I can hear the booming voice of retired ski patrol legend Robin Perry saying, "Don't do it, Speedy!" in his down-home Western drawl.

My first memory of a chairlift is from Mammoth Mountain in California, when I finally proved to be ready to ride the chairlift at age 6. As I inched toward the loading zone, I froze and let two or three empty chairs go by. The adults in the line were extremely unimpressed and started yelling at me things like, "Hey stupid kid, GO!" It was just another excuse to cry, of which there were many, and hate the sport of skiing.

People in lift (and gondola) lines can get unreasonably aggressive. The advent of high-speed lifts made skiing more efficient, but in some sense they sucked some portion of the joy marrow from the bones of the sport. Case in point: It's harder to feel connected to the outdoors from the seat of Ajax Express than it is riding Lift 1A without a safety bar. People used to ski under the lift intentionally to get woo-hoo'd at. It was a thing, doing bump runs under the lift. The thought of crashing underneath the hallowed run 1A Lift Line when the chairs are full keeps me up at night. That would be a stone-cold reputation killer.

Remember when a lady with tight fitting, in-the-boot stretch pants, mirrored I-Ski sunglasses, a headband and big hair would casually ski up to the very front of a gargantuan lift-line and yell "Single?!" with a raucous Texan accent and the ensuing wave of men who would embarrassingly fall over themselves to get the chance to ride up the chairlift with her? The singles line changed that to more of a random lottery dating game. There are probably married couples who met on a chairlift in Aspen.

The chairlift that used to scare the crap out of me was Lift 2 on Buttermilk that went over the daunting Toilet Bowl. The old outside pole two-seater chair used to come whipping around the bullwheel so fast, and the lift operator would grab a handful of the front of your jacket and pants and slam you into the chair as it whooshed you up the steep ski-jump-like loading ramp. I can remember being so small that the bend of my knees wouldn't even reach the edge of the seat so my feet and skis stuck straight-out, wearing a pom-pom hat and a Mother Karen's anorak, with one of those strings going through the sleeves to keep your mittens from getting lost. I was so teeny that I couldn't even extend high enough to put my 100-centimeter red and white Hart Gremlins from Sabatini's in or out of the bus ski rack. Often times the bus driver would have to get out and help me.

The real scary thing was the safety bar. When you're that tiny, it's next to impossible to reach up and get the safety bar down. If you did somehow manage to get the bar down, it was incredibly difficult to get it back up. We used to ride the mighty span over the Toilet Bowl gripped with fear, praying to God (when I still believed that stuff) that the lift wouldn't stop there. Inevitably it did, and the ensuing dip the lift did was hair-raising. The lift would bounce a good 30 feet up and down over the bowl. It's a miracle it never tossed all the kids off. Those old chairlifts were like sketchy roller-coasters.

One day my friend Bruce Burton and I were riding up the locals' favorite (no safety bar) "Oly" chair on Aspen Highlands.

There was a colorful, raucous guy in front of us with shaggy blond hair and funky shades riding single in front of us. He was a Highlands regular. It was a Saturday morning and we were freshman at Aspen High. We had just finished our own chairlift shenanigans and were coming out of the foggy Jug's hill area when the lift started shaking. The guy in front of us was violently jolting around in the chair, murmuring and groaning. He was having a vicious epileptic seizure. We both grabbed onto the lift in shock.

I still get sick to my stomach thinking about it. Just as the chair reached tower 13 near the Cloud 9 restaurant, he slouched forward, went silent, and fell. It all happened in slow-motion right before our eyes. He fell a good 30 feet and landed right on the back part of his head and neck, and augured in. The lift remorselessly kept going. We were screaming for help, and alerted the lift operator at the top of what happened. The patrol headquarters was housed in Cloud 9, so they were on it instantaneously. I skied straight down and went home immediately after seeing that. I never did find out what happened to that poor guy, or if he even lived, but it keeps a healthy fear of chairlifts alive within me.

THE SHERIFF
WE KNEW

I HEARD THE SIRENS BLARING last Friday morning and didn't think anything of it — probably just another horrible accident, and a medical-airlift scenario for some poor soul. When I got home from work, I turned on the computer and saw the breaking news update that former Sheriff Bob Braudis had died.

The bulletin swirled in my mind. I decided to go for a mountain bike ride to try and process the gravity of his passing.

I spontaneously stopped my knobby tired, chrome-molly steed on a bold ridge overlooking the glacial plateau of Aspen — one I usually ride right past. "What's the rush?" I thought to myself. Just then, something fascinating happened. A whirlwind whooshed over town from west to east, whipping up a giant cloud of pollen that overtook the entire downtown core in an instant. You could see the ever-so-slight green tinge that differentiated the unique event from a run-of-the-mill spring dust storm.

It was incredible to experience. My thoughts were that I had just witnessed the spirit of the recently departed Braudis sweeping over town. Because really, pollen is indicative of a healthy forest, and I'd say that as a result of the community-policing ethos that's permeated every nook and cranny of Aspen's renegade freewheeling culture, our community law enforcement "forest" is healthy, overall.

The legacy of kind, thoughtful, engaging law enforcement from Dick Kienast to Bob Braudis to Joe DiSalvo has shaped me personally. They are the reason to this day I always wave at the sheriff and police, and engage with them face-to-face whenever I get the chance. And you know what? I'm always glad I did.

A regret I'm now grappling with is that I didn't hang out more with Bob when he was holding court at the Gonzo Gallery the last couple of years. It's embarrassing to admit, but there was a part of me that was afraid to go talk to him because it looked like he was struggling physically. That's hard to write. I know he was a fan of my writing because he often emailed, telling me so.

He and his stature reminded me of a former NFL player whose body had broken down after years of physical abuse, only his funky brand of abuse was one of a life fully lived. I'm by no means part of his close circle of friends, but I have been known to glance off their orbit from time to time.

I'm really going to miss seeing his hulking figure lurking around town, and hearing passersby say, "Whoa, who was that dude?" If they only knew the people he's met, the things he's seen — the good, the bad and the ugly secrets of Aspen.

Bob Braudis was inextricably linked to the legacy, mythology and methodology of Hunter S. Thompson. My loose understanding is for that reason and others, the "feds" if you will, or the Drug Enforcement Agency, always wanted to arrest him. To me, it seemed the disagreement was always over one particularly pernicious drug: cocaine. Let the legend now seep deep into the bedrock of maverick Aspen.

There always have been and always will be local folklore about Braudis and his relationship with those known to be drug dealers, and his tenuous rapport with federal drug agents. I always thought he should have organized a fundraiser at the Belly Up for out-of-work pot dealers when marijuana was first legalized.

There is definitely a faction of Aspenites and greater Roaring Fork Valley citizens that thinks the entire mindset of our former sheriffs and the current sheriff is garbage. I'd be remiss to attempt to label them. They'd prefer for Aspen's deranged old guard to expire, perhaps even let the feds back into town and generally make the town a whole lot stricter — a"law and order" kind of place. Who knows?

It's for that very reason that I am, without any hesitation whatsoever, voting for Joe DiSalvo in the next election for sheriff. He is effectively carrying that torch of my defiant, messy vitality — renegade Aspen, steadfastly forward — albeit into a remorseless, gale-force headwind of change.

I've always fashioned our local law enforcement to be the "Community School" of law enforcement. Stand alone. Lead by example. Be empathetic and compassionate, warnings being more important than arrests: (I know warnings have carried more weight for me.) Someone asked me if I'd ever been to jail. I told them no, but I did spend the night in the Kienasts' basement once when I got in big trouble.

There's been a glut of death in Aspen lately. Sometimes it seems like you could stack the bodies up like firewood. If bodies were in fact logs, that of Bob Braudis would be more like an oversized one of those Duraflame logs that burns deep into the night with psychedelic colors and is a little more fun to stare at and ponder the wild wacky ride that life is.

From now on every time I see tempestuous pollen, dust, cotton or snowstorm squall over town, I'll think of the spirit of Bob and his gap-toothed, illegal smile, looking over the daily docudramas and keeping his ear cupped on heady conversations in all the stimulating funky social circles of Aspen.

SEMPLE: THE $100 MILLION LISTING

THE LONGER YOU STICK AROUND TOWN, the more you get to see unfold. Just when you thought Aspen real estate couldn't get any more stupendous, or oddly mirror that Bravo reality TV show "Million Dollar Listing," a record-shattering $100 million offering comes along. What we're witnessing right here, right now in terms of real estate is every bit as significant as the silver boom of the late 1800s. We look retrospectively at the historic silver glut as a heyday. I equate today's flabbergasting real estate sales to Aspen's new monetary highpoint.

When I saw Steven Shane's Compass Instagram post alerting subscribers there was an open house on the new listing, my ears perked up, Mr. Spock-style. I did what any self-respecting local columnist would do — I went to it. I'm a big fan of Shane. I used to be his lawn guy when he lived in employee housing at the end of Ute Avenue over by the Aspen Club. He was selling real estate back then, and I'm still mowing lawns. A man's got to know his place. Hosting an open-house luncheon was a really nice thing for him to do. I honestly hope he sells the house.

I'd never been in the mansion before, but I know some people who have. Upon arrival, I was greeted promptly by one of Steven's lovely "angels." There was a bountiful spread of food and beverages, and you were free to walk about and inspect each and every room. I even went into the house's main "engine room," which I found fascinating. Something felt eerily personal walking from room to room, seeing all kinds of family pictures. Walking through someone else's well-feathered walk-in closet, seeing their clothes and shoes, was a curious sociological sensation for me.

I've been in palatial residences previously, but this spread was different. The interior of the house is truly incredible. The house has three stories, ski-in, ski-out access, sweeping views — everything a relatively high-functioning ski bum could imagine. The exterior? Architecture is like anchovies on pizza, and this reminded me of the same architect that designed any Alpine Bank building. But hey, why stick out? Better to hide in plain sight if you ask me. That's why I wear camouflage.

I found it fitting that the house for sale is at the bottom of Ajax, one of the epicenters of our local mining operations. There, it's easy to visualize our town's history, its extracting heritage, where hearty, calloused men realized incredible fortunes by scurrying around in tunnels in filthy canvas clothing, speculatively digging into solid rock with hand tools and explosives, all of the work done by candlelight.

Today's male real estate agents, with their pastel-collared shirts, manicures, finely brushed teeth and loafers without socks, have things a little easier than the miners did. I don't know; it's just a guess. It actually made me wonder for a fleeting moment — could I be a Realtor?

The latest listing probably dumbfounds some locals. Not me. When I first heard of the $100 million listing, honestly it really didn't even register with me on any level of consciousness. That's just how dumbed down and comfortably numb I am to money, having grown up here. Nothing surprises me anymore. How many bowl laps someone did in one day. How fast someone can run up Ajax. How much money someone has. A fancy car or motorcycle passing by. How much this or that costs. I'm literally incapable of feeling any emotion for those types of feats or material possessions.

I attribute this blissful state of apathetic ignorance to the fact that I own real estate (employee housing) in Aspen. Tourism and real estate both paid for my nest. I've worked hard, and I am eternally grateful to those who have chosen Aspen and paid my bills. I'm not one to bite or write on the hand that feeds.

Real estate in Aspen has made a lot of people a lot of money. The industry probably employs more people here than Aspen Skiing Co. Vast fortunes and astounding piles of treasure have been amassed in our short lifetimes.

I used to be resentful of wealth here when I was in my angry 20s, but one day I realized it's a bad look; harboring jealousy or resentments about money make you wildly unattractive. The bitter sentiment feels like a form of prejudice to me. Being upset all the time about town or feeding into the "outrage du jour" can make you physically sick. A local girl taught me that lesson one night over dinner at the Steak Pit. The schooling was tougher than an undercooked artichoke, but well worth the asking price of a romantic dinner for two.

What do I know about real estate in Aspen? Other than being friends with most all of the Realtors in town, not a single thing. I seek and find humor and amusement in local real estate. I view the prices through a lampoon-lit lens, and see the purchases as a comedy of heirs.

Would you buy the house if you had the money? I dare you to indulge your wildest fantasies. I might just start rifling through my email's junk box and see if I can find any of those eager pleadings from long-lost Nigerian relatives in the oil and diamond business, bequeathing me titanic riches of inheritance.

———

ACKNOWLEDGEMENT

AS STUDENTS FROM ASPEN HIGH SCHOOL, we would all like to thank one of our favorite teachers, George Burson. George taught us about history in a way that made us all think more about past, present, and future.

After we wrote these pages for this book it was clear that we needed to get them edited one last time by the person that had edited so much of our past work.

Thanks George from all of us students.

I taught at Aspen High School from 1976 to 2003, and I was extremely fortunate to have had that experience. I met my wife, the French and Spanish teacher Kathie Martinson, there, and the students I taught were usually hard-working, motivated to learn, and a pleasure to teach. My sons, Rob and David, both graduated from AHS and were friends with some of the authors of this book.

George Burson: Circa 1985

I took it as a compliment when Andy asked me to edit this book. It was an enjoyable experience because I was able to learn about the lives of some of my ex-students from their perspective, and to get a feel for their current lives. Thanks Andy.

– George Burson

SPECIAL THANKS

WE WOULD LIKE TO GIVE A SPECIAL THANKS TO SOME OTHER FOLKS WHO WERE MAJOR INFLUENCES IN OUR TOWN, WHETHER US KIDS KNEW IT OR NOT.

Nick and Maggie **Dewolf**, Patti and George **Stranahan**, Dr. Whit and Polly **Whitcomb**, Herbie and Marcie **Balderson**, and Sandy and Mary Lynn **Munro**, and Tom and Cathy **Crum**, Bob and Nancy **Odén**, and Ralph and Marian **Melville**.

THANKS TO ALL WHO HELPED IN THE MANY WAYS IT TAKES TO GET A BOOK OUT.

Amy Blumenstein **Collen**, Kyra Hider-**Jackson**, Courtney **Pomeroy**, Sheridan **Semple**, Mark Ronay, Melanie Malone Love, Rhett Snyder, Erica Balderson, Missy Brinkman, Greg Poschman, Terry Murray, Jody McMurrian (illustrations), Carlos Olivares (illustrations), Ann O'Neal Garcia, Michael Peretz, Tina Collen, Eric Marcus, Susan Sanchez, and Ted Conover.

WE WOULD ALSO LIKE TO THANK ALL THOSE WE GREW UP WITH IN ASPEN HIGH SCHOOL
The AHS classes from 1982-1988.

KEEP IN TOUCH

WE OCCASIONALLY POST NEWS about the book, book signings, and stories on our blog. Also, as this book uses QR codes which may need updating, we'll provide links and/or stickers now and then. **If you'd like to receive notices, please subscribe to our mailing list at: TwistAndTurnPress.com**

More about the books mentioned in our book (blog)

For more about the Aspen related books mentioned in this memoir, scan the QR code or go to:
twistandturnpress.com/post/other-notable-aspen-books — feel free to make recommendations!

Collectible T-Shirts featuring some of the art used in the book (online store)

We hope you've enjoyed this not-so-short trip down memory lane. May our memories leave you with unsupervised plans or half-cocked, rambling memories of your own. Regardless, don't do anything we haven't done. Aspen was a great place to grow up. And if the "good lord's willing and the creeks don't rise," our hope is that it will remain so going forward. If you liked this memoir, leave a nice review somewhere (please). And, please, for all that is holy, we didn't mean it. Please don't sue.

ANDY   LO   DEAN   CHRIS